CISTERCIAN STUDIES SERIES: NUMBER SEVENTY-TWO

Medieval Religious Women II

Peaceweavers

CISTERCIAN STUDIES SERIES: NUMBER SEVENTY-TWO

Medieval Religious Women

Volume Two

PEACEWEAVERS

Edited by
Lillian Thomas Shank and John A. Nichols

Cistercian Publications Inc.
1987

The work of Cistercian Publications
is made possible in part
by support from Western Michigan University.

Available in Britain and Europe from
A.R. Mowbray & Co Ltd
St Thomas House Becket Street
Oxford OX 1 1SJ

in all other areas (including Canada)
from

Cistercian Publications
WMU Station
Kalamazoo, Michigan 49008

Typeset by the Carmelites of Indianapolis

Library of Congress Cataloging in Publication Data

(Revised for vol. 2)
Main entry under title:
Medieval religious women.
(Cistercian studies series; no. 72)
Includes bibliographies and indexes.
Contents: v. 1. Distant echoes — v. 2. Peaceweavers.
I. Nichols, John A., 1939– II. Shank,
Lillian Thomas. III. Series.
BX4210.M345 1987 271'.9'000902 83-2111
ISBN 0-87907-871-5 (v. 1)
ISBN 0-87907-971-1 (pbk. : v. 1)

A fifteenth-century flemish memorial to Marguerite d'Escornaix, abbess of Nivelles (died 25 April 1462).

The kneeling abbess is flanked by the women most important in her religious life: behind her, St Margaret symbolizes the virgin martyrs whose faith triumphed over evil, portrayed by the dragon; enthroned in front is the Virgin Mary, the protector of all who call on her, holds the infant Christ who receives the abbess' prayers. The latin banner overhead reads 'Jesus Christ, son of the living God, have mercy on me, a sinner'.

Brass rubbing and photograph have been provided by John A. Nichols.

TABLE OF CONTENTS

Foreword ix
John A. Nichols

Introduction 1
Lillian Thomas Shank

Living Sermons: Consecrated Women and the Conversion of Gaul 19
Jo Ann McNamara

Female Spirituality and Mysticism in Frankish Monasticism: Radegund, Balthild and Aldegund 39
Suzanne Foney Wemple

The Unique Experience of Anglo-Saxon Nuns 55
Janemarie Luecke

Solitude and Solidarity: Medieval Women Recluses 67
Jean Leclercq

Elizabeth of Schönau and Hildegard of Bingen: Prophets of the Lord 85
M. Colman O'Dell

Divine Power Made Perfect in Weakness: St Hildegard on the Frail Sex 103
Barbara Newman

The Anchoress in the Twelfth and Thirteenth Centuries 123
Patricia J. F. Rosof

The Sacramental Witness of Christina *Mirabilis*: The Mystic Growth of a Fool for Christ's Sake 145
Margot H. King

Clare of Assisi 165

Clare: Poverty and Contemplation in Her Life and Writings 167
Madge Karecki

Following in the Foot Prints of the Poor Christ: Clare's Spirituality 175
Fidelis Hart

Clare of Assisi: New Leader of Women 197
Frances Ann Thom

THE WOMEN OF HELFTA 211

Saint Mechtild of Hackeborn: *Nemo Communior* 213
Jeremy Finnegan

To Be a Full-Grown Bride: Mechthild of Magdeburg 223
Edith Scholl

The God of My Life: St Gertrude, A Monastic Woman 239
Lillian Thomas Shank

Foundations of Christian Formation in the Dialogue of St Catherine of Siena 275
Susan Muto

JULIAN OF NORWICH 289

Julian on Prayer 291
Ritamary Bradley

The Motherhood of God According to Julian of Norwich 305
Charles Cummings

TERESA OF AVILA 315

Teresa of Jesus: The Saint and Her Spirituality 317
Laurin Hartzog

The Foundations of Mystical Prayer: Teresa of Jesus 331
Keith J. Egan

St Teresa of Avila: A Guide for Travel Inward 345
Margaret Dorgan

Two Faces of Christ: Jeanne de Chantal 353
Wendy M. Wright

Epilogue: Cistercian Monastic Life/Vows: A Vision 365
Jean Marie Howe

AFTERWORD: CONCORD HOMESPUN 373
Agnes Day

CONTRIBUTORS 377

INDEX OF PERSONS AND PLACES 383

SUBJECT INDEX 389

Foreword

Background of the Project

Medieval Religious Women: Peaceweavers is a response to a question. In 1980, Sister Lillian Thomas Shank asked if it would be possible to publish a book of articles on monastic women who lived in the Middle Ages. With the appearance of this volume, it is evident that her question can be answered in the affirmative. Indeed, her query was greeted with such enthusiasm that there were enough superior articles to produce, not one, but three volumes on medieval religious women.

This overwhelming reply came from two different groups of persons who were looking into the lives of women religious to ascertain their role and contributions in the past. To one group belonged members of religious communities, both women and men, who were searching for the spiritual roots of their lives. They were trying to discover the manner in which religious women had lived, the ideas these women had had, and the impact they had had on religious thought. To the other group of persons interested in the medieval religious woman belonged members of the academic community who were writing the histories of these women. Since Sr. Lillian is a member of the monastic community of Our Lady of the Mississippi Abbey at Dubuque, Iowa, she was already in touch with one of the groups of persons interested in the lives of the female religious. When she teamed with John A. Nichols, a professor of medieval history and her co-editor of the volumes, a link was forged with the academic community and the two groups came together in a unique collaboration.

The sharing of information between the academics and religious has been a 'learning experience' for both. The academics are expert in researching and writing about women long dead. The religious, on the other hand, are expert in sharing the lives of persons who lived in the past. For the religious of today, medieval women remain very much alive, for the study of their lives and insights aids their own search. The academics have come to realize the impact medieval religious women have on the spiritual lives of contemporary religious. The religious have come to realize that medieval women did not live in a vacuum, but were very much influenced by the social, cultural, economic, and political conditions of the Middle Ages. The result of this collaborative research is a blend of articles in these volumes which balances the historical and spiritual in a way seldom found in other works on religious life.

THE THREE VOLUMES

The first volume, *Distant Echoes*, presents, within an historical frame of reference, the variety of life styles open to religious women from the fourth to the fifteenth centuries. It considers such important factors as economy, enclosure, relationship to bishops, and reasons for the evident lack of information about these nuns. Our contact with them is like a distant echo, often a barely audible reverberation sounding through writings by and about men. This second volume hopes to make those echoes clearer.

This volume, *Peaceweavers*, focuses on individual women and their spiritualities, experiences, and values. They were indeed peaceweavers who drew together into an harmonious whole all peoples by their total consecration to the non-violent Christ. They speak their messages of peace by this living witness, or, as Dr Jo Ann McNamara phrases it, by being 'living sermons' of the gospel message. They speak of devotion to the Crucified Christ and an intensity of womanly love. Often referred to as the 'Handmaidens of Christ' and as *sponsae Christi* (spouses of Christ), they identified with the poor in Christ in purity and simplicity. Called to weave peace by their lives of prayer, in the strong weakness of true humility and in an abounding charity, they challenge us, whether lay or religious, to live this peace in our time. These articles give valuable information on the lives of medieval religious women and re-express for us today the values they embodied.

The third volume, *The Cistercian Monastic Woman: Hidden Springs*, will deal specifically with the nuns of the Order of Cîteaux, few studies of whom exist in English. St Lutgard, Beatrice of Nazareth, Ida of Leau, Ida of Nivelle, Alice of Schaerbeek, St Gertrude and St Mechtild were vessels of living waters whose lives and writings put us in touch with that ultimate spring and source, the Holy Spirit; by their paths of hidden holiness they sought union with God and solidarity with their brothers and sisters in this lived union. Viewing cistercian women from the twelfth to the seventeenth centuries, this volume also seeks to lay basic groundwork in historical and methodological studies. We hope that this beginning will invite even more studies on these fruitful yet hidden springs.

Each volume follows a chornological sequence, and because of the diversity of disciplines and subjects, each contains an epilogue which the editors chose as embodying an important focus of the studies therein.

ACKNOWLEDGEMENTS

In a project of this scope a great number of persons took part in forming the final product. While it would be impossible to indicate everyone who had a share in this adventure, some names must be acknowledged.

From the religious community, Abbot Aidan Carr of Mepkin Abbey, Moncks Corner, South Carolina, and Abbot Thomas Davis of New Clairvaux Abbey, Vina, California, were literary editors who read every article and offered opinions or suggested revisions. Sisters from Mount St Mary's Abbey, Wrentham, Massachusetts—Agnes Day, Gertrude Ballew, and Colman O'Dell—as well as Sisters Regina Keating, Mary Ann Sullivan, Rosemary Durcan, Kathy Lyzotte, and Joanna Daly from Mississippi Abbey, Dubuque, Iowa, made significant contributions in improving the quality of the articles. Once articles were accepted, Sisters Beverly Aiden of Santa Rita Abbey in Sonoita, Arizona, Sister Mary Adorita Hart BVM, of Clarke College, Dubuque, Iowa, and Joseph Bawens of New Melleray Abbey, Dubuque, Iowa, prepared the drafts for the publisher.

From the academic community, Dr Jo Ann McNamara, Professor of History, Hunter College of the City University of New York, offered insightful suggestions. Drs Ann K. Warren, Department of History, Case Western Reserve University, Cleveland, Ohio, and Penny Gold, Department of History, Knox College, Galesburg, Illinois, provided contacts with members of the scholar world. And last but not least, Dr Rozanne Elder, Editorial Director of Cistercian Publications, Kalamazoo, Michigan, served as copy editor for the project.

The collaboration between the religious and academic communities was successful. Both groups learned from each other and as a result produced a collection of volumes on medieval religious women that is unique. May the readers of this series see the fruits of the collaboration and share in the harvest.

J.A.N

Introduction

Lillian Thomas Shank

WOMANHOOD IS GIFT and it is potential; it is bonding, lifegiving relationships; living it fully and holily weaves peace for women themselves and for the world. In this volume we meet integrated, holy women—whole women—walking through the age that was theirs, each of them uniquely different and yet all of them somehow alike. Their lives reflect the art of peaceweaving as well as the deep coupling of the human and divine.[1] Their spiritualities—their characteristic ways of life flowing from the heart—emerged from the beliefs and self-image each held, and we discover they had a positive self-image, despite their many protestations of womanly inadequacy. Human weakness was counter-balanced by an ever growing consciousness of God's presence guiding and emboldening them. Having touched real earth with bare and humble feet, they longed to cross the mystery of time in faith, hope, and love. Having been proven by encounters with both good and evil, they affirmed by their faith and experience the human-divine life within which energized them and let them gradually mature into persons fully human, fully alive.

Spanning thirteen centuries, from the fifth to the seventeenth, the twenty-two articles here have been written by academics and religious; some bring to light recent historical research and some emphasize a post-Vatican II perspective: some are scholarly in tone and others spiritual. Within an historical framework the authors study the shades and highlights of the religious woman, who felt herself called by God to express exclusive commitment to him by her whole way of life, usually by the profession of vows. Several articles focus on facets of the charism of a single woman. Others examine general movements that involved many women. This introduction will look briefly at the origins of, and early models available to, medieval religious women, and then synthesize her values and convictions as they weave the patterns of her spirituality into a brightly-colored tapestry.

ORIGINS

SCRIPTURE MODELS

As society and therefore social roles change, the religious woman seeks to live the Gospel within the culture of her day. Going back to her 'roots', she rediscovers herself in God's Word, in the gold of Scripture. His Word challenges and invites, it echoes within;[2] in this Gospel call the christian woman first becomes conscious of her unique identity. Early christian women sought to live this Word in their world. Medieval religious women looked to these early models, as do today's christian women. Together we form a great interconnected arc as we identify with their aspirations and are inspired by the example of their lives.[3] The events of history are dead, but the spirit of the persons who created the events still lives. Looking back receptively, we can catch this living spirit.

The religious woman commits herself to Christ, and these first christian women touched and loved him. Pondering their lives as we know them through Scripture, liturgy, history, and hagiography, we gain insight into our own quest and come into touch with our human-divine reality. These women transcend time and yet are rooted in this same reality, and from it they drew a sense of wholeness, dignity, and worth.

In the Scriptures we see first Our Lady. Reverent and receptive, she heard the angel's message; in the anguish of uncertainty (for Scripture says, 'she was greatly troubled . . . and asked "How can this be"'. Lk 1:29, 34) she believed and encourages us to believe: 'Behold, I am the handmaid of the Lord' (Lk 1:38). She received the Holy Spirit and bore Jesus in her womb. The simplicity and faith she showed at this Annunciation has empowered religious women also to form, to mother, Christ spiritually in themselves and in others. Mary exulted in God's grace and pondered his word in her heart. The religious woman also praises and ponders as the Word comes to life and is nurtured within her. Many articles make reference to Our Lady who, like a mother, succoured and guided these medieval women. St. Clare counseled her daughters to cling 'to his most sweet mother', for 'as the glorious Virgin of virgins carried him physically in her body, without a shadow of a doubt, you too, by following in her footprints, especially of humility and poverty, in your chaste and virginal body, can always carry him spiritually . . . and so possess him more securely then any passing riches which the world can offer'.[4] Religious women have long believed that Mary, the model of motherhood, accepts and loves us in all our sinful humanness, constantly drawing us into her Son's covenant of peace.

Mary Magdalen, loving and impetuous, followed Christ and with his mother 'stood near the cross of Jesus'. She hastened to the tomb weeping, and heard him call her tenderly by name. Is this the same Mary who sat at his feet at Bethany or the sinner who washed his feet and dried them with her hair? We are not sure, but in all these acts we see a richly warm woman seeking simply 'to be' with Jesus. To medieval women, Mary Magdalen exemplified ardent prayer as well as repentent love.

Anna, the prophetess, was their model of constant prayer and prophecy. Serving God night and day in the temple, Anna had been waiting patiently, longingly, in the wisdom of her age. Watching in attentive prayer, she was called to prophesy, to speak God's message of hope: '. . . and she spoke of him to all who were looking for the redemption of Jerusalem' (Lk 2:38). Like Anna, 'the recluse persevered in prayer' . . . and like Mary Magdalen [sat] at the Lord's feet'.[5] Well known through Scripture and liturgy, these two women provided potent models of the prayer that enlivens and speaks God's Word.

MARTYRS

Scripture also reveals, as a vivid red thread in our tapestry, the witness of martyrdom, men and women suffering side by side for the sake of Christ. The women of the early christian centuries manifested a courage drawn from an interior presence; their example stirred medieval women. Identification with Christ came in the experience of sharing Christ's passion. We see this poignantly in the death (in 177 AD) of the young slave girl, Blandina. She and three others, after being tortured, were taken to the amphitheatre. 'Blandina, suspended on a stake, was exposed as food to wild beasts which were let loose against her. Even to look on her, as she hung cross-wise in earnest prayer, wrought great eagerness in those [others] contending, for in their conflict they beheld with their outward eyes, in the form of their sister, him who was crucified for them.'[6] In a vivid way she had let Christ live in her for the salvation of the world. Blandina's martyrdom dramatically exemplifies the entry into the mystery of Christ that the religious woman must freely choose and live by the grace of her call. Blandina was not a born martyr. Her timid disposition had made some suspect she would be the first to recant under torture. It was her union with Christ in faith and love that overcame her fears.

In the liturgy we come into contact with the virgin-martyr saints of this early period: Cecilia, who died in Rome between 170-180; Agatha who died in Sicily about 249; and Agnes who died probably in 305. Their lives, some fifty years apart, are monuments to the ideal of virginity esteemed by the young christian community; their legends and acts, and the subsequent liturgical Offices honoring them, became formative for religious women from the earliest ages. In the choices they made we discern their spirit. Cecilia's liturgy breathes the joy and hope that is received from prayer and the reading of Scripture. 'To the sound of music Cecilia sang to the Lord.'[7] 'The glorious virgin ever carried the Gospel of Christ in her heart, and by day and by night she never stopped speaking with God in prayer.'[8] Agatha retorted to the judge who was trying her: 'I am free and noble born . . . . I am the servant of Christ . . . . the highest nobility is to be the slave of Christ'.[9] The liturgical Office honoring Agnes shows in depth the exclusive love the *sponsa Christi* had for Christ. Its bridal imagery expresses the highest womanly fulfillment in union with the divine.

> My Lord Jesus Christ espoused me with his ring, and as a bride he adorned me with a crown . . . . He has placed a mark on my face that I should admit no other love than himself . . . . I keep my troth to him alone and commit myself to him with all devotion . . . . at whose beauty the sun and moon wonder . . . . it is Christ whom I love . . . when I love him, I am chaste; when I touch him, I am pure; when I possess him I am a virgin.[10]

Capable of deep human relationships, these women committed themselves to another, Christ, and radically adhered to this commitment, loving with all their being. They move us, just as they have moved men and women throughout history. A spiritual verve emanates from their 'womanly weakness' and their witness has moved others to similar zeal. The story of St Cecilia moved Julian of Norwich to want Christ's 'pain to be my pain: a true compassion producing a longing for God. I was not wanting a physical revelation of God, but such compassion as a soul would naturally have for the Lord Jesus, who for love became a mortal man. Therefore I desired to suffer with him.'[11] Another virgin martyr, St Ursula, murdered (according to medieval legend) by the Huns near Cologne inspired Elizabeth of Schönau and Hildegard of Bingen; the latter wrote in a hymn about the love of this martyr:

> In a vision of true faith Ursula fell in love with the Son of God and renounced man with this world, and looked into the sun, and called to the loveliest youth, saying: 'In great desire have I desired to come to thee and sit with thee at the heavenly wedding feast, running to thee by a strange path as a cloud streams like sapphire in the purest air'.[12]

DESERT MOTHERS

From the crimson hues of martyrs, we move to the obscure blue-browns of the women monks who fled with their brothers to the desert in the fourth-century monastic movement.[13] We catch brief but telling glimpses of these *monachae*. On fire with an intensity of love, these women did not emphasize the externals of the ascetical life. Mother Talida, described as 'the aged handmaiden of Christ', dwelt in her nunnery for eighty years and taught sixty virgins 'the ascetic life in purity'. Dearly loved by her daughters, she led them to holiness by that liberty of spirit 'which she had acquired in Christ'.[14]

Melania the Great, friend of Rufinus, was described by Palladius as a 'holy woman. . . . having been held worthy to be seized upon by divine love . . . being hot with divine zeal and blazing like a flame with the love of Christ'.[15] She described herself simply as 'his handmaiden'. Blessed Olympias, another desert mother, 'was seized with a fervent desire of traveling in the path which leads to heaven. . . . and made herself cling close to the divine books'. She grew in humililty and simplicity, 'and the understanding which is without arrogance and the lowly heart, and the watching of vigil, and the spirit which is without anxious care. . . . she endured great contendings for the sake of the name of Christ'.[16] The way this woman chose summarizes monasticism: she pondered Scripture with a humbled heart, gentle constant watching, and eyes fixed on Jesus. Like the early virgins and martyrs, the first desert mothers were transformed by being conformed to Christ. Purity of heart, ardor, and poverty of spirit radiate from the desert.

Monasticism arose from Christians' desire to live the gospel and share the martyrs' full entry into the mystery of Christ.[17] The spirituality of the desert laid the foundation for the many forms of religious life that developed across the ensuing centuries.

PATTERNS

Having glimpsed our roots and come into contact with our own experience, and thus woven the lives of early christian women into our tapestry of time, we come to the ages spanned by this volume to view the vibrant colors of our medieval peaceweavers and to touch their living spirit. The warp and weft threads of their aspirations and convictions weave ten theme patterns.

SPONSA CHRISTI

'God the Father of heaven and King of kings, deign to wed me within my soul unto Christ the king, your Son . . . Holy Spirit, join my heart forever unto Jesus by that connecting tie of love wherein you do unite the Father and the Son.' So prayed St Gertrude.[18] To become a 'bride of Christ' was the foremost desire of religious women from Aldegund in the seventh century to Jeanne de Chantal in the seventeenth. Although they lived in societies that defined women by marriage, they took the *sponsa Christi* title not as a substitute, spiritualized marriage bond but rather as an expression of a complete personal relationship with 'Him whom my heart loves' (Song of Songs 3:1) in the words of the bride of the Canticle. It symbolized the deepest possible union between the human person and God. Jesus speaks to the Father on behalf of all of us in the Gospel of John: '. . . that they may all be one, even as thou, Father, art in me and I in thee, that they also may be in us . . . I in them and thou in me. . . .' (Jn 17:21–23). Aldegund was told by an angel that she would have only one bridegroom, Jesus Christ; the angel counseled: 'the more one guards the spark of faith in the soul, the more one will burn with the love of Christ'.[19] St Hildegard wrote that the nun is 'one who reorients not only her affections but all the capacities of her being toward the heavenly Bridegroom'.[20] In the thought of Jeanne de Chantal, 'the dying and rising Christ, who was to become the rhythm and source of her own interior music, was also the Christ to whom she was bethrothed, with whom she brought herself to birth, and whom she bore within herself as a reality as yet unborn'.[21] All these women felt called to oneness of union with Christ.

In the love song of the Old Testament the bride says: 'My beloved is radiant and ruddy' (Song of Songs 5:10). The medieval religious heard her speaking of Christ, radiant in his divinity, ruddy in his humanity. In order to become 'a full grown bride', to be transformed, the bride must assimilate the characteristics of Christ. The 'radiance' they interpreted as love, the grace of eternal life, the resurrection; it expressed divine reality. The 'ruddiness' they understood as human reality, the experience of joy or sorrow; it implied immersion in the mystery of Christ and desire for the salvation for all God's people.[22] These women perceived two complementary invitations, one to love of their 'radiant' Beloved, the other to enter into the mystery of the 'ruddy' Christ. In the imagery of Wendy Wright's article, they saw 'the two faces of Christ; the Beloved and the Crucified. As these two calls were accepted and lived out they believed Christ's image was formed within them, the bride and Bridegroom become one, the human and divine were coupled. Rich fruit was borne of a chaste devotion to the humanity of Christ'.[23] Like the martyrs before them these very ordinary brides entered the mystery of Christ with faces both radiant and ruddy.

ANAWIM[24]

These brides are the poor ones, God's handmaids, humble before God. Poverty of spirit is emphasized in every article and expressed uniquely in each woman's life. For Mechtild of Magdeburg poverty meant to 'make your heart crystal clear within and keep yourself outwardly small'.[25] In humility Teresa of Avila found truth: 'His majesty desires and loves courageous souls if they have no confidence in themselves but walk in humility. . . . God is Sovereign Truth and to be humble is to walk in truth . . .'.[26] Truth for Catherine of Siena was 'to know oneself as wholly dependent on God and thus to attain deep humility'. Only the humble, they all thought, can be transformed and drawn by God into the 'fathomless furnace of divine charity'.[27] Clare of Assisi belived humility demanded letting things go '. . . in order to be open and ready to receive the gifts of the Lord in prayer, one's heart must be free of clutter—the clutter of self and of material possessions and securities'.[28] St Hildegard's womanly weakness itself—her 'airiness', she called it—gave her a capacity for God.[29] Some women were asked to be 'fools for Christ', enduring contempt, ridicule, abuse; sharing in the passion of Christ they became empty and poor with the poor Christ.[30] By poverty of spirit these women surrendered and became his servants and handmaids, letting God speak through them. From the *anawim* spirit came a purified heart stripped of its false self and fully open to the Holy Spirit.

PROPHETS

Thus medieval religious women, weaving with the green thread of new life in the Spirit, became prophets and teachers, admonishing us by their lives and writings and sometimes by their visions. Although they were not allowed to preach, their holy lives were believed by many to give witness that the words they spoke came from God.[31] The 'holy woman', whether in reclusion or in a convent, was sought for advice and direction. 'Prophecy was a form of teaching in which a person shared with others the revelations received . . . women seemed to have received this gift more abundantly than men.'[32] Yet Origin said that graces of prophecy are determined 'by purity of heart alone, not by difference of sex'.[33] Like Anna, the prophetess in the temple, many of these women spoke messages to and on behalf of the Church. The message need not have been dramatic but could be simply a prophetic life of 'detachment from the ways of the world, desire for God, contemplative prayer for the good of the whole Church and all mankind'.[34] Sr Colman O'Dell's article exploring the theme of prophecy in Elizabeth of Schönau and Hildegard of Bingen opens with a challenging quotation from Pope John Paul II: 'The present-day world is awaiting everywhere . . . consecrated lives which tell, in acts more than words, of Christ and the Gospel. . . . I ask you, my Sisters, to contribute even more to the prophetic mission of the Church.'

THEOLOGIANS

Besides the bold, if sometimes hidden green of prophecy, these women also offer us the white gold of a rich experiential theology.[35a] They left no technical tracts explaining, with theological exactitude, the procession of the persons of the Trinity, yet their spirituality is deeply trinitarian; nor do we find a concise definition of the relationship of humanity and divinity in Christ, but they fully experienced these truths. Julian of Norwich is described as 'a true theologian with greater clarity, depth, and order than St Teresa: she really elaborates, theologically, the content of her revelation'.[35b] By reflection on her vision, Julian arrived at the theological principle that 'our humanity is incorporated in Christ and thereby joined to divinity'. In a single passage she linked experienced theology and the symbolism of 'my beloved is radiant and ruddy'!

> I saw the red blood trickling down from under the garland, hot fresh and plentiful, just as it did at the time of the passion when the crown of thorns was pressed onto the blessed head of God and Man who suffered for me . . .

Julian saw the 'ruddy' passion of Christ and entered into his mystery. Then:

> at the same moment the Trinity filled me with heartfelt joy and I knew that all eternity was like this for those who attain heaven. For the Trinity is God and God the Trinity; the Trinity is our maker and keeper, our eternal lover, joy and bliss—all through our Lord Jesus Christ.[36]

In the Trinity she found the 'radiance' of divinity—eternal life and our eternal lover.

Mechtild of Magdeburg shared her experience in richly symbolic images: 'There [in heaven] the heavenly Father is the cup-bearer, Jesus Christ the Chalice, and the Holy Spirit the pure wine, and the Holy Trinity together the full plenishing of the Chalice and Love the mighty cellar.' Then in simplicity she described her own experience of the Trinity: 'Lord and heavenly Father, you are my heart! Lord Jesus Christ, you are my body! Lord Holy Spirit, you are my breath! Lord Holy Trinity, you are my only refuge and my everlasting peace'![37]

Besides the theological realities of God, they experienced such doctrinal truths as the existence of heaven, hell, and purgatory. Teresa of Avila tells of 'being carried up to heaven: the first persons I saw there were my father and mother'. Later 'I found myself, as I thought, plunged right into hell . . . . I felt a fire within my soul . . . . I felt . . . as if I were being both burned and dismembered; and I repeat that that interior fire and despair are the worst things of all'. But most of Teresa's experience in this realm of theology reflected her devotion to the humanity of Christ. One day she saw the beauty of his hands and at another time his divine face. Later '. . . I saw Christ at my side—or, to put it better, I was conscious of him . . . . I thought he was quite close to me . . . . I could not but be aware of his nearness to me . . . . I saw the most sacred humanity in far greater glory than I had ever seen before, I saw a most clear and wonderful representation of it in the bosom of the Father'.[38] Theirs was an 'experienced' theology and they became signs of salvation and witnesses to his divinity in the poverty of their humanity. They shared, perhaps without knowing it, the classic definition of the theologian: 'If you are a theologian you truly pray. If you truly pray you are a theologian'.[39] This theology prayer was their life.

PEACEMAKERS

Yet another thread medieval women wove into our tapestry can be seen in the delicately embroidered lavender patterns of peacemaking and mediating. Like Mary who, they believed, mediates for us with her Son, these women by gentleness, compassion, and courage worked for peace. Sixth and seventh-century frankish and anglo-saxon women, raised amid the strife of warring tribes, provided examples of peaceweaving in fostering reconciliation and in establishing the european beginnings of christian monastic life.[40] Not only did individual women mediate conflicts, some convents also acted as intermediaries between 'royalty and divinity'. The author of Radegund's life relates:

> because she loved all the kings, she prayed for the life of each, and instructed us to pray without interruption for the stability [of their kingdoms]. Whenever she heard that they had turned against each other with hatred she was greatly shaken and sent letters to the one and the other . . . . and she instructed us with tears in her eyes to pray for the kings without interruption.[41]

Anchoresses and recluses settled local quarrels, not from positions of power, but by the authority of their lives of prayer and poverty and by the advice they gave to those who had recourse to them.[42] St Clare saved all Assisi from bloodshed by holding the Blessed Sacrament before her at the convent gate to ward off saracen attack.[43] Catherine of Siena wrote indefatigably to the leaders of the Church pleading for reform and peace. In the face of their self-centeredness and the seemingly hopeless cause of peace she heard the Lord instruct: '. . . . let your respite be in glorifying and praising my name, in offering me the incense of constant prayer. . . . and let your place of refuge be my only begotten Son, Christ Crucified'.[44] Because they believed unwaveringly in God's presence in this life and trusted in him, these women strove—often successfully—to bring the peace of Christ to their world.

MONACHAE

Many of the women we will meet in these pages were taught by monastic rules which were, in a practical sense, commentaries on the Gospel; all of them were steeped in Scripture and meditated on Jesus and his Word. The spirit of the monastic life and the gospel values shaped their lives and their actions. These monastic women found in Scripture and The Rules constant exortations to love, and this love, joined to a woman's natural ability to nurture life and to give love, pervades their response to the Gospel, enriching humility and ascetic practices with maternal tenderness and care.[45] Love demanded conversion, change of heart, which is the ongoing process of becoming rooted in Christ. One paper tells of a nun who died and was brought back to life because the necessary business of conversion had not yet been finished. Conversion to God in humility, obedience, and charity began with the woman herself; only then could it extend to the world beyond.[46] A woman's natural ability to love had first to be purified of all possessiveness and cupidity, and this demanded living out the monastic and gospel values.

Obedience prepared the *monachae* to live in the freedom of the Holy Spirit. This obedience St Clare took to mean abandonment, sharing St Francis' 'perfect joy' in imitation of Jesus' own acceptance of the passion. Her 'Poor Ladies' also wished to interiorize that cry of Jesus: 'Father, into your hands. . . . Father, forgive them. . .'.[47] Those who followed the Rule of St Benedict accepted obedience as sharing the obedience of Christ who came not to do his own will but the will of him who sent him. To obey God's will was St Gertrude's desire: 'My heart has fixed itself upon the will of Jesus. . .'[48]

Most of the monastic women we meet here were formed to gospel values through community, their religious community and the community of the Church. Their communities supported them and provided an environment conducive truly to living the christian life. The difficulties inevitably encountered in the demands of community living were often seen as God's choice means to perfect still unpolished virtues of humility and charity. Women used their talents and gifts in community, some as spiritual mothers and leaders, others in the humble everyday service of one another. We see Mechtild von Hackeborn in the mainstream of the common life. As chantress, teacher, and counselor, doing the household tasks, she gave gospel witness: '. . . Mechtild's apostolate was an individual ministry, to manifest the infinite reaches of divine love accessible to every person.'[49]

As bonding shuttle, the deep quiet blue of prayer keeps the weft threads of monastic gospel values in place. Prayer nourished all these women, who understood it as being present to a God who loved them, understood them, trusted them—it was deep relationship sometimes expressed as that between daughter and father (or the Christ mother), sister and brother, bride and bridegroom, friend and closest friend. It allowed the sharing of anguish and disappointments as well as intimate avowals of love and surrender. It was attentive listening to the still small voice within and responding in faith and love. Catherine of Siena reiterated 'the absolute necessity of building in one's soul an interior cell into which one can return to be alone with God and attend to his word and will. . . . continual prayer was nothing else than a ceaseless holy desire for God and a sharing in Christ's hunger and thirst for souls'.[50] Prayer for Julian of Norwich and St Gertrude was growth into union, the intimate communion of face to face vision. Prayer drew them into the mystery of Christ—on the cross, in the resurrection, recognized in every person. The recluse in her hermitage imitated Christ for 'Christ was truly a hermit and the cross was his hermitage',[51] that is, the cross was his place, his experience of prayer. They expressed their prayer through devotion to the Holy Cross, the five wounds of Christ, and the mysteries of his life; through devotion to Mary, and later to the rosary, and then the Blessed Sacrament. To pray truly they found they had to prepare themselves by conversion of life. Love of one another, detachment, and humility, which is the most important, was Teresa of Avila's prescription for preparation for prayer.[52] She herself is described as '. . . a guide for the heights, those moments on the mount of unitive embrace; for the lowlands, when we wonder if we can ever climb out again; for the plateau, when we would just as soon set up a tent and stop moving.[53] In the preparation for prayer, Clare believed, 'at the deepest level poverty readied the heart to receive the gift of the Lord'.[54] The pray-er's purpose was to become prayer, to become a person in whom the Holy Spirit can freely move and pray. Each woman in this book speaks in a manner both intimate and original of her experience of prayer.[55] As each grew in prayer she grew in her oneness with all men and women, with all creation. Lives of prayer cement the ontological unity which exists among all persons; prayer reaches out to everyone in a cosmic dimension from 'solitude to solidarity', as the lives of our recluses and anchoresses reveal.[56] To pray is to travel inward, to come into touch with ourselves at our very center, where God is, and so to come into touch with God. In this continuing contact through love, petition, praise, thanksgiving, and even sorrow and anguish, these women became transformed.

FRIENDS

The religious women we will meet here allowed charity to come to fruition in them by embracing an asceticism of love. As Suzanne Wemple's article explains: 'these women conceived of religious growth as self development through charity;'[57] therefore it is not surprising to find them excelling in the art of friendship and relationship. As spiritual mothers, many developed life-giving relationships with their spiritual daughters and sons. Others simply shared the mystery of Christ and encouraged one another—as did St Gertrude and St Mechtild von Hackeborn of Helfta, who were close friends. We find also a sense of cooperation and friendship between men and women In this volume we discover men and women collaborating in double monasteries, as well as pairs of spiritual friends: Francis and Clare of Asssisi, Jean de Chantal and Francis de Sales, Elizabeth and her brother Egbert of Schönau. In each case they offered one another mutual encouragement, and the insights of one were re-expressed by the other. Mutually enriching each other with their complementary gifts, they could inspire, correct, and advise one another. Not that there were no tensions! But these women were able to handle the quirks of human nature which, after all, afflict women as well as men. Hildegard had such great difficulty with Abbot Kuno of Disibodenburg that she began her own independent monastery at Rupertsburg. Refused communion by a priest, Ivetta received the sacrament from John the Evangelist. Ragdegund protested the usurpations of her local bishop and was protected by her step-son Sigebert.[58] Some protested injustices, some took refuge in God alone. On the whole we find collaboration between men and women growing into a satisfying mutuality as they met the christian religious challenge together, interacting, influencing, loving, and supporting each other as the culture of their time permitted.[59]

WOMEN

A distinct pattern of feminine identity emerges among our medieval women, who are described as mothers, virgins, widows, and brides of Christ. They appear as compassionate, peaceful, sensitive, nurturing, sweet, attuned to the experience of relationship, able to mediate, and to love. Womanly powerlessness made them capable of a potent receptivity to the Holy Spirit. Barbara Newman's paper illumines this quality as she points out many of Hildegard's original insights into the beauty of the feminine. Teresa of Avila countered the poverty of her womanhood with her supernatural anthropology: 'I don't find anything comparable to the magnificent beauty of a soul and its marvelous capacity. . . . it is a beautiful and delightful castle'.

This 'poor' woman knew she was created in God's image and that her soul was 'a brilliantly shining and beautiful castle'.[60] All these women were life-giving, mothers in the deepest sense. Mechtild of Magdeburg saw all persons as one of her three children 'for whom I foresee great trouble. The first child stands for poor sinners who lie in everlasting death . . . my second child stands for those poor souls who suffer in purgatory . . . my third child stands for those spiritual people who are not yet perfect'.[61] Julian of Norwich spoke more startlingly of the 'motherhood of God' and 'the Christ mother'. She saw womanly mercy, tenderness, and lifegiving qualities in Jesus who, of course, has given them to women.[62]

PILGRIMS

Constant movement inward and upward to more profound union, more fervent prayer, greater concern for others, made of these women pilgrims on a quest, an adventure, that involved their whole life. St Benedict instructs that the one great requirement of the *monachus/monacha* is that s/he truly seek God; this quality reveals an interior dynamism at work, a growth. We tend to think of these great saints as living on peaks, static on their saintly pedestals, and we forget the laborious and painful growth and climb that led to the heights. Various articles speak of Julian's growth in prayer, Mechtild's growth in love, and Gertrude's conversion and growth in monastic values.[63] It is perhaps in Margot King's unusual article on Christina Mirabilis that we get the best sense of spiritual growth and its place in a medieval religious woman's life. Christina was seeking a life of contemplation, but found that virtues must be developed by God's gifts; thus results the cycle of growth. Borrowing William of St Thierry's three stages of growth; animal (needing nourishment), rational (needing education), and spiritual (having attained freedom) Dr King traces Christina's growth from basic virtues to mystic heights.

These women, as pilgrims, sought in loneliness, faith, and darkness. Growth in God means letting oneself be stripped of every vestige of the false self, and it is fraught with trials and anguish. Jeanne de Chantal experienced inner desolation, and Mechtild von Hackeborn was tormented by a conviction of her unworthiness and wasted life. All these women experienced a painful spiritual maturing in following their beloved, 'radiant and ruddy'.

CHRISTBEARERS

The desire these women had to put on Christ, to be transformed, made them Christ bearers in every event of their daily lives. But it was particularly their participation in the liturgy that set the mystery of Christ before them. This liturgical cycle was especially important for the women of Helfta, as it is for all those who follow the Rule of St Benedict, but it was also true for the recluses and anchoresses who often recited the Divine Office and made the Mass an important part of their daily devotions. Eucharistic devotion gave a uniquely personal meaning to the pauline phrase: 'I live now, not I, but Christ lives in me' (Gal 2:19–20).

This devotion was expressed in the profession of religious vows which, as a second baptism, made them Christbearers committed to Christ. Each of them put on Christ, and brought his word to their world. In our Epilogue, Mother Jean Marie Howe traces the profound meaning of the religious woman's profession of vows.[64] Only through porousness (receptivity) and in *kenosis* (the emptying of the false self), she says, are we enabled to respond ever more fully to the call to immerse ourselves in Christ and his mysteries. The rich red of chastity is 'fire, energy'; royal blue is loss of self in poverty; yellow gold is union of wills in obedience; these are the threads of his life by which he transforms us. The vows are not techniques but, when received and responded to in freedom, become cords of grace drawing us toward the goal to which all men and women are called: union with the Beloved, union with the Word, who leads us to the Father in the Holy Spirit.[65]

In the concluding Afterword, Sr Agnes Day concisely summarizes the volume, encouraging us to examine carefully this unique and interwoven human tapestry.

The completed weave of warp and weft is the more brilliant because it reflects experiences of earth's deepest realities—suffering, sorrow, joy, love, prayer, faith, and the conflict of good and evil, the meaning of life and death. It guides us through time to 'connect' with these women, and to know and love them. They speak to us of our own conversion and the conversion of our children, teaching us in the Holy Spirit the way to bring Christ and his peace and love to our modern world. They are models for us in their experiences of the human-divine reality which is our life as it was theirs.[66]

NOTES

1. The values and experience of these women will speak to both men and women, religious and lay, Catholic and non-Catholic. We are all called to image this coupling of human and divine. 'So God created man in his own image, in the image of God he created him. Male and female he created them' (Gn 1:27). Fr David Knight in his book *Lift Your Eyes to the Mountain* describes the religious and lay vocation as a deep living of the christian life. We are all called to the same goal but we live it in different ways.

2. This is a reference to our Volume One, *Distant Echoes*. In the concluding article, I explain the cause and meaning of the religious woman's call by the image of an echo within of the call of the Holy Spirit. The Spirit elicits a response from all men

and women. They are the custodians of this Word in the mystery of human history, an intense cooperation between God and men and women.

3. We speak here only of New Testament models and then only the most important, leaving aside Old Testament models.

4. From Fidelis Hart, "Following in the Footprints of the Poor Christ: Clare's Spirituality'. p. 180 below.

5. Jean Leclercq, 'Solitude and Solidarity: Medieval Woman Recluses', p. 77.

6. Eusebius, *History of the Church*, trans. by G. A. Williamson, (Minneapolis: Augsburg, 1965) 193–203. This letter from the Churches of Lyons and Vienne to the Churches of Asia and Phrygia is described as 'one of the most perfect documents of Christian antiquity'. The letter includes also a description of Blandina's death: '. . . the blessed Blandina, last of all like a noble mother who had encouraged her children hastened to them, rejoicing and glad at her departure as though invited to a marriage feast rather than cast to the beasts.'

7. Lauds Antiphon, *Cistercian Day Hours Breviary* (Abbey of Gethsemani, 1961) p. 351.

8. *Cistercian Beviary*, Gethsemani english antiphonary for choral office, 1982.

9. Mourret-Thompson, *History of the Catholic Church* Vol. I, (St Louis: Herder Co., 1946) 383.

10. *The Roman Beviary*, edited by Bede Babo, OSB, (Benziger Bros. 1964) 761–68.

11. Ritamary Bradley, SFCC, 'Julian on Prayer', p. 294.

12. Barbara Newman, 'Divine Power made Perfect in Weakness: St. Hildegard on the Frail Sex', p. 117.

13. The sources used here are from Palladius' works written about 419–420; see also the *Apophthegmata*. More and more research is being done in this area.

14. Palladius, 'The Paradise of Palladius', *The Paradise of the Holy Fathers*, Vol I, trans. by E. A. Wallis Budge (1907, reprint 1972) p. 153.

15. Ibid., 156–60. This fiery prayer is described in Cassian's *Conferences* on prayer as one of the highest forms of prayer.

16. Wallis-Budge, 163–65.

17. The evangelical counsels (Mt 19:12, 21, 29) are the bases of the vows of poverty, chastity and obedience usually taken by religious. They are promises to be chaste for the sake of the Kingdom, to live Jesus' obedience to the Father, and to leave everything in order truly to follow him; they reflect counsels given in the gospel which in the tradition of the Church gradually provided a structure for religious promises.

18. Lillian Thomas Shank, OCSO, 'The God of my Life: St Gertrude, a Monastic Woman', p. 242. See also, the epilogue article in *MRW I: Distant Echoes*, by Dom Jean Leclercq, on the theme of spousal union as a goal for all peoples; it is entitled 'Does St. Bernard have a Specific Message for Nuns?'

19. Suzanne Wemple, 'Female Spirituality and Mysticism in Frankish Monasteries: Radegund, Balthild, and Aldegund', p. 47.

20. Newman, p. 110.

21. Wendy Wright, 'Jeanne de Chantal: Two Faces of Christ', p. 362.

22. For an enlightening commentary on this verse from the Song of Songs see *Secrets of the Interior Life*, by Archbishop Luis M. Martinez (St. Louis, Herder, 1949) p. 195. See Rev. M. Jeanne Marie Howe's article in this volume; 'Monastic Life: Vows/A Vision' for the meaning of 'immersion in the mystery of Christ'.

23. Devotion to the humanity of Christ was strong in all these women. Br Laurin Hartzog, OCSO, treats this theme specifically in his paper: 'Teresa of Jesus: the Saint and her Spirituality'.

24. The *anawim* are the 'poor of Yahweh'. This Old Testament concept describes the biblical person, the one who lives in God's presence, totally committed, fully surrendered, blindly confidant. This poor one becomes God's instrument with the ability to welcome God, to be open to God, and willing to be used by God; a humility before God. This concept is fully developed by Albert Gelin PSS, in *The Poor*

of Yahweh (Collegeville: Liturgical Press, 1963). The *anawim* spirit pervades the New Testament; Mary, the mother of Jesus, with her Old Testament roots exemplifies it.

25. Edith Scholl, ocso, 'To be a Full Grown Bride: Love and Growth in Mechtild of Magdeburg'. p. 230.

26. Hartzog, p. 321.

27. Susan A. Muto, 'Foundations of Christian Formation in the Dialogues of St. Catherine of Siena'. p. 279.

28. Madge Karecki, SSJ-TOSF, 'Clare; Poverty and Contemplation in her Life and Writing'. p. 171.

29. Newman, p. 109. This insight into the positive aspects of womanly weakness is treated fully in her article.

30. See Margot King, 'The Sacramental Witness of Christina *Mirabilis*: The Mystic Growth of a "Fool for Christ's Sake"', pp. 151. See also Jean Leclercq on recluses, (fn 5, p. 77).

31. Patricia Rosof, 'The Anchoress in the Twelfth and Thirteenth Centuries', p. 135

32. Jean Leclercq, p. 80, n. 5.; if it is true that women received the gifts of prophecy more abundantly than men perhaps it was their womanly weakness that made them capable of becoming porous, open, pure of heart.

33. Origin, 'Homily V.2 on Judges, 11' cited by Colman O'Dell ocso in 'Elizabeth of Schonau and Hildegard of Bingen: Prophets of the Lord', p. 86.

34. Leclercq, p. 80, n.5.

35a. In emphasizing experienced theology, we do not imply approval of purely subjective (and sometimes false) experiences that can come from our false self or other sources. We are speaking of an experience of the 'whole' person, as has been fostered in 'monastic theology', which is not just an intellectual evaluation of theology but also the 'experience' of the reality underlying it.

35b. Thomas Merton, *Confessions of a Guilty Bystander* cited by Ritamary Bradley, p. 292.

36. Bradley, p. 294.

37. Scholl, n. 25, p. 225.

38. Hartzog, n. 23: p. 325, p. 326, p. 327, p. 324, p. 320.

39. Evagrius Ponticus, *Praktikos, Chapters on Prayer*, trans. by John Eudes Bamberger, ocso, Cistercian Studies 4 (Cistercian Publications, 1970) p. 65.

40. Janemarie Luecke OSB, 'The Unique Experience of Anglo-Saxon Nuns', pp. 56–58, and Wemple, n. 19, pp. 44–45.

41. Wemple, n. 19, p. 44.

42. Rosof, n. 31, p. 135 and Leclercq, n. 5, p. 78.

43. Hart, n. 4, p. 179.

44. Muto, n. 27, p. 284.

45. Wemple, n. 19, p. 43.

46. JoAnn McNamara, 'Living Sermons: Consecrated Women and the Conversion of Gaul', pp. 28–29.

47. Francis Thom, osc, 'Clare of Assisi: New Leader of Women', p. 202.

48. Shank, 'The God of my Life: St Gertrude, Monastic Woman', p. 250.

49. Jeremy Finnegan, OP, 'Saint Mechtild of Helfta: *Nemo Communior*', p. 213.

50. Muto, n. 27, p.283.

51. Leclercq, n. 5, p. 77.

52. Keith Egan, 'The Foundations of Mystical Prayer: *The Interior Castle*, Mansions 1–3', p. 337.

53. St Margaret Dorgan, DCM, 'St Teresa of Avila: A Guide for Travel Inward', p. 351.

54. Karecki, n. 28, p. 171.

55. See Sr Ritamary Bradley's article on growth in prayer in Julian, Sr Margaret Dorgan and Keith Egan's articles on prayer in Teresa of Avila, Sr Madge Karecki's

article on poverty and prayer in St Clare and Sr Lillian Thomas Shanks' article on St Gertrude.

56. Leclercq, n. 5. pp. 80–81.

57. Wemple, n. 19. p. 48.

58. See Colman O'Dell, 'Elizabeth of Schönau and Hildegard of Bingen: Prophets of the Lord, p.94, Patricia Rosof (n. 31, p.140) and Suzanne Wemple (n. 19, p. 40).

59. See Rosemary Rader OSB, *Breaking Boundaries: Male/Female Friendship in Early Christian Communities* (Ramsey, N.J.: Paulist Press, 1983).

60. Egan, n. 52 pp. 339–40.

61. Scholl, n. 25. p. 229.

62. Charles Cummings, OCSO, 'Motherhood of God according to Julian of Norwich', pp. 306–9.

63. These articles are by Ritamary Bradley, Edith Scholl, Lillian Thomas Shank, p. 290ff, p. 223ff, p. 239ff.

64. To amplify what is meant here I quote from the Letter of Pope John Paul II to the Bishops of the United States 3 April 1983; 'Essential Elements in the Church's Teaching on Religious Life as Applied to Institutes Dedicated to Works of the Apostolate': 'Consecration is the basis of religious life. By insisting on this the Church places the first emphasis on the initiative of God and on the transforming relation to Him which religious life involves. Consecration is a divine action. God calls a person whom He sets apart for a particular dedication to Himself. At the same time, He offers the grace to respond so that consecration is expressed on the human side by a profound and free self-surrender. The resulting relationship is pure gift. It is a covenant of mutual love and fidelity, of communion and mission, established for God's glory, the joy of the person consecrated and the salvation of the world' (Part 5, page 16).

65. The marriage vows also plunge a man and a woman together into the mystery of Christ making each responsible for the growth of Christ's life in the other. The sacraments plunge us all—religious, single, married—into the 'radiant and ruddy' Christ. Baptism is a gift seed of divinity.

66. For a further study of the theology of the human divine reality see: Karl Rahner in *Foundations of Christian Faith*, trans. Wm. V. Dych (New York: Seabury, 1978). Ch. IV: 'Man as the Event of God's Free and Forgiving Self-Communication'. See also: Richard P. McBrien's *Catholicism* (Winston Press, 1981) Vol I, Chapter V and Vol II, Ch. XXVIII.

Living Sermons: Consecrated Women and the Conversion of Gaul

Jo Ann McNamara

> Where now do the words of scripture not resound? Daily they are recited by lectors in the churches and sweetly sung by cantors and soundly explained by preachers. What country, what city, what farm is not honored with the patronage of some saint by special providence of the Creator? And thus, through his members, Our Saviour gleams everywhere. His name pours out like oil, everywhere resounding; always it rains down through the Gospel, through the apostles, through the doctors and through the example of the saints.[1]

IT HAD TAKEN hundreds of years. Lifetime after patient lifetime had been spent amid scenes of violence and death, on a dark field fitfully lit with flashes of the miraculous. Deep-rooted loyalties to old gods and old beliefs gave way only slowly and reluctantly before the christian missionary efforts not only of saintly men but also of saintly women in Gaul.

Only in modern times has this essential contribution of women to the conversion of Europe been ignored, as historians have become increasingly mesmerized by institutional history and increasingly contemptuous of the hagiographic material which commemorated women's achievement. Valuable sources show that in three major ways, saintly women participated actively in the conversion of the Gauls and of their Frankish invaders. First, women acted as a bridge between the gallic christian community and the barbarians, most dramatically in the baptism of their kings. Secondly, women were patrons, foundresses and rulers of monastic communities planted in the deteriorating cities and devastated countryside of Gaul, and these served as an agency for the conversion of other women. The task of the saintly foundress or abbess was to provide pastoral guidance for women brought by a variety of circumstances into the community: to shape their manners, their lives, their personalities to that demanding humility, obedience, and charity which conversion 'to religion' demanded. Finally, women reached out from these communities to the world beyond. Their communities acted as supply bases for the heroic individuals who ventured out over long distances to carry the Gospel to new tribes. More directly, these communities exemplified christian principles to the poor among whom they lived and to the hordes of miserable wanderers who tramped the roads of that war-torn world. What was the immediate effect of their efforts in the Christianization of Frankland? What was the continuing effect of the records of their deeds, re-shaped and molded into living sermons for the continuing instruction of the faithful?[2]

THE CONVERSION OF THE FRANKISH MONARCHY

Gallic Christianity. Late in the second century the Emperor Marcus Aurelius determined to purge his realm of various undesirable influences, Christians among them. As a result, our first records of a christian community in Gaul tell of persecution and the dramatic deaths of the martyrs of Lyon. Among those who spread the faith by the example of their sufferings, first place is given to the slave girl, Blandina, whom the Romans singled out for a particularly grisly ordeal in hopes of securing her recantation.

Even at this early stage, a diocesan network had already been established to maintain the christian community and to expand it, partly by circulating the inspiring account of the martyrs' heroism. Under such adverse circumstances, however, conversion could be only a slow and painful process, with almost as many steps backward as forward; the conversion of the Emperor, the protection of the state, and the patronage of leaders of society were crucial to the conversion of an entire community. Only in the fourth and fifth centuries, therefore, did Christianity begin to make real inroads into the gallic population. Representatives of the roman landed and bureaucratic aristocracies were gradually wooed into the new hierarchy of ecclesiastical administrators. Christian emperors outlawed the public rites of the old religions, and christian bishops began a vigorous offensive against the old cults of the gallic countryside.[3]

The cities of Gaul, with their proselytizing bishops and busy religious communities long remained outposts in a pagan countryside. In the late fourth century, when Martin of Tours moved around his diocese, he was constantly confronted with rituals in pagan temples and hostile crowds determined to defend their sacred trees.[4] Indications in the life of Saint Genovefa in the fifth century suggest that tree worship and other pagan practices still persisted.[5] Saint Radegund, in the sixth century, stopped on her way to dine with a friend to burn down a pagan temple; even with the protection of her bodyguard, it required great personal courage for her to remain seated motionless on her horse confronting the violence of the enraged villagers.[6] The lives of saints well into the eighth century are marked with such incidents, showing the persistence of pagan temples and rites in the very heart of christian Gaul. Moreover, the nature of the fanes centered on sacred wells and groves of trees, or dedicated to known roman deities like Venus and Diana, strongly indicate that these were old gallic cults, not newly implanted frankish centers.

Martin of Tours, who was to become the patron of the entire missionary effort in Gaul, did not find the episcopacy an entirely satisfactory vehicle for the work of conversion. Indeed, he complained that, after his reluctant elevation to the office, he had lost some of the ease with which he had formerly channeled the healing graces of God through himself to the diseased supplicants who came to him.[7] He was therefore anxious to sponsor the spread of the ascetic movement into Gaul. His friend and biographer, Sulpicius Severus, depicts his efforts to introduce gallic Christians to the eastern practices. Their reluctant response gave a strong foretaste of the future of western monasticism.[8] The robust venturer into the 'deserts' of northern Europe was rarely a seeker after solitude. He was far more likely to be an active seeker after new souls for the christian community.

In the east and then in Italy, women occupied an important place in the spread of ascetic communities. The new movement offered them, and they eagerly seized, freedom and scope for the development of their religious aspirations. As the consecrated life became popular in Gaul, the presence of women was therefore felt strongly in the life of the church. In 396, Victricius of Rouen painted a vivid picture of the ascetics of his city as they came out to welcome a translated relic:

> Here there presses the crowd of monks with their faces emaciated by fasting; there the sonorous joy of innocent boys bursts out. Here the choir of devout and untouched virgins carries the ensign of the cross. There the multitude of continent men and widows, wholly worthy of entering the procession for their life is all the more splendid that their lot has proved harder. . . . These women advance in brilliant array, glowing with the gifts of God. Their hearts are filled with the riches of the Psalms. There is no vigil night in which such jewels do not shine forth. There is no religious festival which such finery does not adorn. The crowd of the chaste

> joy of the Saint, the multitude of widows and continents attracts the heavenly powers.[9]

In this period, while the land was still pacified by Rome, consecrated women were an actively present part of the christian community, and thus their presence could directly influence their non-christian neighbors. Bishop Hilary of Poitiers does not seem to have thought that his consecrated virgin daughter, Abra, needed to be housed in a convent.[10] Nor did Sulpicius suggest that a prefect's daughter who was cured of a fatal illness by a letter of Martin leave her home after being consecrated to God.[11] There may have been communities of women living in Tours under Martin's protection, but we do not know of any specific rule of life in general use for women at that time. The writings of John Cassian must have been available for the guidance of the women in his fifth century community in Marseilles, but we have no concrete information as to their application.[12] Certainly, at that time, no authority existed with the power or resources to regulate these communities. Thus no clear line was drawn between consecrated women and their neighbors, leaving the former free to participate actively in the on-going efforts of the ecclesiastical establishment to christianize the population of Gaul.

The arrival of the Franks. The late fifth century preserved the memory of one such life, lived out in an age when the faith of the partially christianized Gauls was being subjected to the onslaughts of the pagan Franks. Unlike most of the saints who drew the attention of hagiographers, Genovefa was a poor orphan of peasant stock whose life was lived among her poor and suffering contemporaries.

Genovefa was marked out for the consecrated life in childhood by Germanus of Auxerre, who could spare her but a single day of his busy life for instruction. She was left to her own devices thereafter, with only a coin embossed with the cross to hang about her neck in token of her sacred purpose.[13] She continued alone and unaided in her path until she was old enough to be consecrated by the bishop. But, despite the fact that other girls were consecrated with her, she did not join any community, nor indeed does there appear to have been a community available.[14] A poor girl, she lived at home, subject to complaints and beatings by her mother when she gave prayer and church attendance priority over her household chores.[15] Apparently she labored to support herself throughout her life, with the occasional assistance of miracles. For example, she was once out with the mowers harvesting her field, when the entire area was threatened with a violent rainstorm. Thanks to her prayers, not a single blade of her corn was even moistened while the tempest raged around her. A humble enough miracle, perhaps, but it is hard to imagine any wonder better fitted to convince a peasant population of the importance of prayer.[16]

After her parents' death she was taken by her godmother to Paris, where she was threatened more than once by persons hostile to her vocation.[17] Her biographer does not say who those detractors were, but if they were Christians, their conversion appears to have been grossly incomplete. Even the most famous deed of her life, the organization of a group of pious matrons to protect Paris from the invading Huns with a wall of prayer, was not accomplished without personal danger. An archdeacon saved her in the nick of time from a mob intent on stoning her as a false prophet leading them to destruction in a doomed and defenseless city.[18]

The life of Genovefa is but one of several accounts of the difficulties of christian life at the end of the fifth century. Successive waves of barbarian invaders constantly threatened the lives of rural and urban dwellers alike. The hoards of the poor and miserable were swollen by crowds of refugees fleeing endless violence.[19] Catholic Christians in southern Gaul and Burgundy were additionally distressed by the hostility of arian barbarians.[20] Gregory of Tours maintained, for example, that the Vandals confiscated the estates of Catholics who refused re-baptism and even tortured at least one Christian virgin to death.[21] For the orthodox, then, the conversion of the Franks not only to Christianity but to Catholic Christianity, was a matter of life and death.

One of those whose lives, preaching, and miracles prepared the invaders for this conversion was Genovefa, tirelessly travelling over the gallic countryside in the critical days when King Childeric was completing his conquest of Gaul. When the Franks were besieging Paris, she persuaded the king to allow her to take a fleet of ships down the Seine to collect food for the city. Of all the miracles which accompanied that progress, perhaps the most astonishing was her reckless distribution of the hard-won food to the poorest and the most helpless people in the city on her return.[22] Like many of her contemporaries, Genovefa worked like a leaven to lighten the hearts of the Franks.

Though he died still pagan, King Childeric must have shared some of the amazement of her contemporaries at these displays of piety and charity. On one occasion, when he wanted to execute some prisoners, he is said to have locked the gates so that Genovefa could not come out of the city until the deed was done. Undeterred, the saint pushed aside the heavy barriers and saved the hapless captives. In all probability, these captives were Christians, like the besieged Parisians. If so, Genovefa's work in bending the pagan king to clemency for his conquered subjects, her efforts to gain his sympathy and respect for their religion, would be an important contribution to the process of mutual assimilation.

A chain of Queens. Although, as in fourth century Rome, a substantial christian population showed itself capable of surviving persecution and hardship, the completion of the conversion of the countryside and of the new ruling class required the protection and patronage of the monarcy. The crucial work of bringing the Frankish king Clovis and his aristocratic following into the christian flock depended on his queen, Clotilda, the first link in a chain of queens who secured the conversions of both pagan and arian monarchs in succeeding centuries. When Clotilda was still a child, her arian uncle murdered her father and mother and drove her sister Chrona into exile. We do not know why he kept Clotilda at his court, but she was there when the emissaries of Clovis came to seek out a wife for their pagan king. Clotilda was a Catholic in that arian court. It is possible that this conflict of religion had something to do with the death of her parents: the fact that her sister became a nun suggests that they were not Arians. But it could also be that Clotilda deliberately embraced that faith later on. Saint Avitus, who converted her cousin Sigismund, may also have influenced her.

The chance, or carefully plotted design, that culminated in Clovis' request for the hand of the orphaned and friendless catholic princess from her arian guardian remains somewhat obscure in the available sources.[23] That Clotilda regarded herself as the agent of her husband's conversion is, however, clear. Once married, she relentlessly cajoled and hectored Clovis, despite his frequent outbursts of anger. At last he submitted to baptism and, with him, the chieftains of the frankish people proclaimed the nation officially catholic.

The baptism of Clovis did not, of course, transform the Franks into exemplary Christians, but the royal family did act as powerful patrons actively engaged in the conversion of their arian and pagan neighbors. From the frankish royal family, a chain of queens anxious to emulate the achievement of Clotilda spread over Europe. Clovis' sister Alboflede was sent to the court of the arian Theodoric. She failed to convert her husband, but this did not deter Bishop Nicetius in 564 from urging the same tactic with his lombard successors in Italy. He urged Clotilda's granddaughter, Clotsinde, to emulate her grandmother by converting her husband Alboin, King of the Lombards, an effort that was completed by Theodelinde in the next generation.[24]

Clotilda's daughter and namesake was married to Amalric, king of the Visigoths, who greeted her efforts to convert him with nothing but abuse, throwing dung at her whenever she went to catholic services. Young Clotilda's brother took the occasion to avenge her and, incidentally, to loot the visigothic kingdom, but the princess died soon thereafter, her task uncompleted. In the next generation, however, the Visigoths were more receptive. When their princess Brunhilda married Clotilda's grandson, she converted to Catholicism and the rest of her family followed soon after.[25] At about the same time, another frankish princess, Bertha, set off for England, where she opened the kingdom of Kent to roman missionaries sent by Gregory the Great.[26]

The conversion of these monarchs brought their peoples under the official authority of the catholic religion and made them accessible to further teaching. At best, however, the mass baptisms they sponsored could only have had the most superficial effects. The urban poor and remote rural populations could not have experienced even this minimal contact with the church. Their conversion would be undertaken over the next centuries by women and men largely based in monastic communities.

THE CONVERSION OF WOMEN

> A certain girl, ill with a paralyzing disease and, what is worse, entangled in the error of a fanatic cult, sought the tomb of the blessed [Martin of Tours]
>
> and, after celebrating a vigil there, was returned to health. Called back again to the vomit of her idolatry, she incurred again the weakness from which she had been freed by the power of the priest.[27]

Promoters of modern evangelical movements have often attested to the ease with which an audience can be inspired, only to revert to apathy in ensuing days. Transformation of transient enthusiasm into a deeply-rooted personal commitment to the principles of Christianity must be the ultimate goal of every missionary endeavor. Where there is no strong permanent local organization to tend the fire kindled by the preacher, it readily sputters out. Similarly the work of Clotilda and her descendants required constant reinforcement from institutions for the conversion and instruction of new Christians.

Monasteries of women, established first in fortified cities and later in the countryside, carried on this work in two ways. They acted as refuges to shelter women who sought to escape the confines of the secular world, and they acted as an evangelizing vanguard, reaching out to the local population.

The cloister as sanctuary. The girl featured in the exemplary tale above could not spend her life in vigil at the tomb of her healer. In the early fifth century, when Paulinus of Nola recorded her story, there does not seem to have been anywhere for her to go except back to the pagan community from which she had come. By the sixth and seventh centuries, however, thanks to the work of rich and noble patronesses, the convent increasingly provided shelter and training for women determined to devote their lives to the pursuit of religion. The age of the heroic individual like Genovefa ended with this development. Saintly women were now directed to monastic discipline. But the presence of these endowed centers also provided an alternative for the relapsed pagan who forfeited both the corporal and spiritual benefits she had achieved by christian prayer.

Clotilda herself spent the years of her widowhood from 511 to 545 in retirement near Martin's shrine at Tours. Contemporary chroniclers were not very clear about the nature of her establishment. Whether or not she regarded herself as a nun, later writers credited her with foundations at Tours, Les Andelys, and other, unnamed places.[28] It was not, however, until the carolingian redaction of her biography that she was depicted as fully ensconced in a monastic setting, working at wool and emerging briefly from her meditations to change water into wine for the thirsty builders at work on her new buildings.[29] In her lifetime, certainly, there was some sort of establishment at Tours, for Gregory says that when a deaf-mute cured by Martin wanted to devote his life to God she placed him in a school where he could receive the necessary training.[30]

Was there at Tours or elsewhere a similar school for women? We have seen that such an institution does not seem to have been available to the young Genovefa, despite the patronage of the great Germanus. But in the years when Clotilda was striving with Clovis for the soul of Frankland, southern Gaul did boast foundations where religious women could receive training.[31] On the fortified island of Lérins, a monastery sheltered women and men dedicated to chastity as well as married couples destined for the episcopal sees of Gaul.[32] We know too that a cloister for women existed under Cassian's rule at Marseille where, in the early sixth century, Caesarius of Arles sent his sister Caesaria for training before he established her as abbess of a new foundation in Arles.[33]

Caesarius' first foundation, outside the city at Alyscamps, was destroyed by barbarian raiders. His rule, therefore, was written for a foundation obliged to settle within the city for the sake of security both from barbarians and from the Arians who were hostile to the monastic movement.[34] During Caesaria's lifetime, the community grew to over two hundred women willing to abide by her brother's rule, which demanded lifetime vows of stability and claustration.[35] This certainly meant that they were to keep themselves out of the dangerous world beyond the cloister.[36] But it did not mean that they lived the sort of strictly secluded life that we associate with later contemplative orders. The nuns' welfare was entrusted to the clergy of the city, and there was considerable coming and going on this account. The nuns went out regularly on various errands and to attend church, and the cloister appears to have been open to any number of visitors.

The fourth abbess of Arles, Rusticula, when accused of giving shelter to one of the king's enemies in the course of the endless internecine wars that afflicted the merovingian dynasty, invoked the rule of claustration in vain. Royal soldiers broke into the convent and it required a miracle to save her life.[37] Even supernatural aid could not prevent the soldiers from taking her to Lyon for royal judgment in the matter. Similarly, soldiers of the Mayor of the Palace broke into Anstrude's monastery at Laon after the murder of her brother Baldwin. Again miraculous intervention saved her life and a public display of divine displeasure even prevented her being forcibly removed from the cloister.[38] In a very real sense, therefore, the rule of claustration seems often to have operated as a defense against intruders rather than as a barrier to the nuns themselves.

The sheltering aspect of the convent is even more pronounced when we look at the circumstances in which many women came into the community. The first patroness to bring Caesarius' rule into northern Gaul was Clotilda's daughter-in-law, Radegund, whose life illustrates very graphically the distance between christian teachings and the customs of the first generation of frankish converts. Chlotar I, the first merovingian prince to receive baptism in infancy, was polygamous. He was also a drunken brute. He won Radegund in a lottery among his brothers after they had killed her parents and captured her in a raid on her native Thuringia. Brought up on one of his farms, she tried to escape her fate but was ultimately forced to marry her captor and to live with him for some years. Only after he had murdered her brother, her only surviving relative, did she succeed at last in forcing a bishop to consecrate her. Thereafter she took refuge in a convent she founded at Poitiers, invoking the rule of stability to prevent her husband from seeking her and possibly demanding her return.[39]

Radegund's community was placed under the rule of Caesarius, which she apparently modified to her own tastes with ascetic practices gleaned from her eager reading and constant inquiry among other ascetics.[40] Though she subjected herself to far more physical misery than she could ever have endured at the royal court, Radegund plainly saw the convent as an asylum and there is reason to suppose that other members of the community shared her sentiment. Her second biographer, the nun Baudinivia, imagined that the convent walls were besieged by a thousand demons which the holy superior kept at bay by the power of the cross.[41] Even the invasion of a raucous nightbird was enough to alarm the gentle hagiographer, who saw Radegund's dismissal of the bird as a miraculous event.[42].

Radegund was a woman of wealth and influence, as were other women able to establish religious foundations. They could thus not only create a sanctuary for themselves, but provide asylum for others whom they recruited to the life of service. A certain Rusticula, for example, was kidnapped as a child by a nobleman who expected to raise her as his wife. The third abbess of Arles, Liliola, rescued her and admitted her as a novice in the monastery at the age of six. This story makes a somewhat ambiguous impression on the reader, since the abbess refused adamantly to return the girl to her bereft mother. This is corrected, however, not only by the girl's own determination to devote her life to religion, but by the appearance of Saint Caesarius to the mother, asking for her services.[43]

The role of the convent as a shelter for abused and helpless women must have been enhanced in the sixth century, when the Synod of Macon conferred on bishops the right to intervene in secular proceedings on behalf of widows, orphans, and freed slaves.[44] Sadalberga's biographer states specifically that she recruited her nuns from both servile and noble classes.[45] Her contemporary, Bishop Bercharius, founded the convent of Puellemoutier with six ransomed slave women as his first recruits.[46]

The most dramatic example of this comes from the seventh century. Queen Baltilda had been captured and enslaved before she attracted the attention of the dissolute Clovis II, who married her. Later, as regent for her son, she interested herself greatly in the ransoming of slaves and the foundation of monasteries. Her life having come full circle, she herself took refuge from her political difficulties in her foundation at Chelles, where young women from her native England were being trained to carry the monastic movement back to their own country.[47]

CONVERSION OF LIFE

In the early middle ages, 'conversion' was often taken to mean conversion to monastic life. The saintly women whose lives form the basis for the present paper attracted the attention of hagiographers as models of such conversion. Their struggles to perfect themselves and to conform to the demands of community life were thus held up as living sermons to future generations of nuns. For the saintliest of women, the struggle to maintain lives of humility, self-abnegation, service, and above all charity, was intense and unending. It was clearly compounded for those who entered the convent with untested or non-existent vocations. Many women who sought refuge in the convent from some intolerable situation in the world found that the consecrated life did not suit them. Still others were brought into the convent as children and trained to be nuns regardless of their basic inclinations. Other women were inclined to a religious life but had not chosen the female community as a vehicle for that life. They were instead steered there as conciliar and episcopal legislation in the sixth century sought to regulate consecrated women under episcopal authority.

The process of conversion, therefore, began in many cases only when a woman entered the convent. Merovingian hagiography is much concerned with the small incidents of disobedience and friction that marred the peace of the cloistered life. It provided the women who wrestled daily with the difficulties of communal life with reminders of past successes and warnings of punishments meted out to those who failed. For these women living lives charged with tension and sometimes ecstasy, or for their biographers, the small events of daily life became charged with elements of the miraculous. A narrow escape from a spilled pot of boiling water, for example, becomes a triumph of divine power over the power of darkness.

In this context, the pastoral responsibilities of the sainted abbess assume the highest importance. Their charges were afflicted with boredom, discomfort, discouragement, and all the abrasive difficulties of intimacy. We can hardly wonder at their tendency to see divine signs and portents in the events of daily life, to magnify and embroider their victories and dramatize their defeats. Shaped and screened by hagiographers, the events are often presented as muted and intimate miracles designed to point a lesson of community life that must have been sorely needed. Saint Bertilla, for example, called back one of her sisters from the dead because she had failed to make a complete reconciliation with her after an exchange of harsh words. With marked impatience, the deceased sister forgave her abbess and then hurried back to the heavenly journey that had been so rudely interrupted.[48]

Bertilla was wise to do this, however great the inconvenience to the deceased. Of all the conversion efforts of consecrated women, none was more important than their own conversion. For the abbess, that conversion depended on her attention to the souls entrusted to her care. Burgundofara was sent back to life from the very judgment seat of God because her nuns were praying for her restoration, fearing that they would be lost without her guidance:

> Go back, for you have not yet fully relinquished the world. Lo, it is written, Give and it shall be given unto you. And elsewhere, Forgive us our debts as we forgive our debtors. But you are not yet acquitted by your companions of the charge that has burdened you. Bear in mind that three wounded souls have borne witness against you. . . . Go then, mind your ways and compose those souls that you have soiled through tepidity or neglect.[49]

THE CONVERSION OF THE PEOPLE

Though the first duty of the consecrated woman was to convert to true religion herself and the sisters of her community, she also engaged actively in the conversion of her neighbors, both pagan and christian. In the sixth century, when convents were few and constant warfare forced their establishment behind city walls, the effort was probably limited to a few centers or the experiments of a few extraordinary individuals. For example, Radegund's biographer does not say whether or not she was a christian when Chlotar captured her and left her to grow up on one of his estates. But during that unhappy childhood, she clearly came to find a refuge in religion and formulated her desire to play the role of missionary and servant of God.[50] Her efforts to organize the other children on the farm into a religious community foreshadowed her later attempts to live as a nun at her husband's court, much to his displeasure.[51]

In the seventh century, despite continuing peril from civil war and the dangers of the unsettled wilderness, the missionary movement became more aggressive and widespread. The inspiration behind the troops of preachers and pilgrims who ventured out into the 'deserts' of merovingian Gaul stemmed from the great irish missionary, Columbanus. His biographer tells us that he was at first reluctant to respond fully to the call of the ascetic life. The conversion of the great converter began with the admonitions of a holy woman near his irish home:

> I have gone forth to the strife as far as it lay in my power. Lo, twelve years have passed by since I have been far from my home and have sought out this place of pilgrimage. With the aid of Christ, never since then have I engaged in secular matters; after putting my hand to the plough, I have not turned backward. And if the weakness of my sex had not prevented me, I would have crossed the sea and chosen a better place among strangers as my home. But you flowing with the fire of youth, stay quietly on your native soil.[52]

Shamed by her admonitions, Columbanus literally stepped over the body of his prostrate mother and departed at once for Gaul. There he found a kingdom torn by the fratricidal strife which seemed endemic among the Franks, a land which, two centuries after the pioneering work of Martin of Tours and one century after the famous conversion of Clovis, seemed to the foreign missionary utterly desolate:

> Either because of the numerous enemies from without or on account of the carelessness of the bishops, the christian faith had almost departed from that country. The creed alone remained. But the saving grace of penance and the longing to root out the lusts of the flesh were to be found only in a few.[53]

Among those few there were women, ready to help him in his work but apparently isolated from one another in their own homes rather than gathered into communities. Fleeing into exile from the court of the angry queen Brunhilda, whose arian background may have given her a distaste for scolding monks, Columbanus was sheltered in the house of the noble Theudemanda.[54] Later, in Nantes, two other noble ladies appeared to bring him food while he awaited passage out of the kingdom.[55]

On his return, Columbanus made his way to a forested place called Luxeuil, where there was an abandoned fortification 'filled with a great number of idols which had been worshipped with horrible rites'.[56] There he built his great monastery for both women and men attracted to the monastic life, and sent them back across Frankland smashing idols, preaching, baptizing, and recruiting new ascetic communities to carry on the work. The records of the lives of the women among this number are, as we might expect, restricted to their conventual experiences. We do not know of any women who roamed about as the male monks did, finding shelter and food with any hospitable family they found on the road. Occasionally, however, we do find commemorations of determined recluses, like Monegund at Chartres or Aldegund at Maubeuge, who braved the wilderness in search of solitude and eventually formed the core of a community of followers. More commonly, an abbess was trained at Luxeuil or one of its daughter foundations and began her community with a cadre of recruits, an endowment from her own family or from an interested sponsor, and a noble or episcopal patron. Some combination of the caesarian, columbanian, and benedictine rules would be applied to the community, with individual adjustments like those supplied in the rule written by Donatus of Besançon for his mother.[57]

These women came from a more isolated and rural world than had their saintly predecesssors of the sixth century. The saintly foundresses whose history we know were generally the daughters of rural aristocrats, recruited almost by chance by missionaries stopping for hospitality along their routes. Thus, Columbanus found a brother and sister, Faro and Fara (or Burgundofara), in the house of Hagneric near Meaux. Faro and his wife separated and entered the monastic life, which suited her so well that she refused his efforts to re-establish their conjugal life.[58] Faro became a bishop and the protector of a female community established by their father for his sister Fara.[59] Similarly, one of Columbanus' successors, Waldebert, found Aldegund in her parents' house and encouraged her vocation. From that conversion stemmed the further conversion of her sister Waldetrude, along with her husband and her two daughters, and, finally, even their mother who long opposed the virgin's determination to live unmarried.[60] Another missionary, Eustatius, converted the family of Sadalberga and supervised the spiritual life of the saint and later of her daughter.[61] All of these converted women eventually became foundresses of their own monasteries, aggressively proselytizing new congregations.

These new establishments were not so firmly tied to cities as had been those of the sixth century. Sometimes, they were situated on the rural estates of the saint's family or near small cities which boasted only minimal christian communities. Without pursuing the complex and perhaps pointless question of the 'double monastery', we need only note that women and men who had put cities behind them needed one another.[62] The autonomy of the convent envisaged by the caesarian rule depended on the active cooperation and support of the local clergy. It was not a suitable instrument for the conditions of seventh-century missions. The process of conversion required men, if only to administer the sacraments, which women were forbidden to do. The rough life of the wilderness made the presence of men a comfort if not an absolute necessity for these pioneering women.

On the other side, the women could provide many services and supplies needed by the men. Traditionally throughout the early centuries of monastic life, nuns produced wool and made clothing. They produced books, and provided shelter to wandering missionaries. They provided an essential center for servicing, sheltering, and training female converts as Christianity expanded.[63] Caesaria II introduced the production of books to the nuns at Arles, an activity at which they long continued to busy themselves.[64] Girls destined for the monastic life were trained to propagate christian doctrine both by instruction and by the copying and transmission of books. Constant reading, indeed, formed part of the monastic life. It was one of the attributes of a female saint that she could read day and night, sometimes even in her sleep. Rusticula, raised in the convent at Arles, was early trained to these habits by a nun who sat by her bed nightly and whispered into her sleeping ear.[65] Gertrude of Nivelles was said to have memorized an entire volume of divine law.[66]

Preaching, except within the community, was generally a task reserved to men. The most direct impact of the saintly woman on the secular public was as a living sermon, a model of the christian life to be imitated by all. Thus, charity in all its aspects was central to their efforts. From Clotilda's time on, saintly women represented a strong force for the redistribution of wealth. What Clovis, his companions, and successors among the frankish warrior class accumulated in loot, his queen and her successors seemed determined to dissipate.[67] Radegund, in particular, was so energetic in her open-handed distribution of gifts to churches, holy persons, and any needy person who came in her way, that Chlotar may finally have been persuaded to let her go through alarm at the inroads she must have been making into his treasure.[68] On her progress to Poitiers, she ostentatiously heaped gold and jewelry on the altar of every church she visited, but she still had plenty left to endow her own foundation.[69] Caesarius of Arles left his fortune to his sister's convent, and the conversion of the child Rusticula assured the community the wealth of her family.[70] Sadalberga, having brought her daughter into the convent with her, designated the community as heir of her patrimony and performed a disciplinary miracle on her deathbed to force her brother to hand it over.[71]

The wealth of these aristocratic families was thus channeled to the support of the hundreds of anonymous women who depended on the convent. It was also distributed among the troops of beggars, vagabonds, and refugees who came daily to the monastery doors. The rule of claustration never prevented the nuns of this period from opening their gates to these suppliants. Here, rather than in the spectacular baptisms of kings, is where the real work of conversion took place. Poor villagers, the miserable wanderers, who came to the convent door might stay only for a meal or a bath or a change of clothes. They might be settled nearby and habitualy dependent on the nuns for supplements to a scanty livelihood. If they were ill they might stay for a longer time to receive care.

Many of the beneficiaries of this active illustration of the gospel message must have been pagans if we judge from the evidence already put forth of the failure of Christianity to penetrate rural areas before the seventh and eighth centuries. Even those who may have received baptism were probably sadly in need of reminders of the true purposes of their religion. Occasionally one of them was believed to be the recipient of some wonderful act of divine intervention. In the hagiographical sources, miraculous cures of every imaginable human ailment abound, and such tales must have been widely spread among those who had lost nearly all other hope in life. But miracles are at best only one end of a continuum of healing and care which all nuns practised.

Most of the sick, starving, beleaguered people who daily came to the convents for assistance did not receive miraculous cures. But a bowl of hot soup, a jug of wine, a hot bath, and clean clothes are perhaps the most potent miracles of all to the outcast. We cannot know whether they greeted the simple homilies of their benefactresses with cynicism or sincere attention. But the sight of the daughters of a proud warrior caste combing the lice from a beggar's head can hardly have failed to make its impression on a population for whom no one else cared.

In other instances, we know that the convents were centers of systematic liturgical practices aimed at improving the religious life of their communities. At Chelles, for example, the Abbess Bertilla attracted converts from as far away as England. For her own neighbors, she reinforced the occasional excitement of visiting preachers by a program of frequent confession and daily communion.[72] At Laon, Sadalberga instituted a popular columban devotion, the prayer chain, and an aggressive program of frequent baptisms, in collaboration with the local clergy.[73] The presence of the holy woman, said her biographer, brought all those debauched by the devil to idolatry, gaming, and homicide, back to the holy cleansing of baptism.[74]

These women were genuine soldiers of God, carrying his conquests into every corner of Frankland. Sadalberga converted her husband and all her children to religion. When she ventured into Laon with a group of virgins to establish a new community she was leaving a flourishing older community firmly planted at Langres. On the day that she led her troop of holy women into Laon, the bishop and his clerks came out singing psalms to greet them. That night, the servants of the bishop reported that they had seen

> . . . wild things and beasts of different kinds at the city gates that night. Some saw bulls, other stags; some bears and others swine, wolves, foxes, lascivious asses and savage lions. All were going away, fleeing the city with many other monsters. . . . What else could be understood by this but that the ancient enemy, who could not tolerate the holiness and vigor of God's handmaids, was fleeing the city with his satellites? . . . For many here still remember . . . that in this town there were then flourishing many rustic louts and stupid men who held games to honor the cunning arts of he [sic] of whom it is written: "He injures us by a thousand arts".[75]

NOTES

1. Hucbald, *Vita Aldegundis*, Prologue, *Acta Sanctorum [*= AA SS] 30 January, 656.

2. The authenticity, style and uses of early medieval saints' lives continue to preoccupy the attention of the Bollandist Society in articles published in the *Analecta Bollandiana*. René Aigrain, *L'hagiographie: ses sources, ses méthodes, son histoire* (Paris: 1953) and Hippolyte Delehaye, *The Legends of the Saints*, trans. Donald Attwater (New York: 1962), provide excellent introductions to the subject. Recent monographs and articles on specific *vitae* are thoroughly covered in Suzanne F. Wemple's magnificently annotated *Women in Frankish Society* (Philadelphia: 1981). I intend to venture further into this problem in connection with a set of translations with John E. Halborg.

3. For further reading on this process see, E. Griffe, *La Gaule chrétienne à l'époque romaine. II. L'Église des Gaules au Ve siècle.* (Paris and Toulouse, 1957).

4. Sulpicius Severus, *The Life of Saint Martin*, in *The Western Fathers*, ed. F.R. Hoare (New York, 1954) 3–46.

5. *Vita de sancta Genovefa virgine Parisiis in Gallia, AA SS* 3 January, 137–153. See particularly 7. 34.

6. Baudinivia, *De vita sanctae Radegundis* 2. 2, ed. B. Krusch, *MGH Scriptores rerum merovingicarum* (Hanover, 1895) 2:358–95.

7. *The Life of Saint Martin* 22–23.

8. Sulpicius Severus, *Postumianus*, in Hoare, 73. The young monk Gallus reacts to the suggestion that he imitate the self-denial of the monks of Cyrenaica: 'It's most inhumane of you to try and force us Gauls to live in angels' fashion, though I suspect that even angels take pleasure in eating.'

9. *De laude sanctorum* 3, in J.N. Hillgarth, ed., *The Conversion of Western Europe, 350–750* (Englewood Cliffs, 1969) 23.

10. *Ad Abram filiam suam*; PL 10; 547–550.

11. *Life of Martin 19*; Hoare 33.

12. For general observations on the problem, see the classic by Lina Eckenstein, *Women under Monasticism, 500–1500* (Cambridge: 1896); S.G. Luff, 'A Survey of Primitive Monasticism in Central Gaul, 350–700', *The Downside Review* 70 (1952) 180–203; Friedrich Prinz, *Frühes Mönchtum im Frankreich* (Munich-Vienna, 1965).

13. *Vita Genovefa* I. 4.

14. *Ibid.* 2, 6.

15. *Ibid.* 2, 5.

16. *Ibid.* 10, 49.

17. *Ibid.* 11, 9.

18. *Ibid.* 3, 11.

19. These stresses are most vividly illustrated in the *life* of Saint Caesarius of Arles, the most relevant sections of which appear in Hillgarth, 31–42. Prinz, *Frühes Mönchtum*, believes the island of Lèrins was first established by refugees as a monastic community, 54.

20. Jonas of Bobbio, *Vitae S. Columbani disciplorumque eius* 2, 24, ed. B. Krusch, *MGH Script. rer. Merov.* 4: 113–152.

21. *Historia Francorum* 2, 2, ed. W. Arndt *MGH Script. rer. Merov.*, 1:39.

22. *Vita Genovefa* 7; 34–40.

23. *Historia Francorum* 2; 28–31. Jane T. Schulenberg, in an unpublished paper read at the international Medieval studies congress at Western Michigan University in May 1978, has pursued the chain of events abbreviated here in some detail, concluding that the christian 'conversion strategy' involved a self-conscious pairing of queens and missionaries.

24. Nicetius of Trier Ep. 8; ed. W. Gundlach, *MGH Epistolae* (Munich, 1978) 3:119–122.

25. Georges Tessier, *Le Baptême de Clovis* (Paris, 1964) surveyed the literature which had accumulated on this event. In his appendix he offers a French translation of Fortunatus' encomium on the conversion of Brunhilda.

26. Bede, *Historia Ecclesiastica* 1. 25. See also, Richard E. Sullivan, 'The Papacy and Missionary Activity in the Early Middle Ages', *Mediaeval Studies* 17 (1955) 46–106

27. Gregory of Tours, *Miracles of Saint Martin* 2, translated by William C. McDermott in Edward Peters, ed., *Monks, Bishops and Pagans: Christian Culture in Gaul and Italy, 500–700* (Philadelphia, 1975) 149.

28. *Vita Chrotildis* 11; *MGH Script. rer. Merov.* 1:341–48. Prinz, *Frühes Mönchtum*, 153, thinks she established a convent at Auxerre. Eckenstein, 46, was more cautious in crediting any of these claims.

29. *Vita Chrotildis* 12. This miracle is a favorite example of the *imitatio Christi* and is credited to several saints of this period.

30. *Miracles of Martin* 7.

31. These monasteries were thoroughly surveyed by Ferdinand Hilpisch, *Die Döppelklöster: Entstehung und Organisation* (Munich, 1928). See also the general overview of conventual life in sixth-century Gaul by Sr Mary Caritas McCarthy, *The Rule for Nuns of Saint Caesarius of Arles* (Washington DC, 1960).

32. Prinz, 51 ff., notes the presence there of Lupus of Troyes and his wife, Hilarius of Arles and his sister, Eucherius of Lyon and his wife among others.

33. *Vita Caesarius* 35.

34. *Ibid.* 21, 32, and 36 serve as a few examples of the dangers encountered by the saint in his lifetime. *Ibid.* 33 recounts the destruction of his original foundation.

35. It is not my intention in the course of this paper to recapitulate the development of monastic rules for women nor to go deeply into the arguments revolving

around the constitutional nature of their institutions. Interested readers may consult Eckenstein, Prinz, and Wemple, already cited.

36. Caesarius of Arles, *Regula sanctarum virginum*, ed. G. Morin, *Opera Omnia*, (Maretoli, 1942) 2:101–27, art. 2; 36–40.

37. Florentius, *Vita sanctae Rusticulae sive Marciae* 9–15, ed. B. Krusch, *MGH Script. rer. Merov.* 4, 339–351.

38. *Vita Anstrudis abbatissae Laudunensis* 11 and 14, ed. W. Levison, *MGH Script. rer. Merov.* 6:64–78.

39. Fortunatus, *De vita sanctae Radegundis* 13, ed. B. Krusch, *MGH Script. rer. Merov.* 6:64–78.

40. *Ibid.* 23.

41. Baudonivia, *De vita sanctae Radegundis* 18.

42. *Ibid.* 19.

43. Florentius, *Vita . . . Rusticulae*, 2–3.

44. Concilium Matisconense, canon 5; *Concilia Galliae, 511–695* ed. C. de Clercq, CCSL 148A:244.

45. *Vita Sadalbergae abbatissae Laudunensis* 18, ed. B. Krusch, *MGH Script. rer. Merov.* 5:40–66.

46. Vita Bercharii 3, *AA SS* 16 October 993.

47. *Vita Balthildis reginae* 9, ed. B. Krusch, *MGH Script. rer. Merov.* 2:477–508. An interesting view of Balthild is given by Janet L. Nelson, 'Queens as Jezebels: The Careers of Brunhild and Balthild in Merovingian History', in Derek Baker ed., *Medieval Woman* (Oxford, 1978) 31–78.

48. *Vita Bertillae, abbatissae Calensis*, 2, ed. W. Levison, *MGH Script. rer. Merov.* 6:95–109.

49. Jonas of Bobbio, *Vitae S. Columbani disciplorumque eius* 2. 12, ed. B. Krusch, *MGH Script. rer. Merov.* 4:113–152.

50. Fortunatus, *De vita sanctae Radegundis* 2.

51. *Ibid.* 5.

52. Jonas of Bobbio, 1. 8 in *Vitae S. Columbani* . . . Peters, *Monks, Bishops, and Pagans*, 77–78.

53. *Ibid.* 1, 11.

54. *Ibid.* 1, 39.

55. *Ibid.* 1, 45.

56. *Ibid.* 1, 17.

57. Donatus of Besançon, *Regula ad virginem*; PL 87; 274–98. The *rule* of Columbanus has been published in PL 80. Surveys of the applications of these rules can be found in Prinz and Hilpisch.

58. Jonas of Bobbio, *Vitae S. Columbani* . . . 1, 50.

59. *Ibid.* 2, 7.

60. *Vita Aldegundis abbatissae Malbodiensis* 1, 4, ed. W. Levison, *MGH Script. rer. Merov.* 6: 79–90.

61. *Vita Sadalbergae* 4.

62. The first, and still classic discussion of this problem is Mary Bateson, 'Origin and Early History of Double Monasteries', *Royal Historical Society Transactions* 13 (1899) 137–198. Subsequent literature on the subject is surveyed by Wemple, 286.

63. The most detailed record of transactions of this sort comes from England in the correspondence between Saint Boniface and the nuns of Wimbourne in the early eighth century; C.H. Talbot, *The Anglo-Saxon Missionaries in Germany* (London–New York, 1954) 65–153.

64. *Vita Caesarius* 58.

65. *Vita Rusticulae* 6.

66. *Vita sanctae Geretrudis Nivialensis* 3, ed. B. Krusch, *MGH Script. rer. Merov.* 2: 453–464.

67. *Vita Chrotildis* 14.

68. Fortunatus, *De vita sanctae Radegundis* 13–14. In the life of Saint Leonard of

Vandoeuvre, AASS 15 October, Chlotar again appears in opposition to the hero's desire to embrace the monastic life, expressing dismay at his desire to withdraw his goods and his services from royal command.

69. Fortunatus, *Radegundis* 14.
70. *Vita Rusticulae* 6.
71. *Vita Sadalberga* 29.
72. *Vita Bertillae* 6.
73. *Vita Sadalbergae* 16.
74. *Ibid.*
75. *Ibid.* 15.

Female Spirituality and Mysticism in Frankish Monasteries: Radegund, Balthild and Aldegund*

Suzanne Fonay Wemple

THE EXPERIENCES, visions, prophecies and influence of women mystics living in the High and Late Middle Ages are being studied intensively in both the United States and Europe. In the shadow of writings by well-known women mystics of the twelfth, thirteenth, and fourteenth centuries, there exists however, a little-known literature of spirituality, inspired and composed during the sixth and seventh centuries by women in the monasteries of the merovingian kingdom. The biographies of two merovingian female saints, Radegund and Balthild, written by nuns who knew them personally, and the visions of St Aldegund, details of which she dictated herself, provide valuable insights into this much neglected chapter in the history of christian spirituality.

Social customs determining the lives of women in the frankish kingdom were so different from ours that we will begin this essay with sketches of the careers of Radegund, Balthild, and Aldegund. This will be followed by an examination of the authorship and date of composition of their *vitae*, including Aldegund's *vita*, the only extant source for her visions. After these preliminary remarks, I will turn to my main theme, analyzing female modes of sanctity and ideals of spirituality as reflected in the three *vitae*.

RADEDGUND

Radegund lived in the sixth century. Of royal stock—a princess of the thuringian nation—she was captured in battle by the Franks in 531. Less than seven years old at the time, she became part of the booty that fell to Clothar I (511–567), son of Clovis. Clothar I reared Radegund to become his bride, and although he married her around 540, she had nothing but contempt for her husband, who not only practiced polygamy, but also had her brother murdered. Determined to leave Clothar, Radegund asked Bishop Medard of Noyon to veil her as a deaconess. When he hesitated, she veiled herself. She then went to Saix where she transformed her villa into a hospice for the poor and the sick. When her husband tried to reclaim her, she turned to Bishop Germain of Paris for help. The saintly bishop persuaded the king to grant Radegund her freedom and help her establish a monastery at Poitiers. Radegund eventually founded two monasteries: one in Poitiers for nuns, and one outside the walls of the city where the nuns were buried and the clergy who ministered to them were housed. She did not assume leadership of the nuns, but installed her friend, Agnes, as abbess. Dwelling in a cell adjoining the monastery in Poitiers until her death in 587, she participated in the life of the community, although she did not observe the obligation of strict enclosure which bound members of the community once she had adopted the *Rule* of St Caesarius for them.

Radegund outlived her husband by twenty-six years, maintaining close relations with her royal in-laws. Her step-son, Sigebert, protected her against a local bishop angered by the exemption from episcopal authority her community gained under the *Rule* of Caesarius. Sigebert's wife, Brunhilda, helped Radegund obtain relics from Byzantium, including a piece of the true cross which greatly increased the respect the monastery commanded. Shortly after Radegund's death, two accounts of her life were composed, one by her friend, the priest Venantius Fortunatus, another by a nun, Baudonivia.[1]

BALTHILD

Born a century after Radegund, Balthild made her mark in history not only as a saint but also as a queen and regent. A saxon slave, Balthild was raised to the throne by Clothar I's great-great-grandson, Clovis II (639–656). Balthild's interests were broader than Radegund's. She was a benefactor of the poor and enslaved and a patroness of churchmen; she restored churches and founded one monastery for men at Corbie and another for women at Chelles. Astute and ambitious in politics, Balthild ruled Neustria as regent for eight years after the death of her husband. Around 664–65, when her son came of age, her enemies forced her to withdraw to Chelles. She lived there as a nun under the abbess Bertila until her death in 679 or 680. Her biographer, writing at Chelles a few years after her death, glorified Balthild as the founder of a dynastic cult center.[2]

ALDEGUND

Aldegund's life was less dramatic than Radegund's or Balthild's. A contemporary of Balthild, Aldegund was not a queen, nor did she ever marry. Of noble parentage, she would have been married at an early age, as was normal for girls of her class, had it not been for the intercession of an older married sister, Waltrud, who interpreted the nightly visions Aldegund was having as indications of a religious vocation. Waltrud persuaded their parents to send Aldegund to Nivelles, where she was educated. Later she founded her own monastery at Maubeuge and became its first abbess. She died at Maubeuge around 689.[3] Aldegund described her visions to Subnius, abbot of Nivelles, asking him to record them, and her biographer claims to have heard a reading of this record.[4]

The life, background and personality of these three women were very different, yet in their biographies we find a common thread. They shared both the experience of founding monasteries and the achievement of developing their foundations into enduring centers of spirituality and culture. Even more significant for the purposes of this essay is the fact that the spiritual growth of these women, their self-imposed asceticism, religious devotion, and mystical visions, were recorded by other women, or in the case of Aldegund, by Aldegund herself.

HAGIOGRAPHY AS HISTORICAL SOURCE

The historical value of merovingian saints' lives has been vindicated by modern scholarship.[5] Although hagiographers often distorted the lives of their protagonists by copying from earlier works and introducing legendary materials for the sake of religious edification, the prevailing view today is that even the most unhistorical *vitae* reflect ideals of sanctity prevalent at the time of their composition. Armed with a better understanding of merovingian culture and social customs, historians in the past twenty-five years have redated several sixth and seventh-century *vitae* as contemporary compositions.[6] Bruno Krusch and Wilhelm Levison contended in the preface to their editions of the *vitae* in *Monumenta Germaniae Historica*, that whenever the *vita* of a merovingian saint was not marred by gross grammatical errors, it must have been the work of a carolingian author. Modern scholars are increasingly calling their judgement on this point into question[7]. By classifying legendary themes in early medieval hagiography, scholars have also succeeded in distinguishing direct observations and authentic experiences from clichées and stereotyped models of behavior.[8] These new methods of scholarship make it possible to study Baudonivia's *Life of St Radegund* and the earliest extant versions of the anonymous *vitae* of St Balthild and St Aldegund as works that reflect truly female expressions of merovingian life.

FEMALE AUTHORS OF MEROVINGIAN SAINTS' LIVES

The exceptional aspect of Baudonivia's *Life of St Radegund* and Balthild's anonymous *vita* is not that they were written by near contemporaries who knew them—an unchallenged claim made by both authors—but that they were written by female members of their communities, who sympathized with and understood female modes of spirituality. The learned Bollandists who began editing saints lives in the seventeenth century, and the distinguished german scholars who reedited them in the late nineteenth century, assumed that the anonymous biographies of male and female saints surviving from merovingian times had been composed by men. The only *vita* in which the author identified herself as a woman and a nun, Baudonivia's *Life of St Radegund*, was dismissed as an exception. Influenced by Krusch's remark that Baudonivia's style was barbarous,[9] scholars have tended to disparage her work as mere compilation, especially in comparison with Fortunatus' skillful and dramatic *vita* of Radegund that Baudonivia intended to supplement.[10] Neither Krusch nor later scholars perceived that Baudonivia had a better understanding of the nature of a woman's spiritual experience than had the learned poet.

The oldest version of St Balthild's life, the so-called *A vita*, was also composed by a nun, a member of the community Balthild had founded at Chelles.[11] The intimate details that the *A vita* gives of Balthild's activities and death as well as the prominent place it accords to the bishop of Paris in the circle of Balthild's friends, leaves no doubt that this version was written at Chelles not long after Balthild's death in 679–80 by someone who knew the queen quite well.[12] A reference in the preface to the *dilectissimi fratres* at whose behest the work was composed, convinced scholars that the author had been a monk at Chelles.[13] A careful scrutiny of the *A vita* reveals, however, that Chelles was not a double monastery, but a single community, when Balthild lived there. The text does not mention the presence of monks. Although there were priests at the bedside of the dying queen, their function was purely sacramental.[14] They were summoned to entrust her 'blessed soul to God'.[15] The fact that when the priests arrived, Balthild told the nuns to leave indicated that the priests and the nuns did not constitute a monastic community.[16] An entirely different picture emerges from the *vita* of Bertila, the first abbess of Chelles, who was installed in that office by Balthild herself and under whose leadership Balthild later lived at Chelles. Composed in the second half of the eighth century, the *Vita s. Bertilae* depicted the monastery as a double institution with a substantial number of monks and nuns.[17] Rather than dismissing one of the lives as an unreliable source, we can resolve the discrepancy in their stories by the explanation that Bertila invited the monks to join the community after the death of her patroness whom she outlived by some twenty-five years, dying around 705.[18]

The author of Balthild's *vita* may have finished her composition after the first monks were admitted to Chelles. I doubt, however, that the *dilectisimi fratres* to whom she dedicated her work were the new brothers. Rather, as Janet Nelson suggested, they were probably the monks of Corbie,[19] a monastery which had also been founded by Balthild and where Balthild's friend, Theodefrid, continued to serve as abbot for some time after her death.[20]

The corrected and revised version of Balthild's *vita* (the *B vita*), was composed in the ninth century and may also have been the work of a woman. Because it refers to Balthild's testament in the convent's archives, Krusch concluded that the author had been the convent's *bibliothecarius*.[21] But the librarian could just as well have been a woman. Neither external nor internal evidence in this later version, nor for that matter in the *Translatio s. Balthildis*, which was composed shortly after 833, exclude the possibility of female authorship.[22]

Baudonivia and the Chelles author introduced female values and ideals into hagiography. They replaced the ideal of the asexual female saint, the *virago*, whose greatest accomplishment was the imitation of male virtues, with a heroine who relied on female attributes to achieve spiritual perfection. To be sure, the conventional *topoi* of monastic lives—humility and self-denial—appeared also in the compositions of Baudonivia and the nun of Chelles. Radegund, according to Baudonivia, served meals to pilgrims and washed and dried the faces of the sick with her own hands. Balthild likewise, according to the author of her *vita*, sought at Chelles such menial jobs as cooking and the cleaning of latrines.[23] But the characterization of the two saints as mother figures, peacemakers, and promoters of dynastic cult centers was an unusual theme in hagiography. It represented the assimilation into religious life of the nurturing and mediatory roles women were expected to play as daughters and wives in merovingian society.

Writing between 609 and 614, Baudonivia was the first to emphasize typically female attributes which do not appear either in Fortunatus' *Vita* of Radegund or in the other sources, such as the *Vita s. Caesarii*, which Baudonivia used. Baudonivia's aim was to compose a guide for her fellow nuns.[24] Not wishing to repeat 'those things that the blessed father, Bishop Fortunatus, has written about', she concentrated on the second phase of Radegund's life, when the saint lived in a cell adjacent to the convent she had built in Poitiers.[25] The prototype of the ideal nun that Baudonivia presented to her sisters was not, however, a self-effacing and sexless abstraction. In contrast to Fortunatus' portrayal of Radegund as the withdrawn wife and reluctant queen whose main objective was to transcend her femininity and escape from her husband, Baudonivia described Radegund as an outgoing and emotional woman who was as concerned about the affairs of the monastery as about the developments in the kingdom.[26]

The childless Radegund in Baudonivia's *vita* assumed the responsibilities of spiritual motherhood, nurturing and testing the spirit of the sisters with boundless energy:

> When the lesson was read, with pious solicitude caring for our soul, she said, 'If you do not understand what is read, it is because you do not ask solicitously for a mirror of the soul'. Even when the least [of us] out of reverence took the liberty to question her, she did not cease with pious solicitude and maternal affection to expound what the lesson contained for the good of the soul.[27]

An extension of Radegund's role as mother was her function as *domina*, which she discharged with strictness and kindness even after her death. The biographer included among her miracles the story of the punishment she inflicted from heaven on her former servant for sitting on her throne, and the pity she showed after the girl had been taught a lesson.[28]

Radegund's attempts to act as a peacemaker and her efforts to set the community up as an intermediary between royalty and divinity were also interpreted by Baudonivia as expressions of her spiritual concerns. While the love of peace was not an entirely new motif in hagiography,[29] this was the first time that a female saint had assumed the role of peacemaker.

The conventional notion that the love of fellow members in a monastery obliterated the memory of parents and husband, one that Baudonivia dutifully introduced,[30] did not prevent her from remembering that Radegund retained close ties with her husband's kin:

> Because she loved all the kings, she prayed for the life of each, and instructed us to pray without interruption for the stability [of their kingdoms]. Whenever she heard that they had turned against each other with hatred, she was greatly shaken and sent letters to the one and the other, [imploring them] not to wage war and take up arms against each other but to conclude peace so that the country should not perish. In the same way, she sent great men to give salutary advice to the illustrious kings so that the country should be made more salubrious both for the king and the people. She imposed continuous vigils upon the congregation, and instructed us with tears in her eyes to pray for the kings without interruption.[31]

The relic that Radegund obtained from the byzantine emperor played an important part, according to Baudonivia, in Radegund's scheme to develop

Chelles into an agency of intercession on behalf of kings. Radegund regarded the piece of the true cross 'as an instrument whereby the stability of the kingdom would be secured' and the salvation of the whole country assured.[32]

The same triple theme appeared in Balthild's *vita*. The emphasis on Balthild's motherly disposition, her sense of mission as peacemaker between warring kingdoms, and the extension of this mission to Chelles, which became under her guidance the source of concord between God and the court, suggests a direct influence by Baudonivia. The nun of Chelles probably had access to Baudonivia's *Life of St Radegund* while she composed her account of Balthild's life towards the end of the seventh century. It would be wrong, however, to accuse her of outright imitation. Balthild, like Radegund and all merovingian wives and mothers, was socialized to serve the family and the broader aristocratic structure as a *mediatrix* of conflicts. The biographer, being a woman herself, found this role admirable. Baudonivia's work, serving as her model, encouraged her to interpret Balthild's actions in the context of the female role.

The Chelles author stressed the motherly aspects of Balthild's activities as a queen, how she looked after the young men in her court as an *optima nutrix* and treated the poor as a *pia nutrix*'.[33] When she described Balthild's rule as regent, she made much of the fact that Balthild was an instrument of divinely-ordained harmony between the warring kingdoms.[34] Finally, when she spoke of Balthild's life at Chelles, she noted how she

> continually consoled the sick, visiting them frequently and sustaining them with holy exhortation. In the spirit of charity, she suffered with the sufferers, rejoiced with the joyful, and often suggested to the abbess that those in need of healing be comforted. The abbess, as a mother, responded amicably to all her requests because, in keeping with the apostolic tradition, they were one in heart and soul, loving each other tenderly and fully in Christ.[35]

As to Balthild's plans for Chelles, the hagiographer recalled Balthild's request that the congregation should offer prayers not only for the king and queen, but also for the royal officials.[36] Balthild apparently knew only too well that, with the magnates running the kingdom, God's help had to be obtained for a broad constituency if Chelles were to serve as a royal cult center.

ALDEGUND'S VISIONS

While Radegund's and Balthild's biographers translated attitudes associated with feminine roles in secular society into ideals of spirituality, Aldegund found her own voice and gave expression to her own spiritual experiences. As we noted earlier, she left a record of her visions by dictating them to Subnius, abbot of the neighboring Nivelles, according to the author of the earliest version of her *vita*. Passages from her visions were apparently read aloud at Meubeuge; the author witnessed Aldegund asking a girl to act as reader.[37]

The allusion of the author to the fact that he had been educated at Meubeuge and had known Aldegund personally was slighted by W. Levison as a conventional *topos* in hagiography. The style of the work, Levison contended, points to an author who had received the benefits of a carolingian education. Because the grammar was still marred with imperfections and Aldegund's name was listed in Hrabanus' *Martyrology*, which appeared either in 833 or 844, Levison concluded that the work had been composed before the reign of Louis the Pious.[38] The belgian historian, L. Van der Essen, took more seriously the author's remark that he had spoken to Aldegund's sister Waltrud the day after Aldegund's death.[39] Van der Essen listed merovingian characteristics in the author's spelling and grammar, although he did not exclude the possibility that the ninth-century scribe, whose copy of the *vita* is the earliest extant manuscript, imposed his own stylistic improvements on the text.[40]

A comparison of the author's description of Aldegund's visions as a young woman to her later mystical experiences adds further weight to his credibility, indicating that he had used, at least for the earlier visions, a work which had been dictated by Aldegund.

The images of Aldegund's earlier visions are more concrete and colorful, richer in meaning, and more self-consciously anchored in biblical passages than the visions the hagiographer attributes to her in later life. A few examples will suffice to show the differences. Aldegund, as a child and young woman, saw heaven as a mansion with seven columns, shrouded in mist and exuding an aromatic fragrance.[41] She was visited by angels in luminous garments;[42] by Christ as a young boy with a beautiful face, holding a palm in one hand and a crown in another;[43] by a young girl dressed in gold;[44] by St Peter with the eyes of a dove;[45] and by the Holy Ghost manifested as the rays of the sun and the moon.[46] Even the devil appeared to her in concrete form as a rapacious wolf and as a roaring lion.[47] Aldegund's later mystical experiences are described in more abstract terms. She continued to see angels blinding her with their luminescence,[48] but the devil did not appear in concrete form in her later visions, even though he did not cease to tempt her.[49]

The imagery of Aldegund's early visions was powerful but not altogether original. Visions of Christ, the Virgin, angels, and the blessed instructing a saint to take a course of action, or serving as premonitions of death and assurances of salvation were common themes in early medieval hagiography.

Christ as bridegroom appeared in Baudonivia's *Life of Radegund*, promising the saint that she would be one of the brightest diadems in his crown.[50] The dying Balthild saw Mary welcoming her to an altar which had behind it stairs flanked by angels and leading up to heaven.[51] Ranging over a broader spectrum of incidents, Aldegund's experiences gathered together many strands of early medieval mysticism, imprinting female values upon this type of spirituality.

Aldegund's first visions—the mansion, the angel, and Christ as bridegroom—served to reveal her call to monastic life.[52] Dreams and visions associated with monastic conversion appear with great frequency in early saints' lives. Aldegund's encounter with the devil was probably inspired by the temptations of St Anthony.[53] Her firm *virilitas* in resisting the demon was a variation of the *virago* motif in roman literature. She was given consolation after this frightening test, experiencing a foretaste of the mysteries of heaven.[54] Angels, blessed souls, St Peter, and the Holy Ghost not only advised her on how to achieve salvation, but also explained to her the sense of mystic phenomena. Angelic messengers and their reassuring words were conventional *topoi* in early medieval hagiography. Even Aldegund's vision of a beautiful young girl sent from heaven by the Blessed Virgin had its parallel in Pope Gregory I's *Dialogues*.[55]

While the imagery and symbolism of Aldegund's visions were inspired by earlier models, the message the heavenly envoys brought to her was new. Instead of instructing Aldegund to abstain from laughing and joking and to hold her tongue if she wanted to join the circle of celestial virgins, the young girl sent by Mary spoke about the commandment of love: 'You shall love the Lord God with all your heart and all your soul, and with all your powers, and your neighbor as yourself' (Mt. 22:37).[56] Love was the message the angel gave when he informed her that she would have only one bridegroom, Jesus Christ: 'The more one guards the spark of faith in the soul', he told her, 'the more one will burn with the love of Christ'.[57] Love was also the advice that St Peter gave to Aldegund when he informed her that she would be summoned to heaven.

> Why are you bewildered? I am Peter the Apostle who has the power to bind and to loose and was sent to you by Jesus Christ. O chaste [virgin!] you are counted among the blessed. The Lord desires your departure. . . . Do not fear, whoever fears is not perfect in love, but 'perfect love casts out fear, for fear has to do with punishment'. (John 4:18)[58]

Unlike the visions of the female saints described by men, Aldegund's experiences were not designed to convey instruction on how women might overcome the weaknesses of their sex. Aldegund's heavenly messengers intended to draw the message of love, a lesson that was also proclaimed in the lives of Radegund and Balthild.

CONCLUSIONS

By giving insights into the nature of women's religious impulses and mystical experiences, Baudonivia, the nun of Chelles, and Aldegund became eloquent witnesses to the meaning of evangelical piety at a time when male contemplatives tended to emphasize not charity, but humility, as the mark of spiritual perfection.[59] The message that these three *vitae* conveyed was that women seeking an active part in spiritual and mystical life were capable of drawing on their own inner resources and did not have to imitate men. Instead of urging women to transcend their nature, they dignified the female role as a source of spiritual perfection. Care and service of others, the normal function of merovingian women, was upheld in the monastic rules as a means of self-discipline, an exercise in humility, and a form of penance. Baudonivia and the nun of Chelles represented these activities in a more positive light, associating the care of others with prayer and identifying it with the virtue of charity. They exalted it as the very essence of monastic life. Charity, understood as solicitude for the welfare of others, was raised to an even higher plane by Aldegund. Accentuating the comforting aspects of God's love, Aldegund described God's relationship to the individual soul as governed by compassion. Through her visions, Aldegund apprehended not only God's charitable nature, but also received personal instruction in charity.

The importance of charity in spiritual life, as this study has indicated, was not a literary *topos* in early medieval hagiography. Radegund, Balthild, and Aldegund actively pursued the ideal of charity and tried to teach it by example and word to their sisters. Trained at an early age to serve others, these women did not feel the need to overcome pride to gain union with God. Like the monks of their time with whom they maintained contact, they did not shirk from ascetic practices. But, unlike their male counterparts, they did not view spiritual life as an exercise in humility and denial of the self. Rather, they conceived of religious growth as self-development through charity, through love of family and kin, and through love of the kingdom and monastic community to the love of God.

Although Baudonivia's *Life of St Radegund*, the anonymous *vita* of St Balthild and the visions of St Aldegund synthesized rather than delineated stages of perfection in the exercise of charity, they conveyed to posterity an awareness of the need and value of love in spiritual life. By recording the impulse of love in the religious development of Radegund, Balthild, and Aldegund, their biographers made an important contribution to monastic spirituality. They introduced a new motif into hagiography, providing an alternative to the male ideal of humility, penance, and renunciation of the self.

The popularity of the three lives is attested by the number of manuscripts that have survived.[60] An investigation of their influence through quotations and paraphrases in hagiographic literature may yield further evidence about the transmission of the ideal of love at the popular level of monastic culture. Research on the veneration of the three saints recorded in martyrologies may also prove useful in this respect. The central place that love occupied in the writings of the twelfth-and thirteenth-century mystics suggests the intriguing possibility that the *vitae* of Radegund and Balthild and the visions of Aldegund may have exerted an influence across the centuries.[61]

The religious experiences of Radegund, Balthild and Aldegund deserve a chapter in the history of spirituality for other reasons as well. They demonstrate that merovingian women were capable of forging their own spiritual ideal by drawing on values associated with the female identity. They also show that under the influence of this ideal created by women, a new form of monasticism arose, representing a balance between the active and contemplative ways of life. In contrast to this mixed form of monasticism, which eventually came to dominate the West, monasteries in late roman Gaul emphasized withdrawal from the world as the *sine qua non* for individual spiritual development. On the other end of the spectrum stood merovingian male monasticism with its missionary zeal and insistence on penance and humility as antidotes for the worldly involvement of monks.[62] As an alternative to these opposite modes of monasticism, the ideal of charity, introduced by women in female and double monasteries of the merovingian kingdom, provided an opportunity for the pursuit of the active and contemplative ways of life in perfect harmony.

Barnard College
Columbia University

NOTES

*This essay, an expansion of part of Chapter Eight of my book, *Women in Frankish Society: Marriage and the Cloister, 500–900* (Philadelphia, 1981), was read at the Sixteenth Conference of Medieval Studies, Western Michigan University, Kalamazoo, May, 1981.

1. Both *vitae* were edited by Bruno Krusch, *De vita sanctae Radegundis libri duo*; *MGH Script. rer. mer.* 2: 358–95. Venantius Fortunatus, *De vita sanctae Radegundis liber I* (pp. 364–77), Baudonivia, *De vita sanctae Radegundis liber II* (pp. 377–95.) Important details of Radegund's activities may also be found in Gregory of Tours, *Historia Francorum*, III.4.7, VI, 29, IX.39.42 (ed. B. Krusch, *MGH Script. rer. mer.* 1/1 [2nd ed.]: 99, 105, 297, 460–63, 470–74), and *In gloria confessorum*, 104 (ed. B. Krusch, *MGH Script. rer. mer.* 1/1; 364–66). On her age at the time of her marriage, see my re-

marks in *Women in Frankish Society*, p. 39 and n. 61; on her life with Clothar, *ibid.*, p. 152. The best account of her activities at Poitiers is René Aigrain's *Sainte Radegonde* (Paris, 1918; 2nd ed., 1952). See also Aigrain's articles, 'Une abbesse mal connue de Sainte-Croix de Poitiers', *Bulletin philologique et historique* (1946–47) 197–202; 'Le voyage de sainte Radegonde à Arles', *Bulletin philologique et historique* (1926–27) 119–27; Dom Pierre Monsabert, 'Le testament de sainte Radegonde', *Bulletin philologique et historique* (1926–27) 129–134, and E. Delaruelle, 'Sainte Radegonde, son type de sainteté et la chrétienté de son temps', *Études mérovingiennes: Actes des Journées de Poitiers*, 1952 (Paris, 1953) 65–74.

2. Sources of Balthild's life include *Vita s. Balthildis reginae*, ed. B. Krusch, *MGH Script. rer. mer.* 2: 482–508; *Vita s. Bertilae abatissae Calenses*, ed. W. Levison, *MGH Script. rer. mer.* 6: 101–9; Bede, *Historia ecclesiae* V. 19, ed. C. Plummer, *Venerabilis Baedae Opera Historica* (Oxford, 1896) 325; *Liber historiae Francorum*, 43–45, ed. B. Krusch, *MGH Script. rer. mer.* 2; 315–17; Fredegar, *Chron. Cont.* 1, ed. B. Krusch, *MGH Script. rer. mer.* 2: 168; *Vita Dagoberti III regis Francorum*, ed. B. Krusch, *MGH Script. rer. mer.* 2: 512–13. For other sources, see W. Levison, *England and the Continent in the Eighth Century* (Oxford, 1946) p. 9, n. 4. Her political activities have been analysed by Eugen Ewig, 'Das Privileg des Bischofs Berthefrid von Amiens für Corbie von 664 und die Klosterpolitik des Königin Balthild', *Francia* 1 (1973) 62–114; Janet Nelson, 'Queens as Jezabels: the Careers of Brunhild and Balthild in Merovingian History', in Derek Baker, ed., *Medieval Women*, Studies in Church History, Subsidia 1 (Oxford, 1978) 31–77.

3. *Vita s. Aldegundis, abbatissae Malbodiensis*, ed. W. Levison, *MGH Script. rer. mer.* 6: 79–90, a partial edition, does not include her visions. The full text is found in *Acta sanctorum Belgii selecta*, ed. J. Ghesquière, 4: 315–24. See also *Vita Ursmari*, ed. W. Levison, *MGH Script. rer. mer.* 6: 459; Alcuin, *Carmina*, 88. 21, ed. E. Dümmler, *MGH Poetae*, 1: 312; Angilbertus, *De ecclesia Centulensi libellus*, 2, ed. G. Waitz, *MGH Script.* 15: 176. For a discussion of the reliability of these sources, as opposed to later legends circulating about her and various members of her family, see L. Van der Essen, *Étude critique et littéraire sur les Vitae des saints mérovingiens de l'ancienne Belgique* (Louvain–Paris, 1907) 219–31. Levison (*MGH Script. rer. mer.* 6: 79, n. 9) lists six possible dates for her death: 678, 684, 689, 695, 706, 712. I am following Van der Essen (*Étude critique*, p. 220) in accepting 684 as the correct date.

4. *Vita s. Aldegundis*, 18; *MGH Script. rer. mer.* 6: 88-89: 'Supradicta . . . Aldegunda de visionibus . . . cuidam viro religioso Subnio abbati de Nivianlensi monasterio narravit ordinanter et scribendo tradidit; ex nostra parvitatae puellae parvulae coram se legere praecepit, satisque mirati fuimus, quia ante ista tempora ultima simile non audivimus, et quae audivimus veraciter credimus.'

5. Among studies demonstrating that the introduction of new ideals into hagiography reflected new political goals and shifts in social psychology, the most relevant for our subject is Maria Stoeckle, *Studien über Ideale in Frauenviten des VII–X Jahrhunderts.* (Munich, 1957). See also, Karl Bosl, 'Der Adelsheilige. Idealtypus und Wirklichkeit, Gesellschaft und Kultur im merowingerzeitlichen Bayern des 7. and 8. Jahrhunderts,' in C. Bauer *et al.*, edd., *Speculum historiale; Festschrift J. Spörl* (Munich, 1965), 167–187.

6. For a defense of the historical value of merovingian *vitae*, and a bibliography of the controversy, see F. Prinz, 'Heiligenkult und Adelsherrschaft im Spiegel merowingischer Hagiographie', *Historische Zeitschrift* 204 (1967) 529–44, and p. 529, n. 1. Particularly useful for an understanding of merovingian culture are the studies of Pierre Riché, *Éducation et culture dans l'occident barbare*, 3rd ed. (Paris, 1973); and 'Les foyers de culture en Gaule franque du VIe au IXe siècle', *Centri e vie di irradiazione della civiltà nell' alto medioevo*, Settimane di studio del Centro Italiano di Studi sull' Alto Medioevo, 11 Spoleto, 1964), translated into English in Sylvia L. Thrupp ed., *Early Medieval Society* (New York, 1967) 221-236. Riché defended the value of merovingian lives in general and the life of St Rusticula in particular. See his 'Note d'hagiographie mérovingienne: La *Vita s. Rusticulae*', in *Analecta Bollandiana* 72 (1954) 369–377.

7. Joseph-Claude Poulin of the University of Laval and Martin Heinzelmann of the *Deutsches Historisches Institut* at Paris announced at the Sixteenth Conference of Medieval Studies, Western Michigan University, Kalamazoo, May 1981, that they are in the process of examining Bruno Krusch's dates.

8. I have found particularly useful for purposes of this study, František Graus, *Volk, Herrscher und Heiliger im Reich der Merowinger* (Prague, 1965).

9. *MGH Script. rer. mer.* 2: 360: 'Scribere nesciens, quascumque legeret vitas sanctorum spoliavit'.

10. For example, Niccolò Del Re, in his article on Radegund in the *Bibliotheca sanctorum* 10: 1351, wrote: 'una delicata e suggestiva *Vita di s. Radegundis* . . . fu scritta da . . . Venanziano Fortunatus . . ., a cui fece seguito una seconda *vita*, piuttosto rozza, complicata dalla monaca Baudonivia'. Graus, *Volk*, p. 409, made a similar remark.

11. Janet Nelson, 'Queens as Jezabels', p. 46, n. 33, has noted that a nun of Chelles wrote the older version of the *vita*, even though Krusch, whose introduction to the *vita* was used by Nelson as reference, did not identify the hagiographer as a woman. Krusch merely noted that the earlier version had been composed at Chelles by a member of the community; *Vita s. Balthildis, MGH Script. rer. mer.* 2: 478.

12. In *Vita s. Balthildis 19, MGH Script. rer. mer.* 2: 506, the author remarked that the events described 'nostris peracta sunt temporibus'. In chapter 5 (p. 487), she listed Chrodobert, bishop of Paris, before Ebroin, the mayor of the palace, in describing the regency after the death of Clovis.

13. *Vita s. Balthildis* 1 (*ibid*., 482).

14. *Vita s. Balthildis* 15 (*ibid*., 501).

15. Levison has noted this in his introduction to *Vita s. Bertilae* (*MGH Script. rer. mer.* 6: 97).

16. See Levinson's remarks, *Vita s. Bertilae* (*ibid*., p. 99).

17. *Vita s. Bertilae 5* (*ibid.* p. 106): 'plurimi viri ac feminae festinabant, quos ipsa Dei famula Bertila . . . recipiebat . . .'.

18. On the date of Bertila's death, see Levinson's preface in *Vita s. Bertilae* (*ibid*., 96). The emphasis in Bertila's *Vita* on the abbess' fame as an administrator and educator, attracting both sexes to the monastery, would not have been appropriate if the expansion had occurred while Balthild was still alive.

19. 'Queens as Jezabels', p. 46, n. 83.

20. On Theodefrid, see Krusch's remarks in *Vita s. Balthildis* (*MGH Script. rer. mer.* 2:478).

21. In his preface to *Vita s. Balthildis* (*ibid*., 479.).

22. *Translatio s. Balthildis, MGH Scriptores* 15:284). On the date of its composition, see Krusch's preface in *Vita s. Balthildis, MGH Script. rer, mer.* 2:479.

23. Baudonivia, *De vita s. Radegundis*, 8, *MGH Script. rer. mer.* 2:383. *Vita s. Balthildis*, 11, *MGH Script, rer. mer.* 2:496: 'ipsa quoque in quoquina ministraret soroibus et munditias vilissimas, etiam deambulationes stercorum, ipsa mundaret'. On menial work as a sign of saintly humility, see Graus, *Volk*, pp. 295–96, 409.

24. L. Coudanne, 'Baudonivie moniale de Sainte-Croix et biographe de sainte Radegonde', *Études mérovingiennes. Actes des Journées de Poitiers, 1er–3 Mai 1952* (Paris, 1953) 45–51.

25. Baudonivia, *De vita s. Radegundis, MGH Script. rer. mer.* 2:378. Radegund's cell was next to the *oratorium*, according to M. Viellard-Troiekovroff, 'Les monuments religieux de Poitiers', *Études mérovingiennes*, pp. 285–92, esp. p. 287.

26. My interpretation contradicts the one advanced by E. Delaruelle, 'Sainte Radegonde, son type de sainteté et las chrétienté de son temps', *Études mérovingiennes*, pp. 64–74, p. 69: 'Fortunate n'a vu en Radegonde que la moniale . . . soucieuse de tout ce qui s'y déroule et usant de son pouvoir encore royale pour y intervenir'. F. Graus (*Volk*, p. 409), rejected this and wrote: 'Fortunat in Radegunde vor allem die königliche Asketin sieht, die Nonne Baudonivia hingegen das Vorbild einer Nonne'.

27. Baudonivia, *De vita sanctae Radegundis*, 9, *MGH Script. rer. mer.* 2:383–84).

Pope Gregory the Great, in his *Dialogues* 4.16, attributed motherly feelings towards her disciples to Redempta; see the translation by O.J. Zimmerman *Saint Gregory The Great, Dialogues* 4.16, Fathers of The Church Series (New York, 1959) p. 209.

28. Baudonivia, *De vita s. Radegundis,* 12, *MGH Script. rer. mer.* 2:385–86.

29. For example, see Graus, *Volk,* pp. 328, 386–87, 413.

30. Baudonivia, *De vita s. Radegundis* 8, *MGH Script. rer, mer.* 2:383: 'Congregationem . . . in tantumque dilexit, ut etiam parentes vel regem coniugem habuisse nec reminisceretur'.

31. Baudonivia, *De vita s. Radegundis* 10 (*ibid.,* 384).

32. Baudonivia, *De vita Radegundis,* 16 (*ibid.,* 388): 'ut ei permitteret pro totius patriae salute et eius regni stabilitate lignum crucis Domni ab imperatore expetere.'

33. *Vita s. Balthildis,* 4, *MGH Script. rer. mer.* 2, 486. *Nutrix* had a broad connotation; it referred to teachers both male and female.

34. *Vita s. Balthildis* 5 (*ibid.,* 488): 'Et credimus, Deo gubernante, iuxta domnae Balthildis magnam fidem ipsa tria regna tunc inter se tenebant pacis concordiam.'

35. *Vita s. Balthildis,* 11, *MGH Script. rer. mer.* 6:497.

36. *Vita s. Balthildis,* 12, (*ibid.,* 498): 'Et conferens sepe cum matre monasterii ut et regem et reginam et proceres cum digno honore cum eulogias semper visitarent, ut erat consuetudo . . .'.

37. See above, n. 4. On Aldegund's visions, see Stephanus Axters, O.P., *The Spirituality of the Old Low Countries,* translated Donald Atwater (London, 1954) p. 11, and Van der Essen, *Étude critique,* pp. 219–60, 282–91.

38. In his preface to *Vita s. Aldegundis, MGH Script. rer. mer.* 6:81.

39. *Vita s. Aldegundis,* 29, *MGH Script. rer. mer.* 6:89: 'Crastina die germana eius Dei famula narravit nobis.'

40. Van der Essen, *Étude critique,* 222–23.

41. *Vita s. Aldegundis,* 5, (ed. Ghesquière, *Acta sanctorum Belgii selecta* 4, 317).

42. *Vita s. Aldegunis* 6 (*ibid.,* 317).

43. *Vita s. Aldegundis* 7 (318).

44. *Vita s. Aldegundis* 10 (319).

45. *Vita s. Aldegundis* 10 (319).

46. *Vita s. Aldegundis* 11 (319).

47. *Vita s. Aldegundis* 8 (318).

48. *Vita s. Aldegundis* 16 (320–21).

49. *Vita s. Aldegundis* 15 (320).

50. *De vita s. Radegundis* 20, *MGH Script. rer. mer.* 2:391.

51. *Vita s. Balthildis,* 13, *MGH Script. rer. mer.* 2:498–99.

52. *Vita s. Aldegundis* 5. ed. Ghesquière, *Acta sanctorum Belgi selecta,* 4:317).

53. Athanasius, *Vita beati Antonii abbatis,* 9; PL 73: 132B: 'Rugiebat leo, occidere volens . . . luporum impetus ingerebantur.'

54. *Vita s. Aldegundis* 8, ed. Ghesquière, *Acta sanctorum Belgii selecta* 4:318. The Lord's angel comforted her by saying, 'Pax tibi, confortare, viriliter age . . .'. On the *virago* motif in roman literature and medieval hagiography, see Marie-Louise Portman, *Die Darstellung der Frau in der Geschichtsschreibung des früheren Mittelalters,* Basler Beiträge zur Geschichtswissenschaft 69 (Basel, 1958).

55. St Gregory the Great, *Dialogues,* 4.18, trans. Zimmerman, pp. 211–12. The young girl found in Pope Gregory's *Dialogues* had a different message than the young girl in St Aldegund's *vita*; see next note.

56. *Vita s. Aldegundis* 10, ed. Ghesquière, *Acta sanctorum Belgii selecta* 4:319.

57. *Vita s. Aldegundis* 6 (*ibid.,* 4:317): 'Quo plus quippe vigilat scintilla fidei, plus accenditur amor Christi'.

58. *Vita s. Aldegundis* 10 (*ibid.,* 4:319).

59. See for example, the passages cited from *Vita s. Corbiniani* by Bosl, 'Der Adelsheilige', p. 182.

60. Krusch lists nine manuscripts for Baudonivia's *Life of St Radegund,* and twelve manuscripts for the Chelles author's *Life of St Balthild* (*MGH Script. rer. mer.* 2:360–

62;479–81). Levison lists seven manuscripts for the *Vita s. Aldegundis* (*MGH Script. rer. mer.* 6:82).

61. Eileen C. Conheady SSJ, *The Saints of the Merovingian Dynasty, A Study of Merovingian Kingship* (Diss., University of Chicago, 1967). Radegund, 179–86 (calendars and litanies telling also the worship of Venantius Fortunatus); Balthildis, 186–89. Otto Dittrich, *St Aldegundis eine Heilige der Franken* (Kevelaer, 1976) 218–19.

62. On the difference between late gallo-roman and merovingian male monasticism, see F. Prinz, *Frühes Mönchtum in Frankenreich* (Munich-Vienna, 1965), and also his 'Heiligenkult und Adelsherrschaft' (cited above, n. 6). The appeal of the combination of the active and the contemplative ways in female and double monasteries may explain the popularity of these types of foundations in the seventh century. On the flowering of female monasticism, in the seventh century, see my remarks in *Women in Frankish Society*, pp. 158–65.

The Unique Experience of Anglo-Saxon Nuns

Janemarie Luecke

ALAIN RENOIR closed a provocative paper of 'Eve's IQ: Two Sexist Views of *Genesis B*' which he read at the 1980 MLA meeting in Houston with the statement:

> If medieval studies had been initiated by female scholars nurtured on the early Germanic tradition rather than by male scholars nurtured on the French and monastic traditions, it might conceivably be that the official teaching today would assert that the Middle Ages unexceptionally assumed the intellectual superiority of women.

By Renoir's own stated intention, such a view is as female-sexist as the usual view is male-sexist. However, if we qualify a few of the terms—if instead of 'the Middle Ages' we say the anglo-saxon era, and if instead of 'unexceptionally' we say 'in general', we have a statement that can be supported in the great poetic literature of the period and in aspects of the works of Bede and Aldhelm. But the implications in such works cannot be understood unless we come to them with a grasp of history enhanced by some degree of feminist awareness. Given such an awareness, we begin to recognize the teutonic heritage which allowed women to figure—sometimes prominently—in the political and economic schemes of their society, and which expected them to advise their warriors, especially in the art of peace. Because anglo-saxon women as such—that is, in their female function, whether married or unmarried—could be so accepted, it was possible for the anglo-saxon nuns, during the few centuries before the danish invasions wiped them out, to exercise a role that is unique for women as a class in the history of the Church and of female monasticism.

Anglo-saxon women began to become nuns in the 630s. The first house for women was probably Lyminge,[1] since tradition held that it was founded by Æthelburh, the daughter of Æthelberht and Bertha of Kent, when she fled Northumbria in 633 after the slaughter of her husband Edwin and the newly christianized people there. Bede tells that AEthelburh's grand-niece Earcongota was a nun of outstanding zeal in the convent of Brie in Gaul, as were two of her aunts on the other side of her family—the daughters of King Anna of East Anglia: Ethelburh, who is characterized as having preserved the 'glory of perpetual virginity', and Saethryth, a stepdaughter.[2] Anna's eldest daughter Seaxburh was Earcongota's mother; she later succeeded another sister, AEthelthryth, as abbess of Ely. AEthelthryth's monastic career must have begun around 670, for she had been the wife of Ecgfrith for twelve years before he released her from the marriage (Bede IV:19). Ecgfrith, who ruled as king of Northumbria from 670–685, was the son of Oswiu and Eanflaed, who was the daughter of the AEthelburh we started out with. Eanflaed ruled Whitby with her daughter, the virgin AEfflaed, after the death of Hild in 680 (IV:26).

Bede did not concern himself with chronological sequence, nor did he usually tell all of any one person's career in one place; hence, it takes some shuffling to come up with the family relationships given above. But such an account introduces two aspects of my thesis: one is that anglo-saxon women, as shown also in the earlier society of *Beowulf*, continued to be married to the kings of alien and often hostile peoples in the heptarchy that comprised what is now England. The other is that Bede mixes his treatment of nuns who were married, those who were virgins, and those who are not designated as either. Both aspects follow from the practice and attitudes inherited from a germanic past that can be traced in *Beowulf*. One element of the second aspect cannot, of course, be found in *Beowulf*—the rhetorical exaltation of virginity preserved. In describing those nuns who remained virgins Bede uses epithets which echo Aldhelm's rhetoric in his *De virginitate*. What is significant however is that neither Bede nor Aldhelm use negative qualifying statements when speaking of nuns who were or are still married.

THE ANGLO-SAXON WOMAN AS PEACE-WEAVER

The reason neither slighted marriage before entry into religion, I think, is that germanic women were traditionally esteemed as females (as a class), especially in their role as *freothu-webbe* (peace-weaver) when they were married to the kings of conquered hostile tribes. In that role they were expected to demonstrate intellectual superiority in matters of peace-keeping, and to provide wise counsel. We see the role exemplified briefly but clearly in *Beowulf*; and in poetry that role for women did not become suspect until the ninth-century *Genesis B*.

Beowulf as we have it is a scop's epic-lay glorifying the warring deeds of heroic men and their pleasures in the meadhall—probably the ceremonial hall occupied only by men in a tribal society in which the role-functions separated the waking lives of men and women. Hence, women figure in the narrative, not in the principal plot of Beowulf's encounters with monsters, except insofar as Grendel's dam is female, but in the surrounding action of feasting and gift-giving and in the digressive episodes designed to complement the main plot. Through these latter we see Wealtheow (whose name probably indicates that she came from a conquered tribe) counselling Hrothgar. Recent studies link her to the valkyrie-brides of norse eddic lays as well as to the christian female-warriors of old english epic—Elene, Judith, and Juliana.[3] We also see Hygd on the death of her husband Hygelac exercising the power to offer the crown to Beowulf, since her son is too young to lead the people. We learn from the Finn episode and from Beowulf's comment on Freawaru that women were given in marriage to seal the peace with a conquered tribe, and we learn also that when the peace was not kept, the woman could be rescued and returned to her tribe, and the marriage dissolved. Since conquering weaker, neighboring tribes was the process through which single tribes became large clans and eventually nations, the women went to these tribes first as ambassadors representing the interests of their own clan, and secondarily as women whose *wif-lufu* (woman's love) would inspire union and also create in children blood-ties between peoples.

On a first reading of *Beowulf*, women may seem little more than pawns in the wheeling and dealing of fighting men; yet the role had power and dignity, as we see in the deliberate and direct speeches of Wealtheow to Hrothgar and his thanes as she performs the ceremonial office of pouring the drink, and it demanded wise, strong women gifted in political and social analysis. It demanded simultaneously men who valued and accepted women as such advisors.

CHRISTIANITY AND THE PEACE-WEAVER

Women played a corollary role in bringing the 'peace' of Christianity to the various petty kingdoms of England. Augustine was not the first to bring roman Christianity to Kent, for example; preceding him was Bertha, the young frankish wife of King Æthelbert who 'had received her from her parents on condition that she should be allowed to practise her faith and religion unhindered, with a bishop named Liudhard whom they had provided for her to support her faith' (I:25). Obviously the bishop would not have been received without her. Bertha and Æthelbert's daughter was the Æthelburh we mentioned earlier who was given in marriage to the pagan North-umbrian king Edwin on the condition that she be free to practise her religion. Edwin was eventually baptized by her chaplain Paulinus (II:9). Æthelburh was important enough as a christian emissary to receive from Pope Boniface a long letter urging her to influence her husband to accept the faith. Their daughter Eanflaed filled a slightly different role since she (a roman Christian) was married to Oswiu (an irish Christian) and thus played a central role in heightening and then resolving the differences between the roman and irish churches.

Eanflaed and Oswiu's daughter Alhflaed was sought in marriage by Peada, son of Penda of Mercia, whom Oswiu had conquered. Peada was refused until he agreed to accept the christian faith. By then more intermarriages existed and Alhflaed's brother, Alhfrith, who was married to Peada's sister, contributed to Peada's acceptance of Christianity (III:21).[4] Nevertheless, the seventh-century history of the heptarchy is one of successive, dominant kings warring on and conquering neighboring kingdoms. When marriage alliances were sought or used to strengthen political bonds, usually the christian wife was expected to bring Christianity to her pagan husband and his people.

Because of the strength of kinship ties, women were not so vulnerable in the role of wife-ambassador to a pagan-hostile tribe as we might assume. They clearly had their kin-clan always behind them, and there is evidence that marriages might be dissolved, although the germanic people were monogamous. More important to their position was the fact that they could own land in their own right, both land they inherited from parents and land their husbands gave them as a marriage gift.[5] Finally, along with the legal and economic rights that follow from the ownership of land and property, anglo-saxon women inherited the respect that continued from a primitive past which included priestesses, mother goddess cults, valkyrie-brides, and perhaps matrilineal tribal bonds. They inherited also the right to a higher *wergeld*—payment for assault or murder—than that assigned men.[6]

Anglo-Saxon nuns, then, enjoyed position and power because women themselves were esteemed in the culture. That esteem weakened with the growth of patriarchy under the influence of Rome and of Christianity, but vestiges of earlier cultural arrangements and attitudes were still operative from the seventh through the ninth centuries. As a result, nuns could own land on which they built monasteries, and they could will that land to the monastery, or to a daughter or relative they named to succeed them, or to a relative outside the monastery. An abbess could wield power and authority equal to that of a bishop and above that of priests, because women were accustomed to exercising persuasive power in political and social analyses, especially in matters of peace. Christianity and monastic life were preeminently concerned with peace. Hence, the fact that men as well as women chose to live under an abbess in the double monasteries seems to me to be simply a logical consequence of the esteem women enjoyed in a society in which men were still primarily engaged in warring on their neighbors or in defending their people against invasion. And during the seventh and eighth centuries at least, women could function in this leadership role primarily because they were women and regardless of whether they were married or unmarried.

BEDE: PATRISTIC RHETORIC AND ANGLO-SAXON CUSTOM

Bede's references to abbesses provide evidence of the adoption of a new, patristic vocabulary exalting physical virginity while maintaining the cultural attitude esteeming women. For example, in writing about the daughters of Anna, he makes much of the fact that Æthelthryth, who became abbess of Ely, had preserved her virginity through two marriages, even though her husband Ecgfrith (with whom she lived for twelve years) promised to give estates and money to anyone who could persuade the queen to consummate the marriage (IV:19). Bede calls her choice 'the glory of perfect virginity', and says that 'the divine miracle whereby her flesh would not corrupt after she was buried was token and proof that she had remained uncorrupted by contact with any man'. He included in the following chapter a long poem exalting the tradition of christian virgins and linking Æthelthryth with Mary, Agnes, and Cecilia in that tradition. In view of his use of such language in reference to Æthelthryth, then, it is significant that Bede in no way denigrates her successor when he says: 'She was succeeded in the office of abbess by her sister Seaxburh, who had been the wife of Eorcenberht, king of Kent'. Earlier he had said that Seaxburh had a daughter called Earcongota who 'deserves special mention' (III:8) because of the wonderful deeds and miracles connected with her. Only in speaking of her burial does he call hers 'the holy body of the virgin'. And he links this narrative to that about her aunt, the Æthelburh who had preserved 'the glory of perpetual virginity which is well pleasing to God', and whose body was 'as untouched by decay as it had also been immune from the corruption of fleshly desires'.

Wonderful things, nevertheless, are associated also with nuns and abbesses who are not characterized as virgins. For example, Æthelburh of Barking is called only 'mother' of the community, and when Hildelith, her successor in the office of abbess decided to transfer the bodies of buried sisters to a new burial place 'the brightness of a heavenly light . . . a wonderful fragrance and other signs also appeared' (IV:10). Abbess Hereburh of *Wetadun* (Watton) appears in Bede's history because she sought and procured a miracle on behalf of one of the nuns who was ill—'her daughter, whom she loved greatly and had planned to make abbess in her place' (V:3).

The largest number of nuns named by Bede are characterized neither as married nor virgin. Among these is Hild, who merits more attention than any other woman. Bede noted that her sister Hereswith, who was a nun in Gaul, was the mother of Ealdwulf, king of the East Angles; but of Hild we learn only that she spent half of her sixty-six years in secular life and the other half as the abbess first of *Heruteu* (Hartlepool) and then of *Streanaeshalch* (Whitby). We get our best insight about life in Anglo-Saxon double monasteries in Bede's chapter on Hild; yet, Bede never calls Whitby a double monastery or distinguishes between his references to men or women. One paragraph of his account reads as follows:

> She established the same Rule of life as in the other monastery, teaching them to observe strictly the virtues of justice, devotion, and chastity and other virtues too, but above all things to continue in peace and charity. After the example of the primitive church, no one was rich, no one was in need, for they had all things in common and none had any private property. So great was her prudence that not only ordinary people but also kings and princes sometimes sought and received her counsel when in difficulties. She compelled those under her direction to devote so much time to the study of the holy Scriptures and so much time to the performance of good works, that there might be no difficulty in finding many there who were fitted for holy orders, that is, for the service of the altar.
>
> We have in fact seen five from this monastery who afterwards became bishops. . . . (IV:23)

Obviously, double monasteries under abbesses required no explanation. Bede makes reference to others at Hartlepool, Barking, Ely, and Coldingham—the only one about which there is an implication of scandal. The monasteries of Repton, Wimborne, Minster (Thanet), and Wenlock were also double, and all of them were ruled by abbesses.[7]

Abbesses not only produced bishops from their monasteries; they sat with them as equals at Synods. Hild is referred to three times in connection with the Synod of Whitby in 664: first, as abbess of that monastery; then, with her community, as being on the side of the Scots and the celtic tradition; and finally by inference as one of those present who 'signified their assent' (III:25). We know from other sources that Abbess ÆElfflaed (Hild's successor) attended the Synod of Nidd and influenced its decision regarding Wilfrid's re-instatement as bishop, and that five kentish abbesses were present at the Council of Beckenham in 694 'and signed the decrees above all the presbyters'.[8]

Hild is never called a virgin by Bede, and the omission is made more obvious when he relates that the nun Begu at Hackness, who saw Hild's death in a vision,'had been dedicated to the Lord in virginity' for thirty or more years. His handling of the rhetoric of virginity without denigrating the celibate married, the mothers, and the widows who are nuns is reminiscent of Aldhelm's similar care and deference in his *De virginitate* which Bede must have known since it was written before 690 and is listed among Aldhelm's works in Bede's *History*, V:18.

PATRISTIC AND ANGLO-SAXON CURRENTS IN ALDHELM'S *DE VIRGINITATE*

Aldhelm wrote the *De virginitate* initially as a letter of some sixty chapters of latin prose to the nuns at Barking,[9] a double monastery. Aldhelm must have expected the monks to hear his letter as well for he included more examples of male virgins than of female; nevertheless, he greeted only Hildelith the abbess, Cuthburg, Osburg, and seven other nuns in his salutation. Among those named, we know that Cuthburg was married (if she is the Cuthburg who was wife of Aldfrith of Northumbria who later founded Wimborne). Abbess Hildelith as well as her predecessor Æthelburh who founded the monastery are among those Bede does not describe as virgins. Hence Aldhelm manipulated his patristic sources in order not to offend the non-virgins in his audience. He did this by changing the Fathers' tripartite hierarchy of female chastity—virginity, widowhood, and marriage, which Ambrose, Jerome, and Augustine had compared to the hundred-fold, sixty-fold and thirty-fold[10]—to virginity, chastity, and conjugality or marriage, and described 'chastity' as the state chosen by her who 'having been assigned to marital contracts, has scorned the commerce of matrimony for the sake of the heavenly kingdom' (XIX, p. 75). By shifting the distinction in this way, Aldhelm was able to accommodate nuns who had followed a custom probably stemming from their germanic background and had dissolved their marriages. Aldhelm even went so far as to say that although chastity occupies a position inferior to virginity, nevertheless nuns in that position may be holier as a result of their continual striving for perfection, whereas virgins were more susceptible to pride. In his characteristic prolixity and florid rhetoric he says of the latter, for example:

> Because they judge themselves to be thoroughly free from all the dregs of filth [of marital intercourse], inflated with [over-] confidence in their virginity they arrogantly swell up and in no way do they turn away the most cruel monster Pride, devourer of the other virtues, with the nose-ring of humility (X, p. 67).

But if Aldhelm's rhetoric is prolix in defense of the chaste and the married, it approaches the *verbosa garrulitas* he wanted to avoid when he praises virginity. For example, he says 'there is as great a distance between the flowers of virginity and the virtues of marriage as is between east and west' (VIII, p. 65). He compared virginity to gold, chastity to silver, and marriage to brass or tin, and piled up additional similes while maintaining his effort not to denigrate marriage: we do not scorn the rough anvil and rusty tongs even though we prefer the studded girdle and royal diadem; the moon does not lose its beauty though the sun illuminates more clearly; the greedy ouzel and the black crow are not despised although the peacock takes precedence:

> the peacock, the beauty of whose feathers now grows golden with a saffron hue, now blushes red with purple sheen, now shines with a bluish depth of colour or glows with the tawny glint of gold. The excellence of its beauty . . . compared, not in vain, to the model of virginity, scorns the other baubles of the world and counts at naught the ornamental trappings of his life, and indeed St Augustine, in his *De civitate Dei* [XXI, 4] testifies that he has found it to be empirically true that the flesh of the peacock is of an incorruptible nature (IX, p. 66).

Aldhelm makes it clear at different points of his letter that he is speaking of men choosing virginity as well as women choosing it; however, his references that debase intercourse are most often to women. For example, his extended simile of the bee ends with the statement: 'Robbing the flowering fields of pastureland of an ineffable booty she produces her sweet family and children, innocent of the lascivious coupling of marriage' (V. p. 62). And commenting on Paul's distinction between the married woman and the virgin, he says: 'In truth a great interval and a large dissimilarity of vast proportion exists between the munificence of divine dilection and the affection of baser love: the one rejoices at being a companion of angelic chastity, the other is pleased to be a kindling of marital wantonness' (XVII, p. 73). The effect of such debasing allusions to married women is the suggestion that they are distinctly inferior—inferior to female virgins as well as to all males, whether virgin or married. Aldhelm's use, then, of a greater number of male virgins for his examples also reflects, whether Aldhelm accepted it or not, the patristic view that the male virgin is the superior model for females to follow.

This effect, however, was not absorbed into cultural attitudes and mores immediately—perhaps not for two hundred years. I suggest that Aldhelm and his audience were in the process of adopting the patristic rhetoric of virginity; and practice always lags behind rhetoric. Certainly Bede, who was writing perhaps twenty-five years later, used the same rhetoric at times, but, perhaps because he was writing history rather than theology, he manifested no bias against the non-virgin. We need, however, a thorough stylistic study of both Aldhelm's and Bede's use of rhetorical epithets for virginity in order to gauge the literary distance at which they stand from the subjectivity of the author.

Bede's later contemporary Boniface, in his exchange of letters with Abbess Eangyth and her daughter Bugga, and in his close association with Lioba, showed the same absence of distinctions. His letters, indeed, are testimonies to the intellectual attainments, advisory functions, and missionary capabilities of the anglo-saxon nuns.[11] Aldhelm's do as well: we marvel at the educational level of the residents of Barking who, we assume, were able to comprehend his letter on hearing it read to them, but Aldhelm also makes explicit reference to the learning of the women he greets and to the 'rich eloquence' of their letters to him.

PATRISTIC ASCENDENCY

Esteem for women as intelligent counsellors had begun to shift before the seventh century from a view that held them wiser than men, which we find in the earlier germanic and celtic legends and myths, to one which in the seventh and eighth centuries proposed something closer to equality with men. Such an equality could not, however, but be eroded by the patriarchal rhetoric in a theological inheritance that consisted almost entirely of the writings of Church *Fathers*. Bede several times speaks of men advising women in the monastic life. He says of Hild that when she was appointed abbess of Hereteu, very soon after taking up monastic life, she 'set about establishing there a Rule of life in all respects like that which she had been taught by many learned men; for Bishop Aidan and other devout men who knew her visited her frequently, instructed her assiduously, and loved her heartily for her innate wisdom and her devotion to the service of God' (IV:23). He records, however, no further incidence of Hild's either seeking or receiving advice from men, whereas her position implies throughout that she gives counsel and direction to them.

The erosion of esteem for women's—and nuns'—intellectual abilities and advice follows upon the erosion of their value as females, that is, upon the gradual acceptance of their inferior status as married women.[12] In other words, gradually only the virgin was thought able to advise or excel. For example, Judith (in the heroic poem of that name) was changed from the hebrew widow of the Old Testament to a virgin; Cynewulf's Juliana is also a heroic virgin, and Elene, who could not be changed into a virgin without losing her position as Constantine's mother, nevertheless becomes heroic long after her adoption of celibacy. Once women were divided into superior and inferior, then it soon followed that even the superior ones cannot be trusted; hence, that all women are suspect.

The poetic fragment called *Genesis B* may exemplify the arrival at that distrust. My own reading of the poem now is that, as Renoir suggested, Eve is still portrayed as intellectually superior to Adam; it is the serpent-Satan whose intellect is superior to Eve's. What is significant, however, and what Renoir does not say, is that even with her superior intellect, Eve's advice to Adam is bad advice; hence, she should not have been trusted in her role, the hereditary germanic role, of advising the male, the warrior. *Genesis B* was not anglo-saxon in origin. It is a translation of a ninth-century old saxon poem, but could have been translated into Anglo-Saxon before the end of that century. And by that time the danish invasions had wiped out all the monasteries.

No double monasteries were refounded in England after the invasions, and the nunneries that were established after the Norman Conquest were not abbacies but priories subject to an abbot. Hence, the experience of the great anglo-saxon nuns was short-lived under the pressure of patristic rhetoric and it remains a unique episode in the history of christian female monasticism.

NOTES

1. Dorothy Whitelock, *English Historical Documents c. 500–1042,* 2nd ed. (1955; rpt. London: Eyre Methuen, 1979) p. 79.

2. *Bede's Ecclesiastical History of the English People,* ed. Bertram Colgrave and R.A.B. Mynors (Oxford: Clarendon, 1969) III:8. Further references to this edition will be given in my text by book and chapter numbers.

3. Helen Damico, *Beowulf's Wealtheow and the Valkyrie Tradition* (Madison: University of Wisconsin Press, 1984).

4. This marriage ended tragically: Bede says three chapters later, without naming her, that three years later Peada was 'most foully murdered . . . by the treachery, or so it is said, of his wife' (III:24). Perhaps if we knew more of the story we would recognize Alhflaed's role in the murder as consistent with the valkyrie tradition and benefitting her own tribe.

5. Whitelock includes a number of charters of such grants of land. The one most clearly concerning bethrothal settlement, p. 467, is from late in the period. The largest number are of grants of land to abbesses; however, No. 68 (p. 494) indicates that the land could be held by married women as well, and that disputes between female inheritors might be settled in lawsuit.

6. David Herlihy, 'Life Expectancies for Women', *The Role of Woman in the Middle Ages* (Albany: State University of New York Press, 1975) p. 8. He adds that even a female fetus (if the sex could be determined) aborted through injury to the mother required twice the wergeld of a male fetus.

7. In another source, *The Letters of Saint Boniface*. ed. and tr. Ephraim Emerton (New York: Columbia Univ. Press, 1940) 319, Abbess Eangith confides to Boniface: 'We are worried, not only by the thought of our own souls, but—what is still more difficult and more important—by the thought of the souls of all who are entrusted to

us, male and female, of diverse ages and dispositions, whom we have to serve and finally to render an account.'

8. G. F. Browne, *The Importance of Women in Anglo-Saxon Times* (London: Society for Promoting Christian Knowledge, 1919) 22–23.

9. My citations are from the translation by Michael Lapidge in *Aldhelm: The Prose Works* (Cambridge: D. S. Brewer Ltd, 1979). Aldhelm later cast the *De virginitate* into 3000 hexameter verses. My references are to the prose work only and are given in my text by paragraph number and the Lapidge pagination.

10. Ambrose, *De virginibus ad Marcellinam* 1.10.60 (PL 16:205); Jerome, *Commentarium in evangelium Matthaeum* 2 (PL 26:92); Augustine, *De sancta virginitate* 45 (PL 40:423).

11. See also Sheila C. Dietrich, 'An Introduction to Women in Anglo-Saxon Society', in Barbara Kanner, ed., *The Women of England from Anglo-Saxon Times to the Present* (Hamden, Conn.: Archon Books, 1979) 37.

12. See Bernice W. Kliman, 'Women in Early English Literature, *Beowulf* to the *Ancrene Wisse,' Nottingham Medieval Studies* 21 (1978) 32–49, for a development of this thesis using the Christian heroic poems, *Judith, Juliana,* and *Elene.*

Solitude and Solidarity

Medieval Women Recluses

Jean Leclercq

AMONG THE FIRST letters I received from Thomas Merton in 1950 is one which shows his interest in the eremitic life generally and medieval recluses in particular. Later, on Holy Saturday 1964, commenting on an article he had just read, he wrote: 'It will help me a little in my work on recluses. I am keeping on patiently and quietly in this, and will I hope eventually begin to get something on paper about Grimlaic. . . '. It seems that Merton never finished, or at least never published, this study. He several times alluded to the problem of solitude and communion, especially in *Mystics and Zen Masters* and *Contemplation in a World of Action*, but he never really got down to dealing with the subject. We shall certainly be faithful to his memory if we try to do so.

In this paper I shall consider only *women* recluses. From the very beginnings of Christianity, women have had an important place in the Church and played an active part in spreading it among the nations. Recently, in connection with a dictionary of biblical proper names, a theologian commented that we find '2,900 men and only 170 women—hardly more than five percent. In the New Testament there is a much higher proportion, and this is a sign of the new place Jesus gave to women by a sort of revolution, one which was quickly reduced by the surrounding masculinity'.[1] Though it may be true that the official role played by women very soon became secondary, their influence has always continued to be real and varied both in works of charity and in that other no less important service in the Church, prayer.

This was true in primitive times as well as in the Middle Ages. The wives of barbarian kings often played a decisive part in the conversion of their husbands, and consequently of the people, to the christian faith. Nuns were closely associated with the work of evangelization carried out by the monks, and from the seventh century on, nuns were real missionaries.[2] Generally speaking, they practised communal prayer, but they also maintained the tradition of solitary prayer, and of course this was particularly true for the recluse.

Thus it is important to set the fact of female reclusion in the context of the tradition which went before it. Having done that, we shall be in a position to examine how medieval women recluses lived this way of life, and how they were actively present to their contemporaries.

RECLUSION IN PRIMITIVE TIMES

Reclusion consisted of a person living in a 'cell'—a cottage or little house. This was one of the more extreme forms of primitive monasticism, and it was sometimes lived in queer and extravagant ways which we find difficult to understand. But reclusion was then considered one of the milder and more reasonable ways of going about monastic living. It had its roots in the desire to do something really great for God and the world. Reclusion was not always absolute, nor even of a difinitive character. It often happened that a person started in total separation from society, and then gradually returned in order to share with others the spiritual experience gained in solitude. Nearly always, recluses communicated with the outside world by a window; their faces remained hidden but their voices could be heard. Whenever they tended to overdo ascetic practices, bishops intervened to moderate their zeal. The monastic institution proved itself worthy of admiration by the astounding flexibility which allowed the living out of so many strange vocations. Authorities were as broad-minded as the institution; they did not impose their own way of thinking but respected the freedom of individuals.[3]

History has recorded more names of men than of women recluses, but we know for a fact that women lived this life. The most famous is St Thaïs, a prostitute, converted by her uncle, the old hermit Paphnutius. The legend about her has been a best-seller right down to our own day. In the nineteenth century, Massenet made the story into an opera, and it is still being quoted, read, and staged. The great french novelist, Anatole France, whose works have been translated into several languages, also mentions Thaïs. Her legend is an illustration of the view so many generations have held of the monastic attitude towards repentant prostitutes. It was an attitude of concern for the soul of a sinning woman, an attitude of practical charity which does something to help. Paphnutius goes to Thaïs in her room and talks to her about God. She repents, gathers everything she has earned through her sins and burns it in the market place as a token of her break with her wicked past. Paphnutius locks her up as a recluse for three years in a narrow cell. Then he consults St Anthony about his penitent. Anthony brings all the brethren together and asks them to pray to God for light. This is a conventual attitude of solidarity, humility, and courage; they were not afraid of being connected with this sort of woman. One of Anthony's disciples, Paul, has a vision of a bed of glory. Everyone thinks it is for Anthony, but a voice from heaven declares that it is for Thaïs. Here again we see the idea that a repentant sinner can be greater in the eyes of God than monks who have spent their entire lives in ascetic living. Paphnutius wanted to set Thaïs free from her reclusion, but she refused and died in peace two weeks later.[4]

'The Rise and Function of the Holy Man in Late Antiquity' has been remarkably well studied by Peter Brown.[5] In his work he has described what he calls those 'ascetic stars' which were needed by oriental peoples at once refined and violent. Each society does in fact provide itself with models, 'stars'. And in those days such models and stars were not beauty queens or sports champions, but men and women who gave proof of inner freedom and—in some cases—of spiritual strength against pressures from the demonic as well as the secular worlds. Once on the fringe, at a distance from pervasive violence, the star Christian had power to pacify people and things. He was seen as a 'man of power' who used his power as an arbitrator and mediator. Sometimes he even went so far as to curse, and frequently he exorcised. 'When little girls played games in fourth-century Syria, they played at monks and demons; one, dressed in rags, would put her little friends in stitches of laughter by exorcising them'.[6]

The social context in which these holy solitaries exercised their influence was that of the villages, in which they were the only authority. They were, in many ways, similar to the innumerable gurus of India today. Nobody ever did anything without asking their advice. It goes without saying that this is very different from the style of certain famous gurus we now see in the affluent cities of the West.[7] Few of these 'holy men' seem to have been women; or at least, few feminine names have been transmitted by historical records. But one has the impression that, in contrast to these rather frightening men of power, women did not curse. They were nonviolent, and this feminine form of christian charity mingled with charm was probably just as effective in pacifying their brutal contemporaries.

RECLUSION DURING THE MIDDLE AGES

Though individual cases differed, certain general features distinguish two main periods.[8] The first period, which extends approximately to the end of the twelfth century, was largely a time of monastic reclusion; men and women undertook reclusion in or near a monastery. These recluses had contact with the community and were under the control of the abbot or abbess. Monastic reclusion seems to have reached its peak in the eleventh century.[9]

From the thirteenth to the fifteenth century, with increasing urbanization, men and women recluses settled in the heart of towns or on their outskirts. They might be near the town gates, close to a church or chapel, in such a position that all who passed could see their window and be assured that someone was praying for the citizens and for visitors. At one time in its history, Toulouse had six recluses, one for each gate. Recluses also lived near hospitals with the intention of praying for the sick or in order to pray for the dead. In such cases, recluses were no longer given material aid by monasteries. The municipality looked after them. And, of course, they were no longer under the control and spiritual direction of an abbot or abbess, but of the bishops and local clergy. Many towns covered the expenses of building cells and supporting recluses. It is easy to understand that one historian interpreted this fact as 'a proof that the people of those times believed with deep faith in the powerful efficacy of the prayer of solitary propitiatory virtue'.[10]

Whatever the social setting, whether monastic or urban, the life-style of the recluse always had the same distinguishing features. Drawing on the fairly numerous sources, historians have collected many a picturesque and sometimes amusing detail about the daily life of recluses. In this field even more than in others, the documents are to be used with caution. We must be careful neither to idealize recluses on the basis of hagiography, which deals with cases of exceptional success, nor to give way to facile irony as occasionally, though rarely, did some writers of fabliaux. Our experience today, even in connection with Thomas Merton, is the same as ever. It shows us that ordinary people have a natural tendency to bring down to their own level men and women greater than they. We must also be on our guard against the professional reformers who tend to magnify deficiencies so that they may have the pleasure of proposing remedies. This seems to have been the case, for example, with Aelred of Rievaulx when he wrote his *Rule for Recluses* somewhere between 1147 and 1167.[11]

Like all the great cistercian writers of St Bernard's generation, Aelred was a reformer. St Bernard, Isaac of Stella, and others proposed programs of reform for every state of life in the Church—the papacy, bishops, clergy, monastic institutions, knighthood. But there was one form of life about which none of these reformers had spoken. So Aelred set himself to do so, and he did it wonderfully well. Before presenting an ideal of extreme fervor and splendid themes for the recluse's meditation, he enjoyed writing a sort of generalized satire of the recluses of his own times. The result is a fairly interesting text, very well written but probably somewhat exaggerated, as reliable as St Bernard's satires against the roman Curia, the pomp of bishops, and the Cluniacs.

The most useful documents for getting to know the truth about the life of recluses, are the *Rules*, like the *Ancrene Riwle* written probably between 1190 and 1230, or the *Lives*, like that of St Christina of Markyate. There, as in other texts written by bishops, the life of recluses bears a stamp of realism, common sense, and a search for that harmonious balance which avoids excess and eccentricities. This life of reclusion is, in the intentions of those who lived it as well as of those who fostered and protected it, marked with a great sense of all that is best in humanity, including joy and humor. The life of a recluse is essentially human, and we find this dimension in several areas.

First of all there is the relationship between the recluse and animals. Christ himself, in the momentous hours of solitude with which he chose to begin his public life, dwelt 'with the beasts of the forest'. Tradition saw in this the symbol of universal reconciliation, prefigured by the strange herd of animals in the prophecy of Isaiah, who foretold that the lion and the lamb would lie together, and that the most incompatible beasts would live in peace. Many an ancient hermit had an animal to help him and keep him company, and we find them mentioned in some pieces of 'hermit poetry' reflecting irish customs in the High Middle Ages.[12] Recluses seem generally to have had a cat, not as a pet but quite simply, apparently, to get rid of mice.

Sometimes however, in assuring the necessities of life, exceptions crept in, and it was against these that the *Ancrene Riwle* reacted: 'Ye shall not possess any beasts, my dear sisters, except only a cat. An anchoress that hath cattle appears as Martha was, a better housewife than anchoress; nor can she in any wise be Mary with peacefulness of heart. For then she must think of the cow's fodder, and of the herdsman's hire, flatter the heyward, defend herself when her cattle are shut up in the pinfold, and moreover pay the damage. Christ knoweth it is an odious thing when people in the town complain of anchoresses' cattle . . . .'[13]

A chronicler reports that the recluse Verdiana, in the thirteenth century, lived with two snakes who shared her food and ate out of the same bowl she did. When the bishop came, he was horrified and wanted to have the serpents killed, but Verdiana persuaded him to let them live because she had prayed God to have them.[14] This is a good example of freedom with regard to a prelate. The story does not say whether or not the bishop held his ground. He probably admitted that this woman of God was able to do things beyond his own capabilities.

As to hygiene, exceptional recluses never washed themselves, or if they did so, rarely. But the *Ancrene Riwle* seems to be nearer the general truth when it says that recluses might wash as often as they considered it necessary. Of course we must remember that this is a british text and it is well-known that northerners have always been greatly in favor of baths and hydrotherapy. Aelred himself mentions that Mary gave her child Jesus his bath.[15] We also know that it was possible for the recluse to air the cell by means of a special window, which was not the same as the one through which she spoke to visitors, nor that through which she could see the altar and attend Mass. To have three windows was a sort of luxury at a time when, as a thirteenth century chronicler states, 'even strong and good houses had few windows, and those of small size; and they lacked light'.[16]

As for food, it had to be sufficient and cleanly prepared but not fancy. The *Ancrene Riwle* states that the recluses are not to complain about the food if it is a bit stale. Should it really be inedible, they were allowed to mention the fact politely. They were to be careful not to grumble and give themselves a reputation for being fussy and difficult. If a recluse did not eat something she received, then she had to give it away to poor women and children.[17]

Historians have often taken pains to stress the longevity of certain recluses. Examples are quoted of people who remained recluses for twenty, thirty, forty, and even fifty years. The record seems to have been held by Agnes Durscher, the daughter of a wealthy middle-class family in Paris, who spent eighty long years, until her death in 1483, as a recluse in a tiny cell at the parish of Sainte Opportune.[18] Historians find this surprising because they tend to compare her living conditions and hygiene with those of modern times rather than those of medieval days. The facts as we know them seem to show that conditions were probably better for Agnes than for the majority of her contemporaries, even those living in castles.

Recluses were not able to beg, of course, but they were allowed to accept alms or whatever was offered them by the monastic communities and towns with which they were connected. Sometimes two recluses shared the same cell, with all the joys and annoyances experienced by students who room together. It does, however, seem that when two or three recluses lived together, they generally had separate cells with communicating windows, It even happened that the recluse in the neighboring cell was a man. St Christina of Markyate had as a neighbor the monk Roger of Saint Albans. They talked about God together, but he saw her only once.[19] The case of a similar spiritual friendship between Herveus and Eva is exceptional in the literary history of recluses, and perhaps even in historical history. But it is a beautiful thing and suggests an ideal. It caused a problem, of course, and this, together with its solution, is admirably expressed in verse by a certain Hilarion, a disciple of Abelard:

> Eva lived there a long time with her companion Herveus. I feel that you are troubled, you who hear such talk. Brother, avoid all suspicious thought; let this not be the cause. Such love was not in this world, but in Christ.[20]

Two main themes stand out from what we know of the life itself and of the rites by which men and women were set into reclusion. First, the idea of freedom. Recluses illustrate this as a sort of peak example and in a paradoxical way. Throughout monastic tradition from its origins down to our own day runs the theme of voluntary captivity not as a punishment for crime, but out of love for Christ who in his passion accepted imprisonment for love of his Father in order to save the world.[21] We now know that legends of women being walled up in spite of themselves are myths, at least in Christianity.[22] Recluses proved that it is possible to shake off the chains of the elementary freedom of being able to go from place to place and so reach the higher freedom of being able to surrender one's entire self to God. That was why, when a person was installed as a recluse, a Mass of the Holy Spirit was sometimes celebrated, because the Spirit of God is the source of all liberty. When we read through all that has been written in the *Rules* and the *Lives*, we realise that being walled up was as much a symbol as a reality; the fact of being closed in was not absolute. The cell was the symbol of voluntary imprisonment, but it was not a prison.

The other spiritual theme of which the recluses were the parable or living metaphor is that of the intense interior life a person can attain who dies to the fulfillment of many natural human capacities. The ritual for being put away in reclusion was sometimes the funeral ceremony—a Requiem Mass which symbolized reclusion as a grave. Recluses even received the Last Sacraments at times, and ashes were thrown on the cell as was customarily done for bodies. These gloomy rites had a practical purpose. If the recluse died suddenly without anyone knowing, then at least she would have been succored by holy mother Church. But there was more to it than that. This quasi-death, mini-death, false or pretended death was also the symbol of the total renunciation of the earthly fulfilment of one's natural faculties. The observances were only the practical consequences of death to the world. In the *Ancrene Riwle* we read: 'There are anchoresses who take their meals with their friends outside the convent. That is too much friendship. . . . We have often heard it said that dead men speak with living men; but that they eat with living men, I have never yet found'.[23] Such separation from our often mediocre way of life opens out to an existence lived in the presence of God alone. This is well expressed by an antiphon which was sometimes sung during the ceremony of enclosing a recluse: 'Here is my resting place forever'.[24] To rest, in such a context, meant to be 'on vacation', at leisure and relaxed—on sabbatical leave, so to speak, for God. This is the life of contemplation.

One interesting case is that of St Ida, who died in 825, but whose *Life*—that is to say, the legend which proposed her as a model of christian behavior—was written by a monk at the end of the tenth century. Ida was a widow; she had been married to Count Egbert whom she greatly loved. They had had several children, five of whom are recorded as living. As husband and wife, they shared their human love in marriage and in so doing they loved God and lived together in communion with his Holy Spirit. When Egbert died, Ida remained faithful to his memory and became a recluse near the chapel he had built and where he was buried. When she died, she was buried with him. A very explicit, dense and legendary *Life* illustrates this example of conjugal fidelity in a reclused widow. Up to her death she had two lovers—an earthly one, her deceased husband, and a heavenly one. She peacefully and happily united these two loves and so left to posterity an example of humanity and humanism.[25]

In the thirteenth century we find an interesting and more likely story in the legend of Blessed Philip Bruizo—a story which is in harmony with the social and religious context of the period. The text is simple and moving. As Philip was walking along a street in the city of Todi, he saw two prostitutes trying to attract clients. Crying out 'God forgive you!', he tried to persuade them to think of the price God had paid to redeem them by his precious blood. At least they should spend the money they earn on works of charity. But the women informed him they had no other means of making a living. Philip replied, 'I beg this grace of you for love of the Virgin Mother of God —do not commit sin for the next three days. Here is some money to support you'. As soon as they took the money from his hands, the grace of the Holy Spirit welled up in their hearts.

The next day they came to him weeping, asking him to obtain forgiveness for them. He gave them God's pardon. They left their sinful lives and entered a cell. Another version which seems less authentic says that it was Philip himself who walled them up so that they could not go back to their former life. Whatever happened, the fact is that the two women stayed in their cell and lived saintly lives until their deaths.[26]

It is not easy to know exactly whether, or how many, repentant prostitutes became recluses in medieval times. But the idea is certainly present in literature. In the tenth century, a certain Hrostwitha, a saxon abbess, wishing to persuade her nuns not to read Terence, wrote in his style a comedy about the conversion of Thaïs. The abbess described all the adventures of Uncle Paphnutius who set out to find his niece and convert her. When he had succeeded, he suggested she should become a recluse. Her lovers (*amatores*) did not agree and tried to dissuade her, telling her she was mad. She hesitated, but Paphnutius intervened and won the day. He then had to find an abbess willing to take charge of this unusual 'captive'. Again he was successful, and described to his niece the sort of life she would lead in the following dialogue:

Thaïs: My vileness does not refuse to go at once where your paternity commands; but there is a certain inconvenience in this dwelling which is difficult for my weakness to bear.

Paph: Now, what is this inconvenience?

Thaïs: I blush to say.

Paph: Come now, don't blush. Be thoroughly honest.

Thaïs: What is more inconvenient, or what could be more disagreeable than having, in one and the same place, to attend to the different needs of nature? Indeed, it would soon become uninhabitable because of the excessive stench.

Paph: Fear the cruelty of everlasting hell, and cease to shudder at things which pass away.

Thaïs: My weakness drives me into terror.

Paph: It is only right that you expiate the sweetness of the pleasure of evil delights by the vexation of an excessive stench.

Thaïs: I do not object, I do not deny that it is not unjust for filthy me to go and live in a foul and squalid little hut; but this I do very greatly deplore, that there is no place left where I may fitly and chastely invoke the name of the Tremendous Majesty.[27]

All this is imaginary. In the Middle Ages, everything was subject matter for literature, and reclusion was no exception. There is always a certain exaggeration in the literary genre of drama. A passage in the *Life* of Christina of Markyate contradicts what Hrostwitha supposes here, while still proving that the time schedule of a recluse was very mortifying: 'What was more unbearable than all this was that she could not go out until evening to satisfy the demands of nature'.[28]

Furthermore, the recluse generally had a maid-in-waiting who went out to get things or take things away. The heroic form of penance attributed to Thaïs makes sense, however, when we realize that most of the dramas written by Hrostwitha, especially the play *Dulcitius*, take for their major theme martyrdom as the witness of christian virgins. This is the 'martyrdom of love' attributed to St Romuald in the eleventh century: *Martyr fuit, sed amoris*.[29] This was not merely a symbol. It is known for a fact that at least one recluse, St Wiborade, was killed by the Hungarians on the second day of May in 926.[30]

Thomas Merton expanded on this idea when he wrote: 'Just as the Church of God can never be without martyrs, so too she can never be without solitaries, for the hermit, like the martyr, is the most eloquent witness of the Risen Christ'.[31] One of the main sufferings in such an existence might well be old age, even though everyone, including the servant, gave the recluse all the medicines known in those days. Today many an old lady would assent to these words spoken by a woman with a sense of humor: 'Had I known how boring it is to grow old, I would have stayed young.' But the solitude of a recluse at the end of her life was probably less painful than that of old people today.

Such was the life of recluses in the Middle Ages, in continuation of the life-style in antiquity. It seems to have been a constant factor in the life of the Church. We know of cases of reclusion in the seventeenth and the eighteenth century in Europe[32] and in the New World. In Canada, near Montreal, Catherine Leber spent twenty years as a sister in a Congregation which had little sympathy for the solitary life—frequently the case in modern times as well. Then for fifteen years, until her death in 1714, she lived as a recluse in her father's house with the approval of Bishop Laval of Quebec, which is also quite normal. Her vocation sprang from reading about medieval recluses.[33]

SOLITUDE AND COMMUNION

Now that we have seen something of the externals of a life of reclusion in the Middle Ages, we must take a look at the spiritual reality which lies at the core of this mystery. We are dealing with a paradox whose meaning and interpretation are a matter of faith. Certainly we may wonder whether anyone has the right to withdraw so absolutely from secular, ecclesiastic, and monastic society. Is this not a form of selfishness which, though disguised under spiritual motives, is nonetheless contradictory to the fundamental requirement of Christianity—a love for all humanity which manifests itself in the sharing of every good thing bestowed by God? This aspect of reclusion has been much less studied than the more picturesque external elements; yet it is the more important aspect, and the documents tell us a great deal about it. They show that recluses shared in every state of the common lot of humankind, from the least to the highest.

The recluse's first and deepest form of solidarity is the knowledge that, like every other human being, she is a sinner. This accounts for the great role given to temptation in the different *Lives* and *Rules* and various other documents. These temptations, which are sometimes described with some degree of exaggeration, make the recluse conscious of her attraction to sin, a tendency in which she is no different from anyone else; she merely had a keener awareness of it, and this increased her responsibility towards others.

It was essential, then, for the recluse to do voluntary penance. Taking into account the majority of texts and the literary exaggeration, however, we realise that physical mortifications were fairly moderate. The author of the *Ancrene Riwle*, for example, states: 'Your meat and your drink have seemed to me less than I would have it. Fast no day upon bread and water except ye have leave' . . .[34] Yet penance, though not excessive, was constant. It was a voluntary way of sharing in the involuntary suffering of all the victims of sin and its consequences. The most important effect of mortification is growth in humility and purification of heart, intentions and motivations. It was because men and women felt recluses were close to them and yet close to God that they had confidence in them. Just as in *Tristan* and other romances, the unhappy lovers take refuge and counsel with a hermit in the forest, so people in every situation unburdened their sorrows and opened their hearts to a kind, compassionate recluse.

Above all, the recluse prayed for everyone. This was one of her forms of solidarity with them—she shared in the absolute solitude of Christ and so shared also in his solicitude for all. A twelfth-century text tells us that Christ was 'truly a hermit, and the cross was his hermitage'.[35] The recluse persevered in prayer like the prophetess Anna in the Temple,[36] and like Mary Magdalen at Our Lord's feet. Furthermore, it should be noticed that, in the mentality of those times, Magdalen was the symbol of the repentant sinner, converted and loving.[37] In addition to her experience of deep solitude, a solitude similar to Christ's, the recluse often had to suffer the severe judgment passed by pharisees on a repentant sinner, and the lack of comprehension which was sometimes accorded her. She was held up to ridicule in cartoon stories (*les contes-a-rire*).[38] Certain churchmen even laid snares in a attempt to seduce her.[39] She had to renounce not only prestige and vainglory but even a good reputation.

Any influence which the recluse may have had arose from this twin experience of humiliation as a sinner and union with Christ as a loving penitent. Exceptionally, she may also have had influence after her death through the recounting of her life story.[40] Or again, her own writings might have been a source of influence. This was the case with Eva of Saint-Martin at Liège and of Ava Göttweig.[41] The recluse was also sometimes considered a healer. But generally her action was more direct and unsensational—perhaps just teaching little girls to read. St Hildegard, who became one of the most cultured people in the twelfth century, first learned to read from a recluse at Disibodenberg. When a recluse engaged in counseling, she usually spoke through the window of the parlor next to her cell.[42]

Historians frequently stress that this window was a source of concern for the authors of the different *Rules* and for the bishops who had to see that they were kept. Obviously, all sorts of abuses were possible, and some did take place. But again we must guard against literary exaggeration in this as in every point concerning recluses and others who live an unusual life. Writers who want to attract a reading public have always been quick to exploit sensation. In actual fact most of the visitors received by recluses seem to have been afflicted people in need of spiritual comfort rather than idle gossips.

The recluse had influence too through her prayer, which is an effective way of being united to the saving prayer of Christ. The recluse read and meditated and is sometimes represented in pictures with a book in her hands.[43] Sometimes she helped to spread new devotions by her example and her encouragement; sometimes she herself started new devotions. It has been written that:

> Some of the devotions which were later to be part of popular piety were already favored by the recluses of the twelfth century. Such, for example, as the devotion to the five wounds, the holy cross, the mysteries of the life of Christ and the joys of Our Lady. About the same time too, people in reclusories began to repeat the short formulas used in the angelic salutation, and this repetition joined to other elements gradually became the most popular of marian devotions, the rosary.[44]

The recluses also recited the psalter, and to the extent that they had liturgical books, the Divine Office. One of the most spectacular developments of the liturgy in the thirteenth century was due to a recluse. Public devotion to the Blessed Sacrament and the institution of the feast of Corpus Christi was mainly due to Blessed Julian of Mont-Cornillon and her friend Blessed Eva, who was a recluse of the Abbey of Saint-Martin in Liège.[45]

Lastly the influence of the recluse was felt through her charity towards all, especially those in her immediate neighborhood. It has been said that the recluse was a 'link between two worlds'. This role of mediation and reconciliation has already been studied in connection with the holy man of eastern villages in late antiquity.[46] It has also been discussed for the Middle Ages in the article by H. Mayr-Hartling, 'Functions of a Twelfth Century Recluse'.[47] She could settle local quarrels without taking sides because she was sufficiently distanced from the passions electrifying the atmosphere. Particularly in prayer she interceded for all the wretchedness of the world. In writing about male hermits, St Peter Damian made wonderful Statements on the theology of universal communion in his treatise *Dominus vobiscum*. He shows that the most solitary of solitaries must pray in the plural, because he prays in the name of all and for the benefit of all.[48] Aelred of Rievaulx has written in the same vein about women recluses more briefly but with no less fervor:

> What good then will you be able to do to your neighbor? Nothing is more valuable, a certain holy man has said, than good will. Let this be your offering. What is more useful than prayer? Let this be your largesse. What is more humane than pity? Let this be your alms. So embrace the whole world with the arms of your love and in that act at once consider and congratulate the good, contemplate and mourn over the wicked. In that act

> look upon the afflicted and the oppressed and feel compassion for them. In that act call to mind the wretchedness of the poor, the groans of orphans, the abandonment of widows, the gloom of the sorrowful, the needs of travellers, the prayers of virgins, the periods of those at sea, the temptations of monks, the responsibilities of prelates, the labors of those waging war. In your love take them all to heart, weep over them, offer your prayers for them.[49]

We find the same emphases in the *Ancrene Riwle*. From the very beginning, in connection with the intentions for which the recluse is to recite the Divine Office, we notice that she prays in the plural: 'Give *them* eternal rest, O Lord . . . Christ, have mercy on us'.[50] The recluse prays in the Church, with the Church, and for the Church: 'For the peace of the holy Church . . ., for all christian souls . . ., O Lord, mercifully receive the prayers of thy Church, that being delivered from all adversities, it may serve thee in security and freedom . . .'.[51] A little further on we read this prayer for every form of suffering:

> Think upon and call to mind all who are sick and sorrowful, who suffer affliction and poverty, the pains which prisoners endure who lie heavily fettered with iron. Think especially of the Christians who are among the heathen, some in prison, some in great thralldom as is an ox or an ass. Compassionate those who are under strong temptations; take thought of all men's sorrows, and sigh to Our Lord that he may take care of them with a gracious eye . . .[52]

RECLUSION AND PROPHECY

It is interesting and revealing to notice that the theologian of spiritual friendship also sketched a theology of the life of reclusion. Aelred of Rievaulx, who was so human and sociable, had a keen sense of the universal role which could be played in the Church by a woman dedicated to God in absolute solitude. Christina of Markyate, Aelred's contemporary, and many others like her lived out his teaching.Friendship can become so intimate as to allow one person to read into another's heart, as do those who have the gift of prophecy. One of the models for the recluse, as we have seen, was the prophetess Anna.[53]

If we try to attach the charism of reclusion to others mentioned by Scripture and Tradition, prophecy seems to be the most appropriate. According to the New Testament and the documents of the early christian centuries, prophecy was a form of teaching in which a person shared with others the prayer and had the nature of a public witness in the Church. After charity, prophecy was the most elevated of charisms, higher even than the active ministry. 'But when it comes to prophecy, men and women were clearly on the same plane', and women seem to have received this gift more abundantly than men.[55] It was something independent of the hierarchy and the clergy.

> In this category belong all those groups organized not for any external ministry but for the spiritual function of praying and bearing witness to the Church's otherworldliness by their lives of prayer and asceticism. Among them are the late widows, the early virgins, and those monastic communities predominantly eremitical rather than ecclesial in spirit.[56]

Reclusion—this great fact of the Church—retained its vitality throughout the Middle Ages. A great abbess like St Hildegard, an illustrious recluse like Christina of Markyate were called prophetesses. And, as we have already seen, some recluses had some kind of active service in the Church. But there were other more obscure women who were just as surely prophets. They all had in common, and this is specific, the task of keeping alive in the Church the characteristics of the 'prophetic life'[57]—detachment from the ways of the world, desire for God, contemplative prayer for the good of the whole Church and all humanity.

Right at the beginning of his study 'Franciscan Heremetism',[58] Thomas Merton stressed the factors common to every form of eremetism: solitude and the desire to help everyone. These two attitudes flow from the same source—love for God in Christ, love for Christ and for all human beings. In 1975, during an ecumenical symposium when Orthodox, Roman Catholics, Anglicans, and other Christians met to discuss ***Solitude and Communion***, one of the participants spoke at length on the words of St Peter Damien, ***solitudo pluralis***, corporate solitude.[59] Another member quoted 'a true hermit, Thomas Merton'.[60] And in its 'Statement on the Solitary Life', the symposium summed up its conclusions in several points, of which the first is the most important:

> The life of solitude, while involving an external separation from society, is at the same time a life lived in profound communion with all mankind. Dwelling 'on the frontier', separated from all, the solitary is at the same time united to all. Living often in conditions of utmost simplicity and poverty, he or she is identified with all men in their need and poverty before God'.[61]

CONCLUSION

Each human being is like a mirror of every other and of the whole universe; personality is the crossroad of the entire world. And the Logos who is in God, who is God, who is the mirror in whom God the Father is reflected in the oneness of their Spirit, is also the mirror of every human being.

Thus there exists an ontological solidarity between all human beings, because solidarity, before belonging to a psychological or spiritual order, is an ontological reality. It is on this basic level that we are in fellowship with one another whether we realize it or not. This ontological reality must be consciously taken up into psychological awareness and spiritual experience—otherwise we fail to understand that what happened to dear little Eve in the garden is of any consequence for us. And we fail also to grasp that what happened on the cross is of benefit to us.

Seen from this perspective of ontological reality and awareness, monasticism reveals itself as a great sacrament, a mystery of solitude and communion, instead of the specialized activity of a chosen few. The nun, the monk, is a person in whom the center of consciousness and the cosmic sense coincide. The monastic person is one who is centered, who *is* the center, who is con-centrated in such a way that in this one person converge as in a single focal point the centers of every other reality.

Such is the purpose of contemplative solitude—to be the center of a center which is everywhere, a center without circumference. Such is the fruit of contemplative solitude—to become totality, to live without the limits of dimension, aware with deep humility of one's condition. This is not empty rhetoric. It is factual, as this letter which I received last fall from a monk in this country illustrates:

> My experience of the contemplative life is that the longer I live it, the more universal I seem to become. Everything is my friend. I think Father Louis [Merton] had a lot to say about that. And it is very wonderful to experience this without even having put it into words and then read something by him . . . which is an articulation of something already there. But I guess that is one of the main dynamics of contemplative prayer.

NOTES

1. R. Laurentin, in a review in *Le Figaro* of O. Odelain and R. Sequineau, *Dictionnaire des noms propres de la Bible* (Paris, 1978).
2. E. De Moreau, 'Le rôle des la femme dans la conversion des peuples païens', *Nouvelle revue théologique* 58 (1931) 317–39.

3. H. Leclercq, art. 'Reclus', *Dictionnaire d'archéologie chrétienne et de liturgie*, 14/2 (Paris, 1939) col. 2155–58.

4. *Vitae patrum; PL* 73:661–2; *Bibliographie hagiographique latine* 8012 –19.

5. In the *Journal of Roman Studies* 62 (1971) 98–100.

6. *Ibid.*, 88.

7. Francis Acharya, 'The Guru: The Spiritual Father in the Hindu Tradition', in John R. Sommerfeldt, ed., *Abba. Guides to Wholeness and Holiness East and West*, CS 38 (Kalamazoo, 1982) 243–75.

8. The history of reclusion has been the subject of many studies: a bibliography may be found in L. Gougaud, *Ermites et reclus. Études sur d'anciennes formes de vie religieuse* (Ligugé, 1928); Peter Anson, *The Call of the Desert* (London, 1966) 265–68; and especially R. Rouillard, 'Reclusione', DIP 6 (

9. This form of reclusion near a monastery lasted much longer. For the fourteenth century, see Morton W. Bloomfield, *Piers Plowman as a Fourteenth Century Apocalypse* (Rutgers University Press, s.d.) 70. He goes so far as to write: 'In Langland's period all monasteries made provisions for recluses and hermits, and many attached themselves to these centers.'

10. J. Hubert, 'Les recluseries urbaines au moyen âge', *L'eremitismo in Occidente nei secoli XI e XII* Milan, 1965) 487.

11. *De institutione inclusarum*, translated by Mary Paul Macpherson as *A Rule of Life for A Recluse* in *Aelred of Rievaulx: Treatises and the Pastoral Prayer*, CF 2 (Spencer, 1971: Kalamazoo, 1982).

12. Texts are quoted in J. Kenneth, *Studies in Early Celtic Nature Poetry* (Cambridge, 1935) 93–109.

13. Quoted according to the edition of James Morton, *The Nun's Rule: Being the Ancreen Riwle modernised*, Introduction by Abbot Gasquet (London, 1905) 316.

14. According to Anson, *op. cit.*, 176,

15. Aelred, *De Jesu puero*, 6, translated by Theodore Berkeley as *Jesus at the Age of Twelve*, in CF 2:10.

16. MGH SS 17:232, quoted here after the translation of G. G. Coulton, *Life in the Middle Ages* (Cambrdige, 1967) part II, pp. 191–2.

17. According to Anson, p. 215.

18. Gougaud, *op. cit.*, 93.

19. *The Life of Christine of Markyate. A Twelfth Century Recluse* edited by C. H. Talbot (Oxford, 1959).

20. Edited Nicholas M. Häring, 'Die Gedichte und Mysterienspiele des Hilarius von Orléans', *Studi medievali* 17 (1976) 928.

21. J. Leclercq, *Libérez les prisonniers. Du Bon Larron à Jean XXIII* (Paris, 1976) 36–59: Monastère et prison.

22. Gougaud, p. 75.

23. Morton, p. 314.

24. Ps 131:14 (Vulgate)

25. AA SS,September II (Paris, 1868) 260–62.

26. *Legenda beati Philippi . . . auctore incerto saeculi XIV* in A. Morini and P. Soulier, *Monumenta Ordinis Servorum S. Mariae*, 2 (Brussels, 1898) 77–78.

27. *Paphnutius. Conversio Thaidis meretricis*, ed. Homeyer, *Hrotsvitae Opera* (Paderborn-Vienna, 1970) 333–34.

28. *Life . . . 4*, ed. Talbot, p. 105.

29. On this text and theme, see J. Leclercq, *La vie parfaite* (Paris-Turnhout, 1948) 148–57; ET Collegeville, MN, 1960.

30. Gougaud, p. 81.

31. Preface to J. Leclercq, *Alone with God* (New York, 1961) xiii.

32. Comtesse Henri de Boissieu, *Une recluse au XVii^e siècle* (Paris-Gembloux, 1934).

33. Sr Ellen Clarkin, 'The Story of a Recluse', *Review for Religious* 19 (1978) 387–92. In memory of Jeanne Leber, the Congregation of Missionary Recluses was founded in Canada.

34. Morton, pp. 313–14.

35. J. Leclercq, 'Pétulance et spiritualité dans le commentaire d'Hélinand sur le Cantique des cantiques', *Archives d'histoire doctrinale et littéraire du XII$_e$ siècle* 39 (Paris, 1965) 41.

36. Cited by Gougaud, p. 110.

37. Aelred, *Rule for a Recluse*, 31; CF 2:91; J. Leclercq, *Monks and Marriage in the Twelfth Century* (New York, 1981).

38. J. J. Jusserand, 'Les Contes à rire et la vie des recluses au XIIe siècle', *Romania* 24 (1895) 122–28. In this article, Jusserand quotes Abelard and concludes that he 'adds to the indications we already had on the thousands of ways in which the stories were built up and how adventures happened, which is the basic material of the fabliaux'. But he does not give any indications about such stories, if they existed.

39. This was the case for Christine of Markyate.

40. Gougaud, p. 85.

41. *Ibid.*, 96–7.

42. *Ibid.*, 102.

43. J. Hubert, 'Les recluseries urbaines au moyen âge' in *L'eremitismo in Occidente*, 486.

44. Gougaud, 110–11.

45. *Ibid.*, 82.

46. See above, note 5.

47. In *History* 60 (1971) 337–52.

48. J. Leclercq, *S. Pierre Damien, ermite et homme d'Église* (Rome, 1960) 265–73: Solitude et communion d' après le 'Dominus vobiscum'.

49. *Rule for a Recluse*, 28; CF 2:77–78.

50. Morton, p. 18.

51. *Ibid.*, 19.

52. *Ibid.*, 25.

53. Sr Mary Lawrence McKenna, *Women in the Church*, Foreward by Jean Danièlou (New York, 1967) 149.

54. *Ibid.*, 155.

55. *Ibid.*, 160.

56. *Ibid.*, 159.

57. J. Leclercq, *La vie parfaite*, 125–60.

58. *Contemplation in a World of Action* (New York, 1971).

59. André Louf, *'Solitudo pluralis'*, in A. M. Allchin, ed., *Solitude and Communion. Papers on the Hermit Life given at St David's, Wales, in the Autumn of 1975* (Oxford: Fairacres Press, 1977) 17–29.

60. A. M. Allchin, 'The Solitary Vocation. Some Theological Implications', *Ibid.*, 16.

61. *Ibid.*, 77.

Elizabeth of Schönau and Hildegard of Bingen: Prophets of the Lord

M. Colman O'Dell

In his first encyclical letter, *Redemptor hominis*, Pope John Paul II stressed that all of the members of Christ's mystical body share in his role of prophet.[1] In many of his recent allocutions to religious women, the Holy Father has challenged them to set about fulfilling this function in the Church. In speaking to the women religious of Zaire during his recent visit to Africa, he said:

> The mission of the Church is in the first place prophetic. She proclaims Christ to all nations and transmits to them his message of salvation. This involves your personal and community life-style in the first place. . . . Is it really luminous [Cf. Mt 5:16], prophetic? The present-day world is awaiting everywhere, perhaps vaguely, consecrated lives which tell in acts more than words, of Christ and the Gospel. . . . I ask you, my Sisters, to contribute even more to the prophetic mission of the Church.[2]

This challenge need not disconcert women who follow the Rule of St Benedict, for they have inherited a venerable tradition that regards christian monasticism as a continuation of the life-style of the ancient prophets.[3] When we scan the vast panorama of christian monastic history, seeking examples of benedictine women who have exercised this prophetic role, our attention is drawn to a pair of rhineland abbesses of the twelfth century: Elizabeth of Schönau and Hildegard of Bingen. Both of these nuns, even in their own lifetimes, were reputed to possess the charism of prophecy. This present study endeavors to present a picture of their lives as prophets and to examine their influence on christian spirituality.

Origen in his *Homilies on the Book of Judges*, commenting on the prophet

Deborah, stated that 'the grace of prophecy is determined by purity of heart alone, not by difference of sex'.[4] Therefore, in this paper we will employ the word 'prophet' as a generic term, referring to a person of either sex who fulfills that role. Since we are concerned specifically with women who have performed this function, we shall use the feminine form of pronouns, in contrast to the conventional masculine form.

WHAT IS A PROPHET?

The most cursory research into the subject soon reveals how much ambiguity exists in regard to a basic definition of the terms 'prophet' and prophecy'. Nearly every writer on these or related topics utilizes the words with nuances of meaning suited to the author's purposes. A monk of our own times, Thomas Merton, himself regarded as a prophet by many who knew him,[5] has given a definition which seems to include the basic components of this vocation. He writes that 'a prophet is one who lives in direct submission to the Holy Spirit in order that, by [her] life, actions, and words, [she] may at all times, be a sign of God in the world of men',[6] Dom Jean Leclercq, commenting on Merton's own prophetic role, expands this concept by saying that 'a prophet is a person of neither vague ideas nor ready-made solutions. He or she is a person who, by reason of the vigor of his or her concepts and the intensity of his or her contemplation, compels other persons to act, giving them worthy reasons for doing so.'[7]

The prophet has received a special summons, undergone an unforgettable experience which convinced her that God has entrusted to her a word or message which she must reveal to mankind, either in words or by her very life. She has not only encountered the Deity; but, more significantly, has yielded herself totally to the experience. She has become a handmaid of God's word, his witness, his sign. The unique character of prophecy would seem to hinge precisely on this personal encounter. In the case of the biblical prophets, this experience is described in phrases such as 'the word of God came to' such and such a person, an identification being made between God and his word.[8]

SPEAKERS IN TIMES OF CRISIS

Authentic prophecy always addresses people in a concrete historical situation. As Jean Leclercq said, it does not indulge in 'vague ideas', nor does it concern itself with platitudes that might apply to anyone or no one. Prophets have been described as people who speak for God in times of crisis, when his interests are at stake.

Some historians regard the period covered by the life-span of Hildegard (1098–1179), and included that of her fellow-prophetess Elizabeth (1129–1164), as one of the most critical periods of western civilization. The spirit of questioning, reform, and re-evaluation of every aspect of social, spiritual, and intellectual life had never been so active. This era saw the Crusades, which reawakened western minds to all the new and old treasures of classical and eastern culture and learning. Trade and commerce revived, especially in the Mediterranean area; town life experienced a rebirth; and a middle social class or bourgeoisie began its long ascent as the guild system developed. Vernacular literature made its influence felt, and the evolution of the gothic style transformed architecture.

In spiritual matters, the monastic life assumed new strength with the emergence of reformed Orders, such as that of Cîteaux. Latin Christendom began to rediscover the riches to be found in graeco-roman philosophy as well as the theology of the Eastern Church. It also encountered the tenets of Islam, often with unsettling consequences. As a result, theologians were stimulated to reappraise their thinking on many doctrines of the faith thitherto taken much for granted.[9]

In ecclesiastical affairs, serious attempts at the reform of simony and clerical morals made progress under the leadership of a series of strong popes. Many of these reformers believed that the root of the many evils besetting the Church lay in the practice of lay investiture, and they actively promoted the abolition of the system. Temporal rulers, however, were determined to maintain their prerogatives of appointing men of their choice to bishoprics and abbacies and of looking upon them as their feudal vassals. As a result, bitter strife broke out betweeen papal reformers and temporal rulers, often ending in armed conflict. Kings and emperors named their own bishops and even popes, and popes crowned rival claimants to secular thrones. Men and women of good will often simply did not know whom to acknowledge as the true pope or as their lawful sovereign. Even our two prophets were divided on this issue.

The formation of the modern european states had begun, but since the fortunes of Church and State were closely linked, the rivalry over investiture convulsed the nations in a series of civil wars that hindered unification and constructive cooperation, especially in Italy and Germany. Leaders of both papal and imperial parties recognized the crying need to reach some agreement, and the Concordate of Worms in 1122 made a valiant, but in the long run ephemeral, attempt to restore some order to the chaotic state of affairs.

Over all the internal confusion brooded the ambitions of the german emperors to renew and enlarge the Holy Roman Empire. Since this involved securing complete control of the italian peninsula, this brought the emperor into direct conflict with the papacy.[10]

Dominated as were those years, for good or ill, by men of the stature of Bernard of Clairvaux, Peter Abelard, and Frederick Barbarossa, in retrospect they appear to have been an exciting time to be alive. To those living through the terror, uncertainty, and heartbreak involved, it was a time to cry out for prophets who could speak or live the truth, and provide valid reasons why people should pledge allegiance to a particular temporal or spiritual leader, or why they should strive to bring their lives into conformity with the gospel. In many respects, our own times mirror theirs, and we also look for charismatic leaders to point the way for us.

PROPHET OF LIGHT—PROPHET OF FIRE

The cry for prophets is answered, as is often the case in spiritual matters, in a way that seems unlikely to promise success, if it is even recognized as being an answer. A twelfth century annalist wrote that 'In these days God made manifest his power through the frail sex, in the two maidens Hildegard and Elizabeth, whome he filled with a prophetic spirit, making many kinds of visions apparent to them through his messages, which are to be seen in writing.'[11]

The pair of nuns are usually treated together by spiritual writers, since they confronted the same historical situation; but a study of their writings reveals more contrasts than likenesses. We may compare them by using the analogies of light for Elizabeth and of fire for Hildegard.

Let us look first at Elizabeth, who has received very little attention from scholars up to our own day.

At a very early age, she was confided to the care of the nuns of the double monastery of Schönau in the diocese of Trier. Since the convents often had a school for girls of respectable family attached to them, she was probably initially enrolled as a pupil. In 1147 she became a nun, and in 1157 was elected *magistra*, or superior, of the feminine section of the monastery.[12]

Never in very good health, she underwent some sort of grave physical and mental crisis, and at Pentecost in 1152 she began to experience a series of ecstatic visions which continued at intervals until her death on 18 June 1164. She, or some of her nuns, wrote down the content of these experiences; and her brother and biographer, Egbert, collated them, as well as compiling her biography. Even in her lifetime these writings enjoyed enormous popularity all over Europe, so much so that she complained to her friend and confidante Hildegard that false letters were being circulated under her name—a sure sign of notoriety.[13]

Modern psychological study has made us wary of giving credence to the authenticity of visions or ecstasies. Medieval thinkers, however, experienced no such difficulty. Spiritual masters such as Richard of St Victor regarded them as necessary concomitants to the higher degrees of prayer, and wrote lengthy treatises on these extraordinary states.[14] Some modern-day biographers would attribute most of Elizabeth's visions and the consequences of their publication to the machinations, deliberate or otherwise, of Egbert.[15] He had been a canon of the cathedral of Bonn, but on the advice of Elizabeth had become a monk and later abbot of Schönau. He was a close friend of the Archbishop of Cologne, Rainald von Dassel, who became chancellor of Germany under Frederick Barbarossa. This warlord bishop is thought by some historians to have been responsible for much of the strife between the Emperor and Pope Alexander III.[16]

Egbert, though he lent his support to the antipope Victor IV, was a man of eminently holy life, and he has left us beautiful meditations in praise of the holy cross and love of God, as well as a treatise against the Cathari, a sect then making its appearance in the region around Cologne.[17] Whatever may have been his influence on his sister, Elizabeth certainly regarded her experiences as coming from God alone. No authentic prophet takes up this office on her own initiative. In fact, as Elizabeth informed Hildegard, she made a deliberate effort to hide her extraordinary gifts; and as a result of this concealment was severely beaten by an angel for her presumption.[18]

Her visionary experiences usually occurred in the context of the liturgical cycle. At the celebration of the Holy Eucharist or Divine Office, she would be 'rapt out of herself', or 'enter into ecstasy', and behold the saint who was being honored on that day, or see some symbolic manifestation relevant to the temporal cycle. At Pentecost, for instance, she saw the Holy Spirit in the form of a dove descending in a ray of light, hovering over the celebrants at the Holy Eucharist and finally coming to rest on the altar.[19]

We have called her a prophet of light, since most of her visions are in some way associated with that element. Repeatedly she would see a great light in heaven, in the midst of which a door would open and the particular saint or saints of the day appear, entrusting some word or message to her which she was to impart to the world at large, or to some individual who may have sought her advice. Often the Blessed Virgin, to whom Elizabeth had a special devotion, would be the center of these experiences. For example, Elizabeth writes:

> On the Purification of the most glorious mother Mary, during the reading of the gospel at mass, I entered into ecstasy; and as I looked, behold, my Lady came down on a ray of light and stood at the right hand of the priest. Near her was a venerable man of great age, having a white flowing beard. When the sisters gave back their candles into the hands of the priest, Our Lady returned to heaven. And behold, a great host of maidens with splen-

> did candles came to meet her. After a short pause, they returned with her to the heights, following her with joy. On the same day at Vespers, when I was again in ecstasy, I saw her once more in heavenly glory. I called upon her most fervently, asking for her help. With all my love and will I pleaded, adding at the end of the prayers: 'My Lady, what shall I hope to receive from you?' And she replied: 'You can hope for good gifts from me, and so will all receive who have faith in me.'[20]

On recovering from her experience, Elizabeth usually uttered some verse of Scripture relevant to what had occurred. For example:

> On the Feast of the Beheading of St John the Baptist, I saw that great light which I was accustomed to see as if through a door, and I hastened to prostrate myself in prayer, and was rapt in ecstasy, and saw blessed John, as I had seen him before, and I said in my heart: 'God the Father blesses us, Jesus Christ watches over us, the Holy Spirit enlightens us'. And I added: 'O Key of David—'and also, 'This is John whom the hand of God consecrated in the womb of his mother, whom we beseech to pray for us when we are in need.' When I emerged from my ecstasy, I uttered these words: 'Help me, Lord my God', and added: 'Through the grace of God, I am what I am'. At Terce on that same day, I again was rapt in ecstasy and, peering through the door, I saw that great light, and my Lady rose from her seat and came towards me, and with her was the blessed precursor of the Lord. I thereupon prayed most earnestly and entrusted to her all my dear ones, and our monastery.... When I recovered, I said: '...among those born of women, a greater has not arisen than John the Baptist. Wonderful is your mercy, O God, who bring salvation to those who hope in you.'[21]

The devotion of monasticism to the holy precursor has always been very marked, and he makes his appearance in many of Elizabeth's experiences.

The connection between these experiences and the liturgical cycle and ritual is significant for Benedictines who devote a large part of their lives to the 'Work of God'. In nearly every religious tradition, music, poetry, and dance have occupied places of honor as means of heightening receptivity to divine influence. Mystics, when they try to describe their experiences, often compare themselves to musical instruments upon which God can play at will. It has been argued that biblical prophets opposed ritual and cult, but a careful reading of Scripture reveals that they held no animosity to ritual unless it became a rival to or substitute for the worship of God in spirit and in truth. Indeed, Peter Comestor wrote that Samuel the Prophet was the first to institute communities of religious who sang unceasingly for the Lord, and that to prophesy is to praise God constantly.[22] Claus Westermann, in his detailed study of Deutero-Isaiah, has pointed out that biblical prophets relied heavily upon ritual for the transmission of their message.[23] Elizabeth was instrumental in promoting devotion to St Ursula and her band of virgin-martyrs, as well as for the liturgical observance of the feast of Our Lady's Assumption. Her visions gave us a great deal of information about twelfth-century liturgical practices in monasteries of benedictine nuns, a matter which deserves further study.

Elizabeth's visions have a simplicity and childlike clarity about them which some readers may find very attractive. It is easy to imagine her in the role of a little child, peeking through her door into heaven. Her sisters took a great personal interest in her experiences, and she was greatly loved in her community. Her writings abound in homely details of everyday convent life: the joy of the sisters at seeing a rainbow, their anxiety and willingness to do penance for her when she was afflicted by evil visions, their concern because she was too ill to receive Holy Communion, their attempts to protect her physically during her ecstasies. All this must have constituted something of a trial for them, yet her election as *magistra* occurred after her visions had begun.

The experiences that exerted the most influence were those which Egbert collated into a small book with the title of *The Ways of God*.[24] In these visions, Elizabeth saw a very high mountain, at the peak of which stood a man whose face glowed with light. His eyes shone like stars and a sharp sword issued from his mouth. Running up the side of the great mountain were three paths: one of blue, one of green, and one of purple hue. The blue path was the way of contemplation, the green that of action, and the purple indicated the way of the martyrs. In subsequent visions, paths of other colors appeared, constructed in different ways and easy or difficult of ascent. These were the paths to be followed by married persons, celibates, widows, hermits, young people, and children. Each vision was followed by a fervent exhortation to live a strictly moral and upright life, according to one's particular state.

This is Elizabeth's advice for those following the blue path of contemplation:

> I was resting on my bed, but not asleep, when the angel of the Lord suddenly came to me and inspired me to speak as follows: 'Give heed, you who have renounced the pleasures of the world, and have chosen to follow in the footsteps of him who has called you into his overflowing light, who himself has given you the title of chosen sons, appointing you to the end of time to judge the tribes of Israel. Consider within yourselves how you should live in humility, obedience, love, without murmuring, detraction, jealousy, and pride; and be careful to keep yourselves from other vices. Love one another, that your heavenly Father may not be blasphemed by you, nor roused to anger at your departing from your path of contemplation.'[25]

The admonition continues with a list of common vices and sins to be avoided by those devoted to divine contemplation. In another vision, the angel again speaks:

> This exhortation of God is addressed to you who have chosen to serve God in the clerical state or according to monastic profession. You have chosen the best part, but be on guard lest it slip away from you. Carefully avoid the sinfulness of those who outwardly bear the semblance of religion but who shame its value by their action. They honor God with their lips, but blaspheme him by their way of life.[26]

The description of the other 'ways' and their exhortations follow the same pattern.

This little book enjoyed enormous popularity in monastic circles, and was widely disseminated by an english cistercian monk, Roger of Ford. He may have had some personal contact with Elizabeth, or with her circle of admirers, since Cîteaux was interested in all types of clerical reform. Roger sent a copy of her book back to his abbey in England, where it received a warm welcome. It was used as material for reading during meals in some cistercian houses, and formed part of the library of Cîteaux.[27]

After Elizabeth's early death, several attempts were made to have her sanctity officially recognized by the Church. No doubts were ever held as to her eminent holiness of life and fidelity to her monastic profession. She had fulfilled the most important rule for any prophet, and practised what she preached, meeting the challenge to live a truly 'luminous' life. But these efforts for canonization came to nothing, probably because she had supported the Emperor and his antipope. Yet popular devotion to her memory continued in the diocese of Trier and the Rhineland, and she is commonly called St Elizabeth of Schönau. Her name was inserted in the roman martyrology in 1584 and her feast is commemorated on 18 June, the day of her death.

Her writings, suffering the fate of many medieval documents, were scattered or confused with those of other spiritual writers. She is commonly referred to only as 'the holy Elizabeth' and her writings have often been attributed to the better-known Elizabeth of Hungary. The solid moral and ethical core of her teaching tended to be overlooked by succeeding centuries. Later fashions of piety favoring the sensational or bizarre found sparse gleanings in her direct, child-like and very scriptural communications. The Ages of Reason and Elightenment, impatient of visions and ecstasies, had no sympathy for her. The protestant movement would regard her insistence on the authority of the Church, her reverence for the ecclesiastical hierarchy and fidelity to the monastic way of life, her deep love for Our Lady, and her devotion to the saints as unpalatable.

Some scholars of our own times might see her as a person psychologically disturbed, or as a second-rate imitator of her better-known contemporary, Hildegard. A thorough study of the content of her visions, however, shows that she had a message uniquely her own. Since an authentic prophet never receives her vocation solely for her own benefit, Elizabeth's experiences revealed to her troubled times that God and the whole community of saints are extremely interested in the affairs of the present world. It is possible for everyone, no matter what his or her state in life, to have a deep person-to-person relationship with God and to all the other members of Christ's mystical body. The very social aspect of all her pronouncements sounds like much of the Church's teaching in modern times. That these elements should be present is not surprising if we consider the great changes which society in the twelfth century experienced.

Elizabeth also teaches us that heaven is not some abstract state of mind, nor is it so far off that there can be no contact between it and our present life. Unfortunately, this also applies to the infernal regions. Satan and his evil forces were very real for Elizabeth and very much at work in the world. Elizabeth's attitude may be a reaction to the bitter rivalries that were splitting Christendom and wracking her own country.

Her love for and interest in all the aspects of the life of Our Lady, especially the mystery of her assumption, stand at the beginning of the great surge of devotion for the humanity of Christ. St Bernard and the so-called School of Cîteaux are sometimes taken as exemplars of this movement. It is interesting to find this trend expressed at so early a date by a woman. This spiritual movement would find its full flowering in the works of other benedictine nuns such as Gertrude of Helfta and the Mechtildes of Hackeborne and Magdeburg, especially in their devotion to our Lord's sacred heart.

A prominent medievalist, Mme Jeanne Ancelet-Hustache, had no hesitation in calling Elizabeth one of the greatest names in the mystical tradition of the religious orders in Germany.[28] It is to be hoped that she will receive more attention from scholars in the near future.

HILDEGARD OF BINGEN

When we turn our attention to Elizabeth's sister-prophet Hildegard, we find ourselves in a completely different atmosphere. This is very surprising when we realize that they were contemporaries with approximately the same background, facing the same historical situation. Hildegard was the elder of the two and, like Elizabeth, came of a good family. She had been enrolled as a student at the convent of Disibodenburg at a very early age, and made her profession as a nun at fourteen. Like Schönau, Disibodenburg was a double monastery, and in 1136 Hildegard became the *magistra* there.

But a significant difference appears between the two prophets. The relationship of the two houses at Schönau seems always to have been a cordial one. The monks were often involved in Elizabeth's experiences and the abbot is spoken of with great affection and reverence. This cordiality did not exist at Disibodenburg, and in 1147 Hildegard began her own independent monastery at Rupertsburg, in the face of fierce opposition from Abbot Kuno of Disibodenburg. This monastery continued to supply priests for the nuns at Rupertsburg; but as late as 1170 difficulties still existed between the two houses, and Hildegard had to appeal to Pope Alexander III for assistance in the matter. Nevertheless, we find no trace of rebellion against authority *per se* in her writings, only determination to follow what she believed God wished her to do and had revealed to her in a vision. This determination and complete conviction of the truth of what she had experienced characterizes all of Hildegard's writings. These works present us with a portrait of a woman strong in will, faith, common sense, and love for God, his Church, and her country.

Like Elizabeth, Hildegard was a visionary, but she differed in not being an ecstatic. In the Preface to her major work, *Scivias* (*Know the ways*), she has left us a description of how her experiences occurred:

> In the year 1142, when I was forty-two years and seven months old, it happened that a great light of brilliant fire came from the open heavens and overwhelmed all my mind, my heart, and my breast, not so much like a flickering flame, but rather like glowing heat, as the sun warms other things on which it sheds its rays. And suddenly I had the power of explaining Scripture, not by a word-for-word interpretation, nor a division of syllables, or cases or tenses. From the time I was a little girl about five years old, I was conscious of a mysterious hidden power and experienced wonderful visions within myself, but told them to none except a few religious with whom I lived. And during that time until the grace of God wished them to be made known, I hid them under strict silence. These visions which I saw were not in sleep nor dreams, nor in my imagination nor by bodily eyes or outward ears nor in a hidden place; but in watching, aware with the pure eyes of the mind and inner ear of the heart. But I received them while wide awake, according to the will of God. How this happened it is difficult for mortal men to understand.[29]

Her emphasis on fire and heat, as well as the element of alertness and self-possession during all of her visionary experiences leads us to call her a prophet of fire. Like Elizabeth, she made an effort to hide her experiences, until she suffered a severe illness as punishment for her efforts to keep God's communications to herself. After seeking the advice of those upon whose holiness of life she could rely, she wrote down what she had seen and heard 'not according to the imagination of my heart or that of other men, but as I saw, heard and understood in the celestial regions, through the hidden mysteries of God'.[30]

Once she had begun to write, a veritable flood of words issued from her pen—or from those of the monks and nuns who served as her scribes. The sheer bulk of her writings is enough to daunt many who attempt to analyze her works. There is no field of spirituality or intellectual endeavor left unexplored by this twelfth-century nun. A theologian, liturgist, poet, commentator on the Rule of St Benedict, dramatist, natural historian, philosopher, physician, musician, cryptographer, spiritual director, and Scripture exegete, she was first of all a woman of prayer who had dedicated her life to God. Her experiences always had the interests of Christ and his Church as their focal point and *raison d'être*.

Only recently has her genius received the attention it so richly deserves. Even now we do not yet have a critical analysis or a complete english translation of even her three major compositions: *Scivias*, the *Liber vitae meritorum*, and the *Liber divinorum operum simplicis hominis*. Of these three, *Scivias* has received the most attention. Most scholars limit themselves to an analysis of only one of her visions, and the detailed theological explanation attached to it.

These visions usually assume a very colorful, highly symbolic form, with liturgical and theological overtones. For instance, in the first vision of *Scivias*, she tells us:

> I saw what seemed to be a great mountain, the color of iron. At its peak sat someone surrounded with so much light that I was dazzled by its radiance. On either side of the form, a wing both broad and long was stretched out like a gentle shadow. Before him, at the base of the mountain, stood a shape covered completely with eyes, so that I was unable to see anything resembling a human form. In front of this shape was another, that appeared like a boy in a pale garment, and shod with white. Upon the head of the latter, he who sat on the mountain shed such a flood of splendor that I could not see its face. The one on the mountain also generated sparks of living light and cast them about both shapes in a beautiful stream.[31]

She then proceeds to hear the explanation of this vision from the one who sat on the peak of the mountain:

> The great mountain, the color of iron, symbolizes the power and the constancy of God's eternal kingdom. . . . And he who is seated . . . on the mountain and dazzles your sight with this glory reflects him in the realm of the Blessed. . . . The long and broad wings like shadows on either side symbolize protection, tender and mild, that curb with warnings and also

> with chastisement. At the foot of the mountain stands the shape covered all over with eyes. In deep humility and oblivious of self, it recognizes the kingdom, and sheltered in the fear of the Lord toils among men eagerly and persistently, with the clear gaze of a good and just purpose.... Beside this shape is another, that of a boy in a pale garment and shod with white. For those who fear God go ahead, and the poor in spirit follow ... inconspicuously clothed in devotion ... joyfully following in the footsteps of God's son.[32]

The vision continues at length in the same vein, with more exact explanations.

In other visions, she saw the universe as an egg wrapped in flame, or as a city with many-colored towers over which the Lord reigns in glory. Multi-hued dragons threaten the people of God. Winds of various types blow to various corners of the heavens. The Church and the Synagogue appear as women of colossal size, gathering their children about them. Fire figures prominently in many visions, great mountains loom up and are washed away. Everything is enormous in size and scope and the reader is left with a sense of being over-powered, either by good or evil. The moral and ethical sense is always stressed, and we are faced with the same necessity of choice that we noted in Elizabeth. But in Hildegard the personal, intimate, and day-to-day aspect of life has disappeared. Everything occurs on a grand and universal scale.

The imagery Hildegard used and the apocalyptic tone of her writing made a deep impression on her critical times, which referred to her as 'the Sibyl of the Rhine'. People of every rank, from the pope and emperor to nuns and monks of obscure abbeys, sought her advice and received it liberally. Her personal correspondence assumed vast proportions.[33] Even there imagery abounds. In her letter to Pope Eugene III she wrote:

> A jewel is lying on the highway, then a bear [the German emperor] comes along; and, thinking it is beautiful, puts out his paw, wishing to take it and put it into his bosom. But suddenly an eagle [the pope] comes, seizes the jewel [the allegiance of the people], wraps it in the covering of his wings, and carries it aloft to the royal palace [the kingdom of Christ]. The jewel gives out so much light before the face of the King, that he rejoices and, for love of the jewel, gives the eagle golden sandals [sign of papal authority], and praises him for his goodness.[34]

Her letters always contain words of exhortation to fulfill the duties of her correspondent's state of life. Even if Hildegard protested that she was merely a poor and lowly woman, she did not let herself be deterred by respect of persons or state from delivering her God-given message. She boldly admonished even the pope and the emperor, lending her support to Alexander III against Frederick Barbarossa and his antipope, Victor IV. Clerics in high stations, monks, and archbishops were targets of her admonitions if they did not live up to their obligations or lead a good moral life.

Naturally she made many enemies, and was calumniated by them as mad, deluded, a fraud, or possessed by the devil. Matters reached such a point that, in 1147, the council of Trier was called upon to pronounce on the authenticity of her utterances. The council fathers appealed to St Bernard for an opinion, and his reply favored her cause.[35]

In addition to her three major works, she has left us interesting commentaries on medicine and natural history which are obviously based on her own practical experience as infirmarian in her own monastery, and deserve further study by historians of medicine.[36] We also have her commentary on the Rule of St Benedict, and on the Athanasian Creed, and her response to questions related to scriptural exegesis and spirituality which were posed to her by Guibert of Gembloux. They deal with such problems as what kind of tongues the angels use to praise God constantly, or why St Paul should say that he was the least of the apostles, when he had worked harder than any of them.[37]

Liturgy was one of her greatest interests, and she composed many antiphons for the Divine Office. In her commentary on the Rule, she advises correspondents to curtail their private prayer if it will keep them from performing the Work of God properly.[38] Her greatest liturgical composition is her morality drama, the *Ordo virtutum*, which dramatizes the search of the soul for salvation. The music demands great skill on the part of the singers. The only character in the drama who does not sing, but instead recites his lines, is the devil.[39]

At the close of her long life, Hildegard wrote the biographies of the patron saints of the two convents with which she had been affliated: St Disibode and St Rupert. These works illustrate medieval hagiography well, dwelling on the intercessory power of the saints, their extreme mortification of the senses, their devotion to solitude and prayer, their contempt for the world, and the enmity they aroused among the forces of evil.[40]

After her death, Hildegard's writings continued to exercise an enormous influence, and were spread to every part of Europe. This was especially true of her apocalyptic works and her letters, which had predicted the age of antichrist and the end of the world.[41] Many spiritual writers later applied her words to the Protestant Reformation, and she is often cited as having foreseen this catastrophe. Joachim of Flora and Peter John Olivi may have been directly dependent on her for much of their thought.[42]

More sober minds saw the value of her solid moral and ethical teaching, and used it in their own instruction. She also received approbation in works such as William Langland's *Piers Plowman*.[43] Even in our own day, Pope John Paul II on the occasion of her eight hundredth anniversary praised her as a model worthy of imitation for her holy life and for her love of the Church.[44] Though never officially canonized, her sanctity was generally recognized, and her feast is celebrated on 17 September, the day of her death.

Scholars have only begun to scratch the topsoil in seeking the treasures hidden in her vast erudition and spirituality. One may ask, 'Where did she get all this?' Given the conditions of the times, the level of education of women in general, and the sources which were probably available to her, we must conclude that there is something out of the ordinary in her achievements. Her works reveal a mind that was not content to accept things at face value. The way she developed the observational and analytical powers of her intellect in an amazing endeavor to find the underlying cause for existing conditions makes her worthy of being considered a forerunner of modern science. She was not afraid to ask questions, but always did so in a manner that reveals her consciousness of her own limitations as a creature. She never succumbed to the pitfall, as do many people of genius, of considering herself as the source of her talents. She referred everything to God, and it is significant that in her *Ordo* it is Humility which is the moving spirit that aids the soul in seeking salvation, and which is called the queen of the virtues.

We may wonder whether Hildegard waged a bitter struggle against intellectual pride all her life. She must have been conscious of her superiority, and may have found it galling to have to submit to the judgment of people who lacked her mental and spiritual insights. But we never find her showing any hint of disrespect for legitimate authority. In fact, she berated those who did not exercise that authority as they should. She may have disagreed with the decisions these people made, but she never objected to their right to make them. We do not find her organizing underground movements to overthrow the emperor or to displace members of the hierarchy who did not meet her high standards. In view of the enormous influence she wielded, these movements might have attracted a large following.

In all her writings, we sense her great love for Christ and his Church and for her monastic life. Her commentaries on the Rule, her biographies of her patron saints, and her letters to wayward monks reveal her love and gratitude for her vocation. Her superior talents and gifts must often have driven her to impatience with her sisters in religion, and may be the chief source of her low esteem for women in general.[45]

Her work lacks the personal touch so distinctive in Elizabeth. It is noteworthy that the faces of the persons in her visions are often obscured, or so brilliant with light or sparks of fire that she is unable to distinguish any individual features in them. They are symbols rather than actual persons. We also find no details of life in her own monastery or of her relationships with her sisters. In some of her letters she objected vigorously to the removal of some of her nuns against her personal wishes, but this was usually because it deprived her of their services as scribes.[46] We receive the general impression of a master addressing her pupils, even if those pupils happen to be popes, emperors, or bishops. Yet she herself often expressed her own inferiority, with a persistence that leaves no doubt as to her sincerity in this belief. She called herself a feather, a handmaid, a mere musical instrument upon which God can play at will. Only in regard to the message which God had entrusted to her was she intransigent, refusing to be silent.

THE MESSAGE OF ELIZABETH AND HILDEGARD

What was the message which had been entrusted to these two nuns? It was that of any authentic prophet—the message which everyone has heard over and over again, and which our hard hearts refuse to heed. They told the people of their times that they must love and serve God above all other interests, especially their own selfish concerns. They must obey God's commandments, follow the guidance of those to whom he had entrusted a share in his authority, fulfill the obligations of their state in life, keeping Christ ever before their eyes, and always strive also to share in his prophetic role.

The modern reader may ask how these two abbesses with their visions, ecstasies, and mental agility can serve as examples for fulfilling a prophetic mission. We remember that the definition of prophet given by Thomas Merton and expanded by Jean Leclercq (quoted at the beginning of this study) said nothing about extraordinary phenomena. It is in the intensity and vigor of their lives of prayer, their dedication to Christ and to the state of life to which God had called them that these women give us leadership. These are the ways in which anyone can fulfill his prophetic function. The extraordinary gifts of Elizabeth and Hildegard may have been more of a hindrance than a help to them in many ways. In dealing with the consequences of the powers in their possession while still remaining faithful to their monastic life of prayer and contemplation, they may have proved their authenticity as prophets most effectively.

God bestows upon us only what we need to do the work he has alloted to us. Christ's words of life, always on the lips of these two prophets, shone like light and fire in their hearts to lead others to the same state. They answered the challenge of God to be his prophets—signs of his presence in the world of their own day. They challenge all Christians, and religious women in particular, to be prophets in our own troubled times.

NOTES

1. See John Paul II, *The Redeemer of Man* (Redemptor hominis) (Boston: St Paul Editions, n.d.) 40–46.

2. Idem, 'To Sisters at Kinshasa, Zaire', *L'Osservatore Romano* (English edition, 19 May 1980) 2–3.

3. See Jean Leclercq, *The Life of Perfection*, tr. Leonard J. Doyle (Collegeville: Liturgical Press, 1961) 43–61; and Claude J. Peifer, *Monastic Spirituality* (New York: Sheed and Ward, 1966) 195.

4. Origen, 'Homily V.2 on Judges, 11', cited by Eberhard Arnold, *The Early Christians* (Grand Rapids: Baker, 1970) 331. Arnold also makes some interesting remarks on the role of the prophets in the early Church, in his Introduction and Survey of the book, pp. 30–41.

5. See *Thomas Merton: Prophet in the Belly of a Paradox*, ed. Gerald Twomey (New York: Paulist, 1978).

6. Thomas Merton, *Disputed Questions* (New York: Farrar, Strauss and Giroux, 1953) 209.

7. Jean Leclercq, 'Merton and History', *Thomas Merton: Prophet in the Belly of a Paradox*, pp. 230–31.

8. This concept has received exhaustive study by scriptural exegetes. See Walther Eichrodt, *Theology of the Old Testament*, 2 vols., tr. J. A. Baker (Philadelphia: Westminster, 1967); and Gerhard von Rad, *Old Testament Theology*, 2 vols., tr. D. M. G. Stalker (New York: Harper and Row, 1965.)

9. See M.-D. Chenu OP, 'Nature and Man: The Renaissance of the Twelfth Century', *Nature, Man and Society in the Twelfth Century* (Chicago: University of Chicago Press, 1968) 1–48.

10. For an overall picture of what was to become the modern state of Germany, the reader may refer to such works as that of John E. Rodes, *Germany; A History* (New York: Holt, Rinehart and Winston, 1964). Rodes also presents a bibliography of standard works at the conclusion of his book. For a more detailed study of the area of Cologne, reference may be made to the study of Paul Strait, *Cologne in the Twelfth Century* (Gainesville: University Presses of Florida, 1974.)

11. *Annales Palidenses*, cited by Lina Eckenstein, *Women Under Monasticism, Chapters on Saint-Lore and Convent Life between AD 500 and AD 1500* (New York: Russell and Russell, 1963) 257.

12. The practice of double monasteries seems to have been fairly common in the twelfth century, probably stemming from a desire to assure the nuns' safety. Usually the superior of the male branch functioned as the juridical head of both houses. A notable exception to this occurred in the Order of Fontevrault, where the female superior fulfilled the role of abbess of both branches.

13. *Epistola 45*; PL 197:215.

14. See Richard of St Victor, 'The Mystical Ark', tr. Grover A Zinn in *Richard of St Victor* (New York: Paulist, 1979) 259–307.

15. This would appear to be the thought of Kurt Koster, DSp 4:584–588.

16. The life of this prelate deserves more thorough study, since it embodies both the positive and negative aspects of the spirit of the twelfth century. The *Chronik der Sachsen*, a late fifteenth-century work, contains a curious woodcut which shows the Archbishop receiving the relics of the Three Kings from the abbess of Milan in whose church they were kept until von Dassel removed them to Cologne in 1164. The Archbishop appears in full armor, with the helmet replaced by his miter. See Margaret B. Freeman, *The Story of the Three Kings: Melchior, Balthasar and Jaspar* (New York: Metropolitan Museum of Art, 1955) 68.

17. PL 195:12–114. This includes his thirteen sermons against the Cathari, his *Praise of the Cross*, and *Meditations*.

18. *Epistola 45*; PL 197:215.

19. PL 195:151.

20. PL 195:144.

21. PL 195:139–140.

22. Peter Comestor, *Commentary on the Book of Kings*; PL 198:1304, cited by Leclercq in *The Life of Perfection*, (above, n. 3) p. 49. For a discussion of the relationship of biblical prophets and cult, see Otto Eissfeldt, *The Old Testament. An Introduction*. trans. P. R. Ackroyd (New York, 1965) 77–81, and Abraham Joshua Heschel, *The Prophets* (New York, 1962) 10–26, and J. Lindblom, *Prophecy in Ancient Israel* (Philadelphia, 1962) 209–19, 317–22, 351–60, 383–403.

23. Claus Westermann, *Isaiah 40–66*, tr. D. M. G. Stalker (Philadelphia: Westminster, 1969) 8–27, 67–79, 102–104.

24. This collection constitutes Book III in Migne, PL 195: 164C–109B. Also in F. W. E. Roth, *Die Visionen der heiligen Elisabeth und die Schriften der Abte Ekbert und Emecho von Schönau* (Brünn, 1884) 88–122.

25. Roth, *Die Visionen*, p. 92.

26. *Ibid.*

27. See Ruth J. Dean, 'Elizabeth, Abbess of Schönau, and Roger of Ford', *Modern Philology* 41:4 (May 1944) 209–220.

28. Jeanne Ancelet-Hustache, 'Rhenish Mysticism', *Cistercian Studies* 10 (1975:2) 93.

29. PL 197:384.

30. PL 197:386.

31. PL 197:385.

32. PL 197:386–387.

33. Migne gives 145 letters and their responses. J. B. Pitra in *Analecta sacra spicilegio Somesmensi parata* 8, pp. 328–440, 518–82, gives as many more.

34. *Epistola 1*; PL 197:147.

33. See St Bernard, Letter 366, SBD 8:323–4. This is letter 390 in *Letters of Saint Bernard of Clairvaux*, Bruno Scott James (London: Burns Oates, 1953) 460.

36. See Gertrude M. Engbring, 'St Hildegard, Twelfth Century Physician', *Bulletin of the History of Medicine* 8 (1940) 777, n.24; and Charles Singer, *From Magic to Science* (New York: Dover, 1958) 230–34. Singer attributes Hildegard's visions to a migraine condition.

37 *Quaestio XIV and XVIII*; PL 197:1045–46. On the topic of the use of scriptural *Quaestio* by medieval theologians see Beryl Smalley, *The Study of the Bible in the Middle Ages* (Oxford: Blackwell, 1952) 66–82. Snalley also makes some interesting comments on scriptural studies for nuns, something advocated by Abelard.

38. *Explanatio Regulae S Benedicti*, PL 197:1058.

39. See Bruce W. Hozeski, '*Ordo Virtutum*: Hildegard of Bingen's Liturgical Morality Play', Diss. Michigan State University, 1969. At the Benedictine Sesquimillenial Symposium held at St Anselm's College, Manchester, N. H. in March, 1981, Sr Victorine Fenton OSB presented a tape recording of the *Ordo*, sung by students from the University of Iowa. A dramatized performance by The Society for Old Music was presented at the 1984 International Medieval Studies Congress, Kalamazoo. The text edited by Audrey Echdahl Davidson will appear from Medieval Institute Publications, Kalamazoo soon.

40. PL 197:1083–1116.

41. Outstanding examples of these predictions appear in Letters 48, 49, and 52. PL 197:243–271.

42. For Hildegard's influence on apocalyptic literature, see Marjorie Reeves, *Joachim of Fiore and the Prophetic Future* (New York: Harper Torchbooks, 1977) 81, 157. See also Lena Eckenstein, *Women Under Monasticism*, 276.

43. Lena Eckenstein, *Women Under Monasticism* p. 276, quotes The Vision of Piers Plowman, line 1401. The source seems to be *Pierce the Ploughman's Crede*, ed. Walter W. Skeat, (London: EETS, 1868) from a 1394 manuscript.

44. John Paul II, 'To Cardinal Volk', *L'Osservatore Romano* (English Edition, 10 January 1979) p. 10.

45. See Bernhard W. Scholz, 'Hildegard von Bingen on the Nature of Woman', *American Benedictine Review,* 31:4 (December 1980) 361–83. Scholz also gives a thorough bibliography of available material relevant to Hildegard, especially her medical works.

46. See *Epistola 5*, PL 197:156–157. In this letter Hildegard protested violently to Henry, Archbishop of Mainz, at the removal of her secretary Hiltrude to serve as abbess at Sponheim. She even went so far as to compare Henry to Nebuchadnezzar. In *Epistola 10* (PL 197:161–163) she communicated more peacefully with Hertwig, bishop of Bremen, whose sister Richardis had been taken from her to serve as abbess at Hildesheim.

Divine Power Made Perfect in Weakness: St. Hildegard on the Frail Sex[1]

Barbara Newman

God chose what is foolish in the world to shame the wise, God chose what is weak in the world to shame the strong, God chose what is low and despised in the world, even things that are not, to bring to nothing things that are, so that no flesh might boast in the presence of God.

St Paul to the Church of Corinth (1 Co 1:27–29)

But I—a poor woman, weak and frail from my infancy—have been compelled in a true and mysterious vision to write this letter. And lying in bed with a serious illness, I have written it by the command and assistance of God to present it to the prelates and masters who are sealed for God's service, that in it they might see who and what they are . . . And I heard a voice from heaven saying: Let no one despise these words, lest if anyone despise them, the vengeance of God fall upon him.

St Hildegard to the Monks of Eberbach[2]

WHEN THE CHURCH of Corinth compelled St Paul to defend his apostolic claims, he took his stand on the unlikely grounds of foolishness and weakness, setting a precedent that has challenged Church leaders ever since. In two millennia of history, few have been able to echo his words more justly than St Hildegard, abbess of Bingen (1098–1179). But the boast is doubly paradoxical, for this famed visionary was richly endowed with what medievals called gifts of nature and fortune as well as grace. Born of a noble family at Bermersheim bei Alzey, she was offered to

God as an oblate at the age of eight, grew up in the hermitage of Jutta of Sponheim near the flourishing monastery of St Disibod, and took her monastic vows ca. 1112–1115.[3] The hermitage meanwhile was growing into a full-fledged convent observing the benedictine Rule, and when Jutta died in 1136, the nuns elected Hildegard as abbess (*magistra*) in her place. Five years later, she received her prophetic call and embarked on the momentous public and literary career which was to continue for nearly four decades. By her death at the age of eighty-one, she had found time and energy to found two monasteries, undertake four extensive preaching tours,[4] and counsel an endless stream of visitors and pilgrims, as well as compose three major theological works, a scientific and medical encyclopedia, a liturgical song cycle, two saints' lives, the first european morality play, and a vast correspondence. It is not easy to take her self-image as 'a poor woman, weak and frail from infancy' at face value.

Mindful of Paul's example and of the need to be (or at any rate to seem) humble, monastic writers throughout the Middle Ages advertised their defects, whether of wisdom or holiness, learning or style. Thus, when St Hildegard's prefaces remind readers of her physical frailty, her scanty education, and her unpolished Latin, she is taking her place in a long line of rhetorically humble monks.[5] Yet her protestations involve more than a mere 'humility topos'. For one thing, she is telling the truth: her health *was* precarious, her schooling (though not her learning) meager, her prose untutored and rough. More to the point, however, Hildegard could lay claim to a more authentic 'weakness' than any of her fellow theologians, for a very simple reason. To be a woman in the twelfth-century Church was, among other things, to be foolish, weak, low, and despised in the world. To be a travelling female preacher, as Hildegard was, could indicate only one of two things: heretical folly, or else divine power made perfect in weakness.

AN EFFEMINATE AGE

One of Hildegard's favorite self-designations is *ego paupercula feminea forma*: 'I, a poor little figure of a woman'. Other self-deprecating labels—wretched, ignorant, feeble—slip in and out of this catch phrase.[6] Whenever she introduces herself with this formula, Hildegard will ascribe the work that follows not to herself but to God, 'the living Light', for obviously she—mere female that she is!—could not be expected to know anything herself. In this way the apologetic tag humbles the writer at the same time that it exalts her authority, while challenging the reader to transcend worldly standards and glorify God in his prophet.[7] Hildegard's sex thus becomes her personal claim to that divine foolishness and weakness which is stronger and wiser than men. And in this case, 'men' means not *homines* but *viri*, for Hildegard was keenly aware of her anomalous role as a woman. In fact, she saw her gender as an essential condition of her prophetic call which, like the Old Testament prophets, she interpreted in broadly historical terms.

The seer's understanding of her mission rested not only on her spiritual experience, but also on the conviction that hers was a *muliebre tempus*, an 'effeminate age' in which men have grown so womanish that God must call women to do men's work. Thus her first prophetic book, the *Scivias* (begun in 1141), opens with a divine injunction to the visionary. Although she is but a weak mortal, 'ashes from ashes', she is to proclaim the word of salvation, for the masters and doctors to whom it was entrusted have grown slack.

> Let those who see the inner meaning of Scripture, yet do not wish to proclaim or preach it, take instruction, for they are lukewarm and sluggish in preserving the justice of God. . . . Therefore pour out a fountain of abundance, overflow with mysterious learning, so that those who want you to be despicable on account of Eve's transgression may be overwhelmed by the flood of your profusion.[8]

Later in the same work, God speaking through the prophet again castigates priests for refusing either to preach or to practise what is right. But alongside the divine voice, we can hear the prophet's anger at the misogynist attacks she must face: God tells her to declare his fiery work even though she is 'trampled underfoot' by the male sex 'because of Eve's transgression'.[9] While admitting the generic frailty of her sex, Hildegard refused to let men use either Eve's feminine weakness or her own as an excuse to ignore their own moral and spiritual weakness. Time and again, she ascribed her prophetic calling to the laxity of male teachers and prelates. At one time, she complains, theologians used to expound the Bible with great zeal, but today their books are greeted with indifference: 'nowadays the Catholic faith wavers and the Gospel limps among the peoples . . . and the food of life—the divine Scripture—has grown tepid'.[10] Hence God must now reveal his mysteries through a chosen vessel who has never been taught by man.

In her autobiography, Hildegard even observes that her birth took place around 1100 in an age when christian fervor had grown cool, clearly hinting that if the times were out of joint, it was she who had been born to set them right.[11] Ever since the reign of Henry IV, she writes elsewhere, society had been plunged 'into feminine levity . . . so that now to the scandal of men, women prophesy'.[12] (The seer's plural may refer to herself and her protegée, Elisabeth of Schönau.) Only the scandal of female prophets will shock the Church into recognizing the greater scandal of men who can and should proclaim the Word, but will not. So to shame them into repentance, God has transformed a frail *virgo* into a thundering *virago*. One of Hildegard's correspondents likened her to the ancient prophetess Deborah, who rose up to fill a similar vacuum: 'The strong men in Israel ceased and held their peace, until Deborah arose—arose as a mother in Israel' (Jg 5:7 Vulg).[13]

In historical terms, then, Hildegard saw herself as a remedy divinely appointed for the ills of her times. An effeminate age calls for a feminine prophet, and an epoch of weakness for the weaker sex. When speaking of this *muliebre tempus*, Hildegard applies the epithet 'female' in a purely pejorative sense. By her showing, the Church of her day had grown soft, sensual, cowardly, and worldly—full of the vices misogynists would impute to women. Yet when she looked at her own feminine 'weakness,' this trait became ambivalent, for she found her physical, mental, and moral failings as a woman offset by a peculiar openness to God. Thus her reflections on womanhood and weakness, initially spurred by her prophetic call and the circumstances of her mission, gradually led her to deeper spiritual insights. The pauline paradox, with its special relevance to the feminine, sheds a new and sometimes surprising light on her own human shortcomings, the mystery of sexual difference, the 'feminine' qualities of inspiration and priesthood, and the saving weakness of the Incarnation itself. Some of her discoveries, though shaped by medieval notions of masculine and feminine which many would now question,[14] can still point the way for women who seek God in and through their own womanhood, instead of pursuing 'equality' through the attempted denial or obliteration of difference.

THORNS IN THE FLESH

Like St Paul, Hildegard had to admit that even the richest grace had yet to extirpate her own thorns in the flesh. Although her illumination had conferred a knowledge of divine mysteries, together with an awesome task, her limitations remained. The fire from heaven did not grant her miraculous healing, or proficiency in grammar, or cheery self-confidence. But while she could accept her ill health and her ignorance of letters as providential, she remained troubled by the diffidence, fear, and insecurity which she perceived as typically female faults. In a letter to Bernard of Clairvaux (1147), the first of her several hundred epistles, Hildegard called herself 'wretched and more than wretched in the name of woman' and contrasted her own fear with the abbot's audacity: 'Two years ago I saw you in this vision as a man looking into the sun, not frightened but greatly daring; and I wept because I only blush and am timid'.[15] The seer's second book, *Liber vitae meritorum*, portrays the vices of *Desperatio* and *Tristitia saeculi* (or in current parlance, depression and despondency) in feminine form.[16] On the other hand, Hildegard tried to correlate the *timiditas* she attributed to women with the biblical virtue of *timor Domini*, 'fear of the Lord':

> God created woman so that she might hold him in fear and fear her husband as well. Hence it is right for a woman always to be fearful (*timida*). For she is a house of wisdom, because things earthly and heavenly are perfected in her. On the one hand mankind is born through her, and on the other, good works appear in her with chaste modesty. . . . The reverent (*timorata*) woman gathers all the riches of good works and holy virtues into her bosom, never ceasing until she has fulfilled all that is good.[17]

Hildegard's culture, of course, strongly encouraged women to behave timidly toward God and their husbands, so it is not surprising that she ascribed this proclivity in her sex to natural law. Moreover, her cloistered childhood and her precocious visions, which exposed her to ridicule as a girl, may help to account for her own fearful character.[18] Yet, after due allowance for psychology and culture, Hildegard maintained that the Creator gave woman a fearful nature not merely because she is subject to man, but because her own dignity deserves a respect which borders on awe. Woman is called to be a 'house of wisdom' (Pr 9:1) whether she elects the vocation of motherhood or of 'chaste modesty' (monasticism), hence she must venerate the one—divine or human—who fulfills and exalts her. What then is the difference between the *timorata mulier* whom the seer praises, and her own fears which she deplores? In modern terms, we might say that she faced the task of transforming neurotic or self-regarding fear into the reverent fear that becomes one in whom 'heavenly things are perfected'. Her correspondent at Clairvaux would contrast the servile fear which is cast out by love with the chaste and filial fear which remains forever.[19]

Another of Hildegard's frailties, according to her self-diagnosis as a physician, stemmed from her peculiar temperament. In medieval medicine, the four physical and psychological types known as complexions or temperaments (choleric, sanguine, phlegmatic, and melancholic) were normally correlated with the elements of fire, air, water, and earth.[20] In addition, the 'warm' elements of fire and air were commonly regarded as masculine, the 'cold' pair of water and earth as feminine.[21] In her medical treatise *Causae et curae*, however, Hildegard presented a theory of humors and temperaments which differed considerably from the standard views.[22] For instance, she found a special affinity between the airy temperament and the nature of woman. God created Adam from the earth, earthy, for he was to till the earth and subdue it; 'but Eve, taken from his marrow, was soft and possessed an airy mind and a keen, delicate life, for the weight of the earth did not oppress her'.[23] The female body needs to be airy—permeable and spacious—to accommodate children in the womb.[24] Eve, the first mother, 'was made like the purest air, for as aether enfolds the inviolate stars, so she—inviolate, incorrupt, without pain—held the human race within her'.[25] Since the Fall, however, woman's airy nature has caused problems. Hildegard writes that women are *fenestrales et ventosae*: their bodies are like windows which freely admit the stormy elements raging without.[26] In consequence, women are especially vulnerable to ailments provoked by the weather, making their health more fragile than that of men.

This theory would now be only an episode in the history of medicine, were it not for the subtle way Hildegard applied it to her spiritual life. She regarded her own nature as even more airy than most women's, and to this defect of her constitution she ascribed the illness which had plagued her from childhood on.[27] Late in her life, however, she came to see a link between her troublesome temperament and her spiritual gifts. Her last great work, the *Liber divinorum operum* (completed in 1173), ends with an autobiographic passage in which the seer speaks of herself in the third person. The Holy Spirit has deigned to anoint her—a *paupercula feminea forma*—with the oil of his mercy, unlearned and feeble though she is. From infancy she has suffered constant pain, as if enmeshed in a net, and her visions themselves cause her great weariness. Moreover her ways are not those of other men; she is like an infant whose veins are not yet full of blood.

> For she is a minister (*officialis*) inspired by the Holy Spirit, and she has a complexion of air. Therefore infirmity is driven into her from the air itself, the rain, the wind, and from every tempest, so that she can by no means enjoy any security of the flesh. Otherwise the inspiration of the Holy Spirit would not be able to dwell in her.[28]

In her old age, Hildegard speculated on the meaning of afflictions that hitherto she could only bear with patience. If the airy make-up of her body and spirit left her exposed to rheumatic fever, the Föhn, the demonic powers of the air,[29] and every other malaise, she knew that it also opened her to that heavenly breath which, like the wind, blows where it will. Her insight rose beyond the abstract recognition that 'suffering builds character' to a full and concrete self-knowledge which embraced body and spirit, human weakness and divine power at once. But eight centuries later, it is not easy to reconstruct—much less to explain—what she meant by certain physical expressions. In a celebrated letter to Guibert of Gembloux (1175), she remarked that her soul 'rises up high in the vault of heaven and in the changing weather' (*in vicissitudinem diversi aeris*) and spreads itself out over faraway peoples 'according to the shifting clouds'.[30] Although her visions were far from ethereal, she hinted that her soul—like Eve's body—somehow expanded to become as capacious as the heavens. Whatever Hildegard's precise meaning, it is clear that the 'airiness' which gives other women the capacity for motherhood had in her become a capacity for God. Physical weakness was but the price that she, like any other fallen woman, had to pay.

PASSIVITY AND PROPHECY

One of Hildegard's most striking images for woman's constitution occurs in the *Causae et curae*, where she compares a woman's body to the frame of a lyre which is pierced to make room for the strings.[31] This same image, like the aeolian harp of the Romantics, served her as an emblem of prophetic inspiration. In another of her third-person epilogues she presents God speaking of his prophet as just such an instrument:

> The person who has seen and revealed these things in writing lives and does not live; a woman of ashes, she perceives and does not perceive; and she reveals the marvels of God not by herself but as one touched by them, just as a string touched by the harper sounds not by itself but by his touch.[32]

Using a comparable image, Hildegard reminded Elisabeth of Schönau that God's elect are like wind instruments which remain mute until the divine musician sounds them. A trumpet does not sing with its own voice, but with the breath of Another: even so the prophet.[33] In several letters, Hildegard compared herself to a little feather (*penna*) soaring on the wings of the wind: she is nothing in herself but, uplifted by the Spirit, the *penna* is mightier than the sword!

> What man can strive against that voice that thundered, mounting up on wings, and vanquished the abyss, resounding under cover of maternal freshness? And what wings of the wind can outrun that voice by their swiftness? Cannot this voice make a little feather fly so that no sword can prevail against that feather?[34]

The prophet felt herself to be essentially passive, sounding or soaring only when the divine breath touched her. Her sense of this irresistible, overpowering voice bears comparison with Abraham Heschel's similar, though more synergistic view of the prophetic stance as 'sympathy with God'.[35]

Hildegard was neither the first nor the last to see an analogy between this state and the attitude of a wife to her husband—though, to be sure, the analogy came easier to medieval minds than it does to modern. The common prejudice which views the passsive role as demeaning and undignified, or at any rate inferior to the active, assumes the absence of this divine point of reference. If human activity seems so far superior to the passive and receptive state, it may be because the creature's essential stance vis-à-vis the Creator is forgotten. But for Hildegard there was nothing shameful in a woman's passivity, any more than it was shameful for the prophet to remain empty and still until the divine word resounded through her. Moreover, we tend nowadays to apply terms like active and passive—or strong and weak—to the human personality as a whole, so that it seems not only demeaning but downright false to characterize a woman's entire being as weak and passive. But Hildegard and her contemporaries used such labels in a far earthier and more limited sense. When she wrote that 'God joined man and woman, that is the strong and the weak, together in marriage',[36] she was thinking primarily of sexual relations in which the roles are simply not reversible. What she envisioned was not a static hierarchy which relegates woman to the inferior place, but a dynamic union in which the woman's potential for giving life will be actualized by the man. Woman's emptiness and frailty are inseparable from her fertility and depth: 'Although man has greater strength than woman, yet woman is a fountain of wisdom and a wellspring of deep joy, which man draws out to perfection.'[37] When Eve was created, Hildegard writes, she gazed at Adam, 'as a soul which longs for heavenly things stretches upward, for she set her hope in the man'.[38] Erotic love in women, as Hildegard saw it, is by nature aspiring and even adoring. We must also bear in mind that for medieval theologians, the natural outcome of every sexual union, were it not for the Fall, would have been conception. According to Hildegard's physiology, woman's physical weakness enhances her ability to conceive. Her fragility, to borrow aristotelian terms, is not sheer impotence but potency vis-à-vis act.

OVERSHADOWED BY THE MOST HIGH

The woman who renounces marriage does not thereby renounce her feminine nature. The nun, in Hildegard's eyes, is one who re-orients not only her affections but all the capacities of her being toward the heavenly Bridegroom.[39] In the process, she becomes spiritually what the Mother of God was physically—a woman so 'overshadowed' by the Holy Spirit that she becomes a vessel of the Word of God. One vision of the *Scivias* records an intimate dialogue between God and the seer—a device common in other prophetic books but rare in Hildegard's—in which she expresses her own sense of unworthiness and terror. God reassures the prophet by reminding her of the Virgin's childbearing: Mary too was a humble maiden, a *pauper-*

cula, yet he made her the slayer of death.[40] She was indeed so humble that, despite the grace of her virginity, she meekly submitted to Joseph, 'for if Mary had had no one to care for her, pride would easily have snatched her, as if she had not needed a husband to provide for her'.[41] Outward submission and obedience, even for the one woman without sin, were necessary to safeguard the humility which made her capable of bearing Christ. How much more, Hildegard implied, should a sinful woman let herself be overshadowed by her husband's authority![42] Far more important, however, was Mary's poverty of spirit before God. When she received the angel's message 'that the High King wished to dwell in her chamber, she looked at the earth from which she was created and called herself the handmaid of God',[43] and the power of the Most High overshadowed her.

Mary's gesture, admitting her own earthiness at the moment of her election, is one which can and must be imitated by all of God's chosen. Hildegard consciously thought of herself, and of all the prophets, as 'overshadowed ones' whose own darkness was both exposed and illumined by the divine light. A revealing text from the ***Liber divinorum operum*** plays richly on the word 'shadow' (*umbra*), which can also denote reflections in a mirror. For the same heavenly light which overshadowed the prophets (and the Virgin) is metaphysically the light of divine Wisdom, which in Hildegard's vision appeared as a luminous fountain reflecting and foreshadowing all creation. In it the archetypes of all creatures—their platonic ideas, as it were—shine resplendent in the mind of God.[44] In a different metaphor, this light becomes the divine creative voice which utters forth the whole world, as well as the specific oracles revealed through the prophets—of whom Hildegard is one. Thus the divine voice proclaims:

> My glory overshadowed the prophets, who by holy inspiration predicted things to come, as all that God wished to make was foreshadowed in him before it came to be. When reason utters its voice, the sound is like thought and the word like a work. From this 'shadow' issued the book *Scivias*, through the form of a woman who was but a shadow of strength and health, for these vital forces were not active in her.[45]

The bright shadow of revelation—what Hildegard would later call 'the reflection of the living Light'—fell on the prophet's own shadowy figure as the voice of divine reason empowered her weakness. And like Mary in her vignette of the annunciation, she paused for a metaphorical glance at the earth from which she was made. Thus the seer deliberately imitated the Virgin Mother, for the new prophetic book revealed 'through the form of a woman' embodied an utterance of the divine voice, a lesser incarnation of the Word. Unlike Mary, however, the prophet must acknowledge the imperfection of what she has conceived, even though the conception is from God. In one of her unpublished letters, she warned that even when the living Light inspires some human soul, the prophet may fall into pride or vainglory and thence into delusion, 'so let what proceeds from truth be heard, and what from lying be removed'.[46] In practice, Hildegard vehemently resisted any attempt to tamper with her visions.[47] But in theory, she admitted that even in the inspired words of prophets the stamp of human weakness remains.

WOMAN AND THE HUMANITY OF CHRIST

The mystery of divine power perfected in weakness, with the feminine coloring that Hildegard gave it, enabled her to relate the fact of sexual difference to the Incarnation in unexpected ways. While discussing the creation of man and woman, she explains how Eve was both complementary and subordinate to Adam, observing that neither sex could exist without the other, and then adds: 'Man also signifies the divinity of the Son of God, and woman his humanity'.[48] At first glance, this analogy seems either misogynist or absurd. Christ was, after all, male, so how can his humanity be specifically symbolized by woman? Or was Hildegard using this comparison as yet another excuse to belabor woman's inferiority? But to notice only the hierarchical ranking of the sexes would be to miss the truly radical anthropology that her statement implies. If woman truly signifies the humanity of God, then the female—not the male—is representative Man: *femina capax Dei*. But given the priority of Adam and the masculinity of Christ, what can this mean? Several answers are possible. In the first place, Christ received his humanity from a woman without the help of man; in the second place, he remains humanly present and incarnate in the Church, which is signified under a feminine form as the Bride of Christ. It is more likely, however, that when Hildegard spoke of the humanity of Christ she referred primarily to his weak, suffering flesh; and she could not help but associate this weakness with the feminine.[49] But this is a weakness which redeems that of the first woman, for 'God himself had created man strong and woman weak, and her weakness gave rise to her fault. Likewise divinity is strong, but the flesh of the Son of God is weak, yet through it the world is restored to its former life.'[50] Hildegard is here replacing the traditional contrast of two women—Eve and Mary—with a contrast between two kinds of frailty. The weakness of Eve put the strong man Adam to shame, but the weakness of Mary's Son confounded the 'strong man' Satan. Death came through the frailty of a woman, and life through the frailty of God—but even in this case, the name of frailty is Woman.

What is more, Hildegard wanted to see the weakness of Eve not only as the cause of her fall, but also as a providential circumstance which lightened her guilt. She even speculated that if Adam had fallen before Eve, the man's stronger character would have hardened him in sin so far that repentance and forgiveness would have been out of the question. But Eve, being softer and weaker, could more easily repent just as she was more easily seduced in the first place.[51] Just as the seer's own airy complexion made her more vulnerable both to illness and to inspiration, Eve's weakness made her more susceptible to sin as well as to grace. Once more, the pauline paradox illumines the ambiguous mystery of the feminine. It is this ambiguity, this frailty at once so perilous and tender, that Hildegard wanted in the last analysis to identify with human (and sometimes all too human) nature.

THE FEMININE DIVINE

Insofar as woman signifies the humanity of Christ, she also signifies the Incarnation itself as a theological mystery—in Hildegard's terms, the 'eternal counsel' by which God willed to become man (Ps 33:11). Like several twelfth-century theologians, she believed in the absolute predestination of Christ, a doctrine which asserts that God created the world and man because it pleased him to be incarnate, regardless of Adam's sin.[52] In Hildegard's visions, Christ's predestined coming in the flesh is represented by radiant female figures—*Sapientia, Caritas, Ecclesia*—inspired at several removes by the feminine persona of Wisdom in the Old Testament.[53] Such visionary forms signify the incarnate Word not as an historical fact, but as the eternal plan of God's loving providence. In these theophanies, the feminine form still signifies the humanity of God, but now as 'the mystery hidden for ages in God . . . as a plan for the fulness of time' (Eph 3:9, 1:10). Here there is no longer any place for human weakness, except insofar as God has foreseen and provided for it. Yet the visions still reveal that weakness of God which is stronger than men: God's weakness is his tender mercy, his forbearance, his love for men restraining his dread judgment.

In Hildegard's first vision of the feminine Divine, she beheld a radiant woman adored by suppliant angels. A voice from heaven identified her as *Scientia Dei*, the Knowledge of God:

> She is awesome in terror as the Thunderer's lightning, and gentle in goodness as the sunshine. In her terror and her gentleness, she is incomprehensible to men, because of the dread radiance of divinity in her face and the brightness which dwells in her as the robe of her beauty. . . . For she is

> with all and in all, and of beauty so great in her mystery that none could comprehend how sweetly she bears with men, and how she spares them with inscrutable mercy.[54]

To 'see' the figure of *Scientia Dei*, as Hildegard did in this vision, meant also to see how she is known by God, for it is this operation of grace which mediates self-knowledge to sinners. The frightened visionary, who was at first overcome by fear and trembling, found herself able to endure the revelation only when it was mitigated by feminine sweetness. For to her sensibility, the form of woman conveyed both the awesome beauty of divine things and the saving restraint—the 'veiled' quality—that makes epiphanies bearable. In a later vision, she saw divine Wisdom as a female figure of dazzling yet tempered splendor, 'for divinity is terrible and mild to every creature'.[55] The figure stands with hands folded reverently before her breast to signify that Wisdom prudently reined in her power, as if 'ordering all things mightily and sweetly' (Ws 8:1), and her feet lie hidden from view because her secrets are manifest to God alone. Out of consideration for human frailty, the Majesty of heaven shows itself discreet and reserved *in feminea forma*, yet even so the vision 'is radiant with such brightness that it bedazzles the gaze of mortal minds'.

In one of her most lyrical visions, Hildegard witnesses to a kind of annunciation in heaven as divine Caritas—the eternal archetype of the Mother of God—proclaims the Incarnation to come. She appears as a virgin arrayed in cosmic glory:

> And I saw one like a lovely maiden, her face gleaming with such radiant splendor that I could not perfectly behold her. Whiter than snow was her mantle and more shining than the stars, and her shoes were of the finest gold. In her right hand she held the sun and the moon and tenderly embraced them. On her breast was an ivory tablet in which there appeared the form of a man, the color of sapphire; and all creation called this maiden Lady. But she spoke to the form which appeared in her bosom, saying: 'With you is the beginning in the day of your power, in the splendor of the holy ones; I bore you from the womb before the morning star.' (Ps 109:3 Vulgate)
>
> And I heard a voice saying to me: 'This maiden whom you see is Love, who has her dwelling place in eternity. When God wished to create the world, he leaned down in the tenderest love and provided all that was needful, as a father prepares an inheritance for his son.'[56]

Allusions to fatherhood and motherhood blend as Caritas, a female persona, utters a psalm verse often used to invoke the Father's eternal generation of the Son.[57] This same verse, however, had acquired marian connotations through the liturgy; in the Office it occurs as an antiphon for Christmas and Candlemas, celebrating Christ's birth in time.[58] Thus the virgin mother Caritas mediates between the eternal and the temporal birth of the Son. Reminiscent of both God the Father and the Virgin Mary, she is identical with neither, for she is an epiphany of that primordial humanity of God predestined 'from before the foundation of the world'.

PRIESTHOOD AND THE MOTHER OF MERCY

Another aspect of God's humaneness—or as Hildegard would have it, femininity—emerges when she speaks of penance and mercy. The virtue of *Misericordia*, or divine grace redeeming sinners, appeared to the seer dressed in a white veil (like Hildegard's nuns) because:

> Mercy, in the person of a woman, is a most fruitful mother of souls snatched from perdition. For as a woman covers her head, so Mercy subdues the death of souls. And as woman is sweeter than man, so Mercy is sweeter than the fury of crimes raging in a sinner's madness before his heart has been visited by God. This same virtue appears in the form of a woman because the sweetest Mercy arose in feminine chastity, in the body of Mary . . .[59]

The beloved marian title *Mater misericordiae* led Hildegard to reflect on the maternal tenderness of God. Like a merciful woman he will soften and sweeten, instead of condemning, the heart embittered by sin; and this yielding quality evokes a similar response in the soul. For when God created male and female in his image, Hildegard remarks, he extended this dual likeness to the soul as well as the body. The male designates strength, courage, and justice in the inward man, while the female denotes mercy, penance, and grace.[60]

Obviously, both men and women seek active virtue as well as repentance and forgiveness, so this notion of a bisexual *imago Dei* in the soul anticipates our current interest in counter-sexual elements of the psyche.[61] While Hildegard was not recommending androgyny, she did strongly urge each sex to cultivate the spiritual gifts of the other. She was herself praised for possessing 'a masculine mind in a female body'—a familiar topos of praise for women, although her own opinion of herself was quite different.[62] Yet she too exhorted women to strive for the masculine virtues of constancy, vigor in pursuing the good and valor in resisting evil. On the other hand, she insisted no less that men, and especially priests, must imitate the feminine grace of God.[63] In a letter to Pope Eugenius III (1153), she begged the pontiff to judge an erring bishop 'in keeping with the motherly heart (*viscera*) of God's mercy', because 'God desires mercy rather than sacrifice' (Mt 9:13).[64] Alardus, abbot of St Martin in Cologne, was advised to teach his monks with maternal tenderness instead of strident words, that they may open their mouths to receive bread instead of thistles.[65] And pastors were to realize that their flocks will be spiritually weakened unless they are allowed to suck 'the breasts of maternal mercy'.[66] Although Hildegard would have been the last to encourage tolerance of sin, she wanted confessors to show the feminine 'weakness' not of laxity but of compassion, as St Paul demanded: 'who is weak, and I am not weak?' (2 Co 11:29). In this way too they will reveal the humanity of the Son of God.

Even at the altar, Hildegard would have the priest assume a feminine role vis-à-vis God. It is striking that, in an age which witnessed a growing emphasis on the priest's unique power to 'confect the sacrament', Hildegard offered primarily feminine role models for the celebrant. Like Ecclesia in medieval paintings of the Crucifixion, the priest stands beside the cross to catch Christ's blood in a chalice and proffer it to the faithful.[67] Or like the handmaid of God, he offers his humble consent to the miracle:

> When the priest repeats the words of God, the body of the incarnate Word of God is again confected. Through that Word all creatures, which formerly had not appeared, came into being; and the same Word was incarnate of the Virgin Mary as in the twinkling of an eye, when she said with humility: 'Behold the handmaid of the Lord'. And the flesh of the selfsame Word of God blossoms forth at the words of the priest.[68]

Thus every Eucharist re-presents not only Christ's passion and resurrection, but also the incarnation of the Word, with the priest as it were impersonating the Mother of God. Hildegard even used the same metaphor of 'overshadowing' for the Virgin Annunciate and the consecrated gifts. As the Holy Spirit once brooded over the Virgin's womb, like a great mother bird, so now it spreads its wings over the offering until the chick hatches and flies to heaven, leaving only a shell (the visible forms of bread and wine) beneath.[69] But why should Hildegard compare the words of institution, which are Christ's own, with Mary's *Ecce ancilla domini*? Parallels between the annunciation and the Eucharist remind the faithful sharply that it is not human power which commands God to descend, but human weakness which receives his coming. The priest is no miracle-worker, but only a servant like Mary consenting to the miracles of God.[70] At the most sacred moments of her life, the Bride of Christ is most feminine, and Hildegard would not let even the gregorian reform obscure this knowledge.

WOMEN IN LOVE

Nowhere is divine power perfected in weakness more plainly than in the martyrs. Not surprisingly, Hildegard showed a special reverence for those women who had offered God the double sacrifice of virginity and martyrdom. Together with Elisabeth of Schönau, she honored the legendary St Ursula whose 'relics', along with those of the eleven thousand virgins supposedly martyred with her, had recently been unearthed near Cologne.[71] In all likelihood this saint never existed, but in any case Hildegard cared less for the ostensible facts of her life than for her role as a type of the heroic virgin Ecclesia. One of the seer's most carefully crafted hymns, addressed to Ursula, begins by juxtaposing Ecclesia as the Bride of Solomon—a figure of more-than-human stature—with the sainted virgin. Ursula herself is portrayed as an innocent girl who (much like Hildegard) fell in love with Christ upon seeing him in a vision and forthwith renounced marriage and the world, desiring to join her Beloved at the heavenly wedding feast.

In a vision of true faith
Ursula fell in love with the Son of God
and renounced her betrothed along with this world,
and gazed into the sun,
and called to the loveliest youth, saying:

'In great desire I have desired
to come to you and sit with you
at the heavenly wedding feast,
running to you by a strange path
as a cloud streams like sapphire in the purest air.'

And after Ursula had so spoken,
the report of it spread through all nations.
and they said,
'How naïve the girl is!
She does not know what she is saying.'[72]

Thereupon the devil and his chorus of scoffers begin to mock the girl, until at last the 'fiery burden' of martyrdom falls upon her. But as she and her companions perish, their blood cries out to heaven and all the elements join with the angels in a symphony of praise:

Let all the heavens hear this
and praise God's Lamb in lofty chorus—
for the throat of the ancient serpent
is choked by these pearls
strung upon the Word of God.[73]

In a startling metamorphosis, the host of virgins have become a necklace of pearls to choke the devil: the seed of the woman crushes the serpent's head (Gn 3:15). Thus the cosmic victory of the Church has been entrusted to a troupe of fragile girls who appear in the world's eyes as so many lovesick adolescents. This triumphant hymn, honoring the power of weakness and the wisdom of folly, brings us full circle to Hildegard's own self-image; for surely in Ursula's faithfulness to her visionary Bridegroom, despite her 'girlish ignorance' and despite mockery and murder, the seer of Bingen found a model for her own unlikely mission.

On balance, Hildegard's theology of the feminine—as expressed in her own spiritual life as well as her teaching—is both radical and conservative. Her assumptions about the nature of man and woman, whether we choose to call them stereotypes or archetypes, belong to the conventional wisdom of her age (and of other ages before and after). Yet the conclusions she drew from them were by no means commonplace, especially when she turned to the mysteries of Christ and the eternal Wisdom. She was the first theologian to reflect at length on the meaning of womanhood, considered not abstractly but from the incomparable depth of her experience. But great as her achievement was, in this respect her influence was slight; centuries were to pass before the Church would resume the task she had begun. Her activity in the public sphere, on the other hand, would be emulated by scores of charismatic women in the later Middle Ages. Yet here too, Hildegard reveals this same blend of respect for tradition and radical novelty. Perhaps no one has summed up her attitude—reserved, ever mindful of her frailty, yet finally and triumphantly free—better than the friend and secretary of her last years, Guibert of Gembloux. To justify the seer in view of her inevitable detractors, the Flemish monk writes:

> The Apostle does not permit a woman to teach in the Church. But this woman is exempt from this condition because she has received the Spirit, and with a heart instructed in wisdom by his teaching, she has learned through her own experience what is written: 'Blessed is the man whom you have instructed, O Lord, and out of your law you have taught him' (Ps 94:12). And she may be unskilled in speaking, yet not in knowledge, for by her wholesome teaching she instructs many, pouring forth abundantly as if from two breasts the milk of consolation for the young and the wine of correction for those who are stronger.

But although the anointing of the Spirit, like a school-mistress, teaches her all things inwardly and bids her, as it is told in her writings, to offer confidently in public what it has taught her in secret so as to instruct her hearers, she is nonetheless mindful of her own sex and condition, and especially of the aforesaid prohibition. Yet she obeys the Spirit, not him whom the Spirit sends...

Likewise the Apostle commands women to veil their heads, partly for decency's sake and partly to commend a certain just submission. But this woman is free, not indeed from every law, but at least from the one which orders brides to wear veils. For she has transcended female subjection by a lofty height and is equal to the eminence, not of just any men, but of the very highest. Beholding the glory of the Lord with unveiled face, she is being transformed into the selfsame image as by the Spirit of the Lord, from glory into glory.[74]

NOTES

1. The themes of this essay are treated more fully, in their historical context, in the author's *Sister of Wisdom: St. Hildegard's Theology of the Feminine* (Berkeley, 1987).

2. *Ep.* 51; PL 197:268C. All translations are mine.

3. The chief source for Hildegard's life is her *Vita* by the monks Gottfried of St Disibod and Dieter of Echternach (PL 197:91–130), trans. Adelgundis Führkötter, *Das Leben der hl. Hildegard von Bingen* (Düsseldorf, 1968). A useful short biography is Kent Kraft, 'Hildegard of Bingen', in Katharina Wilson, ed., *Medieval Women Writers* (Athens, Georgia, 1984) 109–23.

4. Between 1158 and 1159 Hildegard travelled along the Main, preaching at monastic communities in Mainz, Wertheim, Würzburg, Kitzingen, Ebrach, and Bamberg. Her second trip in 1160 took her to Metz, Krauftal, and Trier, where she preached publicly. Within the next three years she visited Boppard, Andernach, Siegburg, and Werden, addressing clergy and people together at Cologne. After 1170 she undertook her fourth and final journey in Swabia, preaching at Rodenkirchen, Maulbronn, Hirsau, Kirchheim, and Zwiefalten.

5. See Ernst Curtius, 'Devotional Formula and Humility', in *European Literature and the Latin Middle Ages*, trans. Willard Trask (Princeton, 1953) 407–13.

6. For examples see Ep. 1 (PL 197:145C), Ep. 7 (159A), Ep. 51 (264D); *Regulae S. Benedicti Explanatio* (1055A); *Explanatio Symboli Sancti Athanasii* (1078C); *Liber divinorum operum* Prol. (742A) and III.10.38 (1037C); *Vitae S. Disibodi Prooemium* 8, ed. J.-B. Pitra, *Analecta Sacra* 8 (Monte Cassino, 1882) 357. This edition will henceforth be designated 'Pitra'.

7. Such inversion of standards is a commonplace of biblical prophecy; cf. Jr 1:6–7, Dn 10:16, Am 7:14–15.

8. *Scivias* I.1; ed. A. Führkötter, CCcm 43–43A (Turnhout: 1978) 8.

9. *Scivias* II.1; Führkötter, p. 112.

10. *Scivias* III.11.18; Führkötter, p. 586.

11. *Vita* II.16; PL 197:102CD. Portions of the *Vita*, narrated in the first person, comprise Hildegard's memoirs as dictated to her secretary and biographer, Gottfried.

12. 'Ein unveröffentlichtes Hildegard Fragment', IV.28; ed. Heinrich Schipperges, *Sudhoffs Archiv für Geschichte der Medizin* 40 (1956) 71. Cf. Ep. 49; PL 197:254CD.

13. Ep. 75; PL 197:297C. Cf. *Vita* II.24; PL 197:108C.

14. Conventional views of male and female character are encapsulated in the oft-

repeated derivations of *vir* from *virtus* or *vis* (strength) and *mulier* from *mollities* (softness); see Isidore of Seville, *Etymologiae* XI.2.17–18 (PL 82:417A). Two concise reviews of sexual stereotyping in the Middle Ages are Marie-Thérèse d'Alverny, 'Comment les théologiens et les philosophes voient la femme', in *La Femme dans les civilisations des Xe-XIIIe siècles* (Poitiers: 1977), 15–40; and Vern Bullough, 'Medieval Medical and Scientific Views of Women', *Viator* 4 (1973) 485–501.

15. Ep. 29; PL 197:190AB. For a corrected text of this letter see M. Schrader and A. Führkötter, *Die Echtheit des Schrifttums der hl. Hildegard von Bingen* (Cologne-Graz: 1956) 105–108.

16. *Liber vitae meritorum* III.50, V.48; Pitra, pp. 125, 202.

17. *Liber vitae meritorum* I.96; Pitra, p. 44.

18. *Vita* II.16; PL 197:103AB.

19. Bernard of Clairvaux, *Liber de diligendo Deo* XIV.38 (ET *The Book on Loving God*, CF 13:130).

20. A standard humoral chart can be found in Isidore of Seville, *De natura rerum* 11; PL 83:981–82.

21. 'Scientists call these two elements [fire and air] masculine, but water and earth feminine. For the former lie above, the latter below; the former are active, the latter passive.' Alberic of London ('Third Vatican Mythographer'), ed. G. H. Bode, *Scriptores rerum mythicarum latini tres*, I (Cellae, 1834) 163. Cf Thierry of Chartres, *De sex dierum operibus*, ed. N. M. Häring, *Commentaries on Boethius* (Toronto, 1971) 562; and William of Conches, *De philosophia mundi* I.23 (PL 172:56): 'the warmest woman is colder than the coldest man'.

22. See R. Klibansky, E. Panofsky and F. Saxl, *Saturn and Melancholy* (London, 1964) 110–11; H. Schipperges, 'Menschenkunde und Heikunst bei Hildegard von Bingen', in Anton Brück, ed., *Hildegard von Bingen, 1179–1979. Festschrift zum 800. Todestag der Heiligen* (Mainz, 1979) 295–310.

23. *Causae et curae*, ed. Paul Kaiser (Leipzig: Teubner, 1903) 46. On this general subject see Bernhard Scholz, 'Hildegard von Bingen on the Nature of Woman', *American Benedictine Review* 31 (1980) 361–83.

24. *Causae et curae*, p. 59.

25. *Ibid.*, p. 104.

26. *Ibid.*, p. 105.

27. For the alternative theory that Hildegard saw herself as a melancholic woman, see Peter Dronke, *Women Writers of the Middle Ages: A Critical Study of Texts from Perpetua (†203) to Marguerite Porete (†1310)*, (Cambridge, 1984) 181–82. Although the airy temperament was normally regarded as sanguine rather than melancholic, such an anomaly will not surprise readers familiar with Hildegard's originality.

28. *Liber divinorum operum* III.10.38; PL 197:1038A; Gent Universiteitsbibliothek MS Cod. 241, ff. 391–92.

29. *Vita* II.27; PL 197:109–10. For evil spirits as 'powers of the air', cf. Eph 2.2.

30. Ep 2; Pitra, p. 332.

31. *Causae et curae*, p. 105.

32. *Liber vitae meritorum* VI.68; Pitra, p. 244. For the textual correction *vivit* for *vidit*, I am indebted to Dronke, *Medieval Women Writers*, p. 308, no. 38.

33. Ep 45; PL 197:217D.

34. Ep 34; Pitra, p. 520. Cf. Ep 77 (Pitra p. 540), Ep 1 (PL 197:146B), Ep 58 (PL 197:277BC).

35. A. Heschel, *The Prophets* (New York, 1962).

36. *Scivias* II.6.78; Führkötter, pp. 291–92.

37. Ep 13; PL 197:167B.

38. *Causae et curae*, p. 136.

39. Ep 141 (PL 197:372B): 'For she must remain such as Eve was before God presented her to Adam, because then she looked not to Adam but to God'. Cf. Ep 116 (PL 197:337D–338A): The virgin 'stands in the simplicity and the beautiful wholeness of Paradise which will never fade, but remain forever green . . . Virgins are wed-

ded in the Holy Spirit to holiness and the dawn of virginity; therefore it befits them to come to the High Priest as a whole burnt offering consecrated to God.'

40. *Scivias* III.1; Führkötter, p. 330. Cf. *Scivias* I. 2.33, p. 37.

41. *In vigilia nativitatis Domini, Expositiones Evangeliorum* 1; Pitra, p. 245. The notion that virginity without humility is of little worth was a commonplace: cf. Augustine, *Enarratio in Psalmos* 75.16 (CCSL 39: 1049); Bernard of Clairvaux, *Homilia super Missus est* 1.8, (SBOp 4:20); Rupert of Deutz, *Commentariorum in Apocalypsim* 2.3 (PL 169:900D).

42. Nonetheless, the prophet herself had no qualms about obeying God in defiance of her superiors. She successfully fought her abbot's resistance to her move from St Disibod to Bingen (1150), and at the end of her life defied a bishop's interdict (1178) in order to avoid desecrating a grave.

43. *Liber divinorum operum* I.1.17; PL 197:750CD.

44. *Ibid.* III.8.2 (PL 197:981A): 'The purity of the living God is indeed a leaping fountain, resplendent with his glory. In that splendor, God with great love embraces all things whose reflections appeared in the leaping fountain before he bade them come forth in their own forms.' For instances of this widespread christian Platonism cf. Augustine, *Tractatus in Joannem* 2.1.16 (PL 35:1387); Eriugena, *De divisione naturae* 3.16 (PL 122: 667A); Honorius, *Liber XII Quaestionum* 1 (PL 172:1178C); Rupert of Deutz, *De Sancta Trinitate, In Genesim* I.5 (CCcm 21:132–33).

45. *Liber divinorum operum* III.8.2; PL 197:979D–980B.

46. Berlin MS Lat. qu. 674, ed. and trans. Dronke, *Women Writers*, pp. 185 and 256–57.

47. See Ep 29.25–27 (Pitra pp. 431–33) for Hildegard's heated argument with her secretary Guibert of Gembloux over his desire to rewrite her works in a more urbane and elegant Latin.

48. *Liber Divinorum operum* I.4.100; PL 197:885C. On this theme, see Caroline Bynum, '"... And Woman His Humanity": Female Imagery in the Religious Writing of the Later Middle Ages', *Gender and Religion: On The Complexity of Symbols*, edd. Caroline Bynum, Steven Harrell, and Paula Richman (Boston, 1986).

49. Cf. Elisabeth of Schönau's vision of a sorrowing woman clothed with the sun, identified as 'the sacred humanity of the Lord Jesus'. *Liber visionum* III.4; ed. F. W. E. Roth, *Die Visionen der hl. Elisabeth* (Brünn, 1884) 60–62.

50. *Liber vitae meritorum* IV.32; Pitra, p. 158.

51. *Causae et curae*, p. 47. Cf. *Scivias* I.2.10; Führkötter, p. 19.

52. For this doctrine cf. Honorius, *Libellus VIII quaestionum* (PL 172: 1187C), Rupert of Deutz, *De gloria et honore Filii hominis, super Mattaeum* 13 (CCcm 29:415), *Glossa Ordinaria*, Si 24:14 (PL 113:1208D).

53. See especially Pr 8:1–9:6, Si 24, and Ws 6:24–8:1. A fine study of these texts is Gerhard von Rad, *Wisdom in Israel* (London, 1972) Ch. 9.

54. *Scivias* III.4.15; Führkötter, p. 401.

55. *Ibid.* III.9.25; Führkötter, p. 538–39. Hildegard anticipates Rudolf Otto's famous definition of the Holy as *tremendum et fascinosum*.

56. Ep 30; PL 197:192D–193A.

57. Ambrose, *De fide* 4.8 (PL 16:634) is one example among many.

58. Georges Frénaud, 'Le Culte de Notre Dame dans l'ancienne Liturgie latine', in *Maria*, VI, ed. Hubert du Manoir (Paris, 1961) 193, 198.

59. *Scivias* III.3.8; Führkötter, p. 380.

60. *Liber divinorum operum* II.5.46; PL 197:952A.

61. For a recent Jungian treatment of this theme, sensitive to the nuances of spiritual life, see Ann Belford Ulanov, *Receiving Woman: Studies in the Psychology and Theology of the Feminine* (Philadelphia: 1981).

62. Ep 136; PL 197:363D. Cf. Ep 84; PL 197:305CD.

63. This theme is also extremely common in cistercian writers. See Caroline Bynum, *Jesus as Mother: Studies in the Spirituality of the High Middle Ages* (Berkeley: 1982) Part IV.

64. Ep 1; PL 197:148B. For a corrected text see Schrader and Führkötter, *Echtheit*, p. 114.

65. Ep 41; PL 197:208D.

66. Ep 83; ed. Francis Haug, 'Epistolae S. Hildegardis secundum codicem Stuttgartensem', *Revue bénédictine* 43 (1931) 67.

67. Cf. the lost Rupertsberg MS illustration of *Scivias* II.6, repr. in Führkötter, plate 15.

68. Ep 47; PL 197:225B. Cf. *Scivias* II.6.15; Führkötter, p. 244.

69. *Scivias* II.6.36; Führkötter, pp. 264–65. Cf. Ep 47; PL 197:238B. Parallels between the annunciation and the Eucharistic consecration are common in Eastern liturgies; see John of Damascus, *De orthodoxa fide* IV.13 (PG 94:1141A, 1145A). For Western analogues cf. Ambrose, *De mysteriis* 9.53 (CSEL 73:112); Paschasius Radbertus, *De corpore et sanguine Domini* 3 (CCcm 16:27).

70. For Mary as priest cf. Ernaldus of Bonneval, *De laudibus beatae Mariae*, PL 189:1727A; Elisabeth of Schönau, *Liber visionum* I.5, ed. Roth, p. 6.

71. Cf. *Liber revelationum Elisabeth de sacro exercitu virginum Coloniensium*, ed. Roth, pp. 123–38; Guy de Tervarent, *La légende de Ste. Ursule dans la littérature et l'art du Moyen- âge* (Paris: 1931).

72. 'De Undecim Milibus Virginibus', ed. P. Barth, M.-I. Ritscher, and J. Schmidt-Görg, *Hildegard von Bingen: Lieder* (Salzburg, 1969), No. 54, pp. 270–72.

73. *Ibid.* 'Hoc audiant omnes caeli/ et in summa symphonia laudent Agnum Dei,/ quia guttur serpentis antiqui in istis margaritis/ materiae Verbi Dei suffocatum est.'

74. Guibert of Gembloux, Ep 16; ed. Pitra, p. 386.

The Anchoress in the Twelfth and Thirteenth Centuries

Patricia J. F. Rosof

THE TWELFTH and thirteenth centuries mark a change in the way the anchoretic life was lived as well as a time when the number of female recluses was at its height. Female recluses or anchoresses had existed from the early days of monasticism, and the church had regulated for recluses by implication as early as the fifth century, and more specifically in the seventh.[1] By the late eleventh century, however, a confluence of economic, demographic, and religious circumstances worked to bring about a preponderance of female over male recluses as well as a move in the location of numerous anchorholds away from monasteries to towns. By the twelfth century, towns and cities were springing up throughout Europe. By this time, too, women had come to outnumber men, particularly in these cities.[2] At the same time these towns, with their majority female populations, were developing, new religious sentiments and movements began appearing. An eremitic spirit which had begun in Italy with men such as St Romuald and Peter Damian, by the twelfth century had moved to northern Europe, particularly western France. The forests of Craon, Nyoiseau, and Rennes were filled with hermit-preachers and their followers. Among these followers were numerous women, who by their presence attested to the attraction this spiritual way of life held for them. Soon, monasteries were built for women, Robert of Arbrissel's Fontevrault being the most famous. All these preachers and convents were outpaced, however, by the Cistercians, who made no provision for female followers. On the contrary, they did all they could to discourage women from joining their reform. In 1134, the cistercian abbots formally declared that they would not accept women's houses into the order.[3] The Premonstratensians, who had begun with double houses, by 1198 had received papal permission not to receive any more sisters.[4] Just less than a century later even their own nuns were allowed to enter other orders.

GENERAL RELIGIOUS ENVIRONMENT

Thus we find in the twelfth century women as attracted as men to the new, ascetic, more solitary way of life, but with far fewer means of expressing that attraction. As religious men were absorbed into the new flourishing Cistercian Order, or the even more austere Carthusians, spiritually inclined women were left floundering. Nor could they seek refuge in the old Orders. Cluny, which dominated eleventh-century Europe, made only a small, belated provision for women. The traditional, non-cluniac Benedictines had women's monasteries, but they were fewer in number than the men's houses, and would not answer, at any rate, the new spiritual longings for a stricter life.

A few statistics illustrate the disparity in religious outlets for men and women in this period. In England and Wales, during the period 1100 to 1350, the number of monasteries for women ranged from about ten to fourteen percent of the total number of houses.[5] The number of nuns ranged from about fifteen to nineteen percent of the total number of religious. This meant that there were far fewer houses for women than men, and these houses were usually more crowded. Since these statistics do not include the military orders, priests, and hermits, the discrepancy between religious outlets for men and women was even larger.

While the number of female monasteries remained small the female population increased. Since a number of men—monks, canons, hermits and priests—were required to remain unmarried, and a number of widows remarried, a large number of women never did marry, and a significant percentage of them lived in towns and cities. The solution for those who were sincerely religiously motivated seems to have been enclosure as recluses. Enclosure was in keeping with the solitary, eremitic spirit of the age. In the twelfth and thirteenth centuries the small cells of recluses appear to have dotted the medieval landscape, and the majority of their inhabitants were women. M.-C. Guigue reports that based on his study of Lyon, 'The great period of reclusories in Lyon appears to have been the eleventh, twelfth, and thirteenth centuries. During this period, most were inhabited by women, at least the female recluses of the city appeared in the majority in acts and obituaries.'[6] A document from Rome ca. 1320 indicates the presence of two hundred forty female recluses in this city of four hundred thirteen churches, and makes no mention of male recluses.[7] Similarly, documents from Flanders indicate only three known medieval male recluses: two from the seventh century and one from the twelfth.[8] Yet we can cite by name a number of female recluses as well as male hermits. An analysis of the names in the Appendix of *The Hermits and Anchorites of England* also offers dramatic results. The author has located two hundred forty-seven anchorites of known gender from the eighth through sixteenth centuries.[9] Study indicates a ratio of over two women to every one man or about sixty-nine percent female. For the years 1075–1325, the statistics are more impressive. There are ninety-two known women as compared to twenty known men.

Of course, women had always been recluses. In the early medieval period, when there was a dearth of women's benedictine houses, women were welcomed as recluses at men's benedictine monasteries. Throughout our period, we shall continue to see anchoresses attached to monasteries, but they will include the new Orders as well, and recluses who were never nuns. We shall, however, also see an increasing number of town anchoresses, with their cells along city gates or next to one of the many town churches. Just as the friars were a thirteenth-century religious solution to increasing urbanization, so too was the church anchoress a solution to the increasing number of religious townswomen, especially at a time when monasteries sought less responsibility for women. Similarly, just as the friars originally spoke to and drew from a different class of people than the monks, so too the recluses in this period were drawn from a wider variety of economic and social backgrounds. While the traditional nobility remained attracted to monasticism, members of the urban middle class and even some poor women became recluses. Like monasticism, the institution of female enclosure responded to the changes of the twelfth and thirteenth centuries.

THE ATTRACTION OF THE ANCHORETIC LIFE

The reasons women became recluses, as well as the lives they led and the advice they were given, while similar in many respects to those of male recluses, were not identical. Although it is impossible to generalize about women recluses in terms of economic class or marital status, certain character traits stand out. Female recluses were strong, highly motivated women. They often became anchoresses in spite of great pressure to follow other directions, the strongest being their parents' pressure to marry. It was a scenario played again and again. A girl is pious from childhood. Her parents want her to marry. Sometimes she convinces them of her strong desire to be the bride of Christ, and they acquiesce. More often, the young virgin is forced to run away or marry against her will. Later she is widowed and rejecting a second marriage, often at the cost of fighting off pressure to remarry, she can at last follow her initial religious impulses. The best known example of a virgin forced to flee home to preserve the virginity she had vowed to Christ is that of a twelfth-century Englishwoman, Christina of Markyate.[10] Although a marriage was forced upon her, she fled to a recluse named Alfwen before it could be consummated. The Italian Chelidonia (c. 1152) provides another example. From the time she was a little girl she devoted herself to learning the psalter, hymns, and simple prayers.[11] Because her parents wanted her to remain in the world, she left them and found a deserted spot in the rocks where she could devote herself to prayer, fasting, and divine contemplation. Humilitas (d. 1310) represents a noble maiden with pious inclinations who was forced to marry against her will.[12] She, with much weeping and under the pretext of bodily ill-health, convinced her husband to enter a double monastery with her. Later she became a recluse. The venerable Hildeburgis (d. 1115) provides an example of a noble Frenchwoman almost forced to marry a second time. Her friends and son feared she was too young to remain unmarried and chaste.[13] She had succumbed to their pressure and was dressed for the wedding ceremony when she fell to the ground and injured herself badly at the hips. This she took as an unmistakable sign that she was not meant to remarry, and remained a widow, later becoming a recluse.

The factors which influenced religious women to choose the life of a recluse over that of a nun varied with individual circumstances. Widows often exhibited a certain weariness with the world. Hildeburgis seems to have been one of these. Her sons were frequently engaged in wars with neighbors, making a peaceful existence difficult for her. She finally obtained from her son some land which was his by hereditary right, and went to Pontisara, where she became a recluse. She had given alms to many houses and could have undoubtedly gained admittance to some nunnery. Clearly she preferred the solitude of the anchorhold. Other women, less wealthy, probably found anchorholds better financial alternatives than convents. No dowry was demanded on admittance, and one could maintain private property for self-support. It was also easier to find a benefactor to help support a recluse than a nun. Even for the wealthy there was the problem of a shortage of nunneries and available spaces. A woman of resources, on the other hand, could always build her own cell, as long as she could find a willing church or monastery to provide for her needs. Thus, where money was a problem or monasteries for women were lacking in a particular area, an anchorhold made a good alternative for a religious life for spiritual women.

Others chose this way of life because it was more removed from the world, closer to the desert, and they hoped, nearer to God. This choice is clearest in the case of nuns who became recluses, for they were women who had tried the communal life and found it lacking. We have already mentioned Humilitas, but there are other, less dramatic, examples. Iustina (d. 1319), for example, was an Italian who entered the monastery of St Mark when she was thirteen.[14] She lived as a nun for more than four years before she obtained license to be enclosed with another solitary named Lucia, purposely choosing a harsher life. Eve of St Eutrope (d. ca. 1125) was another such recluse. She was originally a nun at the english monastery of Wilton, which she entered as a child of about seven.[15] Like Iustina, she desired a stricter life. She went abroad to Angers, where apparently another Englishwoman named Benedicta already lived. Eve occupied a cell at St Laurent of Angers until about 1102 when, for unknown reasons, she moved to another cell at St Eutrope.

There is no doubt that these women were moved by a desire to live a stricter than monastic life, closer to the one the desert fathers had lived. Such a desire does not, of course, rule out other motives as well. Some women might have preferred the privacy of a reclusory to the communal living of a nunnery. Medieval society did not provide many outlets for individuals with private temperaments, and an anchorhold was one of the few acceptable ways of creating private space. The religious element, however, must always be considered uppermost. Women were affected by the same religious currents and movements as men, the same longing for a contemplative existence. Given fewer monastic alternatives than men to fulfill these spiritual longings, women might naturally turn to the life of a recluse. It was not simply a matter of too few women's monasteries, but of too few diferences among the monasteries. Micheline de Fontette makes a good point in distinguishing between men's reformed monasteries and women's. 'The differences of *form of life* become, among the monks, one of an ideal pursued, and the appearance of monastic orders corresponds to spiritual necesssities. . .', while with women 'the chance of geographic proximity or the ascendance of a strong personality determine the choice more than the recognition of a pursued idea.'[16] She goes on to note that the internal arrangements of women's monasteries did not vary as greatly as did that of the men's. Men could choose between the rich liturgical life of a cluniac monastery, where most of their time would be spent in choir, and the austere life of the Cistercians in which agricultural labor held a place. Women, in contrast, had to choose between 'religious families [which] have the same face in regards to their interior rules'.[17] The choices for women were starker than for men: communal life in the monastery or the life of a recluse.

Some recluses, recognizing their needs early, became recluses without ever having been nuns. The Spanish virgin Auria (d. ca. 1100), a lover of virtue from early adolescence, spurned all delicacies, wearing rough clothes, and devoting herself to reading, prayer and fasting.[18] Not content with this, she was enclosed by the male monastery of S Aemiliano of Suso, donning a monastic habit herself.

Finally, some women became recluses by necessity. These were women who dedicated themselves to virginity but who could maintain that vow only by being recluses, not nuns. Christina of Markyate falls into this category. Talbot says concerning her:

> Whether Christina would have chosen the life of a recluse if left to her own devices is not at all certain . . . even after Burhred [her husband] had released her from her obligations and offered to provide a dowry so that she could enter a convent, it is doubtful whether the bishop of Lincoln would have allowed any community to accept her.[19]

Christina became a recluse because she was fleeing home, and the life of a recluse, being an enclosed life, was the most secret and safest. Even if a young fugitive virgin could find a nunnery that would risk accepting her, she would have had no money for a dowry. Since it was generally not acceptable to move from an anchorhold to a nunnery, the former life being considered the higher state, even a fugitive virgin forgiven by her family would remain a recluse. Young women in Christina's position, however, undoubtedly viewed the choice as one between virginity and marriage, not one between the life of a recluse or that of a nun.

Other women were driven by economic necessity rather than the necessity of flight. After the decision was taken to remain a virgin and devote one's life to God, the issue became what route could best fulfill that purpose. Verdiana (d. 1242) was born in the diocese of Florence, Italy, to poor parents. Like Auria, she early showed an inclination for pious exercises, wearing an iron chain, and being assiduous in vigils, prayers, and fasts, even before she turned twelve.[20] A rich and noble relative took her into his house to aid his wife and provide her with companionship. Not long after Verdiana entered this man's house, there was a great famine. Verdiana, moved by pity for those suffering, distributed a large container of beans belonging to the nobleman. He, meanwhile, unaware of what Verdiana had done, had sold the beans and accepted money for the sale, and when he discovered the empty vat, he was quite angry. Verdiana spent the night in prayer, and the next day the container was filled with beans again. News of the miracle quickly spread around the province, and Verdiana's reputation grew. It was further enhanced when she accompanied some matrons on a pilgrimage. Word of her patience, piety, and charity *en route* reached Florence. By the time she returned home, the townspeople begged her not to leave again. Verdiana acquiesced on condition that they build a cell for her where she could live a solitary existence. The townspeople agreed. Verdiana went on one more pilgrimage while the cell was under construction and then she was enclosed.

Given her choice, Verdiana probably would have become a recluse. Certainly she showed great devotion to that way of life. However, she did not have a totally free choice. She could not have afforded a dowry for a nunnery nor, coming from a poor background, would she necessarily have been welcome in one. It is unlikely that the townspeople would have agreed to pay her dowry, for then she would have been just one among many nuns. As a recluse, she was uniquely *their* recluse, whose prayers would be especially efficacious for them. It was a mutually satisfactory relationship for Verdiana and the townspeople.

CHARACTERISTICS OF ANCHORESSES

The story of Verdiana brings us to the question of the economic and social class of recluses. While there were always noble recluses, the anchoretic life opened up to the middle classes in the twelfth and thirteenth centuries. In fact, it is the relative openness of the life which is striking, relative to the much more class-conscious nunneries and to the much nobler recluses of earlier centuries. There was no social class totally excluded from this calling. Verdiana is representative of the new recluse, an urban woman dedicated to virginity, poverty, and a solitary contemplative existence, supported by the town in return for her prayers. We can also cite examples of rural, poor recluses. There was in Cudot, France, a virgin named Alpais, who became a renowned recluse. The eldest child of very poor farmers, Alpais worked in the fields and led the oxen.[21] When still young, she became seriously ill and emitted such fetid secretions that she was isolated in a hut separate from her family. The Virgin Mary healed her of her ulcerous wounds, but Alpais was left paralyzed. The bishop of the diocese, by a miracle, became convinced of the virgin's sanctity and made for her a recluse's cell out of her poor hut. A church of canons was built adjacent to her wall, with a window into the church level with her bed.

A poor religious woman like Verdiana or Alpais had first to prove her sanctity in order to find support. She followed a harder path to enclosure than did wealthier women. She did, nevertheless, enjoy the opportunity of a sanctioned religious vocation.

One trait all recluses had in common was a strong commitment to their way of life. When a woman, whether a young virgin or a widow experienced in the ways of the world, chose this life, she did so with open eyes. There is no evidence of a recluse having permanently regretted her choice, although many were severely tried and tempted. In the rare case where a recluse left her enclosure, she did so to become an abbess at the strong urging of others.[22] Entrance into a cell meant not only acceptance of a solitary, lonely existence, but also of a barely changing daily routine which would continue for years and years. Recluses were long-lived (Verdiana lived enclosed for thirty-four years,[23] and Eve of St Eutrope for forty-five,[24] to give just two examples), and no one became a recluse, not even widows, as she might a nun, *ad succurendum*. A woman about to be enclosed knew she would face many years—thirty, forty, fifty—in a small room with one window providing her only contact with the outside world. There were mitigating factors, but when all were considered, it remained a life attractive only to the truly contemplative.

THE ANCHORESS AND ECCLESIASTICAL AUTHORITY

By the twelfth century, the ecclesiastical hierarchy was actively involved in licensing recluses. The first step towards becoming a recluse was taking a vow of virginity or chastity. These vows, as church councils remind us with great regularity, were supposed to be taken only with the counsel of priests, especially in the case of vows by women.[25] The approval of male relatives was often specifically mentioned as well. If a woman wanted to be consecrated as a recluse, she needed not only the consent of these men but also that of the bishop of her diocese. This required consent of laymen, priests, and bishops served to test the determination of the woman desiring enclosure, weeding out those who were weak in their commitment. While none of the synods or decrees from this period make reference to a specific period or type of probation,[26] a woman gaining consent from the various required men underwent a very real testing. This might take the form of family pressure, illness, pious acts such as alms-giving and pilgrimage, or a more traditional monastic life for a while. The diocese put various questions to the prospective recluse before granting a license, a procedure which we know was not always *pro forma*. The bishop was responsible for the recluses in his diocese, a responsibility which, with good reason, was taken seriously. If a woman were too easily approved for enclosure and then caused scandal, the disgrace would reflect on the bishop. If a woman he had approved as a recluse could no longer live by the work of her hands or by alms, the bishop would become responsible for her support. On the other hand, it was important to approve serious-minded women. A fervent woman rejected by her church might fall into one of the several heresies of the period. The bishop had to provide valid religious outlets for such women. Nor would this be a totally unwelcome burden. In an era when bishops found themselves losing popularity first to Cistercians and then to friars, and power to papal legates, they found that recluses, especially female recluses, remained strongly dependent on them. Anchoresses required a diocesan license to be enclosed and needed confessors. They often turned to the bishops in time of need, although if a bishop wished, he did not have to concern himself with the recluse beyond enclosure. Priests or abbots of particular churches or cells might control an anchoress's daily life. Bishops generally responded well to this responsibility. Unlike monks, they did not have to fear being drawn away from their contemplative existence; theirs was a pastoral calling.

Even monks and abbots, unwilling to help women's convents, showed themselves ready to assist anchoresses, who were less threatening to the monk's way of life. It was the business of monks to live in community, praying and working together. Monks sent to a sister monastery to act as confessors and administrators would be cut off from their communal life. They might even be carnally tempted. Money which could be spent on monks might have to go to support the nuns. The monks and friars, as we saw, reacted by trying to avoid responsibility for nuns. In the case of a recluse, the situation was different, even if her cell were dependent on a monastery. No special Mass had to be performed for her, because she could follow the Mass in the priest's church or monastic church through her little cell window. There were none of the administrative problems which arise in a community. A recluse could receive income or live off alms; in any case, arrangements for material support were generally made before enclosure. Since she was usually attached to a church, the anchoress could have her spiritual needs served by the parish priest. Even in cases where a woman was enclosed next to a monastery, the problems were not like those connected with a convent.

Furthermore, the anchoress was, in a sense, the perfect female religious. Beginning with the foundation of the Cluniac convent of Marcigny, strict enclosure became synonymous with the ideal religious life for women,[27] a tendency which reached its epitome with the promulgation of a papal bull in 1299 demanding strict enclosure for all nuns.[28] The models women were given to emulate were the contemplative Mary and the Virgin Mary, who was presented as a model of little speech. Who fit this model better than the anchoress, whose life was dedicated to enclosure and silence? As we shall see, the advice given anchoresses and the fears for them centered on this silent aspect of their lives.

There was no authoritative rule for anchoresses;[29] rather anchoresses received advice from their confessors. The emphasis in every case was on advice rather than prescription. An anchoress lived alone and therefore, within the general framework of following the hours of the Divine Office, was to move from prayer to reading to working depending on what best served her contemplative goals at a particular moment. Indeed, one of the attractions of this way of life was the flexibility which the recluse had in ordering her daily existence. Moderation was urged upon the recluse, for her very existence was considered a sacrifice and mortification. From the moment of enclosure in a public ceremony, the recluse was to consider herself as in a tomb, silent and unknown to the world.[30] She was to live in the world of church services and in the world of her mind and spirit. If she was reminded of the temporal world, it was to know that sooner or later she would leave it physically as she had already done in part. Eve of St Eutrope was told 'What if you think you are buried here or if you consider this cubicle your tomb? By bearing the cross after Christ, you will rise from the tomb. Do not fear the burial of resurrection.'[31] The english author of the thirteenth-century *Ancrene Riwle*, writing to the three recluses in his care, tells them that anchoresses should think often about death. 'They should scrape up earth every day, out of the grave in which they shall rot.'[32] Death was a constant reality to an anchoress from the time of the enclosure ceremony, when the Mass for the Dead might have been celebrated, her cell sealed, her body powdered with dust. The fact that this very cell might be her place of burial, and certainly of her death, was a constant reminder, whether or not she actually dug up the earth or prepared her tomb. Her cell's decoration was the cross, an instrument of death and a sign of life after death. Her view was of the altar with the Holy Sacrament, again a reminder that true life was after bodily death. Even alive, the anchoress was sealed off from the world as in a tomb.

While the emphasis on the cell as a tomb and the constant reminder of death were the same for male and female recluses, the female recluses were reminded much more insistently that their chief role was to be one of total silence, their greatest temptation the window to the outside world. The Cistercian Aelred of Rievaulx, writing to his recluse-sister, vividly describes the possibility of an old woman sitting before the anchoress's window, spreading rumors, particularly about monks and clerics,[33] and then entertaining the anchoress further with tales of girls and widows until, even after she is gone, the recluse finds herself musing on her stories rather than giving herself to God. The author of the *Ancrene Riwle* also warns about a 'prating gossip who tells her all the tales of the land; a magpie that chatters to her of everything that she sees or hears.'[34] Women were neither to receive visitors at the window nor talk to them. Even if a holy man came to visit, the anchoress was to listen and learn, not speak or teach.[35] Summing up the general guiding principle of modest and moderate speech, Aelred says, 'For if this pertains to an honest man, how much more to a woman? how much more to a virgin? how much more to an anchoress? Sit therefore, my sister, and be silent.'[36]

In works addressed to women, female models were cited to support this rule of silence and contemplation. The first was Mary the contemplative, the sister of Martha.[37] Another was the Virgin Mary who, the author of the

Ancrene Riwle mentions, spoke only four times, but her words were important and forceful.[38] In guides to men, the issue of silence is dealt with much more expeditiously and less colorfully. The Carthusian prior Bernard uses one short sentence to warn a recluse, Rainaldus, not to listen to tales or rumors.[39] There is no colorful story of old women coming to gossip. The recluse was to hear only worthwhile talk from those who visited, and was to say only religious things in return. There was a much greater mutuality of speech allowed between male recluse and visitor than between female recluse and visitor. The cluniac abbot Peter the Venerable also wrote to an anchorite about the window, but his fears were different from those of authors dealing with women. While Aelred feared what the anchoress would hear, Peter the Venerable feared what the anchorite would say. He rebuked the recluse who sought diversion by acting as an oracle or prophet, drawing the picture of an anchorite who imagined himself a bishop, judge, or abbot ruling thousands.[40] The models given to men were the desert fathers St Paul and St Anthony, as well as St Jerome and St Benedict. Elijah and Christ were cited, but the story of Martha and Mary was absent. The Virgin as exemplar also went unnoticed. The male counsellors of anchoresses feared not only that the anchoress at her window would be distracted from her greater calling or would speak to a degree unbecoming a woman, but that her reputation might be sullied. Thus anchoresses should consult with women rather than men and when possible have a third person present.[41]

SPIRITUAL TEMPTATIONS AND TRIALS

While the authors of these guides seemed to locate the women's greatest temptation at the window, the story of the recluses's lives would indicate that they faced a much greater internal temptation. Isolation, silence, a world practically devoid of human companionship and the human voice could give rise to great temptations and doubts. Anchoresses lived on an intense spiritual plane. The inner world became their reality. Belief had to be absolute. If any doubts set in they easily became serious. Although temptation was considered necessary for the practice of humility and virtue, the normal tempations were pride, illness or carnal thoughts. Anchoresses, however, were subject to much more serious temptations touching the very basis of faith. A couple of stories from Caesarius of Heisterbach illustrate the point. One story concerns a rich young virgin, who after considerable difficulty finally convinced her parents to let her become a recluse. After having been enclosed for a short time, she came to question the reason for her enclosure. She said to the cistercian abbot responsible for her care, 'Who knows if there be a God, or any angels with him? or any souls? or any kingdom of heaven? Who has ever seen such things, who has ever come back to tell us what he has seen?'[42] She begged to be released from seclusion. The abbot convinced her to stay one more week. When he returned he found her full of joy and consolation. Her soul had been rapt from her body and she had seen the angels and the blessed. The story illustrates both the despair and ecstasy open to an anchoress, who spent her existence on the spiritual plane and for whom the spiritual world had to be the real one.

Another story also demonstrates the totality of doubt possible if faith began to slip. A priest while saying Mass spilled wine on a corporal and could not wash it out.[43] He went to the scholar Rudolf of Cologne, a man of great reputation, for advice. Rudolf asked the priest if anyone in his parish had doubts concerning the sacrament. The priest replied that a recluse had frequently doubted it. Rudolf told the priest to show the corporal to her, since perhaps the stain had been miraculously indelible to strengthen the woman's faith. This was done and, after the recluse's faith had been restored, the linen returned to its pure color. The sacrament was not only at the heart of the system of belief, but also at the heart of the recluse's existence. It was an object of her daily attention. To doubt its veracity must have made every day an agony, just as belief in the sacrament furnished mystical experiences for many anchoresses. Such serious spiritual doubts and temptations illustrate the reality of the spiritual realm to anchoresses.

The writers of rules concerned themselves primarily with the temptation of the window, and with the possibility that gossip or sexual fantasies would be used to cure idleness and boredom. They did not deal with the possibility of that most severe temptation, a loss of faith. It is possible that the male writers of Rules, even a male recluse such as the canon Walter who wrote the *Regula reclusorum*, could not imagine the intensity of the isolation an anchoress experienced. A cleric who became a recluse still heard confessions and gave spiritual advice. He had a legitimate reason, even if, as Peter the Venerable feared, he abused it, to concern himself with the window. The anchoress had no such excuse. Furthermore, the priestly recluse could say Mass himself. The anchoress was in a totally passive position, waiting for the eucharist to be celebrated in the adjacent church, waiting for communion to be offered. Unlike a priestly recluse, her only direct contact to the spiritual realm was the eucharist offered her by a priest or her visions. Interestingly, there is no mention in the rules of *acedia*, the bane of monks and nuns. Anchoresses who began to doubt their life seem not to have fallen into lethargy but into despair. A recluse had either to scale the spiritual heights or return to contact with the world by breaking her rule of silence and opening her tomb to the gossip of the world.

Contact with other spiritual persons was permitted and even to an extent encouraged. Anchoresses could be in contact with each other through intermediaries and were often visited by spiritually inclined women whom they encouraged to undertake a religious vocation. A recluse named Mechtildis convinced the virgin Hildegund to go to Schönau, where she became a monk in male guise.[44] The nun Juliana of Mont Cornillon often visited Eve of St Martin and for a while took refuge with her,[45] and Eve of St Eutrope seems to have been drawn to the anchoretic life by her compatriot Benedicta.[46]

VISIONS

Anchoresses were equally dependent on contact with male religious, most importantly the confessor. Yet other men of religion were regular visitors as well and appeared in the recluses' visions. Anchoresses often saw into the thoughts of such men, foretold their actions or deaths, or had visions of them after death. The vision was, in a sense, the preaching medium of the anchoress, and visions concerning those already dead acted as a warning to the living. Anchoresses were not allowed to preach, but they were considered particularly capable of being touched by the prophetic spirit. Alpais, for example, learned in a vision that the abbot of Fontis Ionannis had been freed from purgatory, where he had been sent because he had not checked the speech of his monks.[47] While Alpais might have had difficulty warning an abbot to control his monks, the same abbot might gratefully heed the hidden message in a vision of the holy virgin. Powerful individuals often did not hesitate to ask an anchoress for advice or guidance concerning God's will. In one way the female recluse was most qualified to give this kind of advice. No one questioned the holiness of these women or the fact that they were capable of having visions. Everyone knew that a woman was not supposed to preach, especially not to a cleric. The words she spoke had to come from God, whose agent she was. Proud men who could not take advice from an equal in the world, from other men who might be equally sinful and who might be vying for positions of power, could accept the humble warnings of an anchoress with no stake in the world. The anchoress was an accepted agent of social conscience. A woman, humble in social position and unable to preach or give advice, was for that very reason acceptable as a visionary. The very humbleness of her position and the fact that she was outside the power structure gave what she said great weight, and kept it from becoming threatening in a social sense. Only a lay male hermit could begin to equal these conditions, but even his maleness could make him more threatening, especially if he had been a nobleman of consequence.[48]

The vision of an anchoress had the immediacy which a sermon lacked. A priest could preach on the dangers of usury, but Alpais *saw* the souls of three usurers in torment.[49] She *knew* with her innermost knowledge what happened to three sinful men. Alpais needed a priest to disseminate her knowledge, and the priest could make pastoral use of the visionary experience of the recluse.

We have varied evidence of anchoresses filling the role of advisor and corrector. To use Alpais as an example again, we are told that in one vision she was visited by St Benedict, who ordered her to inform the abbot of les Écharlis how each brother was observing the Rule.[50] Another abbot went to a recluse who had a holy reputation and was accustomed to receive revelations to inquire whether he should maintain his abbatial office.[51] After prayer, the recluse informed the abbot he could not maintain his office because he had tricked his simpler brethren into electing him. The abbot recognized the truth of what the recluse had said and immediately went to the abbot of Clairvaux to confess.

Visions could also serve a purpose for the recluses themselves, giving them the advice and consolation which they needed, and acting as their consciences. The anchoress Auria had a vision in which she was visited by the queen of heaven and a retinue of virgins.[52] Mary urged Auria to soften the harshness of her existence and to stop using the hard pavement as her bed, and warned her she would soon die. One can imagine how many times Auria had probably been urged by her confessor to moderate her existence, but a celestial vision made it possible for her to do so without guilt.

Anchoresses valued the visionary visits of celestial figures, especially the Virgin Mary and Jesus. Mystical experiences, having the spirit 'rapt' out of one's body, were the high points of an anchoress's existence. The trigger for this mystical experience, according to the author of the *Ancrene Riwle*, was the Mass. 'After the kiss of peace in the Mass, when the priest communicates, forget the world, and be completely out of the body, and with burning love embrace your Beloved Saviour who has come down from heaven into your heart's bower, and hold Him fast until He has granted you all that you ask.'[53] The Virgin Mary was prominent in these visions. The presence of her image in the cell, her role as mother of Christ, and her example as ideal woman all served to give her this central position. It was the Virgin who appeared to Auria to tell her to soften her life and who healed Alpais of her oozing wounds.[54] The visions concerning the Virgin show her as a symbol of mercy and compassion, as well as the mother of the boy Jesus.

According to Gougaud, devotions which later became popular among the general laity were already central to the devotional exercises of the recluses of the twelfth century.[55] These practices included a devotion to the five wounds of Christ, to the holy cross, to the mysteries of the life of Christ and the joys of the Virgin Mary. Also in regular use was the psalter, while the use of devotional beads was gaining in popularity.

Indeed the very nature of the anchoress's cell and life worked to make them innovators in matters of the interior life, dedicated to the eucharist, the cross, and the Virgin Mary. The few items allowed in their cell, in the room where their entire religious life was spent, were the cross, an altar, and the image of the Virgin and perhaps one more saint. When looking through the church window, their eyes lit on the altar and the holy eucharist. The cross or the sacrament was in almost constant view. Furthermore, the singularity of the life, the fact that it was for one individual and so emphasized substance not form, the fact that recluses were encouraged to find the best spiritual mix for themselves, to favor short meaningful prayers over long drawn-out ones, all encouraged mystical, interior experiences.

Contemplation upon the cross conspicuously displayed in the recluse's cell could touch off a mystical experience. Once, when the devil came to Alpais in the person of a doctor, the recluse turned her eyes away from him to another part of the wall where the crucifix hung.[56] When she saw this, the memory of the passion of Christ welled up in her and she forgot about her dangerous visitor, falling into holy meditation. Jesus himself appeared to Christina of Markyate carrying a cross of gold. He gave her the cross, telling her to hold it firmly and promising comfort in her tribulations.[57]

Contemplation of the passion naturally led to contemplation of the consecrated eucharistic host. This was especially so because it was in continuous sight on the altar of the church which the anchoress viewed from her window. It was the object of her meditation. Anchoresses showed a special devotion to the host. We are told of one recluse who always kept it on the altar in her cell.[58] Alpais lived on the sacrament alone. Unable to swallow any food without great difficulty, when she was healed by the Virgin, she was promised from then on her only food would be the food of the Lord.[59] Matthew Paris tells of another recluse who existed solely on this holy food. For seven years before her death, all she took into her body was the body and blood of Christ on Sundays. The truth of this was verified, he tells us, by the bishop of Lincoln.[60]

The devotion to the sacrament was epitomized in Eve of St Martin who, inspired by her friend Juliana, was an avid advocate of the feast of Corpus Christi.[61] Her devotion to the feast was recognized by Urban IV, who sent her a letter announcing its institution, and calling it the desire of her heart.[62]

The number of times an anchoress communicated varied, depending on the inclination of her confessor. The author of the *Ancrene Riwle* stipulated fifteen times a year, on the theory that what is done less often will be more highly valued.[63] In contrast, the *Regula reclusorum Dubliniensis* permitted communion every Sunday.[64] If, however, this was impossible, it was not to be a cause of concern. The anchoress could still listen to the Mass and should remember that the desert fathers did not communicate regularly.[65]

Anchoresses sometimes felt the availability of communion to be too much at the whim of the priest. The eucharist was central to the spiritual lives of anchoresses. It was a means of coming close to their Spouse, a path to meditation, the central mystery of their existence. Yet a priest could refuse a recluse communion without explanation. This points again to the truly isolated, silent position of the female recluse. The recluse was powerless to effect the most important spiritual activity of her existence.

The importance of the Mass and communion, and the sense of powerlessness which could be experienced by recluses, is illustrated in a story told by Caesarius of Heisterbach. A certain recluse had a special relic, the tooth of St Bartholomew. A priest who learned of her prized possession forced her to divide the tooth by threatening to stop celebrating the Mass for her if she refused.[66] Reluctantly she agreed, but as the priest was about to cut the tooth, blood gushed out of it, terrifying him. Thus both the recluse and the relic were spared. Without divine intervention, however, the recluse felt compelled to yield to the priest's demand in order to preserve contact with the Mass. Recluses unable to communicate would occasionally receive communion in their visions from heavenly figures. Alpais received communion from Jesus himself,[67] while a recluse named Herluca received it many times from St Laurence.[68]

The Example of One Anchoress

Various aspects of the anchoretic existence already discussed become clearer if we look closely at one anchoress. Ivetta of Huy, Belgium, is a representative, if not typical (there being no one type), recluse.

Ivetta lived enclosed as a recluse for thirty-six years, dying at the age of seventy in 1228.[69] At the time of her enclosure she had been a widow for fifteen years, her husband having died after five years of marriage and three children. Ivetta, like many women who became recluses, had never wanted to marry. Her aversion to marriage came not just from her natural piety but also from what she had observed of the dangers of pregnancy, the burdens of educating children and caring for the family, and the dubious nature of husbands. While she did not flee the marriage bond, she resented it. Like the venerable Hildeburgis, Ivetta was urged to marry a second time, pressured by her father and the bishop because of her youth. Ivetta was called before the bishop and other distinguished men to justify her attachment to widowhood. She acquitted herself so well that the bishop ordered her father, who served as cellarer and creditor to the prelate, not to bother her any more. Afterwards she led a pious life at home for five years, and then spent ten more serving the lepers outside the walls of the city of Huy. Only gradually did Ivetta come to her calling as an anchoress.

When Ivetta first went to serve the lepers, the church for them was very poor and badly served. Ivetta's father, converted by her prayers, had built himself an anchorite's cell adjacent to this poor church, but had then chosen the monastic life instead, joining the cistercian monastery of Villiers. When Ivetta was ready to be enclosed, therfore, she had a cell already available to her, as well as a special tie to the Cistercian Order where first her father and then her son had become monks. Thus, it was the cistercian abbot of Orval (her son's monastery) who enclosed her in her 'hole in stone', and she donned the cistercian habit.

By the time of her enclosure, Ivetta had undergone a long probation, first by accepting the burden of an unwanted marriage, next by defending herself before the bishop, then by pursuing pious works and almsgiving as a widow, and finally in serving lepers.

Once enclosed she led a severe life, measuring everything she ate and drank, even water, lest by slightly increasing her intake she rekindle in herself a concern for the flesh. Because of this abstinence she suffered a weakness in the limbs and heart. She wore out her body with fasts, vigils, flagellation, and prayers performed on bent knees. She slept on a hard bed, girded herself with iron and hung a board from her shoulders. Yet prudent and religious men were eventually able to convince her to temper this rigorous routine, citing arguments from the Fathers and Scripture. Thus Ivetta like many recluses used the internal freedom of the anchoretic life to make harsh demands upon herself, while the pious men whom she attracted urged her to moderation in accordance with the advice given in the rules for recluses.

As Ivetta's reputation grew and she attracted followers, both a leper's church and a recluse's cell were rebuilt. The new cell was much more spacious, consisting of two floors, with the window to the outside on the lower level, and Ivetta's room on the upper level.[70] Also enclosed in this larger cell was a girl named Agnes, who had received her license from the bishop of Liège. Ivetta had a maid as well, who was considered enclosed by the bishop but who had permission to go out to get whatever was necessary for Ivetta in her old age.[71] All but Ivetta were enclosed by the bishop. Ivetta surely had an episcopal license to be enclosed, but she put herself under the guidance of the cistercian abbot to whom she felt closest.

There is a story in the Life which illustrates the bishop's role in enclosure. A certain virgin had vowed herself to seclusion. The bishop of Liège had inherited several anchoresses from his predecessor and refused to acquiesce to her petitions. No one presumed to ask the bishop why he refused the girl. The virgin begged Ivetta for her prayers and was reassured by her. The next time she sought the permission of the bishop, he gave her the license, which he had rarely given anyone. The story indicates the importance of episcopal permission, the extent to which success in fulfilling a private vow could depend on the inclination of the diocesan bishop, and the prophetic powers of Ivetta who reassured the virgin of her ultimate success.

Like many recluses, Ivetta saw herself as having a special relationship to the Virgin. While Ivetta was still leading a pious life in her own home, a distant relative tried to sneak into her bed one night. The Virgin protected Ivetta by appearing to Ivetta in a brilliant light, but in such a way that the evil young man could hear footsteps but see nothing, thus causing him to flee in terror. She also reconciled Ivetta to Christ the judge. It was unusual for an anchoress to see Christ in any way but as a loving spouse or as a child, but Ivetta had tremendous guilt over her hostile feelings to her late husband. When Christ, accompanied by angels, came to judge the newly-enclosed recluse, Ivetta, groaning on bent knees, appealed to the Virgin, who then sought mercy from her son. When she was accused of having despised the bonds of matrimony, the Virgin replied that the recluse had not known the magnitude of her sin and had since done penance. Christ then remitted the sin and entrusted the recluse to the special care of his mother. After this unusual vision, Ivetta saw Jesus in the more common and comforting role of spouse and felt his presence in a physical way. Once she saw herself decorated in gold and valuable gems by orders of angels and so presented to her heavenly spouse.[72] Like other recluses, she had a deep devotion to the eucharist, and twice received the sacrament from Christ himself. This led to such sweetness that whenever she devoted herself to private prayers she continued to feel his presence.[73] Another time she was greatly upset by being arbitrarily refused communion by a priest. While she slept St John the Evangelist led her into the church, celebrated the entire Mass, revealed to her the secrets of the sacraments, and communicated her. He then explained the reason for the priest's refusal: he had recently slept with a harlot and did not dare touch the body of Christ.

It is clear that Ivetta served her society first by aiding lepers directly and then by attracting money for their church and care by her holy reputation. Yet she also performed the more usual service of giving prophetic advice, acting as corrector and guide to a spiritual existence. For example, a sacristan in a church of Huy slept with a woman of the city in the church. The details of this occurrence were made known to Ivetta through the spirit. The woman, whom she knew, was brought to her, confessed, and thanked the Lord that he was watching over her through his handmaiden. The clerk, obstinately refusing to heed Ivetta's summons, died soon afterwards without communion. Another woman who was seduced by a priest in church did not confess before her death because this priest convinced her she was not going to die. In a vision Ivetta saw the Virgin pleading for vengeance for this woman. She summoned the priest to her and when he came warned him about the vision. Although he first denied the truth of the vision, he later confessed and vowed to enter the Cistercian Order to do penance. Unfortunately for his soul, he lapsed shortly after. Again, when a premonstratensian brother left his cell without abbatial permission, Ivetta became aware of his presence at the visitor's window, although she had been intent on oration. She went below, asked him why he had left without license, consoled him and promised to help him fight his temptations. Others she convinced to join monasteries, beginning with her father and brother but including many who were not relations.

Thus Ivetta, like many recluses, a member of a distinguished although probably not noble family, entered slowly upon the anchoretic course but lived it fully for thirty-six years. She was never a nun, although she wore a monastic habit, and was attached to a church outside but near the city. She underwent a very real, although not a monastic, period of probation. She showed a special devotion to the sacrament, receiving it at various times from Christ himself, St John, and upon her death, the Virgin, to whom she was especially devoted. She served her community as prophet, and consoler. Ivetta, like the anchoresses of our period, was clearly a strong-willed woman who knew her mind and arranged her spiritual life in a way proper for her but with respect for those who advised her.

CONCLUSION

The female recluse of the twelfth and thirteenth century was a well-known figure in that society, and one increasingly associated with town churches rather than monasteries. She could have begun life as a virgin or widow as well as a nun, and could be middle class or even poor as well as noble. Set before her as examples to emulate were the Virgin Mary and the contemplative Mary. The anchoress had a great deal of control over the ordering of her daily existence, while urged by her confessor or advisor to be moderate in her regime, since her entire life was one of sacrifice and mortification. Being shut off from the world, she could vary between despair and ecstasy, finding comfort in the visionary presence of Mary and her spouse Jesus. Central to her existence was the cross and the eucharist, the symbols of the human and suffering Jesus, with whom the recluse could identify. Yet despite living in the realm of the spiritual, and indeed because of it, the anchoress could serve a special function for her society. She could correct even male clerics through her visions and attract new recruits to the religious life. She witnessed, by the very existence, to her faith and provided women with an alternate model to the nun or the matron.

NOTES

1. In 465 at the Council of Worms and 646 at the Seventh Council of Toledo, Johannes Dominicus Mansi, *Sacrorum Conciliorum et Amplissima Collectio* (rpt. Graz, Austria: Akademisch Druck—U. Verlagsanstalt, 1961) 7:954, 10:769–70.

2. Fritz Rorig, *The Medieval Town* (Berkeley: University of California Press, 1969) 115. See also David Herlihy, 'Life Expectancies for Women in Medieval Society', Rosemarie Thee Morewedge, ed., *The Role of Women in the Middle Ages*, (Albany: State University of New York Press, 1975) 111–13.

3. Micheline de Fontette, *Les Religieuses àl'âge classique du droit canon: Recherches sur les structures juridiques des branches féminines des ordres* (Paris: J. Vrin, 1967) 29.

4. Simone Roisin, 'L'Eflorescence cistercienne et le courant féminin de piété au XIIIe siècle', *Revue d'histoire ecclésiastique* 39 (1943) 350.

5. David Knowles and R. Neville Hadcock, *Medieval Religious Houses, England and Wales* (New York: St Martin's Press, 1971), percentages drawn from statistics in Appendix II, p. 494.

6. M.-C. Guigue, *Recherches sur les recluseries de Lyon* (Lyon: Henri Georg, 1887) 4.

7. P. Livarius Oliger, 'Regula Reclusorum Angliae et Quaestiones Tres de Vita Solitaria Saec. XIII–XIV', *Antonianum* 9 (1934) 265–66.

8. L. Detrez, 'L'Eremitisme septentrional', *Bulletin du comité flamand* 14 (1951) 20–21.

9. Rotha Mary Clay, *The Hermits and Anchorites of England* (1914, rpt. Detroit: Singing Tree Press, 1968), Appendix C, pp. 203–63.

10. C.H. Talbot, ed. and trans., *The Life of Christina of Markyate, A Twelfth Century Recluse* (Oxford: Clarendon Press, 1959) 41.

11. *AA SS*, (Oct. 13) Oct. 6:366. (Antwerp).

12. *Ibid.*, (May 22) May 5:206.

13. *Ibid.*, (June 3) June 1:362.

14. *Ibid.*, (March 12) March 2:243–44.

15. André Wilmart, 'Eve et Goscelin (II)', *Revue bénédictine* 50 (1938) 82–83. See also C.H. Talbot, 'The Liber Confortatorius of Goscelin of Saint Bertin', *Analecta Monastica*, ser. 3, *Studia Anselmiana* 37 (1955) 22–23.

16. Fontette, p. 10.

17. *Ibid.*, p. 154.

18. *AA SS*, (March 11) March 2:101.

19. Talbot, *The Life of Christina of Markyate*, intro., pp. 15–16.

20. *AA SS*, (Feb. 1) Feb. 1:257–58.

21. *Ibid.*, (Nov. 3) Nov. 2:168, 175–78. See also 'Alpais', *Dictionnaire d'histoire et de géographie ecclésiastique* (Paris, 1912–) 2:673–74.

22. The recluse Humilitas, having attracted many women to cells around hers, was asked by bishops, abbots and clerics to build a monastery for women, which she did. *AA SS*, May 22, 5:208.

23. *AA SS*, (Feb. 1) Feb. 1:258.

24. Wilmart, p. 83.

25. Mansi, 22:681, 731, 735; 23:330, 425, 714. An additional clause to the 1236 provincial constitutions of the Archbishop of Canterbury (appearing in Mansi 23: 425) which concerns the diocesan license for enclosure appears in J.V. Bullard and H. Chalmer Bell, edd. *Lyndwood's Provinciale*, London: Faith Press, 1929) 87.

26. The earlier church councils had demanded a period of monastic probation. See Mansi, 10:769–70 (Seventh Council of Toledo of 646) and 11:963 (Council of Quinisextum, *In trullo* of 691).

27. Noreen Hunt, *Cluny under Saint Hugh* (London: Edward Arnold, 1967) 188.

28. Eileen Power, *Medieval English Nunneries c. 1275–1535* (Cambridge, 1922) 344.

29. We have two rules written specifically for women: Aelred of Rievaulx, 'De institutione inclusarum', ed. C.H. Talbot, *Opera Omnia,* I, *Opera Ascetica,* CCcm

(Turnhout, 1971), translated by Mary Paul Macpherson, in CF 2 and the anonymous *The Ancrene Riwle,* trans. into modern English M.B. Salu (London: Burns & Oates, 1955), which was written for three sister recluses in the early thirteenth century. Aside from these we have Goscelin of St Bertin's letter of advice written ca. 1082–83 to Eve of St Eutrope when he learned she had decided to become a recluse. This is the *Liber Confortatorius,* ed. and intro. C.H. Talbot, *Analecta Monastica,* ser. 3, *Studia Anselmiana* 37 (1955) 1–117, text from 26. Another letter of encouragement was written to Eve by Geoffrey of Vendome ca. 1102 (*ep.* 48; PL 157:184–86). Another letter of a general nature is from Bishop Hildebert of Mans to a recluse Athalisa (*ep.* 21; PL 171:193–97). Two further english rules from the thirteenth century were written with both men and women in mind and have been edited by P. Livarius Oliger. The *Regula reclusorum Dubliniensis* (*Ordo anachoritalis vitae*) appears in 'Regulae Tres Reclusorum et Eremitarum Angliae saec. XIII–XIV', *Antonianum* 3 (1928) 170–90 while the *Regula reclusorum* appears in 'Regula Reclusorum Angliae et Quaestiones Tres de Vita Solitaria saec. XIII–XIV', *Antonianum* 9 (1934) 53–84. Other letters specifically for men also exist.

30. We have two enclosure ceremonies from the twelfth century and one from the thirteenth. These are, from twelfth-century England, the 'Ad recludenum anachoritam', ed. H. A. Wilson, *The Pontifical of Magdalen College with an Appendix of Extracts from other English MSS. of the Twelfth Century,* Henry Bradshaw Society, 39 (London, 1910) 243–44, and from Soissons the 'Ad reclusum faciendum', in Martène, ed., *De Antiquis Ecclesiae Ritibus Libri,* 2, 2nd ed. (Antwerp, 1736) 498–99. From thirteenth-century England we have the 'Ordo includendi famulam Dei', ed. W.G. Henderson, in *Liber Pontificalis Christopher Bainbridge Archiepiscopi Eboracensis,* Surtees Society, 61 (1873) 81–86. This last, although originally considered as sixteenth century, has since been accepted as thirteenth century. We also have descriptions from the lives of two saints, that of Verdiana in *AA SS* (Feb. 1) Feb. 1:258, which is fairly full, and a shorter one of Humilitas, *AA SS* (May 22) May 5:207.

31. *Liber Confortatorius,* bk. 3, *Studia Anselmiana* 37:79.

32. *Ancrene Riwle,* part 2, p. 51.

33. Aelred of Rievaulx, Instincl 2; CCcm 1:638, trans. CF 2:46.

34. *Ancrene Riwle,* part 2, p. 39.

35. *Ibid.,* pp. 28–29.

36. Aelred of Rievaulx, Instincl 5; CCcm 1:641, CF 2:51.

37. Aelred of Rievaulx, 28; CCcm. p. 660; Goscelin, *Liber Confortarius* bk. 3, Studia Anselmiana 37: 89; *Ancrene Riwle,* part 8, p. 183.

38. *Ancrene Riwle,* part 2, p. 33.

39. Bernard, *Portarum Prior,* I, *ep.* 3; PL 153:892–93.

40. Peter the Venerable, 'Ad Servum Dei Gislebertum Silvanectis Inclusum', *ep.* 20, in Giles Constable, ed., *The Letters of Peter the Venerable* I (Cambridge, Mass: Harvard University Press, 1967) 32–33.

41. *Ancrene Riwle,* part 2, p. 30; Aelred of Rievaulx, 7, CCcm p. 642.

42. Caesarius of Heisterbach, *The Dialogue on Miracles,* bk. 4 trans. H. von E. Scott and C.C. Swinton Bland, (New York: Harcourt, Brace and Co., 1929) vol. l: 235–36.

43. *Ibid.,* bk. 9, 2; 125.

44. *AA SS* (April 20) April 2:786. See also Caesarius of Heisterbach, bk. 1, 1: 54–55.

45. *AA SS* (April 5) April 1:452, 466, 473.

46. Wilmart, p. 83.

47. *AA SS* (Nov. 3) Nov. 2:187–88.

48. H. Mayr-Harting, 'Functions of a Twelfth-Century Recluse', *History,* 60 (Oct. 1975) 337–52 discusses the social usefulness of recluses as outsiders, focusing on the male recluse Wulfric of Haselbury.

49. *AA SS* (Nov. 3) Nov. 2:195–96.

50. *Ibid.,* p. 186.

51. Caesarius of Heisterbach, bk. 4, 1: 428.
52. *AA SS* (March 11) March 2:101.
53. *Ancrene Riwle*, part 1, p. 14.
54. *AA SS* (Nov. 3) Nov. 2:178–80.
55. Louis Gougaud, *Ermites et reclus. Études sur d'anciennes formes de vie religieuse* (Vienne: Abbaye Saint-Martin de Ligugé, 1928) 110–11.
56. *Ibid.*, p. 198.
57. Talbot, *The Life of Christina of Markyate*, p. 107.
58. *AA SS* (April 13) Apr. 2:172.
59. *Ibid.*, (Nov. 3) Nov. 2:178.
60. Matthew Paris, *Chronica Majora*, 3, Rolls Series (London, 1876) 1225, 101.
61. *AA SS* (April 5) Apr. 1:465.
62. The text of the letter appears in Mansi, 23:1076–77 and *AA SS* (April 5) Apr. 1:477.
63. *Ancrene Riwle*, part 8, p. 182.
64. *Regula reclusorum Dubliniensis*, ch. 6, p. 178.
65. The example of Mary the Egyptian who communicated only at the point of death is specifically cited.
66. Caesarius of Heisterbach, bk. 8, 2: 63–64.
67. AA SS (Nov. 3) Nov. 2:183.
68. *Ibid.*, (April 18) Apr. 2:555-56.
69. *Ibid.*, (Jan. 13) Jan. 1:863–87. All the following information on Ivetta comes from her life in *AA SS*.
70. The cells of recluses could vary vastly in size. The recluse Iustina had a cell which she shared with another recluse, Lucia, which was so low and narrow that she could not remain erect (*AA SS* (March 12) Mar. 2:244). Goscelin of St Bertin assumed that Eve's cell was eight feet in width and height (*Liber Confortatorius*, 3, p. 72). On the other hand, a late thirteenth-century english recluse by the name of Emma of Shrewsbury appears to have had an anchorhold consisting of three rooms, providing space for a maid and guest, a visiting nun perhaps, or a would-be recluse (Henrietta Mary Auden, 'Shropshire Hermits and Anchorites', *Transactions of the Shropshire Archaeological and Natural History Society*, ser. 3, 9 [1909] 104). Thus, Ivetta in her own life seems to have experienced both extremes in the accomodations of a recluse.
71. The writers of rules assume the existence of a maid to provide the recluse with her necessities as well as to act as a buffer between the anchoress and the outside world. Nonetheless, not all recluses had maids.
72. *AA SS* (Jan. 13) Jan. 1:876.
73. *Ibid.*: 882.

The Sacramental Witness of Christina *Mirabilis*: The Mystic Growth of a Fool for Christ's Sake*

Margot H. King

THE REMARKABLE OUTBURST of a specifically female apostolate in the Lowlands at the end of the twelfth and the beginning of the thirteenth century has not, until recently, received the attention it deserves from the general public.[1] At its peak, it numbered its followers in the thousands[2] and was marked by a profound mysticism which expressed itself in an active and energetic ministry. Essentially a grass-roots movement, it never received official approval from the hierarchy and by the fifteenth century its momentum had died and it soon disappeared.[3]

The holy women who made up this movement either lived alone as recluses or solitaries,[4] or as nuns in regularly constituted monasteries, or as semi-religious called Beguines in loosely organized communities outside the effective control of the Church. Francis of Assisi wanted to visit them[5] and had actually started off on a pilgrimage to Belgium in the summer of 1217 when his voyage was interrupted in Florence by Cardinal Hugolino,[6] later Pope Gregory IX. Jacques de Vitry championed their cause and wrote a life of Marie d'Oignies around whom the movement is said to have revolved.[7] Thomas of Cantimpré, an augustinian canon turned Dominican,[8] wrote lives of four of them: Christina of Saint Trond,[9] Margaret of Ypres,[10] Lutgard of Aywières,[11] and Marie d'Oignies in a supplement to the life by Jacques de Vitry.[12]

The *vitae matrum* written by Thomas shed much light on this new movement, but only the lives of Margaret and Lutgard have received a sympathetic reading. That of Christina (1150–1224)), written by Thomas about

1232, has recieved an almost universally bad press in the last century. The criticisms levelled at the *vita* are based on the historicity of the events recounted by Thomas, despite Jacques de Vitry's laudatory reference to her in his preface to the Life of Marie d'Oignies.[13] It is an undeniably odd story. After living a solitary and devout life as a shepherdess, Christina died at the age of thirty-two but, during her funeral Mass, was restored to life. As she explained to her thunderstruck sisters, God had sent her back to earth to warn sinners of the fate which awaited them if they persisted in their sins. Her literal re-enactment of the purgatorial torments, accompanied by amazing feats of endurance and ascetic pyrotechnics, was misunderstood by the townspeople of Saint Trond and it was not until impelled by the Holy Spirit, she immersed herself in the baptismal font at Wellen that she was able to explain her behaviour and hence became an effective witness to God's justice and mercy. She died at the benedictine abbey of Saint Catherine's in Saint Trond but was never a member of a canonically established Order.[14]

Simone Roisin, the authority on the hagiography of this periord, called the life of Christina 'a tissue of extravagances'[15], and a few years later Herbert Thurston not only attacked the life as 'a preposterous narrative' and 'utterly untrustworthy', but accused its author of 'deliberately romancing'[16]. More recently, Brenda Bolton has discussed the life of Christina in an excellent survey of these *vitae matrum* but refrained from passing judgment on its historical or hagiographical content.[17]

It is clear that the reason why critics have either attacked or dismissed Thomas's life of Christina arises from the outrageousness of her behavior. They have accepted her historical existence on the basis of Jacques de Vitry's witness but have ignored his testimony concerning the details of her life. In his prologue to the life of Marie d'Oignies, he presented himself as an eye-witness who obviously believed what he had seen:

> I saw another in whom God wrought wondrously for, after she had lain dead for a long time but before she was buried, her soul returned to her body and she revived because she had received permission from God to undergo purgatory in this world. Accordingly she was wondrously afflicted by God so that sometimes she rolled herself in fires, at other times she would stand for long periods in freezing water in the depths of winter, and sometimes she was driven into the tombs of the dead. Finally, however, when her penance was finished, she lived in great peace and God gave her such grace that often, ravished in spirit, she led the souls of the dead into purgatory or conducted them into heaven without any harm to herself (*VMO* 549, 8).

Most critics quote this passage and, trusting Jacques de Vitry's good faith ('a man of much more sober judgment than Thomas de Cantimpré', said

Thurston[18]), accept the events of Christina's later life when, it would appear, she behaved more rationally than during the period immediately after her resurrection. They balk, however, at the descriptions of Christina's self-inflicted purgatorial punishments and seem to have forgotten that, even after 'her penance was finished [and] she lived in great peace', this peace was only relative, since she continued to act as a constant reminder to those around her of the inevitable punishment which awaited sinners and, on one occasion at least, voluntarily assumed half the purgatorial pains of a particularly dear spiritual friend.

In previous centuries, the life of Christina was accepted as an historical account of an other-worldly vision. What today is classified as a literary genre,[19] was then accepted without question to be historical fact, simply another example of God's intervention in human affairs. All Christina's torments are found duplicated in accounts such as the so called *Apocalypse of Paul*,[20] or in the much later *Purgatory of Saint Patrick*[21] and *The Vision of Alberic*.[22] Although Pinius had included Christina in the *Acta Sanctorum*, the Bollandists later became unwilling participants in a silly quarrel which centered around the 'authenticity' of the *vita*, and expressed doubt about the literal historical truth of the events of her life in a note in *Analecta Bollandiana*.[23] A Redemptorist, H. Nimal, had written a pious and uncritical account of Christina[24] and, objecting to a bad review by Godefroid Kurth,[25] had focussed attention on the authenticity of her life in a series of polemical articles.[26] The Bollandists, while admitting Thomas's goal of edification, questioned 'the authority and historical value of the tale' and called Nimal's evidence 'completely foreign to the methods and ideas of scientific hagiography' (p. 58). The result of this disapproval has been that, with one exception,[27] Christina has been assigned to the dust-heap of pious folklore.

Since many Christians in the pragmatic and rationalistic world of the late twentieth century question even the probability of divine intervention in human affairs, this paper will not discuss the likelihood of whether Christina's miraculous actions actually took place or not. Rather, it will attempt to read her life as a hagiographical and sacramental expression of thirteenth century mysticism. That it was so read before the twentieth century is clear from the testimonies of those devoted to her cult. There is extant a translation into Middle English[28] and, apart from the witness of Jacques de Vitry, we have testimonials from Denis le Chartreux[29] and Cardinal Bellarmine,[30] among others. In the nineteenth century Görres considered Christina to be spirituality incarnate,[31] and Shouppe, following Bellarmine, read her life as a theological tract on purgatory.[32]

The critics who have dismissed Christina's *vita* seem not to have wondered how its gullible author was able, fourteen years later, to write the life of Lutgard of Aywières which has been praised as 'a masterpiece'[33] and 'the summit of mystical biography'[34]. Simone Roisin unconvincingly argued that this change was due to the author's growth in spiritual maturity arising from either his sojourn in Paris and Cologne or 'his association with the Cistercians' (p. 555). She condemned the *VCM* on the grounds of its emphasis on 'external mystical phenomena' (p. 552) and because of its structure which she called 'purely chronological' (p. 555). This paper will try to show that the author of the *VCM* was, far from being the credulous biographer condemned by Roisin, a highly accomplished and subtle hagiographer.

It must not be forgotten that Thomas was a Dominican, trained in the art of preaching, where the *exemplum* was used to show how the entire material universe mirrored the workings of God within society. This *vita matris* is one such *exemplum*[35] and its reliance on 'external action', so criticized by Roisin, is nothing more than the visible manifestation of what she considered to be the achievement of his later works: a concern with 'the virtues and the interior life' (p. 552). The *VCM* shows, in an explicit manner, the mysticism which lies at the foundation of his other works and is a coherent statement of that visionary mode of perception of what M. D. Chenu called 'the sacramental universe'[36]. Northrop Frye, speaking of Blake, described the visionary as one who 'creates, or dwells in, a higher spiritual world in which the objects of perception in this one have become transfigured and charged with a new intensity'. He then quotes a passage from *The Marriage of Heaven and Hell* which could be read as a gloss to the *VCM*:

> I then asked Ezekiel why he eat dung, & lay so long on his right & left side? he answer'd, 'the desire of raising men into a perception of the infinite'[37].

Once the universe is looked at in this visionary manner, it is surely beside the point to question the validity of the *VCM* on the basis of its historicity as did Kurth or to criticize it because of its reliance on 'external phenomena' as did Roisin. Nor need one read it as a precise and literal representation of an historical occurrence as did Nimal. To do so is to misunderstand not only Thomas's spiritual perspective but that of the whole medieval mystical tradition. The seen and the unseen, the material and the supra-material were inseparable during the Middle Ages. The drift of society during this period was towards what Stephen Medcalf has called 'acted symbol', that is, the identification of 'the objects of religion, God and the new life, with something *within* the phenomenal experience'[38] (italics mine). If the *VCM* is read in this context, what Christina did and what Thomas described without comment is simply a concretization of what in other writers was presented as an other-worldly vision. While twentieth-century pragmatists can dismiss most of these visions as hallucinations and accept Dante's vision as a 'literary device', with Christina we are left with the unnerving spectacle of 'a flying saint' who not only believed what she had witnessed in heaven and purgatory, but lived it as well. Through Thomas's narration, we are brought into a stark confrontation with the medieval belief in the absolute reality of the other world which penetrates and envelops this world. If we believe that there is something to be learned from the medieval mystics, we must somehow learn to inhabit their universe, to see the other world not as something alien to us but rather to see it, as did Julian of Norwich, as God's clothing 'that for loue wrappeth us'[39].

Ironically, Roisin fell into the trap of 'literalism' when she objected to the 'purely chronological' structure of the *VCM* and took Thomas's statement in the prologue at its face value:

> First of all we will tell how Christina was raised (*nutrita*), then how she was educated (*educata*), and finally we will describe her actions (*eius gesta*) as we have learned from most reliable and truthful witnesses (*VCM* 650, 3).

Roisin's literal interpretation of this crucial passage is surprising in view of her usual sensitivity towards the spirituality of this period. If, however, one examines the writers, especially the Cistercian writers whom Thomas may have encountered in his travels,[40] one is immediately struck by the similarities between this division of Christina's life and William of Saint Thierry's description of the growth of the soul according to the animal, rational, and spiritual levels.[41] In the *Exposition On The Song of Songs*,[42] William had examined the gifts God gives to the soul in each of these three stages: nourishment in the animal stage (I. 46), education in the rational (I. 43), and freedom in the spiritual (I. 1). In his treatise, *The Nature and Dignity of Love*, William had compared the ascent of the soul towards God to the three stages of human life:

> First of all, let us begin this series of narrations at the origins of love and then develop it, as it were, through its successive stages until we come to a rich old age which is full not of senile sadness but full of rich mercy. For as the various stages of life increase or decrease, so a lad develops into a young man, a young man into a mature man and a mature man into an old man. There are changes in quality, so there are chages in the names of each stage. In the same way, the will according to the development of [its] virtue grows into love, love into charity and charity into wisdom.[43]

In the context of this kind of microcosmic mysticism, it would seem logical to interpret the terms *nutrita, educata,* and *gesta* as 1) the divine nutrition necessary for beginners; 2) the charismatic education given those who are laboring towards perfection; and 3) the deeds worked in and through Christina by God. This interpretation makes more sense than to read Thomas's statement literally. The real narrative of the *vita* begins at Christina's first death. To ignore this first death and the bargain struck between her and God is to ignore the supernatural dynamic which provides the necessary motivation for the entire *vita*.

If one reads the *VCM* according to this progressive structural plan, it falls into three distinct parts, each part divided from the other by a miracle. These miracles not only serve the purpose of marking the divisions of the *vita* but, as external manifestations of grace, they set in motion the action of each part. These miracles are intended to be understood sacramentally or, as Thomas expressed it elsewhere, for the purpose of 'a signifying of grace' (*ad significandam gratiam, VLA* 194, 16).

The first stage of Christina's spiritual development, her nutrition, was marked by a spectacular miracle. Shortly after her resurrection, she fled society because she was unable to endure the smell of humans after her experience of the divine fragrance.[44] Unable, however, to live without physical nourishment, God showed His mercy towards her weakness and frailty:

> Turning her eyes to herself, she saw that, against the laws of nature, her shrivelled breasts began to drip a sweet milk. . . . Receiving the dripping milk as food, she was thus nourished for nine weeks by this milk from her chaste breasts (*VCM* 652, 9).

Sickened by her contact with sinful humanity, Christina had fled it with horror. Although she had willingly accepted her divinely ordained mission of expiation, acceptance of a submission to the very real suffering it entailed came only slowly. An intellectual acceptance of the Divine Will is, as the mystics have pointed out, quite a different matter from the slow and frequently agonizing submission of self to physical and spiritual suffering. In Christina's case, this suffering was caused by a revulsion at the stink of sinful humanity. It was so repellent to her that she would flee into the forests or perch in trees or sit on the tops of high buildings (*VCM* 652, 9; 653, 16). Like the Stylites before her,[45] she wished to effect a complete material separation from the world in order to live a life devoted to contemplation. This, however, was not the reason why she had been sent back to earth. Her vocation was to serve humanity *within* society.

After some time spent in this kind of solitude, Christina found that she was not the pure spirit she had been in heaven and that, despite her immensely spiritualized body (*subtilisimum corpus*), she could not live without food. She therefore prayed to God for help and, *mira res*!, he miraculously provided her with nourishing milk. Elsewhere Thomas refers to 'the milk of the humanity of Christ' (*VLA*, 193, 13), and one is irresistibly reminded of the milk of the Bridegroom's breasts to which William refers, which must be sucked for nourishment in the animal stage. This milk, he says, is

> the milk of all the mysteries (*sacramenta*) accomplished in time for our eternal salvation in order to attain to the food which is the Word of God, God with God. Christ, in his humility, is our milk; God, equal with God, he is our food. Milk nourishes, and food brings about growth (*lac nutrit, cibus pascit*) (*Cant* 1.46).

In this stage, the animal stage, man prays with his will, 'but his understanding is unfruitful' (*Cant*, Praef. 14) and his prayer is impetratory, 'a prayer for something apart from God' (*ibid.*). The thing 'apart from God' for which Christina prayed was material and physical food, the one thing which society could offer that was unavailable in solitude.

Having thus been nourished (*nutrita*) by 'the milk of the humanity of Christ', Christina was now ready to move on to the more solid food that promotes growth (*pascit*). On her return to the town of Saint Trond, she still found proximity to humans intolerable, and continued to find her rest in unlikely spots. Not surprisingly, her predilection for heights was greeted with incomprehension by her family and friends, who thought her mad. They therefore caught and bound her but, as always, she managed to escape. This time, however, instead of fleeing to the 'secret deserts', she ran to Liège, 'hungering for the sacred meat of the sinless Pascal Lamb' (*VCM* 652,10). After some difficulty, she persuaded a priest to give her Communion but, still unable to live comfortably with other humans, she fled society again by crossing the river dry-shod.

This miracle of divinely and inwardly generated food is repeated just before Christina's final rehabilitation into society. Immediately after partaking of the sacramental nourishment provided both by the milk from her own breasts and by the Eucharist, she began to undertake her divinely ordained mission. Those around her, however, still did not appear to understand the reason for her behavior although she suffered her purgatorial pains loudly and dramatically. Even though she was now living in society, she seemed to have little effective communication with it. Human stench remained the barrier to her ministry. When not occupied with throwing herself into hot ovens or standing upright on revolving mill-wheels in icy waters or doing equally anti-social things, she continued to flee the presence of humans by praying on the tree-tops, steeples, or fence palings.

Christina's family were by now at their wits' end and, horrified by her actions, thought that she was demented. Here Christina greatly resembles those Christians who are called 'fools for Christ's sake',[46] *saloì*, by the early chroniclers of egyptian monasticism,[47] and *gelta* by their irish counterparts.[48] Choosing to follow the Lord's commands with complete obedience and disconcerting literalness, they seemed to isolate themselves from the society they wished to serve. In Christina's case, the pain of the purgatorial torments she voluntarily assumed was compounded by the physical and mental abuse she suffered at the hands of her contemporaries who had not paid attention when she had warned them not to be disturbed by her actions 'because they [were] above the understanding of men' (652, 8).

Christina arrived at spiritual understanding only after much mistreatment by her increasingly distraught family. In desperation, her tormentors shackled her to tree where, like Christ at his passion, she willingly suffered both ridicule and physical pain. Having been bound tightly with a wooden yoke, her buttocks began to fester and bleed from the constant rubbing. 'But', says Thomas,

> in order that Christ show in her the remarkable miracle of his strength, He suffered her to be overcome and to endure tribulation for a time. . . . When no one had compassion on her wretchedness, the Lord took wondrous pity on her and wrought in her that great miracle, unheard of in all previous centuries: her virginal breasts began to flow with a liquid of clearest oil. She took that liquid and used it as a flavoring for her bread which she ate as food [*pro pulmento*] and she smeared it on the wounds of her festering limbs as ointmment [*pro unguento*] (*VCM* 654, 19).

This miracle, like the first, effected a change in Christina's relationship with society. Her family

> struggled no more against the miracles of the divine will in Christina. Releasing her from her chains, they knelt down and begged for mercy for their injuries to her and let her go (*VCM* 654, 19).

Christina herself was also taught by means of this miracle. For the first time she showed an awareness of the potential scandal her actions might create and, in fact, did create. Once again she fled into the forests but this time she did so, not to avoid human stench, but

> because she feared that this highest marvel might exceed human understanding and that the carnal minds of men might see in these divine operations an occasion for evil (*VCM* 654, 20).

With her family praying for her restoration to 'the common state of humanity', Christina was stirred by the Spirit and, finding a baptismal font in the church of Wellen, about nine kilometres from Saint Trond, she completely immersed herself in it and, says Thomas,

> when this event occurred, it was said that afterwards the manner of her life was moderated with regard to society and thereafter she acted more quietly and was more able to endure the odor of men and live among them. (*VCM* 654, 21).

This portion of Christina's life can be considered the period in which she received her 'education' and hence can be called, to use William's terminology, the rational stage. Fed by the nourishing milk of Christ and the solid food of the Eucharist which promoted her spiritual growth, she now received 'the unction of the Holy Spirit which teaches the soul concerning all things' (*Cant* 1.43). The oil which flowed from her breasts recalls, as Pinius pointed out (*VCM* 654, F), the oil which dripped from the fingers of Lutgard 'as a sign of spiritual consolation' (*VLA* 194, 16). Having spent some time in prayer and contemplation, Lutgard was filled with such a sweetness of spirit that her fingers began to drip a kind of oil. 'See', she said to Iutta, the recluse with whom she was staying,

> how the Almighty treats me from his superabundant grace. I am so filled with inward grace that it overflows outwardly even to my fingers which are now exuding a kind of oil as an outward manifestation of grace (*ad significandam gratiam*).

This last phrase has overtones of scholastic terminology, which are surprising in this context,[49] but it unmistakably places the miracles in both the *VCM* and VLA in their proper context. Although mammary wonders such as these may offend our contemporary sensibilities, this kind of imagery was common among the Cistercian writers of the twelfth century.[50] Commenting on *The Song of Songs* 1:1–2, for instance, St Bernard had referred to 'the richness of the grace that flows from your breasts' [i.e. the breasts of the Bridegroom] and, he continued,

> if we persevere [in prayer] there comes an unexpected infusion of grace, our breasts expand, as it were, and our interior is filled with overflowing love; and if somebody should press upon it then, this milk of sweet fecundity would gush forth in streaming richness.[51]

The oil which dripped from Christina's breasts could thus be considered a sacramental sign, 'the visible sign of an invisible grace'.[52] What more effective a symbol of this overflowing grace which God effects in the human than by channelling this grace through chaste but fecund breasts? Lutgard's fingers pale by comparison.

By means of this second miracle, Christina was not only gladdened and consoled in spirit, but healed of her wounds as well, and her symbolic Baptism effected her final healing with regard to society. Now, finally, she ministered to society in the way in which God had intended. This is not to say that she became less of a 'holy fool', for her behavior continued to be as peculiar as ever, but it was now accepted for what it was: the manifestation of God's will within, and for the benefit, of society.

Having been taught by 'the oil of gladness and the unction of the Holy Spirit' (*Cant* 7.86), Christina was ready to use 'her liberty for permissible things and she [was granted the grace] to find pleasure in suffering torments for the sins of men' (*VCM* 654, 20). This freedom, says William, 'accompanies illuminating grace [which] comes when we are no longer under a tutor',[53] because' "where the spirit of the Lord is, there is liberty" ' (2 Co 3:17). Before the miracle of the dripping oil, Christina's freedom had been limited by her 'animal' understanding. Once she received the gift of illuminating grace, however, her liberated spirit found its pleasure in a vicarious suffering for sinners. It was only because of the freedom which comes from the Holy Spirit that Christina's joy in her vocation was not tinged with the slightest suspicion of masochism.

The final stage of Christina's journey godwards occurred after a period of active ministry to society and was marked by a miracle of the more traditional kind, although still in keeping with her flair for the dramatic. Once while praying, she was rapt in ecstasy and her body rolled round and round like a hoop:

> Then a wondrous harmony sounded between her throat and breast which no mortal person could understand nor could it be imitated by any artificial device.... This voice or spiritual breath did not come out of her mouth or nose, but the angelic voice sounded only from between her breast and her throat (*VCM* 656, 35).

When Christina was 'restored to her former self', she 'rose up like one drunk and, indeed, she was drunk', says Thomas (656, 36). When told of what had happened to her, 'she fled . . . and thought herself a fool'. Thomas elaborates on precisely the same theme in the *VLA*. On returning to Iutta's *reclusorium* after the miracle of the fingers, Lutgard acted

> as if she were drunk and, indeed, she was drunk. This was not surprising for she had been led into the wine-room by the Divine Bridegroom and there spent her time in dalliance with the Lord. Afterwards, like one beloved [*ut cara*], she ate the bread of penance with toil; then, like one more beloved [*ut carior*], she drank the fulness of his grace; and, finally, like one most beloved [*sicut carissima*], she became drunk and was filled with exceeding and ineffable joy and with a spirit of folly [*desipientium spiritu*] (*VLA* 194, 16).

Just so was Christina's folly. In the first stage of her 'folly for Christ's sake', that is to say, in the animal stage, she had been nourished with the food of Christ's Body and did penance *ut cara*. In the second stage, the rational, she was taught, *ut carior*, by the unction of the Holy Spirit which dripped from her breasts. In the third stage, the spiritual, her body was entirely taken over by God and, *sicut carissima*, in her worship her song was united with the music of the spheres, that expression of the identification of the sacramental universe with its Creator. Thus did Christina's material and spiritual life mirror the eternal cosmic order which obeys those 'laws of equality, unity and order' found in music.[54]

It must be remarked that even after Christina reached the final, unitive stage of mystical contemplation, her relationship with society continued to be uneasy, not surprisingly in view of her other-worldy experience. Despite this unease, however, she had come to a full realization of her social apostolate and her actions now manifested the divine mercy as shown through the sacrament of penance. While she never forsook her divinely ordained ministry of teaching sinners the lesson of divine justice, towards the end of her life there was less emphasis on the negative aspects of this justice. The climax of this stage of Christina's apostolate occurred when she heard the death-bed confession of Louis, count of Looz, which Thomas is at pains to point out, she did 'not for absolution, which she had no power to give, but rather that she be moved to pray for him by his repentance' (656, 48). This act of compassion shows how far she had progressed in spiritual perfection since the time when she had first simply manifested the purgatorial pains without comment or explanation.

In these last years of her life a new dimension was added to Christina's witness of divine justice. She now suffered *with* society, while still remaining aloof from it. Her act of expiation for the sins of Count Louis marked the final chapter of her life on earth. Dwelling more and more in solitude, she re-entered society only to save souls or to partake of food. Characteristically, Thomas does not tell us which kind of food was required for her increasingly spiritualized body. She was now so taken up with the Spirit, that

> she passed above the ground like a spirit and people could scarcely tell whether it was a spirit or a material body that had passed by because she barely seemed to touch the ground. And indeed, in the last year of her life, the Spirit possessed almost all her material body to such a degree that mortal minds or eyes could hardly look at her shadow without fear and trembling (*VCM* 658, 46).

Having now presumably reached the highest peak of spiritual perfection attainable by humans, Christina died. But even now her earthly purgatory was not over and, not content to leave her in peace, society reached beyond the grave to make one further demand upon her. For a moment, Christina's apparent imperviousness to suffering cracked and, at the very end of her life, we are shown a human Christina for the first time, impatient and a little cranky. After she had received the sacraments of the Eucharist and Extreme Unction, Beatrice, one of the nuns of St Catherine's where Christina had been living, begged her to 'make known certain things before she died' (659, 51). Too preoccupied with God to listen, Christina died without answering this request. Beside herself with frustration, Beatrice

> fell on the dead body and, shouting at the top of her lungs, vehemently asked the dead woman why she had gone to the Lord without her permission. Placing her mouth over the mouth of the dead woman, she cried: 'O Christina, you were ever obedient to me in life. I adjure you now and demand, through the Lord Jesus Christ Whom you loved in this life with an ardent desire, that you obey me. Because you are powerful[55] and can do what you want, [I demand] that you return to life and tell me what I have asked' (*VCM* 659, 52).

Mira res! Christina once again came back from the dead but this time, understandably irritated, she

> heaved a great sigh and, with a distressed look on her face, chided her who had called her back: 'O Beatrice! Why did you call me back when I, just now, was being led before the face of Christ? Ask me quickly what you want and then I beseech you to allow me to return to him whom I have desired for so long' (*VCM* 659, 53).

Giving in to the importunate Beatrice, Christina accepted the fact that she had yet again to postpone that final union with God which she had so profoundly desired for the twenty-four years she had lived on earth since her first resurrection. She therefore granted Beatrice's request and, at last, died for good.

Funny and touching as this story is, it does underline the main theme of the *VCM*. Christina's material presence in the world was a sacramental witness to society. By emphasizing the miracles which God effected through her person—the external mystical phenomena to which Roisin took exception—Thomas shows how God's love is manifested for the benefit of humanity. Through the sacraments and through the charismatic gifts God gives those who follow His path, her inward spirit learned to live in peace with the outward world of matter. Her material and spiritual being found its humanity by serving humanity with compassion. No longer superhuman in her sanctity, in her final moments Christina becomes one of us in her weakness and impatience. Surely it is no accident that this is the first time that Thomas has shown Christina succumbing to the temptations of human frailty for an instant and then recovering herself to continue her ministry of active love.

If the *VCM* were an ordinary narrative dealing chronologically with external phenomena, this would be the end of the story. As must be clear by now, however, Thomas's *vita* is not a simple narrative and Christina's death does not mark the end of the story.[56] Seven years after her burial, says Thomas, the Benedictines moved the monastery of St Catherine's from Saint Trond to Nonnemielen and opened Christina's tomb. Then, in the presence of all the citizens and the monks and nuns of the convent,

> a grace of such sweetness seized everyone individually and collectively that they all cried out together with one mind and one voice: 'Christina, you were marvellous (*mirabilem*) in life and, now after death, you are no less glorious!', for no one doubted the grace of healing which had been effected in them who had come to the tomb with faith (*VCM* 659, 54).

Thus did Christina's body perform its most miraculous feat. By means of it, *all* parts of society were united in peace and reconciliation. With this manifestation of God's healing power, Thomas's description of Christina's life and the deeds (*gesta*) worked through her by God comes to an end. In this final scene we are shown how, even after death, God continued to use her material body as a sacramental witness of his power. As God's instrument, Christina manifested this power through her body in death as well as in life.

In this way, Christina's three deaths parallel the three stages of the ascent of the soul towards God. The first death and resurrection had opened the scene for the manifestation of divine justice by revealing the punishments and rewards meted out by God. This lesson is appropriate for those who are beginners and still in the animal stage. Her second death and resurrection had shown her compassion which mirrored the divine mercy. This sense of solidarity with humanity is in harmony with the gift of spiritual consolation which characterizes the rational stage. The third death shows how the divine power continues to work within society through the agency of a lifeless material body and is in accord with the liberation of spirit which is the mark of the spiritual stage.

This structure is surely not simply chronological but, rather, dynamic and progressive. By means of it, Thomas has taught a profound lesson. As mortals, human beings must operate within the material world and use it to achieve the union with God which their souls so greatly desire. The message which Christina was sent to bring back to earth was not simply that God punishes sinners. Her torments were signs to society of the divine justice; her non-canonical use of the sacrament of penance showed the workings of the divine mercy; and her relics were the means whereby the divine power is shown to work within the material universe. That Thomas intended this life to be read as an *exemplum* is brought out clearly in his epilogue:

> Thus is the necessary argument finished for those who are sleeping, who forget the day and the hour and who do not wish to keep vigil with a lamp filled with the oil of good works and the worthy fruits of penance. . . . By the example of her life, by her many exhortations, tears, lamentations, and boundless cries, she taught more than anyone we have known before or since who, by writing or preaching, has told of the praise and glory of Christ Who, with the Father and the Spirit, lives and reigns for ever and ever, Amen (*VCM* 659, 56).

It is clear, therefore, that Christina was, herself, a living sermon. The lesson she taught through 'external mystical phenomena' and which Thomas taught through his remarkably subtle *vita* is that the greatness and glory of God can best be shown to human beings by example, by an *imitatio Christi*, for it is through the material universe that God works for the salvation of humanity.

St. Thomas More College
Saskatoon, Saskatchewan

END NOTES

*Thanks for the incentive to complete this paper are first due to the generous and sympathetic support given me by Valerie Lagorio, without whom it surely would have withered on the vine. I would also like to thank Donald Ward and Colleen Fitzgerald, my godson and goddaugher-in-law, whose warmth ever sustains me, and Rev. Dan Callam, CSB who has firmly but kindly curbed my occasional excesses. Above all and as ever, I thank Sarah, Bernard, and David for ensuring that I put first things first and who bless my life with their love.

1. First-rate studies have been published on this movement. See especially Ernest W. McDonnell, *The Beguines and Beghards in Medieval Culture* (1954; rpt. New York: Octagon Books, 1969); Alcantara Mens, *Oorsprong en Betekenis van de Nederlandse Begijnen- en Begardenbewegung* (Leuven: Universitetsbibliothek, 1947) and his *L'Ombrie Italienne et l'Ombrie Brabançonne: Deux Courants Religieux Parallèles d'Inspiration Commune* (Paris: Études Franciscaines, 1968); Simone Roisin, *L'Hagiographie Cistercienne dans la Diocèse de Liège au XIIIe Siècle (Louvain: Bibliothèque de l'Université, 1947) and 'L'Efflorescence Cistercienne et le Courant Féminin de Piété au XIIIe Siècle', RHE* 39 (1943) 342–78; Herbert Grundmann, *Religiöse Bewegung im Mittelalter* (Berlin: Emil Ebering, 1935); Brenda Bolton, '*Vitae Matrum*: A Further Aspect of the *Frauenfrage*' in Derek Baker, ed., *Medieval Women* (Oxford: Blackwell, 1978) 253–73, '*Mulieres Sanctae*' in Derek Baker, ed., *Sanctity and Secularity* (Oxford: Blackwell, 1973) 77–95, and 'Some Thirteenth Century Women in the Low Countries: A Special Case', *Nederlands Archief voor Kerkgeschiedenis* 61 (1981) 7–29; John B. Freed, 'Urban Development and the "Cura Monialium" in Thirteenth Century Germany', *Viator* 3 (1972) 311–27; and Dennis Devlin, 'Feminine Lay Piety in the High Middle Ages: The Beguines' in Lillian Thomas Shank and John A. Nichols, edd., *Distant Echoes, Medieval Religious Women*, 1 (Kalamazoo: Cistercian Publications, 1984) 183–96. A fine recent study which, however, does not deal with the Lowlands, is that by Jean-Claude Schmitt, *Mort d'une Hérésie: L'Église et les Clercs face aux Béguines et aux Béghards du Rhin Supérieur du XIVe XVe Siècle* (Paris: Mouton, 1978). There is a vast bibliography on this subject; see McDonnell, pp. 575–612.

2. For instance between 1275 and 1350 about one hundred and sixty-nine houses of Beguines were founded in Cologne (Freed, 'Urban Development', 312–14), and Jacques de Vitry commented on the 'great crowds of holy women in the lily gardens of the Lord [who were found] in diverse places' (*Vita Maria Oigniacensis*, ed. D. Papebroeck in *Acta Sanctorum [AA SS]* (23 June) Junius 5 (1867) 547). Thomas of Cantimpré set the number of Beguines in Nivelles in the mid-thirteenth century at 2,000 (*Bonum Universale de Apibus* 2, 54, 10, cited by McDonnell, p. 64), and Matthew Paris wrote that '2,000 have been reported in Cologne and the neighboring cities' (*Chronica Major* 4. 278, cited by R. W. Southern, *Western Society and the Church in the Middle Ages* (1970; rpt. Harmondsworth: Penguin, 1979) 319.

3. According to Southern, by 1400 in Cologne all beguines lived in convents (*Western Society* p. 35).

4. I use these terms carefully, following the lead of Dr Ann Warren ('The Nun as Anchoress: England 100–1500' in *Distant Voices*, 197–212, especially 198–201). Unlike the solitary, the recluse was, in these late centuries, almost invariably enclosed by the bishop by means of a liturgical ceremony and, to this degree, could be considered to have been officially recognized by the hierarchy. The solitary, on the other hand, whom Dr Warren has called a 'hermitess', lived a religious life without the official sanction of the Church. See the basic work of Dom Louis Gougaud, *Ermites et Reclus* (Ligugé: Abbaye Saint Martin, 1928); Rotha Mary Clay, *The Hermits and Anchorites of England* (London: Methuen, 1914); and Dr Warren's Anchorites and Their Patrons in Medieval England (Berkeley: University of California Press, 1985.) See also *L'Eremitismo in Occidente nei Secoli XI e XII: Atti della Seconda Settimana Internazionale di Studio Mendola . . . 1962* (Milan: Società Editrice Vita e Pensiero, 1965). See also the many fine studies by Jean Leclercq, notably his *Saint Pierre Damien: Ermite et Homme d'Église* (Rome: Edizione di Storia e Letteratura, 1960); and Peter F. Anson, *The Call of the Desert: The Solitary Life in the Christian Tradition*, 2nd ed. (London: SPCK, 1973).

5. 'He loved France [for which read, according to the Bollandist Suysken (*AA SS* Oct. 2: 835: *Analecta de S. Francisco* part. I, n. 104), *Galliam-Belgicam*] as a friend of the Body of the Lord, and he longed to die there because of its reverence for sacred things' (Thomas of Celano, *Second Life of St Francis* 201, translated by Placid Hermann in *St. Francis: Writings and Early Biographies: English Omnibus of Sources*, ed. Marion A. Habig, 3rd ed. (Chicago: Franciscan Herald Press, 1973) 523. See also Thomas of Celano's *First Life* 74 (*ibid*, p. 291) and *Speculum Perfectionis* 65, ed. Paul Sabatier (Paris: Librarie Fischbacher, 1898) 118–19; translated by Leo Sherley-Price in Habig, p. 1191: 'And at once he said to them with joy, "In the Name of our Lord Jesus Christ, of the glorious Virgin His Mother, and of all the Saints, I choose the Province of France, for it is a Catholic nation, and they show an especial reverence to the Body of Christ above other Catholics. This is a great joy to me, and because of this I will most gladly live among them."'

6. See André Callebaut, 'Autour de la Recontre à Florence de S. François et du Cardinal Hugolin (en été 1217)', *Archivum Franciscanum Historicum* 19 (1926) 530–58; and Mens, *L'Ombrie Italienne et l'Ombrie Brabançonne*, 44–46.

7. *Vitae Mariae Oigniacensis*, ed. D. Papebroeck, *AA SS* (23 June) Iunius 5 (1867) 542–72; *BHL* 5516, hereafter cited as *VMO* in text, followed by page and paragraph number. See also his *Historia Occidentalis*, ed. John Frederick Hinnebusch (Fribourg: University Press, 1972); *Lettres*, ed R. B. C. Huygens (Leiden: Brill, 1960); and *The Exempla . . . of Jacques de Vitry*, ed. Thomas Frederick Crane (1890; rpt Nedeln, Liechtenstein: Kraus, 1967).

8. Thomas of Cantimpré (1201–1270/2) transferred to the Dominicans about 1230 and studied in Cologne under Albertus Magnus c. 1232–1238, and in Paris 1238–1239/40. His best known works are the *De natura rerum*, edited by H. Boese (Berlin-New York: Walter de Gruyter, 1973) and the *Bonum universale de apibus* edited by Georgius Colvenerius (Douai: B. Belleri, 1627), hereafter cited as *BUA*. For a discussion of Thomas's view of the society in which he lived, see Robert God-

ding, 'Vie Apostolique et Société Urbaine à l'Aube du XIIIe Siècle', *Nouvelle Revue Théologique* 104 (1982) 392–721.

9. *Vita Christinae Mirabilis*, ed. J. Pinius in *AA SS* (24 July) Iulius 5 (1868) 637–60; *BHL* 1746, hereafter cited as *VCM*, followed by page and paragraph number; translated by Margot H. King, Matrologia Latina Translation Series, 5 loosely and, on occasion, inaccurately translated by H. Nimal *Vies de Quelques-Unes de Nos Grandes Siècles au Pays de Liège* (Liège: H. Dessain, 1897) 100–43 and translated from the Flemish of Fr Henckens by A. Giron, *Sainte Christine l'Admirable de Saint-Trond, Vierge* (Bruxelles: Victor Devaux, 1866); (Saskatoon: Peregrina, 1986); in the second half of the thirteenth century this *vita* and that of Lutgard was translated into Middle Dutch verse by Brother Geraert, a Franciscan, at the request of Maria van Hoye, cellarer at the Benedictine abbey of Nonnemielen at Saint Trond: *Leven van Sinte Christina de Wonderbare, in Oud-Dietsche Rijmen, Naer een Perkementen Handschrift uit de XIVde of XVde Eeuw*, edited by J. H. Bormans (Gent, 1850). Another translation into Middle Dutch prose is extant: see J. Deschamps 'Een Middelnederlandse Prozavertaling van de "Vita Sanctae Christinae Mirabilis" van Thomas van Cantimpré', *Jaarboek van de Federatio der Geschied- en Oudheidkundige Kringen in Limburg* 30 (1975) 69–103.

10. *Vita Margarete de Ypris*, ed. G. Meerseman in 'Les Frères Prêcheurs et le Mouvement Dévot en Flandres au XIIIe Siècle', *Archivum Fratrum Praedicatorum* 18 (1948) 106–30; *BHL* 5319.

11. *Vita Lutgardis Virgine . . . Aquiriae in Brabantia*, ed. G. Henschenius, in *AA SS* (June 16) Iunius 4 (1867) 189–210; *BHL* 5319, hereafter cited as *VLA*, followed by page and paragraph number. Brother Geraert's translation into Middle Dutch verse has been edited by J. H. Bormans: 'Het Leven van Sinte Lugardis: een Dietsch Gedicht, ten Laetste van de Tweede Helft der XIVde Eeuw, Naar het Oorsponkelijk Handschrift van Broeder Geraert' (Amsterdam, 1857), and *De Dietsche Warande* 3 (1857) 37–67, 132–65, and 285–322, 4 (1858) 155–70. See also Guido Hendrix 'Primitive Versions of Thomas of Cantimpré's *Vita Lutgardis' Cîteaux* 29 (1978) 153–206. For the general background of this saint, see Simone Roisin, 'Sainte Lutgarde d'Aywières dans Son Ordre et dans Son Temps', *Collectanea O.C.R.* 8 (1946) 161–72; and Thomas Merton, *What Are These Wounds? The Life of a Cistercian Mystic: Saint Lutgard of Aywières* (1948; rpt. Milwaukee: Bruce, 1950).

12. *Vita Mariae Oigniacensis, Supplementum*, ed. Arnold Rayssius, *AA SS* (23 June) Iunius 5 (1867) 572–81; *BHL* 5517.

13. *VMO* Prologus 8: 'Vidi etiam aliam, circa quam tam mirabiliter operatus est Dominus, quod cum diu mortua jacuisset, antequam in terra corpus ejus sepeliretur, anima ad corpus revertente revixit; et a Domino obtinuit, ut in hoc seculo vivens in corpore, purgatorium sustineret. Unde longo tempore ita mirabiliter a Domino afflicta est, ut quandoque se volutaret in ignem, et quandoque in hieme in aqua glaciali diu moraretur, quandoque etiam sepulcra mortuorum intrare cogeretur. Tandem in tanta post peractam poenitentiam vixit in pace, et tantam a Domino gratiam promeruit, et multoties rapta in spiritu, animas defunctorum usque in purgatorium, vel per purgatorium sine aliqua laesione usque ad suprema regna conduceret.'

14. Christina was not a Benedictine although she lived with the benedictine nuns of Saint Catherine's in Saint Trond at different periods of her life. On her deathbed she was reminded of the obedience she had previously given Beatrice, one of the nuns present. Clearly, however, this was not a formal vow of obedience. In his emphasis on the living sermon (*exempla*) Christina displayed to society, Thomas showed himself as the Dominican he was. The mystical thrust of the *VCM* seems to partake of the cistercian spirit and the only glimmer of sectarianism that I have found in these *vitae* occurs in the *VLA* where, Merton notwithstanding, Thomas makes Lutgard the great patronness of the Dominicans, not the Cistercians of which Order she was a member.

15. Simone Roisin, 'La Méthode Hagiographique de Thomas de Cantimpré', in *Miscellanea Historica in Honorem Alberti de Meyer* I (Louvain: Bibliothèque de l'Université, 1946) 546–57.

16. Herbert Thurston, 'Christine of Saint Trond' in *Surprising Mystics* (London: Burns & Oates, 1955) 149.

17. Bolton, '*Vitae Matrum*', 257.

18. Thurston, 'Christine of Saint Trond', 180.

19. The basic study of this tradition is that by Howard Rollin Patch, *The Other World* (1950; rpt. New York: Octagon Books, 1970) and a still useful work is that by Ernest J. Becker, *A Contribution to the Comparative Study of the Medieval Visions of Heaven and Hell, With Special Reference to the Middle English Versions* (Baltimore: John Murphy, 1899). See also the recent study by Jacques Le Goff, *The Birth of Purgatory*, translated by Arthur Goldhammer (Chicago: University of Chicago Press, 1984). For the Irish, see St. John Seymour, *Irish Visions of the Other-World* (London: SPCK, 1930) and C. S. Boswell, *An Irish Precursor of Dante: A Study on the Vision of Heaven and Hell Ascribed to the Eighth Century Irish Saint Adamnan* (London: David Nutt, 1908).

20. *Apocalypse of Paul*, trans. H. Duensing in E. Hennecke *New Testament Apocrypha*, ed. W. Schneemelcher (London: SCM Press, 1965) pp. 759–98. See also Theodore Silverstein, *Visio Sancti Pauli: The History of the Apocalypse in Latin* (London: Christophers, 1935).

21. *Étude sur la Purgatoire de Saint Patrice*, ed. Cornelis Mattheus van der Zanden (Amsterdam, 1927). See also Philippe de Felice, *L'Autre Monde; Mythes et Légendes: Le Purgatoire de Saint Patrice* (Paris: Honoré Champion, 1906); translated by Jean Marchand in *L'Autre Monde au Moyen Age: Voyages et Visions* (Paris: E. de Boccard, 1940) pp. 81–115.

22. [Visio Albericis], ed. Francesco Cancellieri in *Osservatione Promosse . . . Supra l'Originalità della Divina Commedia* (Rome: Presso F. Bourlie, 1814) pp. 132–207; trans. Jean Marchand in *L'Autre Monde*, pp. 119–183.

23. *Analecta Bollandiana* 19 (1900) 58, 365–66.

24. H. Nimal, 'La Vie de Sainte Christine l'Admirable; Est-Elle Authentique?' *Revue des Questions Historiques* 132 (1899).

25. *Archives Belges* 1, no. 8, 25 octobre 1899.

26. *Réplique a M. Kurth et aux Analecta Bollandiana au Sujet de: La Vie de Sainte Christine l'Admirable, Est-Elle Authentique? Extrait de la Revue des Questions Historiques; suivi de, Un Mot de Réponse au Archives Belges* (Liège: Dessain, 1900).

27. Louis Massignon, 'L'Apostolat de la Souffrance et de la Compassion Reparatrice au XIIIe Siècle' in *La Cité Chrétienne* no. 101, 5e année (5 janvier 1931) 188–95, and reprinted in *Christina de Wonderbare: Gedenkboek 1150–1950: Studien en Essais* onder Leidung van P. Clerinx (Louvain: Bibliotheca Alfonsiana, 1959) 40–57.

28. 'Þe Lyfe of Seinte Christin le Meruelous', ed. C. Horstmann in 'Prosalegende: die Legenden des Ms. Douce 14', *Anglia* 8 (1885) 102–196.

29. Denis the Carthusian, *Liber de Quatuor Novissimis*, art. 50; *Dialogus de Judicio Particulari Animarum Post Mortem*, art. 33, 10; quoted by Pinius *VCM* 638, 8.

30. Robert Bellarmine, *De Gemitu Columbae* 2, 9 in *Opera Omnia* 6 (Naples: Joseph Guiliano, 1862) 369.

31. J Görres, *Le Mystique Divine, Naturelle et Diabolique* (Paris: Poussielgue-Rusand, 1861–62) 1, 347; 2, 184, 340, 348; 3, 520.

32. F. X. Shouppe, *Purgatory Illustrated by the Lives and Legends of the Saints* (1893; rpt. Rockford, Ill.: Tan Books, 1973) 34–37.

33. Merton, *What Are These Wounds?*, p. ix.

34. Roisin, 'La Méthode Hagiographique', . p. 554.

35. Thomas calls his life of Christina an *exemplum* (*VCM* 659, 56) and quotes Christina as saying to her sisters that the torment she is about to endure is an *exemplum* (*ibid.*). See Claud Bremond, Jacques Le Goff and Jean Claude Schmitt, *L'Exemplum* (Turnhout: Brepols, 1982) 40: 'It must be emphasized that the medieval *exemplum* never refers to a person but to an account, a tale, which, in its entirety, is to be taken as . . . an instrument of teaching and/or learning.'

36. M.-D.Chenu, 'Nature and Man—The Renaissance of the Twelfth Century', *Nature, Man and Society in the Twelfth Century* (Chicago: University of Chicago Press, 1968) 35.

37. Northrop Frye, *Fearful Symmetry: A Study of William Blake* (1969; rpt. Princeton University Press, 1972) 8, 13.

38. Stephen Medcalf, 'Medieval Psychology and Medieval Mystics', in Marion Glasscoe ed. *The Medieval Mystical Tradition in England: Papers Read at the Exeter Symposium July 1980*, (Exeter: University of Exeter, 1980) 128–29.

39. *A Book of Showings to the Anchoress Julian of Norwich*, The Long Text, ch. 5, 1. 5, edd. Edmund Colledge and James Walsh (Toronto: Pontifical Institute of Mediaeval Studies, 1978) 2:299.

40. I have not, thus far, found any direct proof that Thomas borrowed specifically from William of St Thierry. Nevertheless it is clear that, although a Dominican, Thomas was steeped in the cistercian thought and spirituality which was all-pervasive at the time. The parallels are so startling, however, that one is tempted to postulate a direct influence.

41. See especially Louis M. Savary, *Psychological Themes in The Golden Epistle of William of Saint Thierry* (Salzburg: Analecta Cartusiana, 1973) and E. Rozanne Elder, 'The Way of Ascent: The Meaning of Love in the Thought of William of St. Thierry', in John R. Sommerfeldt, ed. *Studies in Medieval Culture* (Kalamazoo: Western Michigan University, 1964) 39–47.

42. William of St Thierry, *Expositio super Cantica Canticorum*, ed. J. M. Déchanet, trans. M. Dumontier, Sources Chrétiennes, 82 (Paris: Cerf, 1962); trans. Mother Columba Hart, *Exposition on the Song of Songs*, Cistercian Fathers Series, 6 (Spencer, Mass.; Cistercian Publications & Shannon, Ireland: Irish University Press, 1965). Hereafter cited as *Cant*.

43. *De natura et dignitate amoris* 4, ed. and trans. M. M. Davy in *Deux Traités de l'Amour de Dieu* (Paris: Vrin, 1953) 74–75; trans. Thomas X. Davis, *The Nature and Dignity of Love* 3, Cistercian Fathers Series, 30 (Kalamazoo: Cistercian Publications, 1981) 53.

44. In the writings of the mystics, the sweet smell of God is frequently used to describe and emphasize the experiential *unio*. On the other hand, a foul stench was one of the characteristics of the devil, hell, and purgatory. See Wolfgang Riehl, *The Middle English Mystics* (London: Routledge & Kegan Paul, 1981), p. 116; and Becker, *A Comparative Study*, p. 61.

45. Curiously, Christina shows many "stylitic" characteristics and has marked affinities with that branch of the stylites called dendrites, that is, those people who preferred the unstable environment of trees to the relative security of pillars. Nora Chadwick in *The Age of the Saints in the Early Celtic Church* (London: Oxford University Press, 1963), p. 109–11, drew a tantalizing analogy between the *gelta* ("wild men") "of the Irish Christian Church [see below, no. 48] . . . and the recluses of the Syrian desert, referred to by Greek writers as *boskoí* 'Grazers' and *dendrîtai* 'Tree Dwellers.'" See especially Hippolyte Delehaye, *Les Saints Stylites*, Subsidia Hagiographica, 14 (1923; rpt. Brussels: Société des Bollandistes, 1962); and H. Leclercq, "Dendrites," *DACL* (Paris, 1920) 582–83. There is an extraordinary reference to a community of women stylites living in Syria around Gethsemani and described by the monk Epiphanus in the ninth century. In one of the two extant MSS, the number of these communal stylites was set at 100(!). See H. Delehaye, "Les Femmes Stylites," *Analecta Bollandiana* 27 (1908), 391–92. If, indeed, there is a connection between Christina and these Eastern dendrites, this influence could only have come to the Low Countries via Ireland and the Irish missionaries. See I. Sneiders, "L'Influence de l'Hagiographie Irlandais sur les Vitae des Saints Irlandais en Belgique," *RHE* 24 (1928) 586–627; 828–67.

46. See the fine book by John Saward, *Perfect Fools: Folly for Christ's Sake in Catholic and Orthodox Spirituality* (Oxford: Oxford University Press, 1980).

47. Palladius, for instance, described one such apparently mad woman (*salè*), a nun, whose sanctity was recognized by the anchorite Piteroum only after many years of vilification by her community (*The Lausiac History* 34, ed. Cuthbert Butler [Cambridge: Cambridge University Press, 1898–1904] 99.

48. The most famous of these Irish 'wild men' was Buile Suibhne who has reappeared in modern guise and with an anglicized name in the Sweeney poems by T. S. Eliot. The original can be found in *Buile Suibhne; (The Frenzy of Suibhne) being, The Adventures of Suibhne Geilt: A Middle Irish Romance*, ed. and trans. J. G. O'Keeffe (London: Published for the Irish Text Society by David Nutt, 1913).

Christina shares many of the characteristics exhibited by the Irish *gelta* and listed by O Riain in an article entitled 'A Study of the Irish Legend of the Wild Men', *Eigse* 14 (1971–1972), 182 ff.: '(B) THE STATE OF MADNESS: The madman (i) takes to the wilderness; (ii) perches on trees; (iii) collects firewood; (iv) is naked, hairy, covered with feathers, or clothed with rags; (v) leaps, and/or levitates; (vi) is very swift; (vii) is restless and travels great distances; (viii) experiences hallucinations; (ix) has a special diet' (quoted by Saward, *Perfect Fools*, p. 41). Christina's pattern of behavior is identical to this description except for (iii) and, depending on one's point of view, (viii).

49. According to Thomas himself, the *VCM* was written about 1232: 'I wrote these things not more than eight years after [Christina's] death', which occurred in 1224 (*VCM* 650, 2). It was only after he had composed this life that he left to pursue his studies in Cologne and Paris. In the *BUA* he tells us that he had studied under Albertus Magnus (2, 57, 50; p. 576), and the work contains anecdotes of many of the first-generation Dominicans, including Thomas Aquinas. Despite these encounters, however, there is little evidence of scholastic thought in Thomas's *vitae*, although occasionally, as here, faint echoes of its distinctive phraseology can be heard.

50. See Caroline Walker Bynum, *Jesus as Mother: Studies in the Spirituality of the High Middle Ages* (Berkeley: University of California Press, 1982), and especially Chapter IV, 'Jesus as Mother and Abbot as Mother: Some Themes in Twelfth-Century Cistercian Writing'.

51. Bernard of Clairvaux, *On the Song of Songs I: Sermons*, 9, 6 trans. Kilian Walsh, Cistercian Fathers Series, 4 (Kalamazoo: Cistercian Publications, 1981) 57–58.

52. One of the most popular definitions of the term *sacramentum*, this formula was attributed to Augustine by Berengar, according to Jaroslav Pelikan *The Growth of Medieval Theology* (600–1300), The Christian Tradition, 3 (Chicago: University of Chicago Press, 1978) 207–208.

53. William of St Thierry, *Speculum fidei* 18, ed. and trans. M. M. Davy in *Deux Traités sur la Foi* (Paris: Vrin, 1959) 40–41; trans. Thomas X. Davis, *The Mirror of Faith* 9, Cistercian Fathers Series, 15 (Kalamazoo: Cistercian Publications, 1979) 25.

54. As God unites all things in the universe, so too does number, the basis of music (Augustine, *De musica* 6. 16. 53). Thus should human action reflect the cosmic order of 'the poem of the universe' which obeys 'the laws of equality, unity, and order' (*ibid.* 6. 2. 29). See Kathi Meyer-Baer, *Music of the Spheres and the Dance of Death: Studies in Musical Iconology* (Princeton: Princeton University Press, 1970); and 'Psychologic and Ontologic Ideas in Augustine's *De musica*,' *Journal of Aesthetics & Art Criticism* 11 (1953) 224–30.

55. See the fine article of Elizabeth Petroff on the power which emanated from these medieval women mystics and which so impressed those around them: 'Medieval Women Visionaries: Seven Stages to Power' *Frontiers* 3 (1978) 34–45 and, for a more feminist interpretation, the introduction to her translations of the *vitae* of four thirteenth century italian holy women: *Consolation of the Blessed* (New York: Alta Gaia Society, 1979).

56. Thomas's *vita* ends at Ch. 56 in Pinius's edition, but two more paragraphs were appended at the end by an unknown hand. This further account tells of the appearance of an aged woman, clothed in white, at the monastery in about 1249. She had been sent, she said, 'by divine revelation to tell you that the body of that holiest of women, Christina, is left unattended and that you should exhume it. If you do this', she continued, 'this monastery will receive the grace of her merits, prayers and glory. If you neglect this task, you will incur the displeasure of the divine will' (*VCM* 660, 57). Saying this, the woman disappeared. The monastery did as it was commanded and immediately after the exhumation, a paralytic woman was cured. Given

Christina's pattern of behavior throughout the entire *vita*, this woman was probably Christina herself who, as Thomas had said, dressed in white: 'her clothing consisted of a white tunic and a white scapular which covered her whole body to her feet and was often sewn up with no other thread than the inner bark of a linden tree or with willow twigs or little wooden spikes' (*655, 25*). Although this later ending seems to follow logically upon Christina's inability to remain dead, it does not compare with the artistry of Thomas's original ending.

Clare of Assisi

When people hear the expression 'contemplative nun' nowadays they immediately conjure up a picture of St Clare of Assisi, the charming companion of St Francis in his chivalric service of Lady Poverty. The popular imagination finds rich material in the external features of the early life of this spiritual daugher of the little Poor Man. In this volume, three of Clare's spiritual daughters give us a more profound study of several different elements in Clare's role as a contemplative follower of the poor Christ and as a spiritual mother.

The *kenosis* of Christ and the vision of his cross in all its reality have always provided pivotal points in franciscan spirituality. Sr Madge Karecki explores the *depth* of Clare's contemplation, rooting it firmly in a poverty based on love for and a desire to imitate the poor Christ. Sr Fidelis Hart shows us the *heights* of joy and love which filled Clare's heart as she followed Christ on his upward way to calvary, a way which she encouraged all of her sisters to follow, singing as they climbed. In Sr Frances Ann Thom's study we see Clare reaching out with all the *breadth* of her wide ability as a leader and spiritual mother to encourage and guide her sisters in following Christ, and protecting and building up his Church.

Together, these three studies form a triptych of a fascinating woman who continues to exert a powerful influence on monastic and contemplative life today—a woman as attractive as the young girl who ran away from home to embrace the poor Christ, singing her own Canticle to the Sun, and becoming a 'new captain of womankind'.

Clare: Poverty and Contemplation in her Life and Writings

Madge Karecki

CLARE OF ASSISI (Chiara de Favorone)[1] has been called the most faithful follower of St Francis. She gained this reputation because of her fidelity to the way of life he outlined for her in the *formula vitae* which he gave her at the beginning of her life at San Damiano. Though it seems that this document was no more than a few paragraphs long, it contained directives about the two basic concerns of Clare's entire life—poverty and prayer. Within her life there was a direct relationship between economic poverty, evangelical poverty, and contemplation. A look at her background, conversion and development will illuminate the place of poverty and contemplation in her life and in her instruction of others.

Clare was born in 1194 and grew up as part of the nobility of Assisi. Clare's family belonged to the prosperous and well-established Offreduccio clan. They were known for their gallantry and courage, prudence and foresight, power and wealth.[2] Clare had seven knights in her ancestry and many others who distinguished themselves in public service. Little is known about Favarone, Clare's father, except that he provided his family with a spacious well-built house close to the cathedral of San Rufino.[3] It is also known that when war flared up in Assisi, Favarone took his family to the home of his brother, Monaldo, in Perugia to insure their safety. According to Fortini, who has done extensive research in this area, they remained there until 1205.

These were the crucial years during which the commune of Assisi was trying to organize—a task which was not fully realized until 1208–1209. Merchants had initiated the formation of the commune and Favarone seemed to have wanted no part of it. Such a movement challenged the place of the nobles within the social, political, and economic areas of life. The merchants insisted that the nobles give up part of their wealth and their privileges. The merchants were motivated not by some magnanimous concern for the welfare of the poor, but rather by a desire to increase their own wealth through trade.

Clare grew up in the midst of this struggle between the nobles and the merchants and could not have been untouched by it. The place of money, and wealth, in general, as a means of attaining status must have loomed large in the conversations of the townsfolk of the commune.

Clare's father, no doubt, looked forward to a future marriage for her, the eldest of three daughters. Messer Ranieri di Bernardo d'Assisi, a family intimate and witness in the canonization process of Clare, stated that

> Since she was of a beautiful countenance the question of her marriage was discussed; and many of her relations begged her to consent to accept a husband . . .[4]

Though Favarone would have had to provide the usual dowry, he no doubt saw the marriage of his first-born daughter as a way of securing the family's influence in Assisi if Clare would accept the proposal of the right suitor. If she would marry into an even wealthier family than her own, surely her future would also be made secure. Despite the urgings of her relatives Clare was listening more intently to the promptings heard only in her heart.

An anonymous medieval biographer, thought to be Thomas of Celano, described the young Clare as a person 'with a docile heart' whom 'the Spirit worked within and formed into a most pure vessel of grace'.[5] It was also said that she was generous toward the poor and others in need, taking from her own table all that was superfluous, and giving it freely to them.

She grew up under the influence of her mother Ortolana, who was herself solicitous towards the poor people of Assisi. Furthermore, in the common understanding of christian living, the rich had the duty of sharing with the poor.[6] To do so was to act honorably and was considered in keeping with their social station. Clare assimilated all these attitudes and integrated them into her naturally gracious and sympathetic personality.

Early in 1211, Francis, the son of the wealthy merchant Pietro di Bernardone, began preaching in the Cathedral of San Rufino. Three years earlier, he had taken up a life of poverty, and Clare had undoubtedly heard about him, for he and his little band of followers were frequently the topic of conversation in the commune. He had come from one of the most prosperous merchant families in Assisi, but renounced that way of life, choosing instead a way characterized by poverty, penance, and preaching. He and his followers, among whom were some of the finest young men of Assisi, were known as 'The Penitents of Assisi'. Rufino, Clare's cousin, had joined the group, to the great dismay of the family. Now Clare was fascinated by the fiery words of the ragged Francis and hoped for an opportunity to meet him.

Bona di Guelfuccio, a friend and confidante of Clare, arranged for a conversation between Clare and Francis.[7] These meetings continued throughout the year. These were times during which Francis instructed Clare in the rudiments of the way of life he had begun under the inspiration of the Lord.

Slowly, through this on-going contact with Francis, she began to realize that something was being asked of her beyond generosity toward the poor. Like Francis she was being asked to identify with the poor, to share their lot and to carry their burden. She reflected that this was, after all, what Jesus had done in giving up the status that was rightfully his as the Son of God. She surely was familiar with the early christian hymn recorded in the Letter to the Philippians.

Though he was in the form of God,
he did not deem equality with God
something to be grasped at.
Rather he emptied himself
and took the form of a slave,
being born in the likeness of men. (2:6–7).[8]

She must have reflected on these words and sensed the depth of the Father's love for all humankind and self-emptying obedience of the Son.

A year later, in 1212, Clare decided to follow Francis' example. She gave up her status as a wealthy young woman, a benefactor of the poor, to become one with her poor brothers and sisters in Christ. Through her contact with Francis, she began to understand in a very concrete way that God is the great Almsgiver and the benefactor of all people, everyone being poor in the light of his richness. Benefactor was a role that belonged to the Father. Her role was simply to receive his generous gifts with gratitude and share them with others.

Clare began to see herself as a recipient of many of God's gifts—gifts meant to be used for the good of her brothers and sisters in Jesus. She found that the less she provided for herself the more she could see God providentially caring for her beyond her expectations. This realization of God's tender and extravagant care for her led her to renounce the heritage that was hers as the daughter of the wealthy Favarone di Offreduccio.

Francis' fresh approach to Gospel living set her heart afire. His words, his example, and his willingness to endure all things for the sake of the Gospel attracted Clare. It became the way for her to make her dependence on God very real.

At one of her meetings with Francis, she made the final plans for her departure from home. She would attend the Palm Sunday services at San Rufino, dressed in the finery befitting the royal nuptuals that would take place later that night in the tiny Church of St Mary of the Angels, which had become home for Francis and his brothers.[9]

The service at the cathedral was rich in the symbolism of the Church's liturgy. Clare was so taken up with the mystery of God's love enfleshed in his Son and boldly recounted in the Passion narrative that she forgot to go up to receive her palm from Bishop Guido. The bishop, not wanting to overlook the beautiful daughter of one of his most generous patrons, approached Clare with a palm. From that night on she would walk in the footprints of Jesus, gradually being transformed into his image through poverty, penance, and prayer.

History tells us that after she had stayed briefly at the benedictine monasteries of San Paolo delle Ancelle di Dio and Sant' Angelo di Panzo, Francis took Clare and her sister Catherine (Sister Agnes), who had joined her, to San Damiano, one of the churches that he had repaired. There, in the same place Francis had received his mission to repair the Church, she and other young women of Assisi who soon joined her, would also repair the whole Church through their poverty and prayer. A medieval biographer of Clare says it well:

> That this rivulet of heavenly blessing which had sprung up in the valley of Spoleto might not be confined within such narrow boundaries, it was turned into a broad stream that 'the stream of the river might make joyful the whole city' of the Church.[9]

Clare's life of poverty and contemplation was rooted in her image of the poor, humiliated Jesus. It shaped her spirituality and informed her decisions.

Her words to Agnes of Prague, daughter of King Ottokar of Bohemia, bear this out:

> Look upon him who for you became the object of contempt, and follow him, making yourself contemptible for his sake in his world. Your Spouse, though more beautiful than the sons of men, became, for your salvation, the lowest of men, despised, struck, scourged untold times in his whole body, and then died amid the sufferings of the Cross. O most noble Queen, ponder him, marvel at him, contemplate him, as you desire to imitate him.[10]

She counseled Agnes in this way, because it was the way of life followed by the nuns at San Damiano. Her advice to Agnes was the product of her experience and that of the other sisters. Clare had quickly learned that it was only through constant contact with the Lord in prayer that one could assimilate the message of the Gospel and make it the norm of one's conduct.

For Clare, a life of economic poverty was the environment in which one could be most attentive to the Lord as well as give credibility to evangelical poverty. It was her way of following in the footprints of Jesus and the way to the kingdom of heaven. In the eighth chapter of her Rule[11] she encouraged the sisters not to be ashamed of this way of life because it was the way of Jesus.

> Nor should they be ashamed, for the Lord made himself poor for us in this world. This is that sublimity of the highest poverty which had made you, my dearest sisters, heirs and queens of the kingdom of heaven: poor in goods but exalted in virtue. May this be your portion which leads to the land of the living. . .[12]

All that she learned about the ways of the poor suffering Jesus she shared with Agnes of Prague. Clare could identify with Agnes' struggle to follow Jesus in a lifestyle of poverty and prayer because she herself had come from a wealthy family. Clare had experienced God's love deep within her heart and she knew that no sacrifice was too great to make to keep this love alive. She would have no part of anything that would take her attention away from her Beloved. In her prayer and in her poverty she believed that she already possessed the kingdom of heaven through love. She had the assurance of the Lord himself in the first Beatitude, in which he pronounced the poor the heirs of heaven. Clare instructed Agnes out of this firm conviction of hers.

> You know, I am sure, that the kingdom of heaven is promised and given by the Lord only to the poor: for he who loves temporal things loses the fruit of love.[13]

Clare knew that poverty and love were intimately related. Her counsel to Agnes reflects her own experience: in order to be open and ready to receive the gifts of the Lord in prayer, one's heart must be free of clutter—the clutter of self and of material possessions and securities. That kind of freedom was also at the heart of love of one's neighbor.

At the deepest level poverty readied the heart to receive the gift of the Lord. In directing Agnes' spiritual growth in this area Clare utilized spousal imagery to describe the gifts that the Beloved gives to the person who waits in readiness for him. In this relationship of union it is the Lord himself who

> . . . Adorned your breast with precious stones and has placed priceless

> pearls in your ears and surrounded you with sparkling gems as though blossoms of springtime and placed on your head a golden crown as a sign to all of your holiness.[14]

Clare was no doubt using images that were meaningful to the women who were part of the community during those first decades, women who had turned their backs on lives of luxury and self-indulgence. Her words express the enduring truth that poverty, alive and real, enables the heart to turn more readily to the Lord in prayer.

Clare was so convinced of the special role of poverty in shaping her prayer and her way of life that she had its place assured through the *Privilege of Poverty*,[15] first granted her by Innocent III, and renewed and confirmed by Gregory IX.

The *Privilege of Poverty* resulted from an unprecedented request. Clare had asked Pope Innocent III for the privilege of possessing nothing. The pontiff observed that never had such a privilege been asked of the Court of Rome. In essence it prohibited anyone from forcing the Poor Ladies at San Damiano to accept possessions. Like Francis, Clare wanted common poverty, not common property. She held to the principle of non-ownership.

> The Sisters shall appropriate nothing to themselves, neither a house nor place nor anything. And as pilgrims and strangers in this world (1 Peter 2:11), serving the Lord in poverty and humility, let them send confidently for alms.[16]

Through the *Privilege of Poverty* the nuns could concretely express their dependence on God. This was essential, in Clare's mind, in keeping the spirit of prayer alive in the community.

The radical nature of such a request shocks the mind and heart that are unfamiliar with the ways of faith. No other monastic community of women or men asked for or lived by such faith in divine providence. Clare brought a fresh insight into the medieval understanding of the monastic vocation. She rooted it firmly in her vision of following in the footprints of Jesus who became poor for our sake.

Clare linked contemplative prayer and evangelical poverty to real economic poverty. She did so with confidence because once she had decided to follow Jesus in this radical way, she experienced within her own person the intrinsic bond which exists between poverty and contemplation. In reality she trusted in the Lord and had taken him at his word. He had proved himself true.

Those of us removed from Clare by some seven centuries can find within her writings truth enough to inspire us and mystery enough to challenge us to discover anew the central role of poverty in the christian life. Poverty which has long been matter for heated debate can, if we follow Clare's guidance, become the way to the kingdom of God. We can grasp the full measure of Clare's words in her hymn to poverty. In it we find the fruit of a life of contemplation in the context of economic poverty: an in-depth understanding of evangelical poverty.

O blessed poverty
    who bestows eternal riches on those who love
        and embrace her!
O holy poverty
    to those who possess and desire you
    God promises the kingdom of heaven
    and offers indeed eternal glory and blessed life!
O God-centered poverty
    whom the Lord Jesus Christ,
    Who ruled and now rules heaven and earth,
    Who spoke and things were made
    condescended to embrace before all else.[17]

Poverty is the thread running through all of Clare's Writings. It is integral to understanding her life and thought. To examine its role in Clare's life is to witness God's magnificent action in the life of one of his saints. To probe the pre-eminent place of poverty in Clare's Writings is to be exposed to one of Christianity's most profound sources for understanding the way God works in every human heart.

NOTES

1. Arnaldo Fortini, *Francis of Assisi* (New York: Crossroad, 1981) 327–28, note 1. Fortini has proven that Clare's father was Favarone, son of Offreduccio. At one time it was believed that her family name was Scifi. Research has proven that 'Scifi' was a late malformation of the name of her uncle, Scipione, who was the father of her cousin, Brother Rufino who joined Francis.

2. Fortini, 328.

3. *Ibid.*, 327, note a. This note gives a summary of the controversy that went on between Fortini and Abate concerning the family home of St Clare.

4. Text of the testimonies in the cause for canonization for St. Clare can be found in 'Il processo di canonizzazione di S. Chiara di Assisi', *Archivum Franciscanum Historicum* 13 (1920) 403–507. The specific reference in the text is to Witness 18.

5. Ignatius Brady, ed., *The Legend and Writings of St. Clare of Assisi*, (St Bonaventure, N.Y.: The Franciscan Institute, 1953) 20.

6. Lester K. Little, *Religious Poverty and the Profit Economy in Medieval Europe* (Ithaca: Cornell University Press, 1978) 4.

7. Fortini, 337.

.8 Text taken from *The New American Bible* (Camden: Thomas Nelson Inc., 1969) 1301.

9. Brady, 26.

10. This is now in print. "Second Letter to Bl. Agnes of Prague," 19, in Regis Armstrong and Ignatius Brady, *Francis and Clare: The Complete Works* (New York: Paulist Press, 1982) p. 197.

11. Clare began writing her own Rule around 1247 because she could not accept the idea of ownership of property allowed in the Rule given her by Pope Innocent IV. Her Rule was given papal approval on 9 August 1253, just two days before her death. Cf. Brady, 4–8 and Fortini, note t., 365. She is believed to be the first woman in the history of the Church to write her own Rule. By approving this Rule of St Clare, Innocent IV waived Canon 13 of the Fourth Lateran Council, which would have bound Clare to take an existing Rule.

12. Brady, 75.

13. First Letter, #25 in Armstrong, p. 193.

14. *Ibid.*, #10–11, p. 191.

15. Brady, 12–13. The texts of each version of the *Privilege of Poverty* can be found in Brady, 103–4.

16. *Ibid.*, 75.

17. First Letter, #15–17, in Armstrong, p. 192.

Following in the Foot Prints of the Poor Christ: Clare's Spirituality

Fidelis Hart

What you hold, may you [always] hold,
What you do, may you [always] do,
and never abandon.
But with swift pace [and] light step
and feet unstumbling, so that your steps
stir up no dust,
go forward:
securely, joyfully
and swiftly
on the path of prudent happiness[1]

These compelling words from the heart of our Foundress and Sister, Clare di Favarone Offreduccio (1194–1253) tell us that she saw her gospel way as a way of life, a life-giving way. The phrases breathe movement, strength, and joy; the path of happiness is Christ the Way, whom she loved in complete surrender.[2] This focus on the God-Man is found at the very core of Clare's living and teaching. Clare reflects the pristine thought of her teacher, Francis of Assisi, who heard the call to follow the poor Christ. Like Francis, a man with a song, Clare was a woman with a song, and her song was Christ.

THE POOR CHRIST

The following in the footprints of a poor Christ was ever in her thought With this in mind she urged her Sisters to union with him:

Like a poor virgin, embrace the poor Christ.[3]

There are few pages in the *Legenda* of Thomas of Celano, her own writings, and the ecclesiastical documents on her life[4] that do not mention this beloved poverty, a poverty more than material, a radical poverty arising from the call to a poor gospel life characteristic of a century that saw increasing urbanization and its manifest disparity between great wealth and abject penury.[5] It was a call of the Spirit to openness, availability, and surrender to God. For Francis and Clare poverty was an emptying of self, after the example of Christ and his mother, for the service of others. She saw herself and her sisters as co-workers and fellow servants with Christ in building up the Body of Christ.[6] Her concept of poverty oriented her toward mystical union with the Word of the Father.

STRONG, TENDER, AND OF GREAT CHARITY

Only a cursory glance at the documents mentioned above gives us the clear impression of a gentle, strong, and caring woman. Clare walked in loving confidence, in fidelity and joy, along her gospel way. The sisterhood had two dimensions: 1) growth in the likeness of Christ, and 2) the witness of their lives and sisterly charity to the larger community, the Body of Christ. The life was austere, the buildings poorly constructed, and the food scant. The presence of Clare made the austerity of the little convent a path of happiness.[7] The miracles recorded in the ecclesiastical documents assembled at the time of her canonization,[8] center around the care and healing of her Sisters, and the many sick persons brought to the convent. In the bull of canonization we read:

> She was truly a noble and lofty tree with wide-spreading branches, which bore the sweet fruit of religion in the field of the Church, to the delightful shade and beauty of which so many daughters of the faith have gathered, and still continue to gather to pluck the fruit thereof. She was the *new woman* of the Valley of Spoleto, who poured forth a new fountain of the water of life to refresh and benefit souls.[9]

SOURCES OF HER SPIRITUALITY

It is impossible to think of Clare and her vocation apart from Francis. Her union with him, both in mind and heart, was real and harmonious. St Bonaventure says of her:

> St Clare was especially dear to God. She was the first flower in Francis'

garden, and she shone like a radiant star, fragrant as a flower, blossoming white and pure in springtime. *She was his daughter* in Christ and foundress of the Poor Clares.

(*Major Life* of Francis, c. 1263)[10]

Thomas of Celano, in his Legend of Saint Clare, written about 1255–56 at the order of Pope Alexander IV, as well as in his First and Second Lives of St Francis, written about 1228 and 1246–47 respectively, is clear and precise on the part Francis played in Clare's call and spiritual development.[11] The witness of Clare herself in her Rule (Chapter 6.3) attests to this:

> And that we and those who were to come after us might never fall away from the highest poverty which we had chosen, shortly before his death he again wrote to us his last will, saying: 'I, little Brother Francis, wish to follow the life and poverty of our Lord Jesus Christ most high, and of his holy Mother, and to persevere therein to the end. And I beseech you, my ladies, and counsel you always to live in this most high form of life and poverty. And guard well, lest by the teaching or counsel of anyone you ever in any way depart from it?[12]

THE SACRED SCRIPTURES AS SOURCE

Francis and Clare believed themselves to be called to the perfection of the Gospel. Both the Rule of the Friars Minor and Clare's Rule begin by stating that their form of life is to observe the Gospel of Our Lord Jesus Christ, living in obedience, without anything of one's own and in chastity. In his Testament[13] Francis wrote:

> When God gave me some friars, there was no one to tell me what I should do; but the Most High himself made it clear to me that I must live the life of the Gospel. I had this written down simply and briefly and His Holiness the Pope confirmed it for me.[14]

One has only to read the Rules and Writings of these two saints to discover the wealth of scripture quotations that seemed to flow from hearts nourished and inspired by what Francis called 'the fragrant words of my Lord, which are spirit and life'.[15] In his *Major Life* of St Francis, Bonaventure pointed to a scene in the Portiuncula, the little Church given to the Friars by the Benedictines, as the important moment of decision:

> As he was living there by the Church of our Lady, Francis prayed to her who had conceived the Word, full of grace and truth, begging her in-

sistently and with tears, to become his advocate. Then he was granted the true spirit of the Gospel, by the intercession of the Mother of Mercy and he brought it to its fruition. He was at Mass one day on the feast of one of the apostles, and the passage of the Gospel, where our Lord sends out his disciples to preach and tells them how they are to live according to the Gospel, was read. When Francis heard that they were not to provide gold or silver or copper to fill their purses, that they were not to have a wallet for the journey or a second coat. No shoes or staff, he was overjoyed. He grasped the meaning of the passage immediately in his love for apostolic poverty and committed it to memory. 'This is what I want', he said. 'This is what I long for with all my heart'. There and then he took off his shoes and laid aside his staff. He conceived a horror of money, or wealth of any kind and he wore only one tunic, changing his leather belt for a rope. The whole desire of his heart was to put what he had heard into practice and to conform to the rule and life given to the apostles, in everything.[16]

From this time on, Bonaventure declared in this same Life, Francis strove after Gospel perfection and his words were full of the power of the Holy Spirit. His love and understanding of sacred scripture seemed to have impressed Bonaventure for he wrote:

St Francis had never studied sacred Scripture, but unwearied application to prayer and continual practice of virtue had purified his spiritual vision, so that his keen intellect was bathed in the radiance of eternal light and penetrated its depths. Free from every sin, his genius pierced to the heart of its mysteries and by affective love he entered where theologians with their science stand outside.[17]

Like Francis, Clare desired nothing but to follow Christ wholeheartedly according to the Gospel. Because of the different circumstances of her life, she seemed to draw more heavily on the Gospel for practical norms for her way of life than did the friars. The constant prayer of Christ and his union with the Father inspired her own prayer life.

Texts from the liturgical feasts and the Divine Office shine through Clare's writings and they reflect the manner in which Clare nourished her prayer life and made the prayer of the Church her own.[18] The IV Lateran Council (1215) had called, among other reforms, for an increase in devotion to and respect for the Eucharist. Celano and the cause of canonization speak of Clare's great devotion to the Blessed Sacrament.

How great was the devotion of Blessed Clare to the Sacrament of the Altar, is shown by its results. For during the illness which confined her to bed, she had herself raised up and supported by props and sitting thus she would spin the finest linens. From these she made more than fifty cor-

> porals, and enclosed them in silken or purple cases, and then had them sent to the different churches of the plains and mountains of Assisi.
>
> When she was to receive the Body of the Lord, she shed burning tears and would approach with awe, for she feared him no less hidden in the Sacrament than ruling heaven and earth.
>
> (Celano, *Legenda*, 18.28)

The Sisters recounted that a great sweetness radiated from her person and that her speech was full of grace when she came to join them after prayer.[19] Clare's great confidence in the Eucharist is illustrated by the story of her reaction to news of a Saracen horde at the convent gates. We read that Clare who had counseled her daughters not to fear, but to trust in the Lord Jesus Christ for assistance, at the critical moment fell on her knees and prayed.

> Lord, look upon your poor servants, for I cannot guard them. Soon from the mercy-seat of the covenant a voice as of a little child sounded in her ears: I will always defend you.
>
> (Celano, *Legenda*, 14.22)

Then, with the ivory bound silver ciborium containing the sacred host she had herself led to the door. Routed by her prayers, the Saracens left in confusion.[20] This trust did not arise from a moment of prayer but from a lifelong dedication to her sacramental Lord.

Her greatest devotion, growing out of her love of Christ and his servant, St Francis, was to poverty. The last will of Francis to the Clares at San Damiano stated that he wished to follow the life and poverty of our Lord Jesus Christ and of his most holy mother. Then he continues:

> And I beseech you all, my Ladies, always to live in this highest form of life and poverty.

Clare, too, always added to the following of the poor Christ, the phrase: and of his most holy mother. In her Rule we find several brief but concise precepts in this regard. The Sisters are asked in chapter two to wear only poor garments for the love of the all holy and most dear Babe, who was wrapped in swaddling clothes and laid in a manger and of his most holy mother. Each time the Sisters are urged to virtue, poverty, or observance of the gospel way the same phrase is used. Agnes of Prague was told to cling to his most sweet mother. In a very beautiful section (24–27) of her third letter to Agnes, Clare reveals her love of Mary and adds the idea of being pregnant with the Word of God:

> As the glorious Virgin of virgins carried him physically in her body, without a shadow of a doubt, you too by following in her footprints, especially of ***humility*** and ***poverty***, in your chaste and virginal body, can always *carry* spiritually him by whom you and all things are contained in being, and so possess him more securely than any passing riches which the world can offer.

THE RULE

Francis received oral permission for his Rule in 1210, a rule that did not envision or embrace the foundation of a women's Order. When he placed Clare in San Damiano in 1212 he gave her only a form of life similar to his own profession of evangelical poverty. When the Fourth Lateran Council in 1215 directed that all new movements adopt a rule already established, Clare asked Innocent III for the Privilege of Poverty. The essential privilege lay in the fact that Clare and her sisters were not to be obliged to hold property. Thus they lived according to St Francis' form of life by this privilege.[21]

> As you have thus petitioned Us, so we confirm by Apostolic favor the proposal of highest poverty, granting you by the authority of these Letters present that you can be compelled by no one to receive possessions.[22]

The complex development of the sisterhood and Clare's Rule must be viewed in the light of the demand of the Lateran Council. In 1217 the former camaldolese abbot of San Silvestro on Mount Subiaso, Hugolino di Segni, then Cardinal-Archbishop of Ostia, attempted to comply with its requirement by providing a canonical form for the Poor Clares at San Damiano and anyone following their example, by giving them the following documents: The Rule of St Benedict, the Constitutions of Saint Peter Damien, and the Constitutions of the Benedictine Monastery of San Paulo on Mount Subias.[23] He then drew up a Rule based upon these documents and placed the houses on which they were imposed within the benedictine family. A year later, Hugolino obtained from Honorius III, (1216–27) in the bull *Litterae tuae*, permission to secure estates for the maintenance of religious houses for women.[24] In 1219, by means of the bull *Sacrosancta Romana Ecclesia*, of Honorius III, dated the ninth of December 1219, he imposed this Rule on Saint Clare and her sisters. Francis was away on a misisonary journey to convert the Moors, but Clare and her sisters resisted these Hugoline Constitutions, because they did not follow the teaching of Francis and violated the freedom from possessions granted them by the *Privilege* of Innocent III. Francis returned in 1220, and it is possible that it was he who persuaded Hugolino to rescind the part of the Rule that affected the fundamental issue of poverty. It was not until September 1228, however, that Hugolino, now Gregory IX, granted the earnest requests of Clare, and then he restricted the privilege to Clare and the sisters at San Damiano. The incident is recorded in Celano's Life of Clare.

> As he, Gregory IX, was trying to persuade her one day, in view of the vicissitudes of the times and the dangers of the age, that she should own some possessions for the benefit of the community, which he at the same time liberally offered out of his own means, she resisted with an unshaken resolve, and would in no wise yield to his entreaties. To whom the Pontiff said: 'If it be the vow that hinders you, we absolve you from that vow'. Whereupon she replied: 'Holy Father, never will I consent to be absolved from *following Christ*'.

Clare's firm response marks poverty as the foundation upon which the life of the sisterhood was constructed. Complete poverty was part of the whole-hearted following of Christ which she had learned from Francis.

The question of the corporate possession of property was once again raised by Innocent IV (1243–54). He attempted to impose uniform regulations upon all the convents of Clares, whom he designated as belonging to the Order of San Damiano. Clare and her sisters strongly rejected this new Rule and used this opportunity to write her own Rule. In 1252, she received a final confirmation of the Privilege of Poverty, as well as a profession of that poverty according to the directions she had received from Francis in the first form of life he had written for her at the beginning of her religious life, and she incorporated this into her own Rule.

CLARE'S RULE OF 1253

On 9 August, Clare received final approbation of her Rule in the bull *Solet Annuere.* The Rule itself is not free from the influence of the Hugoline Constitutions and the Rule of Innocent IV in matters to enclosure, silence, visits to the parlor, and fasting. Did Clare freely incorporate these sections? Were they common church law for convents of religious women? We do not know. Clare received the Rule on her deathbed, she gratefully kissed it we are told, but she died two days later.

On the whole the Rule is a franciscan document, based on the Rule of 1223 that Francis wrote for the Friars Minor. There are also passages from the rule of 1221, the *Regula non Bullata.*[25] The beginning is wild and sweet, it is the echo of the friars' way of the freedom of the gospel call.

> The form of life of the Order of Poor Sisters which blessed Francis founded

> is this: To observe the Holy Gospel of our Lord Jesus Christ, by living in obedience, without anything of one's own, and in chastity.
>
> Clare, the unworthy handmaid of Christ and little plant of the most Blessed Francis, promises obedience and reverence to the Lord Pope Honorius, and to his successors, canonically elected, and to the Roman Church.
> (RI, 1–3)

It is a form of life, the gospel way, along which her sisters and those who were to come after them were to walk as pilgrims and strangers, without anything of their own. There was to be no baggage; instead there was to be time for sunrise and sunset, for each other, for the sick, and for upholding the frail and weak members of the Body of Christ.

She is the little plant of Francis, for a plant is a growing life drinking in sunlight and rain. To the very end, she will keep this freshness and her path of happiness will be an adventure, an encounter with the Lord.

The promise of obedience is repeated twice in Chapter Six, and in her letters. She repeated this promise to his successors as an indication of the close ties she and her sisters had, and hoped to preserve, with the Friars Minor. The early documents and Francis himself state that Clare and her sisters had been entrusted to him by God. The sixth chapter of her Rule, one that contains no remnants of earlier Rules, speaks directly to us of her vocation. The text reads like an exultation:

> And after the most high celestial Father deigned to enlighten my heart to do penance after the example of our most blessed Father's saint Francis, together with my Sisters, I voluntarily promised him obedience shortly after his own conversion.
>
> But when our Blessed Father saw that we feared no poverty, toil, sorrow, humiliation, or the contempt of the world, but rather that we held these in great delight, moved by love he wrote for us a form of life as follows:
>
> Since by the divine inspiration you have made yourselves daughters and handmaids of the Most High and Sovereign King, the Heavenly Father, and have espoused yourselves to the Holy Spirit by the choice of life according to the perfection of the holy Gospel: I will and promise for myself and my friars always to have for you as for them the same diligent care and special solicitude.
>
> As long as he lived he faithfully kept this promise and wished it always to be kept by the friars.
>
> And that we and those who were to come after us might never fall away from the highest poverty which we had chosen, shortly before his death, he again wrote us his last will saying:
>
> I, little Brother Francis, wish to follow the life and poverty of Our Lord Jesus Christ most high and of his most holy Mother, and to persevere

therein to the end. And I beseech you, my ladies, and counsel you always to live in this highest form of life and poverty. And guard well, lest by the teaching and example of anyone you ever in any way depart from it. And as I myself together with my sisters have ever been solicitous to observe the holy poverty which we have promised the Lord God and Blessed Francis, so likewise the abbesses who shall succeed me in the office, and all the sisters are bound to observe it inviolably to the end; that is to say they are not to receive or have any possessions or property either of themselves or through an interposed person, or even anything that might reasonably be called property; save as much ground as necessity requires for the becoming seclusion of the monastery, and this land is not to be tilled except as a garden for the needs of the Sisters.[26]

This chapter contains two quotations from the writings of Francis which are preserved nowhere else. They are valuable because they contain Francis' vision of the life of the Poor Sisters. The chapter also contains Clare's sense of community. While she rejoices in her vocation she is careful to include the sisters:

I, with my sisters,
we were afraid of no poverty
we held these to be our greatest delights
moved by love he wrote for us
And as I myself together with my sisters.

'The land is not to be tilled except as a garden'. This little phrase is crucial. It shows Clare's wisdom and determination to preserve the franciscan ideal of the sisterhood. Land that would become fruitful, would bring with it the attention of greedy nobles who would attempt to have the monastery converted into a benefice. She addressed this deplorable practice of the Middle Ages once again in speaking of the election of officers in chapter four:

> And none shall be elected who is not professed. If, however, a sister is elected or otherwise chosen who is not professed, she is not to be given obedience until after she has professed the form of our poverty.

Clare knew her times, she knew her Church, she knew the nobles and their greed. In a firm, sensible way she faced possible abuses, and calmly did whatever was possible to protect her sisterhood with reasonable legislation.

Her Rule places the abbess in the midst of her sisters rather than above them. She is to observe the common life in all things, and should she prove incompetent, 'the sisters are bound to elect another as abbess and mother as soon as possible' (Rule 4.5). Charity or reverential love was to be the guiding spirit of the community. Clare exemplified this love. She cared for the sick, chose the lowliest task, and lived among them as one who served. Taken as a cohesive whole, the Rule, while concise, provides all that is needed in such a document. The Rule begins with Gospel, moves to Church, poverty, unity, and back to Church, to poverty and Gospel. Poverty is the pearl, the way of Christ. It ends with the prayer that 'We may forever observe the poverty and humility of our Lord Jesus Christ and of his most holy Mother, and the holy Gospel which we have firmly promised'.

THE LETTERS OF CLARE

Her writings are few, but we will find a sharing of her prayer life, and her sureness of approach when she spoke of contemplation indicates that she knew her subject through personal experience. There are four letters to St Agnes of Bohemia, and very possibly one to Ermentrude of Bruges, foundress of the Poor Clares in Flanders.[27] *The Testament of St Clare*, a collection of selected writings from her Rule, letters and other sources and always very close to the hearts of her daughters, has come under scrutiny by scholars, because of a dearth of early manuscripts.[27] The internal evidence of the manuscripts indicates that Clare was a good latinist, skillful, eloquent, and poetic. She used a medieval style of address that may seem foreign to the modern reader, for Clare was a woman of her time. The symbols and romantic imagery she used were understood by those to whom she wrote. Her clarity of thought and her precision are in no way obscured by her style. St Agnes of Bohemia, the recipient of these letters, in 1234 entered the monastery of Poor Clares which she herself had founded. This royal princess, the daughter of Ottocar I of Bohemia and sister of Wenceslas, his successor, sought permission from Gregory IX to sever her betrothal to Emperor Frederick II in 1233. She wanted to renounce her inheritance and become a Franciscan. The authenticity of these letters has been accepted by franciscan scholars, critics and the Bollandists. There is some difficulty in determining the exact date of their composition. The first letter is usually assigned the date of 1234, some time before Agnes' entrance into the convent in Prague. The other three letters refer to Agnes more as a sister of the Order than does the first. The last letter is usually assigned the date 1253, preceeding the death of Clare in August of that year. Clare herself gives the reason for the scarcity of letters in her fourth letter:

> do not wonder or think that the fire of love for you flows less sweetly in the heart of your mother. No, this is the difficulty: the lack of messengers and the obvious dangers of the road.

The second letter, which follows in full, has been quoted because in it Clare presented her vision of the contemplative life for the followers of the gospel way, as lived at San Damiano.

To the daughter of the king of kings, the handmaid of the Lord of hosts (Rev 19:16), the most worthy bride of Jesus Christ and, therefore, the most noble queen, Lady Agnes: Clare, the useless and unworthy servant (Lk 17:10) of the Poor Ladies: greetings and a wish for your perseverance in a life of the highest poverty.

I give thinks to the Giver of grace from whom, we believe, every good and perfect gift proceeds (James 1:17), because he has adorned you with such splendors of virtues and signed you with such marks of perfection, that, since you have become such a diligent imitator of the Father of all perfection, (Mt 5:48) his eyes do not see anything imperfect in you.

This is that perfection which will prompt the King himself to take you to himself in the heavenly bridal chamber where he is seated in glory on a starry throne because you have despised the splendors of an earthly kingdom and considered of little value the offers of an imperial marriage. Instead, as someone zealous for the holiest poverty, in the spirit of great humility and the most ardent charity, you have held fast to the footprints (1 Pt 2:21) of him to whom you have deserved to be joined as a spouse.

But since I know that you are adorned with many virtues, I will spare my words and not worry you with needless speech, even though nothing seems superfluous to you if you can draw from it some consolation. But because one thing alone is necessary (Lk 10:42), I bear witness to that one thing and encourage you, for love of him to whom you have offered yourself as a holy and pleasing sacrifice (Rm 12:1), that, like another Rachel (cf. Gen. 19:16), you always remember your resolution and be conscious of how you began.

What you hold, may you [always] hold.
What you do, may you [always] do and never abandon.
But with swift pace [and] light step
and feet unstumbling,
So that even your steps stir up no dust,
go forward
securely, joyfully and swiftly
on the path of prudent happiness.

Trust nothing, give in to nothing which would dissuade you from this resolution or which would place a stumbling block for you on the way, so that you may offer your vows to the Most High in the pursuit of that perfection to which the Spirit of the Lord has called you.

In all of this, so that you may walk more securely in *the way of the com-*

mandments of the Lord (Ps 118:32), follow the counsel of our venerable father, our brother Elias, the Minister General. Prize it beyond the advice of the others and cherish it as dearer to you than any gift. If anyone would tell you something else or suggest something which would hinder your perfection or seem contrary to your god-given vocation, even though you must respect him, do not follow his counsel, but as a poor virgin embrace the Poor Christ.

Look upon him who for you became the object of contempt, and follow him, making yourself contemptible for his sake in this world. Your spouse, though *more beautiful than the sons of men* (Ps 44:3), became for your salvation, the lowest of men, despised, struck, scourged untold times in his whole body, and then died amid the sufferings of the cross. O most noble queen, ponder him, marvel at [him,] contemplate him, as you desire to imitate him.

> If you suffer with him, you shall reign with him;
> if you weep with him, you shall rejoice with him;
> if you die with him on the cross of tribulation,
> you shall possess heavenly mansions in the splendor of the saints
> and your name in the book of life shall be called glorious among men.

Because of this you shall share always and forever the glory of the kingdom of heaven in place of earthly and passing things, and everlasting treasures instead of those that perish, and live forever.

Farewell, most dear sister and lady, because of the Lord your spouse.

Commend me and my sisters to the Lord in your devout prayers, for we rejoice in the good things of the Lord which he works in you through his grace.

Commend us truly to your sisters as well.

The letters should be read against the entire background of the theology of the contemplative life to which she was heir. In the twelfth century the works of such masters as Hugh of St Victor, William of St Thierry, Aelred of Rievaulx, and above all the great St Bernard of Clairvaux were available and popular. St Bernard's doctrine of the love of God, the bridal relationship of the Word as spouse of the soul, profoundly affected the life of the Church. We can trace in Clare's writings a familiarity with St Bernard's sermons on the *Song of Songs*.

The greeting, though somewhat formal in tone, was written in the words of a considerate woman who was Agnes' social equal. It expresses the belief that they were one in heart and mind, and that both understood the depth of the *kenosis* called for in seeking a life of highest poverty. Clare pointed out that the royal princess Agnes, although she had given up everything, was still royal as the bride of Jesus Christ. But Agnes had only taken the first steps; Clare, looking ahead, expressed a wish for perseverance. Clare then broke out into thankful praise:

> I give thanks to the Giver of grace . . .
> since you have become such a diligent imitator. . . .

She gave thanks to the Father for the grace given, as well as for Agnes' openness to the Spirit. She then moved into the bridal mystique: 'This is that perfection which will prompt the King himself to take you to himself in the heavenly bridal chamber', she wrote. Then she compared the splendors of this union to the earthly values of the imperial marriage which Agnes had refused. Clare then acknowledged Agnes as one of the little poor ones, as also the four virtues through which she has held fast to the footprints of Christ: the holiest poverty, great humility, ardent charity, and perseverance.

> As someone zealous for the holiest poverty in the spirit of great humility and most ardent charity, you have held fast to the footprints of Him to Whom you have offered yourself as a holy and pleasing sacrifice.

She saw Agnes as she saw herself, a daughter of the most high King, a child of the Father looking at the Son, a woman impregnated by the Spirit with the word of God. Again the faith vision reflected the full flowering of the gospel way. She encouraged Agnes, but as a true spiritual guide she urged her ever onward to 'more'.

> One thing alone is necessary
> and I bear witness to that one thing.

Clare simply and truthfully appraised her own life, bearing witness to her life of contemplation. She once again returned to the thought of perseverance, urging Agnes to recall the grace of conversion and her loving response to Christ,

> that like another Rachel you always remember your resolution and be conscious of how you began.

The reference to Rachel here has a fuller meaning than the one found in Genesis (29:16). Rachel is used as a sign of maturing love, she will lead to truth, the only Reality. There could be a reference to the work of Richard of St Victor *The Twelve Patriarchs*, in which Rachel is seen as the symbol of contemplative love and Leah active love.[28] The 'Seraphic Life' of St Francis quotes the bull of canonization by Gregory IX, as saying of Rachel and contemplation:

> Wrapped in his beautiful contemplation and clinging in his embraces only to Rachel, he [Francis] descended the mountain and entered the forbidden abode of Leah, lest he should benefit only himself. He led his flock made fruitful by twin offsprings to interior parts of the desert to seek living pastures.[29]

Clare then broke out into a song of life and joy, of love and encouragement: 'With swift feet, light step and feet unstumbling, so that your steps stir up no dust', she began her little canticle and then added:

> securely, joyfully,
> and swiftly
> on the path of prudent happiness.

Since the Son of God has become our way, the path can be securely trod. He is our goal and our guide. The sureness of touch, and the pace of the movement, speak of Clare's personal prayer experience. This little gem is a testament of her own pilgrimage of faith. She continued the exhortation, reminding Agnes that in pursuing this path she would offer her vows to God in search of that perfection 'to which the Spirit of the Lord has called you'.

Clare was clear regarding the divine inspiration of Agnes' call, a call of the Spirit of the Lord. Clare took a positive approach; the Spirit has called, the Spirit will strengthen Agnes if she keeps her gaze fixed on her divine spouse and Saviour. The movement of life and joy recalls a passage in a very early franciscan document (1227) the *Sacrum Commercium*.[29] This relates the story of Francis' search for Lady Poverty, whom he sought because she was the spouse of Christ. Francis was advised to take some companions and together attempt the ascent of the mountain fastness where she was said to dwell. The friars with him became fearful of the arduous climb, and the danger from brigands. Francis encouraged them with these words:

> Put off the burdens that weigh upon your wills and cast away the freight of your sins, and gird yourselves and be valiant men. Forgetting what is behind, strain forward according to your abilities to what is before. I say to you that whatever place the sole of your foot shall tread upon will be yours. For the Spirit before your face is Christ the Lord, who draws you to the summit with bonds of love.[30]

Agnes likewise was to be led to the summit of the mountain. This was Clare's goal: to follow in the footprints of the poor Christ. 'Go, forward', she exclaimed, with joy and security along this path, that is at the same time one of total insecurity, and risks of love relationship. Clare was well aware of the risks, but she was confident that on their small plot of land she and her sisters, working with their own hands, would succeed. This, she believed, is the folly of the cross that had been reflected in these words of Francis, her teacher, in the Friars' Rule of 1221, the *Regula non Bullata*.

> Nothing then must keep us back, nothing separate us from him, at all times and seasons, in every country and place, every day and all day, we must have a true and humble faith and keep him in our hearts.
>
> (Rule of 1221, Chapter 23)

Like Francis, Clare believed that the gospel message could be lived out in its fullness only by those who were poor in spirit, who were stripped of all things save the love of Christ. In this way she could truly urge Agnes not to turn her eyes away from the Crucified but 'as a poor virgin, embrace the poor Christ'. The passage that follows sums up in a characteristic swiftness of expression and clarity of thought, a teaching on contemplative prayer:

> Look upon him who for you became an object of contempt and follow him . . . most noble Queen, ponder him, marvel at him, contemplate him, as you desire to imitate [him].

There is a call to silence, to stillness, here. In effect, she was saying to Agnes; this is the one you want to see: fix your gaze steadily upon him, and with desire imitate him. *Intuere, considera, contemplare, desiderans imitari.* These words follow the pattern of Clare's own spirit of prayer. The idea of imitation in Clare's day was not so much imitation as conformity. The prefix *con* had an active meaning, the soul became one with Christ. It was, as it were, a putting on or a being brought to, the form of Christ, so that the image of God within us is restored to the divine likeness.

The letter ends with a note of joy and another recognition of Agnes as one of the Poor Sisters:

> Farewell, most dear sister, and lady, because of the Lord your Spouse. Commend me and my sisters to the Lord in your devout prayers, for we rejoice in the good things of the Lord which he works in you through his grace. Commend us truly to your sisters as well.

THE THIRD LETTER TO AGNES OF PRAGUE

A note of joy pervades her third letter. In the greeting she wishes Agnes 'the joys of redemption in the Author of salvation and every good thing which can be desired'. And continues:

> I am filled with such joys at your well being, happiness, and marvelous progress, through which you have advanced in the course you have undertaken to win the prize of heaven (cf. Phil 3:14) and I sigh with such happiness in the Lord, because I know and see that you make up most wonderfully what is lacking both in me, and in the other sisters, in following in the footprints of the poor and humble Jesus Christ. I can rejoice truly and no one can rob me of this joy. (Letter 3, lines 3–5)

The sisters who lived with her at San Damiano testified that Clare 'was always joyful in the Lord'; this letter allows some of this joy to shine out. Perhaps the word joy may not fully designate this characteristic of Clare's personality. The joy is more akin to an awareness of blessings to herself, to Agnes, and to all the Poor Sisters. St Bonaventure in a sermon preached at the dominican house in Paris, spoke of the consistent practice of prayer, and wrote that *exsultatio* must follow close after such prayer. It is difficult to translate this word, for Bonaventure's choice of words was always distinctive and deliberate. His own meaning is given in another sermon.

> Passionate joy ought to follow close after prayer for its polishing. This joy is welcome and is an awareness of blessing.
> (Sermon 2.9, after Pentecost)[31]

Clare was joyful about the blessings of God's presence evident in the life of her own sisters and the life of Agnes. She rejoiced that 'by humility, virtue of faith and the strong arms of poverty', Agnes has obtained possession of the treasure hidden in the field. Again the sense of solidarity, and the Church as mystical body, appears:

> And to use the words of the Apostle himself in their proper sense (Cor. 3:9) I consider you as a co-worker of God himself and a support of the weak members of his ineffable Body [the Church]. (Letter 3, line 8)

Clare's joy approached the joy of Our Lady, who sang:

> My soul proclaims the greatness of the Lord
> and my spirit exults in God my saviour.
> (Lk 1:47–48)

She was, like Mary, a woman of dynamic hope and strong faith.

CHRIST CENTERED, STRONG AND TENDER

From this brief study of the Rule and letters of our foundress and sister, Clare of Assisi, there emerges a portrait of a prayerful, Christocentric, strong, and tender woman. The letters to her from the prelate who caused most of the tension and the delay in approval of the Poor Sisters' Rule indicate the esteem in which he held her:

> To the beloved sister in Christ and mother of his salvation, the Lady Clare, handmaid of Christ, Hugolino, miserable and sinful man, Bishop of Ostia, commends himself all that he is, and all that he can be.
>
> Dearest Sisters in Christ! From that hour when the necessity of returning separated me from your holy conversation and tore me away from that joy of heavenly treasures, such bitterness of soul has overcome me, such abundance of tears and cruelty of sorrow, that unless at the feet of Jesus I had found the solace of his unchanging compassion, I fear I would have fallen in to such straits that my spirit would perhaps have fainted away, and my soul melted within me. And with good reason, for as the sorrow of the disciples was exceeding great when the Lord was taken away from them and nailed to the gibbet of the cross, so I being deprived of that glorious joy with which I discoursed with you on the Body of Christ, when I was celebrating Easter with you and the other handmaids of Christ, am now rendered desolate by absence from you.
>
> (Cardinal Hugolino to Clare)[32]

In this letter he continued to praise Clare and her sisters and to consider his life sinful in comparison with the life at San Damiano. Then in an appealing request for her prayers, he ended:

> For I certainly believe that you will obtain from the Most High Judge whatever the insistance of your devotion and the flood of your tears demand.

In another letter to them, this time as Pope Gregory IX, the same Hugolino, after paying tribute to their holy life and seeking their prayers for him under the burden of the papacy, ends with this recognition of their Christlike spirit and unity

> so that as you walk more and more in virtues, you cause God to be glorified and fill up Our joy, who cherish you with a deep love as our closest daughters, [nay] if the word is not out of place, our ladies, for you are the brides of our Lord. Now, because we have become convinced that you have become one spirit in Christ, we beg you always to lift up your hands to God in unceasing supplication. . . . (Brady, p. 112)

Clare cherished a very great reverence not only for the vicar of Christ, but for all the clergy. It was for the little churches in the mountains and on the Umbrian plains that she occupied herself spinning fine linens during her long years of illness. Her lifelong struggle for the recognition of a franciscan Sisterhood, and for the privilege of poverty, was characterized by quiet strength and gentle patience. With the papal confirmation of the privilege, she knew that Francis' words to the Poor Sisters 'never to depart from this highest poverty through the teaching of anyone' had been honored.

She was a tender woman with a great sense of community. There is a trust and freedom for the individual in her Rule. In her third letter to Agnes, she wrote on the subject of fasting:

> On ordinary Thursdays everyone may do as she wishes, so that she who does not wish to fast is not obliged.

Aware that her own fervor had led her to excess in mortification until she had undermined her health, she warned Agnes, in the same letter that 'our flesh is not of brass nor our strength stone'. She asks her to refrain from indiscretion in austerity and fasting, and then ends:

> I beg you in the Lord to praise the Lord and offer your reasonable service to him by your very life, with your sacrifice always seasoned with the salt of wisdom. (Letter 3, line 41)

With a light, joyful step Clare ever responded to Christ, like the bride in the Song of Songs. There is a passage in her fourth letter to Agnes, written shortly before Clare's death, in which we hear the melody of her own heart.

> Draw me
> We will run after you
> in the fragrance of your perfumes
> O heavenly Spouse!
>
> I will run and not tire,
> Until you have brought me into the drinking room
> Until your left hand is under my head
> and your right hand happily embraces me
> and you will kiss me with the happiest kiss
> of your mouth.

Here we have the *Song of Songs* used freely to express the fullness of the desire of her heart and all the love it can summon. It is about spiritual marriage that Clare sings in this passage. The drinking room is the special room reserved for the bride and friends of the Bridegroom. The spanish mystic John of the Cross also sings of this in his *Spiritual Canticle*: 'I drank deeply in the cellar of my friend'.[33] According to Bernard of Clairvaux, the kiss of the mouth is the Holy Spirit:

> When the bride asks for the kiss therefore, she asks to be filled with the grace of this threefold knowledge, filled to the utmost capacity of mortal flesh. But it is the Son whom she approaches, since it is by him it is to be revealed, and to whom he wills. He reveals himself therefore, and the Father as well, to whom it pleases him. And it is certain that he makes this revelation through the kiss, that is through the Holy Spirit, a fact to which St Paul gives witness: 'These are the very things that God has revealed through the Spirit.[34]

On the fruitfulness of Clare's life of contemplation the bull of canonization is profuse. The latin text begins: *Clara, claris praeclara meritis*, and the entire text is a play on the meaning of her name, light. She is a light that, burning in an enclosed community, shed its rays in the wide world; though Clare was silent, her fame cried out. She was a burning light that broke out and illuminated the whole house of the Lord. Amid all this profusion of light and clarity, there is one simple sentence that rings with the deep sound of the human Clare.

> she was a vessel of humility, a shrine of chastity, a flame of love, the essence of kindness, the strength of patience, the bond of peace, and the source of loving unity in her community: meek in word, gentle in deed, lovable and beloved in all things.

The text also uses the symbol of water; she is likened to a new fountain of life to refresh and benefit souls. Water reflects light, whether dew or gentle rain. In a sermon preached in Paris on the second Sunday of Lent in 1251 on the gospel account of Jesus taking Peter, James and John up a high mountain, Bonaventure spoke of this reflection. He remarked on how mountains share generously, for they pour everything they receive, such as the bounty of rain, onto the level plains. Contemplatives then should be:

> beacons of rain-fresh reflections or irrigation ditches for showers, or even dew-drops of charismatic gifts on Mount Sion to give to others through the word of witness and the model of dialogue.[35]

Clare may have been a great light, but she was also a rain-fresh reflection of Christ, of whom her whole life sang. In her lowliness she was like a dew-drop; in her fruitfulness an irrigation canal, bringing life and nourishment to others.

NOTES

1. Letter 2, translated by Regis Armstrong OFM Cap, and Ignatius Brady OFM, *Francis and Clare, The Complete Works*, (New York: Paulist Press, 1982) 195. The translations of Clare's letters have been taken from this work.

2. Letter 3; Armstrong-Brady, p. 200.

3. Letter 2; p. 197.

4. Thomas of Celano, *Legenda of St Clare*, translated by Ignatius Brady, (St Bonaventure, New York, 1953) 103–12.

5. Cf. Brenda Bolton, 'Mulieres Sanctae', in S. M. Stuart, ed., *Women in Medieval Society*, ( ) 141–47.

6. Nesta de Roebeck, *Clare of Assisi*, (Milwaukee, 1951) 183. The original text of the process of canonization is lost. De Roebeck's text is a translation from the Italian of Zeff. Lazzeri in *Archivum franciscanum historicum* 12 (1920).

7. Letter 3, Armstrong and Brady, p. 199.

8. De Roebeck, pp. 183–85.

9. Bull of Canonization, in Brady, *Legenda*, p. 107.

10. Bonaventure, *Major Life of Francis, Francis of Assisi. Omnibus of Franciscan Sources*, (Chicago: Franciscan Herald Press, 1973) 167 (hereafter referred to as *Omnibus*).

11. Cf. Thomas of Celano, *Life of Francis*, in *Omnibus*, pp. 243–45.

12. Rule of Clare, in Brady, *Legenda*, p. 74.

13. Testament of St. Francis; *Omnibus*, pp. 67–70.

14. *Ibid.*, p. 68.

15. Letter to All the Faithful, *Ibid.*, p. 93.

16. Bonaventure, *Major Life* 3.1; *Omnibus*, p. 646.

17. *Ibid.*, 11.1; p. 711.

18. Rule of Clare, in Brady, pp. 69–70.

19. Process of Canonization, in Nesta de Roebeck, pp. 183–85.

20. *Ibid.*, p. 184.

21. See Brady, pp. 121–22.

22. Privilege of Seraphic Poverty 4; Brady, pp. 103–104. The original text of the written confirmation of Innocent III given between the Fourth Lateran Council, 1215, and his death in 1216, is no longer extant. Doubt has been expressed as to whether he actually granted it. The Legenda is quite clear, however, and all internal and external evidence suggests that Innocent III, and not Gregory IX or Innocent IV, granted it. Cf. Zeff. Lazzeri OFM. '"Il Privilegium Paupertatis" concesso da Innocenzo III e che cosa fosse in origine', *Archivum franciscanum historicum* 11 (1919) 275–76.

23. Cf. Armstrong-Brady, *Francis and Clare*, p. 209.

24. Walter E. Seton, *New Sources for the Life of Blessed Agnes of Bohemia* (London: Longmans, Green and Co., 1915) 7–15.

25. See I. Bocalli, *Concordaniae Verbales S. Francisci et Clarae* (Assisi, 1976) 204–205.

26. Cf. 'Investiture Struggle', *New Catholic Encyclopedia* (New York, 1966) 3:611.

27. *Sainte Claire D'Assise* (: Societé de Sainte Augustin, 1915) 145–47.

27A. Regis Armstrong (*Francis and Clare*, p. 226) points to several fourteenth and fifteenth century manuscripts. Whether from the hand of Clare or another, the *Testament* is a rich source of her spirituality.

28. Richard of St Victor, *The Twelve Patriarchs*, translated by Grover Zinn (New York: Paulist, 1980) 129–30.

29. Placid Hermann OFM, *Via Seraphica* (Chicago: Franciscan Herald Press, 1959) 52.

30. *Ibid.*, p. 65.

31. Translation by Marigwen Schumacher, 'Reverence and Relevance', *The Cord* 22 (January 1972).

32. Letter of Cardinal Hugolino, in Brady, p. 111.

33. Spiritual Canticle, 17; translated by Kavanaugh-Rodriguez, *The Collected Works of John of the Cross* (Washington: Institute of Carmelite Studies, 1973) 714.

34. *Sermon 8.5 on the Song of Songs*, translated by Kilian Walsh, ocso in *Bernard of Clairvaux: On the Song of Songs* 1; CF 4:478.

35. Bonaventure, Sermon 1 for the Second Sunday of Lent, *Opera Omnia*, (Quarachi, 1902) 9:col 217b; translation by Marigwen Schumacher in 'Sight and Insight', *The Cord*, 25/2 (Feb. 1975) 44.

Clare of Assisi: New Leader of Women

Frances Ann Thom

Lo, Assisi, lost in the Umbrian hills;
Barely a dot on man's horizon—
Have not your hillsides blushed with many wars
And raised a wail of sorrow to heaven?
How, then, has God favored you with not one,
But—two—saints of peace!

EARLY IN AUGUST 1253, Clare of Assisi lay near death after almost thirty years of illness. Having been received by Francis into his Order on Palm Sunday 1212, and having become foundress of the second franciscan Order (the Poor Ladies as they then were called), she enjoyed approximately twelve years of fairly good health during which her excessive fastings and austerity took their toll. She was very austere in food and drink, and her abstinence was such, that on the second, fourth and sixth days of the week she took no food to support her body; on other days she so reduced the quantity of what she ate that all marvelled how she could live on so little.[1] She was, however, still able to continue the guidance and direction of her small community to found a new expression in the Church of the monastic tradition.[2]

LEADER OF A NEW EXPRESSION IN THE CHURCH

Clare, following the example and inspiration of Francis, had patterned her life-style on the Gospel. Having been introduced to the benedictine form of life by her brief stay at the monastery then at Bastia, San Paolo, and a three or four week stay at 'another benedictine convent, Sant' Angelo in Panzo, on the slopes of Mount Subasio and just outside of Assisi',[3] Clare desired a place where she could live the franciscan way of life for which she yearned. 'She was not a benedictine, and the life of a benedictine community was not at all what she had bargained for. . . . It was the franciscan way . . . the way of adventure and hardship, and she was not finding this in the settled way of life of the Black Nuns.'[4]

Francis was able, with the blessing of the Bishop of Assisi, to install Clare and her sister Agnes in the Church of San Damiano, the first church he had rebuilt after hearing God tell him to repair his crumbling Church. This was also the church in which he had dreamed that someday holy ladies would dwell. Now his dream would be realized. At first there was little organization and no proper Rule to follow, but since Clare regarded herself and her followers as part of the same movement of friars, they lived, as much as possible, in the same manner and with the same rule of life as the friars.

Although Clare occupied the place of leadership, she would not allow herself to be called mother superior or abbess, for she wished to remain in subjection and desired that all the sisters should have equal status in the service of the Lord.

> It was not humility alone that had caused Clare to refuse the title of Abbess; it was also her concept of a Franciscan superior, who was not to be like a Benedictine Abbess in dignity and authority. However, since the Fourth Council of the Lateran, (11–30 November 1215) had decreed (Canon XIII) that no new religious Rule was to be approved but that Orders henceforth were to adopt an older Rule, the Monastery of San Damiano accepted at least formally the Benedictine Rule, and Clare could no longer decline the office of Abbess.[5]

However, the benedictine *Rule*, as given them by Hugolino, the protector of the Order, to give them status in the Church, by no means eliminated those values which had been given them by Francis in the *Formula vitae*, on the contrary, he assured them: 'We give you the Rule of St. Benedict . . . It will in no way run counter to those provisions for living your life (which were given to you by us) and which you have taken as proper to your way of life'.[6]

> Another point which gratified Clare and clarified the status of the Poor Ladies somewhat was that Hugolino had obtained from the Holy See the right for the Poor Ladies to be known as the Second Order of St. Francis. Hugolino's rule did state that the sisters had the right to own nothing except their house and chapel which while not quite the total dependence on providence that Clare desired, was still a step forward. She knew that Cardinal Hugolino's efforts were aimed solely at 'enabling them to fulfill their divine vocation', and Clare was grateful'.[7]

Still another aspect in which the community differed from the traditional monastic style was the type of poverty which they professed. While the benedictine ***Rule*** allowed the community itself to hold properties and benefices, Clare insisted:

> . . . though enclosed, she and her sisters should have no property and no settled income. The vow of individual poverty, which every religious house took, was not enough. There must also be with them, as with the friars, corporate poverty. The right to have no settled income, which came to be known as the ***Privilegium Paupertatis***, was obtained for the sisters at San Damiano by Francis from Innocent III shortly before he died.[8]

How strictly enclosure was enforced is difficult to determine.[9] In fact, it has sometimes been questioned whether Clare really wanted strict enclosure or whether she would have preferred going among the sick and poor as Francis and his brothers did. Since Francis' ideal of gospel living included activity and adventure, conjecture that the sisters performed works of charity outside of the enclosure or even within the enclosure during the early years should not surprise us. These works may have been done, however, by the lay sisters who performed essential external works. Sr Chiara Lainati, moreover, asserts that the contrast of evangelical poverty lived by Francis and the 'well-being that came with monastic landholdings . . . proves . . . very well her intention "to live enclosed" '.[10]

Jacques de Vitry has left us written observations of the nuns' life-style in 1216:

> The sisters lived by their own work or on alms collected for them by the friars or given to them by the people of Assisi. . . . living in various hospices near the towns. They will accept nothing, and live entirely by the labours of their hand. . . . They made a little money by spinning and making altar linen, and grew a few vegetables in their garden; but they remained very poor.[11]

Poverty was indeed honored not only to the letter, but most assuredly in the spirit. We are told that, 'Clare wore only the simplest and roughest of clothes, slept on the floor, and ate so little that it is hard to know how she lived at all'.[12] The others followed her example in all things, as they were able. Except when saying the daily offices, they engaged in useful work. Indeed, the manner in which the offices were recited and the nuns' preference for manual labor were two of the elements which fundamentally distinguished the monastery of St Clare from the numerous benedictine monasteries scattered about the area of Mt Subasio. Since Francis wanted his friars to concentrate on the text rather than a chant melody, Clare and her sisters recited the office without the psalm tones customary in traditional monastic choirs.

Thus, Clare and her sisters remained a sign that was complementary to the friars in the fields, yet equal to theirs in every aspect. Somehow, she and her sisters would be missionaries, preachers, healers, and restorers of churches while remaining behind monastery walls.

The evidence that Clare had truly established a new expression of the monastic tradition is based on the fact that 'in addition to the new foundations, a number of Benedictine and other nunneries obtained permission to change over to the stricter rule of the Poor Clares'.[13] Indeed, Clare's sister, Agnes, was sent to Florence to direct a benedictine community there which had 'turned Poor Ladies'.[14]

PEACE OF SOUL

By now Clare had reached the point for which she had yearned these long years since 1212; the point of perfect union with him whom her soul had loved intensely. In her awareness of the approach of death, she spoke to her soul. 'Go forth, for thou wilt have a good escort on thy journey.'[15] It is obvious that she was comfortable with the prospect of her release from this world, as though she had practised it many times. There is not the least evidence of anxiety over what awaited her, for she knew she had walked in the footsteps of Christ. Testimony of this is found in the Bull of Canonization:

> As the 'footprint of the Mother of God,' she became the 'new leader of women;' her example is as valid for us today as it was for the world over seven hundred years ago. Clare is still 'the lofty candlestick of holiness that burned in the tabernacle of the Lord' and we may still light out own lamps from that clear bright flame.[16]

Clare's whole existence had been one of harmony with her surroundings. True to the ideal of Francis, she praised and loved all God's creatures and instructed her sisters to do the same. In the Process for Canonization, Sister Angeluccia testified:

> When the holy Mother sent the extern sisters outside the monastery, she admonished them that whenever they saw beautiful leafy or flowering trees they should praise the Creator; and, likewise, whenever they saw any human being or any other creature, they should always and in all things praise the Creator. (Process XIV.9)[17]

SENSITIVE LEADER

That Clare's harmony with creation heightened her sensitivity to all of mankind is very obvious from Sr Angeluccia's testimony, but her sensitivity to her Lord was even more obvious. God was not to be outdone in generosity. On Christmas eve of 1252, not long before her death, Clare was much too ill to attend Matins in the friars' oratory. Some of the Sisters wished to remain with her, but she would not hear of depriving them of the joy they would experience at the festivities. She urged all of them to attend and was left alone. It was a tremendous sacrifice on her part for it was her delight to honor the Holy Babe of Bethlehem, as Francis had done so many years earlier,[18] but this evening she had to relinquish that joy.

Being alone on such a wondrous night can be a problem, even for a saint, and Clare indulged in a bit of self-pity. She began to weep and complain to the Lord, but, no sooner had she uttered her complaint when:

> . . . suddenly the wondrous music that was being sung in the Church of San Francesco began to resound in her ears; she heard the glad voices of the friars at their psalms, she listened to the harmonies of the singers; and even perceived the sound of the organ. Yet the place was by no means so near that she could have heard all this in a purely human manner. Either the solemnity was carried to her by some divine power or her hearing was given a superhuman acuteness. But what surpasses even this marvel is that she was worthy also to see the manger of the Lord.[19]

When she came to herself, the first rays of dawn were filtering through the narrow window. How surprised her sisters were when she related to them the festivities held at the Church of San Francesco! Indeed, the church was more than a mile away and while it would be possible to hear the bells which Brother Elias had installed, certainly the singing and the sound of the organ could not have carried so far. This great basilica, while seeming a bit elaborate for the poor friars, had been built by the generous alms of the people to honor St Francis and, in accord with his desires, they gave only the best for the Lord. All the items used there, including the vestments, were used for the glory of God, and hence at Christmas, which Francis dearly loved, the basilica would have been decorated more elaborately than usual to honor the infant Saviour.[20]

Another instance of God's response to Clare's pleas occurred when the sisters were down to their last loaf of bread. Clare's order to have half of the loaf given to the friars who begged for them puzzled the sister who was to carry it out. 'Thereupon the blessed mother ordered the witness [the sister] to divide the half loaf into fifty portions and to set them before the sisters seated at table.' At hearing this, Sister Cecilia asked if the miracle of the loaves and fishes was about to take place again. Clare responded: '"Go and do as I have told you." And the Lord so increased the loaf that she was able to make of it fifty good portions as Saint Clare commanded.'[21] Through such experiences the sister learned from Clare to have complete trust in God.

TOTAL ABANDONMENT

It was in 1226, when Francis died, that 'Clare became the most conspicuous champion of the ideal of total abnegation and complete dependence on God'.[22] She became a mother, a director of souls, and a comforter for many of the friars Francis had left behind, for the countless Third Order members living in their homes, and for the Poor Ladies in the many monasteries which had been established during her life time. She can be compared to Mary, the Mother of God, who remained behind to help the infant Church grow.

> Among the friars who came to see her, the most regular and the most welcome visitors were those who preserved the Franciscan spirit of the first days. Like her blessed Father, Clare was especially fond of Brother Juniper, of joyous and happy mien, of Brother Leo who had copied out a breviary for her, and of Brother Giles who improvised a sermon one day which afforded her so much pleasure.[23]

As time passed and the first friars as well as the friends of Francis died, Clare was sought out more and more as the last of the real bearers of the torch of poverty. That poverty which had inspired Francis and had moved her to leave all, burned brightly behind the walls of San Damiano. She had proved that Christians could live like the poor Christ and his mother anywhere: on the highways, in the missions, in cities, or behind cloister walls. Poverty lived on as long as one consistently attempted to abandon oneself to God's will. And this was evident at San Damiano.

For Francis total abandonment found expression in perfect joy.[24] It is not a popular concept, even among Franciscans, and like so many of the things Francis said and did, it seemed to be beyond the ordinary person. Yet, Francis had learned this concept from Christ himself. The story of perfect joy is none other than the scourging, the crowning, the mockery, the abandonment by friends, and the final cry of 'Father, forgive them . . .'. Thus, Francis stated: 'I tell you that if I kept patience and was not upset that is true joy and true virtue and the salvation of the soul'.[25]

During his short life, Francis had acquired the wisdom to see that when one looks at the Crucified, one cannot be offended by anything done to oneself. His day-by-day abandonment, his day-by-day self-emptying brought him to the summit of perfect joy with Lady Poverty. And Clare was right behind him. She had divested herself of title, position, family inheritance, and now her very life for her Lord. She had pleaded with two popes for the privilege of the highest poverty and had fought for permission to have her own Rule.

> This Rule was indeed a triumph for S. Clare. It forbade the holding of any possessions, and it bound the Order closely to the friars; but it applied only to the community of San Damiano or to such houses as chose, and were allowed, to adopt it as their own.[26]

Clare saw clearly that to abandon oneself into the hands of the living God was an awesome thing and that she and her sisters must be convinced themselves before they could convince others that total abandonment is the key to being a pilgrim and a stranger. Her abandonment, as we know, caught on rapidly so that by the time of her death in 1253, fifty sisters[27] were living at San Damiano and over twenty monasteries of Poor Ladies had sprung up.

CONCERNED LEADER

Of her tender concern for her sisters it is said:

> It was she who sent round to see if anyone were in trouble, who would cover up any sick sister with warm blankets, who thought of everyone's physical, as well as spiritual, well being. Like Francis she was always insistent on the care of the sick—when the sick person was not herself.[28]

Her own severe penances and fasting did not make her harsh or severe toward others; contrarily, the witnesses for her canonization emphasized her 'great sympathy and compassion, her unfailing gentleness and kindness'.[29] She even placed this concept in her Rule:

> As to the sisters who are ill the Abbess is strictly bound to make solicitous inquiry herself and through the other sisters of all that their infirmity requires both in matter of good advice and in food and in other necessities, and according to the resources of the monastery charitably and compassionately provide for them.[30]

It is worthy of note that responsibility for the sick rested on the Abbess and then on the other members of the community. 'Because all are bound to care and serve their sisters who are ill as they would wish to be served themselves were they suffering from any infirmity.'[31] This obligation is written into the Rule of most religious communities, but the fact emphasized here is Clare's fulfillment of the written word, not as a duty, but as an act of love.

While Clare insisted her nuns do this type of service for each other, she was also aware of, and she made allowances for, human frailty. She wrote into the Rule that those who need them may have the use of a feather pillow and a mattress and even woolen stockings, if necessary.

COURAGEOUS LEADER AND MAKER OF PEACE

As a youth, Francis had dreamed of victory in battle and of becoming a great knight. After his first attempt, around 1204, he began to realize that peace is not won through war. His greeting to everyone he met became 'PEACE AND ALL GOOD', and one of his last acts during his final illness was the reconciliation of the mayor and the bishop of Assisi.

The Canticle of Creatures which he wrote at San Damiano during his last illness, expresses a cosmic view on three levels; heaven, air, and earth; it is basically a great poem of praise in which the Son of God destroys spiritual darkness much as the sun destroys material darkness. After considering the four elements—earth, air, fire and water—as great friends of man, he turned to man himself, praising the reconciliation which brings harmony, peacemaking by which one resembles the son of God, and conformity to the will of God through submission or humility. The stanza which transformed the attitudes of the antipathetic bishop and mayor is:

> All praise be yours, my Lord, through those who grant pardon
> For love of you; through those who endure
> Sickness and trial.[32]

Clare never dreamed of being a knight nor of going into battle, but she showed herself the courageous leader and the intercessor of peace, when the battle came to her. Twice in her life Clare pleaded with the Lord to spare her beloved Assisi a battle which threatened to devastate the entire area, and each time the Lord answered. The most often-repeated story concerns an actual event, although some details differ from other accounts. In 1240, Frederick II had been excommunicated. He brought saracen troops with him from Sicily and permitted them to run rampant over the italian countryside. A band of them approached the little monastery of San Damiano outside the walls of Assisi. The attackers climbed the monastery walls and began to invade the nuns' cloister. The sisters, of course, were terrified having lived in peace there since 1212. The particulars of the incident are told to us through one of the witnesses for the canonization of Clare:

> Asked what she had especially noted in St Clare, she told how on one occasion the Saracens had entered into the cloister of the monastery whereupon St Clare had herself brought to the door of the refectory and caused the sacrament of the Body of Our Lord Jesus to be carried before her in a little box. She prostrated herself in prayer upon the ground and in tears among others prayed in these words: 'Lord, look upon thy poor servants for I cannot guard them'. Then the witness heard a voice of wonderful sweetness saying: 'I will always defend thee'; whereupon St Clare prayed also for the city saying, 'Lord, be pleased also to defend this city', and again that same sweet voice answered: 'The city will suffer many dangers, but will be defended'.
>
> Then the Lady Clare turned to the sisters and said to them: 'Do not be afraid; I am your safeguard and no harm will come to you, now or in the future nor at any other time as long as you obey God's commandments'. And the Saracens departed without doing any harm or damage.[33]

LEADER AS SERVANT

Neither Clare nor Francis lacked the ability to govern, or the moral commitment to the task. But in studying the life of Christ, both of them wished to follow as the least of the members, after Christ's example. Once the role of leader was thrust upon them, however, each saw clearly that in that role was a tremendous channel for service and an even greater channel for personal sanctification. It is difficult to say which of them excelled in service to others. The most remarkable of Francis' services was his work among the lepers; Clare's was among the infirm in her own household. How often their services went unnoticed or unappreciated is not known, but human nature does not change with religious garb, so we may assume there were such instances and that these were precious events for them in the light of a joy which perfects through willing sacrifice which goes unnoticed.

Francis, as founder, had no choice but to assume the leadership of the friars, although his intention had been, not to found an Order, but only to follow his own call. Clare, too, had avoided a title even though the leadership was clearly hers. Her sense of being the servant of others did not accord with being a superior in a traditional monastery. For three years the group grew and lived and became a closely-knit unit governed by their love for Francis and living in complete conformity to his ideals. Now, however, even Francis had to make Clare realize that she must assume not just the obligations of a superior but also a title. While he wholeheartedly approved of her stand that she should be on an equal footing with her sisters, he also knew that this little group needed some form of Rule and a recognized leader.

The Rule which he wrote for her was probably much like the 'primitive Rule of the friars . . . quite short and composed largely of texts from the Gospels',[34] and like the Primitive Rule for the friars it has long since disappeared. Although the Rule included regulations about fasting and poverty, and the promise of 'obedience to S. Francis while he, in turn, promised to take care of her and her sisters',[35] Pope Gregory IX, formerly, Hugolino, the Cardinal Protector of the Order, felt it was not solid enough a Rule.

It was at this same time that Clare was persuaded to accept the title of abbess. This, however, was not to minimize her role of service, but if anything, to increase it. For as she submitted to the Pope, to Francis, and to the Lateran Council, she seemed more completely to submit herself to her sisters:

> She never shrank from any menial task, so that at table she usually poured the water on the hands of the Sisters, assisted those who were sitting and served those who were eating. Only reluctantly would she give an order; she would rather do a thing of her own accord, preferring to perform a task herself than to bid others to do it.[36]

According to Sister Pacifica, who testified at the canonization:

> . . . the blessed Mother was most humble, benign and loving toward her sisters, and while she was well she served them, and washed their feet and gave them water for their hands, and she washed the seats used by the sick. Asked how she knew this, she answered that she herself had seen it many times.[37]

LEADER AS FAITHFUL DISCIPLE

Clare's illness was an accepted fact for almost thirty years. She had prayed and worked rarely apart from her bed all the years after 1124–5, but the shock of her death was still overwhelming for those who loved her dearly. She was one of those persons who, it would seem, should never die. When the news of her death reached the town, hasty preparations were made to protect the body of the saint.

> The Podesta at once set guards round the monastery, for it seemed only too likely that relic hunters would try to rob Assisi of its second great

> treasure. The next day the Pope came from Perugia accompanied by the cardinals, by the Bishop of Assisi and other bishops, and a multitude of friends. The friars began the Office of the Dead when the Pope remarked that it would have been more suitable to sing the Office of Virgins; and indeed he would have wished to canonize her on the spot. But Cardinal Raintaldo observed that the Church's ritual should be followed and so the Office of the Dead continued.[38]

Clare had fulfilled her life-time dream, the work which God had given her to do. With Francis, she had established an Order which would continue to live the Gospel, emphasizing poverty, behind enclosed walls, becoming a church within a Church and as loyal a daughter as the Church would ever know.

> Far from opposing ecclesiastical dignitaries, Clare counted Popes and Cardinals among her dearest friends. Innocent III so respected her love of poverty that 'with his own hand he wrote the first draft for the Privilege she sought' (*Leg.* 14). Gregory IX 'loved the Saint dearly with fatherly affection (*loc. cit*) and had such confidence in the power of her prayers that he shared with her the weightiest problems of his pontificate (*Leg.* 27). Innocent IV 'considered her to surpass all the women of our time,' and hastened with the whole Roman Curia to her death-bed (*Leg.* 41). The story of Clare's friendship with the highest authorities of the Church is sufficient proof of their esteem for her. Clare 'the new leader of women; was in every respect a most faithful daughter of the Church whom she served with all her strength and for the whole of her life'.[39]

The Church itself was not slow in honoring the saint, the disciple who lived Gospel poverty and legalized it with a written statement of all it entailed, the disciple whose own Rule had been approved on her death-bed, the disciple whose charity and miracles would be sorely missed by all classes of society. About two months after Clare's death, Innocent IV commissioned the archbishop of Spoleto to record her virtues and miracles. Innocent was not to have the privilege of canonizing her, for he was called by God in 1254. Cardinal Rainaldo, Alexander IV, presided at her canonization on 12 August 1255, a brief two years after her death.

> In her obedience to the Church as well as in her life of Gospel perfection, Clare was the faithful follower of the Seraphic Francis. Her glorious canonization was the voice of the universal Church proclaiming the significance of her life for all Christendom.[40]

In the Bull of Canonization, Alexander poetically declared:

'Her feet stood upon earth while her soul was already in heaven'.[41]

Lo, Assisi, lost in the Umbrian hills;
 Two saints recline within your walls!
You need no longer blush nor cry nor be ashamed,
 For God has raised you above other towns
With perfect joy and holy peace!

NOTES

1. Nesta deRobeck, *St. Clare of Assisi* (Milwaukee, 1951) 234.
2. Sr Chiara Augusta Lainati, OSC 'The Enclosure of St. Clare and of the First Poor Clares in Canonical Legislation and in Practice,' Cord 28/1 (Jan. 1978) 9.
3. John Moorman, *A History of the Franciscan Order*. (Oxford, Clarendon Press, 1968) 33–34.
4. *Ibid.* p. 34.
5. Ignatius Brady, OFM. *The Legend and Writings of St. Clare of Assisi.* (St Bonaventure, New York: The Franciscan Institute, 1953) 161.
6. For a concise reading and better understanding of the intention behind giving the Poor Ladies the Rule of St. Benedict read: John van de Pavert, OFM, 'St. Clare and the Rules', FIA Contact, 4/2 (May, 1983) [Franciscan Institute of Asia: Philippines] pp. 2–11.
7. Sr Mary Seraphim, PCPA, *Clare: Her Light and Her Song*. (Chicago: Herald Press, 1984) 154.
8. Moorman, p. 35.
9. *Legend and Writings*, p. 174. n.5.
10. Lainati, 'The Enclosure of St. Clare . . .', 10–11.
11. Moorman, 36.
12. *Ibid.*, 207.
13. *Ibid.*, 208–9.
14. *Legend and Writings*, 14.
15. *Ibid.*, 50.
16. *Ibid.*, 153.
17. *Ibid.*, 175, n.26.
18. Omer Englebert, *St. Francis of Assisi: A Biography*. (Chicago: Franciscan Herald Press, 1965) 299–301, an account of the crib at Greccio.
19. *Legend and Writings*, 39.
20. de Robeck, 205.
21. *Ibid.*, 206.
22. Moorman, 205.
23. Englebert, 174.
24. For a more perfect understanding of Lady Poverty read the '*Sacrum Commercium*' beginning on p. 1533 in *St. Francis of Assisi: Omnibus of Sources* Marion Habig, ed. (Chicago; Franciscan Herald Press, 1972).
25. *Omnibus*, 1502: Francis' concept of perfect joy.
26. Moorman, p. 213.
27. deRobeck, p. 88. The number fifty is attested to by a listing on the lecturn in the choir at San Damiano (of which I took a picture when I visited there). Nesta deRobeck, however, counts only forty-two on her list.
28. *Ibid.*, 49.
29. *Ibid.*
30. Ignatius C. Brady, OFM, trans., *Rule and Constitutions of the Order of St. Clare.* (New Orleans; Monastery Print Shop, 1973) 12.
31. *Ibid.*

32. *Omnibus*, p. 131.
33. deRobeck, p. 209–10.
34. Moorman, p. 35.
35. *Ibid.*
36. *Legend and Writings*, 27.
37. deRobeck, 184.
38. *Ibid.*, 135.
39. *Legends and Writings*, 129–30.
40. *Ibid.*, 130.
41. deRobeck, 136.

The Women of Helfta

Called the crown of German cloisters, the monastery of Helfta was the home of three renowned women of the thirteenth century: Gertrude the Great, Mechtild of Hackeborn, and Mechtild of Magdeburg. Contemporaries and friends, they have bequeathed to us a treasure rare in the history of women, a collection of spiritual writings. During the Peasants' Rebellion in the sixteenth century the books and manuscripts of Helfta were destroyed, but by strange good fortune, the works of these three women survived. They reveal the spirituality of women full of compassion, courage, and love, women who experienced joy and sorrow, and share with us the adventure of their journey to God. Our authors paint a portrait of these unique women, drawing from their writings.

Sr Edith Scholl, using the rich poetic verse of Mechtild of Magdeburg shows this fiery beguine's growth in love—her journey to the 'top of the mountain' and to becoming a full grown bride.

Sr Jeremy Finnegan portrays Mechtild of Hackeborn, not as a great mystic, but as the ordinary nun, hidden, poor, grateful, cheerful. She entered into the simple tasks of daily life in a spirit of loving prayer and unostentatious service to others. *Nemo communior*, Sr Jeremy describes her, 'No one was more companionable, less singular'.

Sr Lillian Thomas sketches St Gertrude as integrated monastic woman and draws from her writings Gertrude's own feminine description of the traditional monastic values. We have very few monastic women writers from whom we can study these values. An original aspect, Gertrude's philosophy and theology of life and death, is then outlined. These are dominant, but hidden, themes in Gertrude's spirituality. Her vision of the meaning of life and death have much to offer our contemporary world.

These three individual women knew and loved each other, experiencing the monastic life together amid the spiritual vitality of Helfta's environment. Yet the message of each article is unique enriching the many previous studies of these famous women.

Gertrude of Hackeborn governed her community for forty years during one of the most troubled periods in the history of Germany. She and her sister Mechtild belonged to a prominent family, the barons of Hackeborn. Many of the other distinguished families of the region sent their daughters to Helfta to be educated. Abbess Gertrude was convinced that if literature were neglected, the Scriptures would no longer be understood. She took pains to get books for the library and insisted that her nuns be diligent in their studies. She agreed with St Bernard of Clairvaux that the spouse of the Lord should not be a dolt. St Gertrude was probably the most scholarly of the nuns; yet the sister who wrote her biography (Book One of the *Legatus divinae pietatis*) quotes Bede, Augustine, Bernard, Gregory, Benedict, and Hugh of St Victor.

All the nuns undertook the ordinary duties of a large household, and the abbess was often the first at work. Realistic scenes of homely household activity provided Gertrude with 'similitudes' for her illustrations of spiritual truths.* In addition to their spiritual treatises the nuns also wrote letters giving counsel and sympathy to lay persons, and some of St Mechtild's correspondence is quoted in the *Liber specialis gratiae.*

At Helfta the steady pursuit of learning and holiness was maintained despite the distractions inseparable from conducting a school, the pressure of acute financial anxieties, and periods of grave danger when marauding nobles threatened the monastery. Poverty and the terror of feuding barons demoralized Saxony and Thuringia during and after the Great Interregnum between the death of Frederick II in 1250 to the election of Rudolph of Hapsburg in 1273. Many of the nuns were related to the warring nobles but family ties afforded no protection; on the contrary, they involved the community in local feuds. In spite of the perilous times, this group of nuns —about one hundred in number—made a major contribution to the cultural life of the region. The works of the three mystics of Helfta form a large part of this achievement. Though they were closely associated, each has her distinctive themes. St Gertrude's individual style is so pervasive in the *Liber specialis gratiae* that the Solesmes editors agree that she was the chief recorder of St Mechtild's revelations.

With the death of St Gertrude the Great in 1301, at the age of forty-five, the community lost its last outstanding member. She had been preceded in death by the Abbess Gertrude of Hackeborn and the two Mechtilds. Within the next fifty years local disturbances and attacks on the monastery led the community to transfer to Eisleben. The golden age of Helfta had passed and only scattered records remain. Nevertheless by a special providence the writings of Gertrude the Great, Mechtild of Hackeborn, and Mechtild of Magdeburg have come down to us as reminders of a place where learning and art, courtesy and holiness flowered in a dark season.

Jeremy Finnegan, OP

*S. M. Jeremy, 'Similitudes in the Writings of St. Gertrude', *Mediaeval Studies* 19 (1957) 48–54.

Saint Mechtild of Hackeborn: *Nemo Communior*

Jeremy Finnegan

'A MAYDEN THARE was fro here berth gracyouslye blessede of oure lorde godd . . .' So begins the first chapter of *The Booke of Gostlye Grace*, a fifteenth-century translation of the biography of Saint Mechtild of Hackeborn.[1] The sources of our information about her and her remarkable community are the *Legatus divinae pietatis* and the *Liber specialis gratiae*. The former is the biography of St Gertrude the Great, written in part by herself and in part by an anonymous *compilatrix*. The biographical memoir of St Mechtild was almost certainly written by St Gertrude and another nun. The definitive edition of these works has been issued by the Solesmes Benedictines.[2]

The title of St Mechtild's memoir, *The Book of Special Grace*, reflects the particular graces conferred upon her. Hers was not a prophetic or reforming mission inspired by the situation of the contemporary Church. Rather, by extension of her special graces, Mechtild's apostolate, primarily to individuals, manifests the infinite reaches of divine love accessible to every person. It is the purpose of this paper to demonstrate her role in her community.

Mechtild was a child of seven in 1248, when her mother brought her to the monastery to visit her elder sister Gertrude, the future abbess. The little girl went from nun to nun, begging to stay. When they all joined their pleas to hers, her mother consented, and Mechtild became one of the abbey pupils. Her education progressed under the direction of her sister, who in 1251 was unanimously elected abbess. When Mechtild herself was about seventeen, she was received into the community. Her formal consecration followed in due course.

The title *Domna cantrix* (Lady chantress) distinguishes Mechtild from the other members of the community. She had a singing voice of remarkable beauty and eventually became directress of the choir as well as a teacher in the abbey school. One of her charges was the young Gertrude, later known as 'the Great', a child of unknown parentage who had been brought to the abbey at the age of five. This Gertrude is not to be confused with the Abbess Gertrude of Hackeborn, Mechtild's sister.

As choir mistress Mechtild instructed the novices in the ceremonies of the choral office and assisted them in memorizing long liturgical texts. Her own spiritual life was rooted in the liturgy, particularly in the great chants and hymns of the Divine Office. 'Mechtild's mysticism is steeped in the Opus Dei' says the editor of the *Booke of Gostlye Grace.*[3] The French translators of the *Liber Specialis Gratiae* speak of the intelligent piety that she brought to the melodies of solemn prayer.[4] Jean Leclercq has noted that the Cistercians' preface to their reformed antiphonary makes clear that 'ideas of musical technique were adapted to spiritual consideration'.[5] Many passages in the *Liber specialis gratiae* illustrate Mechtild's adaptations. Music was not only a bridge between heaven and earth, it was the meeting place for all members of the Mystical Body. When she intoned an anthem, the angels continued it along with the community. She told her pupils that any deed performed for the worship of God, however small it might be, resounds everlastingly as a soft melody from the heart of the person to the heart of God.

Mechtild's intense devotion during the Office and at Mass moved the other nuns to similar fervor. Her prayers for the community were usually from the Divine Office. As directress of the choir she paid particular attention to the rubrics, instructing the novices to pay homage to the incarnate Lord as they bowed low at the beginning of each liturgical hour.

Her own glorious singing was not without its cost. Sometimes it seemed to her that she was too exhausted to draw breath, yet she continued to sing with all possible fervor. Sometimes the visible presence of Christ sustained her, enabling her to persevere. The role of the chantress is essential to the maintenance of tone and tempo in the performance of the office. St Mechtild's devoted accomplishment of this duty contributed greatly to the stability and richness of the common life at Helfta.

For forty years Mechtild's lovely voice trained and led the choir. Passage after passage in the *Liber* refers to her as a musician, the nightingale of Christ. In thus serving him, she experienced a mysterious relationship with the Lord, whom she repeatedly hailed as *Cantor cantorum*. Once, having prayed for a nun who found her duty (in choir?) burdensome, Mechtild saw her standing before Christ, who asked, 'Why does she sing for me unwillingly since I shall gladly sing for her through all eternity?'[6]

TEACHER AND ADVOCATE

It was not only as musician that Mechtild served her sisters. Many passages refer to her as teacher, particularly in the abbey school. Christ had said: 'I entrust to you the simple innocent children symbolized by the lamb; you are to teach them, preparing them to know and love me.'[7] She gives practical advice on the rearing of children: 'When they reach the age of twelve, they should be taught what is right and their faults seriously corrected. If this were done, there would not be so many lost in religious life and on the way of virtue.'[8] Gertrude and Mechtild, both teachers, often use comparisons drawn from academic situations, and refer to Christ as the best of teachers.

Like her sister the abbess, Mechtild emphasized the importance of study. She enjoined the novices to read and listen willingly to Scripture, to obey the Rule carefully, and to be humble in all circumstances, neither comparing themselves to others nor looking down on them. She offered penances on behalf of clergymen who neglected the study of Scripture or indulged in it only for show.

Besides her teaching and choral duties Mechtild shared the ordinary household work of the community. Spinning, dyeing, and cooking were regular duties. She helped another sister by mending her clothes; her own were covered with patches. She took it as a special sign of God's favor that this person caused her much suffering. At the service of everyone, she was so generally useful that it seemed, says Gertrude, that God wished none of his gifts to her to escape notice.[9] She gave valuable assistance to her sister the abbess in both spiritual and temporal matters.

Passages in the *Legatus* of St Gertrude and the *Liber* of St Mechtild show the close association both had with their community. Charity in the care of the sick is an index to the fervor of a religious house. Mechtild often ministered to the needs of those who were ill, although her own health was far from robust. To a sister who was afraid of dying she brought Christ's reassurance: 'What shipman would cast his goods willfully into the sea when he is coming to the harbor in peace? No shipman would do so; no more will I with her. But I shall take her soul joyfully to myself and not cast it from me.'[10] She also helped a sister who because of illness was unable to restrain her tears and seemed actually to be in danger of losing her eyesight. She begged Mechtild and all the community to pray that she might be cured of this humiliating and dangerous affliction. Upon her sudden restoration Mechtild urged her to ask God to transform the useless tears into tears of love and repentance.

The community regarded Mechtild as their special advocate with God. At a time of great difficulty—perhaps during the 1290s when the canons of

Halberstadt imposed an interdict 'on account of certain pecuniary matters'—the nuns recited the entire psalter. They asked Mechtild to offer these prayers to God on their behalf.[11] In 1294, while marauding soldiers of the Emperor Adolph of Nassau were in the neighborhood, Mechtild prayed for the protection of the monastery. After receiving the response, 'You will not see a single soldier', she persisted: 'Will this promise also keep them from damaging the monastery?' The community soon experienced the protection she had elicited.[12]

FRIENDSHIP AND CHARITY

It was not only in times of urgent necessity that Mechtild prayed for her community. Her constant petition was that God would always sustain the nuns in his service, multiply his graces in them, make them fruitful in virtues, and prosper them in all good works. After receiving a grace, she often prayed that her friends might receive the same blessing. The *Liber* gives the impression that she had at least four close friends, among whom Gertrude the Great was the most intimate. Mechtild, the senior by approximately fifteen years, was a member of the local nobility while Gertrude was apparently a nameless orphan, yet they were united in a profound spiritual relationship. They shared an intense devotion to the mysteries of the incarnation, a personal love of Christ, and a dedication to the welfare and ideals of their community. Their love of music also formed a bond. Gertrude sometimes substituted for Mechtild as chantress. Both moreover were endowed with intellectual gifts of a high order.

Another friend who particularly appreciated Mechtild was the former beguine, Mechtild of Magdeburg. She had come to Helfta in her old age, after having aroused much opposition in Madgeburg by her outspoken criticism of the clergy. Before coming to Helfta she had completed the first six books of *Das fliessende Licht der Gottheit,* and she dictated the seventh to the nuns at the monastery. Her subject was the ways of God with her soul and the ill-conduct of her contemporaries. In writing of her spiritual experiences she used the language of court and chivalry, sometimes breaking into lyric rhythms.[13]

When she first came to Helfta, she was enchanted by Mechtild's conversation and more impressed by her than by St Gertrude. Both nuns, for their part, spoke respectfully of the old refugee whom they attended in her illness and blindness. Her dying words attest to her gratitude: 'I take leave of all my dear friends. I thank God for them that they have been my help in my need. Were I to be longer here, I should ever be ashamed of the lack of virtue they must have seen in me.'[14]

In their warm kindness to the 'weather-beaten old sibyl', as Hans Urs von Balthasar calls her, Gertrude and Mechtild showed a serene acceptance of individuality.[15] Mechtild had said that souls differ as birds do: some are nightingales, enamored of God; some are larks, who perform good works with joyous humility; some are doves, simple souls who quietly receive the gifts of God without discussing their doings or those of others. This understanding of divergent personalities kept Mechtild from rigidity in her dealings with her many companions.

SPIRITUAL COUNSELOR

Desiring that all the nuns might share the grace of intimate union with Christ, she would in spirit take his hand in hers and lead him to her companions to bless each one. The sisters, finding in Mechtild a model as well as a teacher, sought her out and listened to her, says Gertrude, 'with all the attention they would give to a preacher.[16] Her advice was practical, as the following typical examples show:

> If any obstacle arises in our service of God, whether from the attitude of others, from external circumstances, from our own desires, memories, or from any other cause—whatever the impediment, we should take it as a messenger from God, sending it back to him, so to speak, with praise and thanksgiving.[17]
>
> Three things very pleasing to God are: first, never to abandon one's neighbor in his needs, and to excuse his shortcomings and sins as much as possible; second, in tribulation to seek refuge only in God, abandoning to him alone all that disquiets the heart; third, to walk with him in truth.[18]
>
> When it is time to eat or to sleep, say in your heart: 'Lord, in union with the love with which you created this useful thing for me, and yourself made use of it when you were on earth. I take it for your eternal praise and for my bodily need.'[19]
>
> We should be lovingly grateful not only for the spiritual blessings God gives us, but for all bodily necessities such as food and clothing, receiving them with a sincerely thankful heart and considering ourselves unworthy of them.[20]
>
> What best pleases God in members of religious orders is purity of heart, holy desires, gentle kindness in conversation, and works of charity.[21]

Mechtild was not unaware of her sisters' faults, often accusing herself of the same ones. She mentions sleepiness and sloth ('slugerye and slewth' in *The Booke of Gostlye Grace*), particularly during community prayers. In keeping with her conviction that Christ's merits can compensate for all human failings, she offered his labors during his youth in reparation for them. She reacted sensitively to any lack of reverence. It is said that if anyone spoke of the passion of Christ without devotion, her face and hands became as red as a boiled crab (*in modum decocti cancri apparerent*).

To those who came to her for advice Mechtild taught that meditation on the passion is the remedy for spiritual maladies. In her diagnosis of these maladies she says that timid souls afraid to trust themselves to God's love have a trembling paralysis. Those who do everything languidly and half-heartedly have a sleeping paralysis. Others, she says, are flighty and inconstant; thoughts run helter-skelter through their minds, and a single word is enough to make them impatient or angry.

'Everyone who sought her came away either comforted or enlightened', said Gertrude. 'Everyone loved her and wanted to be with her, and in the end this was a great burden.'[22] Sisters who suffered from scruples, who found it hard to obey their superiors, who were overwhelmed by their duties, all fled to her for comfort and relief. She prayed compassionately for the overburdened portress, who was frequently summoned from Mass to attend to guests. 'Tell her', said Christ, 'that I count each step she takes.'[23] As she prayed for a woman weighed down by heavy manual labors, she saw her kneeling before Christ, while he poured upon her uplifted hands a healing balm from his own. To a sister who was discouraged she brought this message from Christ: 'Why is she troubled? I have given myself to her for the fulfillment of all her desires. I am her father by creation, her mother by redemption, her brother in the sharing of my kingdom, her sister by sweet companionship.'[24]

Both Gertrude and Mechtild encouraged the nuns to receive communion frequently, particularly those who hesitated because of indolence or scrupulosity. Mechtild urged them to be generous in praying for others. 'One should be as liberal as a queen at the king's table.'[25] He is pleased when we confidently expect great things of him. She had tremendous confidence in Christ's mercy and accessibility. 'He is more easily possessed than a bit of thread or straw. A single wish, a sigh, is sufficient.'[26]

Mechtild usually presented spiritual counsel as if she had learned it from someone else. 'Blessed be God', wrote Gertrude, 'for giving us such a mediatrix, who shows a mother's tenderness to the unhappy by her constant prayers, zealous instructions, and consolations.'[27]

Deeply affectionate as she was, Mechtild came to realize that divine love was infinitely greater than her own and that not all faults are remediable. She confided in Gertrude, 'In the light of eternal truth I now see clearly that all my love for those who were dear to me in this life is no more than a drop in the ocean in comparison with the love of the Sacred Heart for them. I see also why God permits persons to keep certain faults that humiliate and discipline them on the way of salvation.'[28]

Not only the community, but friars and laypersons, sought Mechtild's advice. That they came great distances in unsettled times when travel was unsafe gives some indication of her influence. Her knowledge of court life and the customs of the nobility would have made her familiar with the needs of these suppliants. Many passages in the *Liber* reveal her acquaintance with the manners of the aristocracy. It is likely that her relatives were among the visitors to the monastery. She wondered whether Christ had maintained communication with his kinsmen after the return from Egypt to Nazareth. Her question was answered when she recalled the text, 'They [Mary and Joseph] sought him among their relatives and friends'.[29]

Undoubtedly the number of visitors could have been wearisome to the nuns. Mechtild's prayer for the portress has already been noted. The *Legatus* reports that St Gertrude once took to her bed to escape the tumult of visitors. It is recorded that Mechtild prayed for 'an ill-tempered man' and for another 'who thought himself wiser than his superiors'.[30] She gave a forceful reply to a Friar Preacher who was experiencing temptations: 'Those temptations cannot hurt you any more than gnats can destroy a mountain.'[31] With the sure instinct that attracts the faithful to those close to God, these visitors to Helfta asked Mechtild's prayers and were not surprised when she was able to read their hearts. In spite of her best efforts she was not able entirely to conceal her mystical graces. Once, when the force of divine love overcame her, says Gertrude, 'even guests and strangers became aware of the heavenly intoxication she had so long kept hidden'.[32]

Evidently Mechtild sometimes corresponded with those who asked her help. The monastic letter is a recognized genre in medieval literature. The *Liber* contains four of her letters. The first, addressed 'Dearly beloved daughter in Christ', is representative of Mechtild's counsel, combining instruction and encouragement. Written in the present tense, it opens with the confident assertion, 'The lover of your soul is holding your hand in his right hand.' Then Mechtild assures her correspondent that Christ's virtues can supply for her deficiencies—a characteristic theme in Mechtild's spiritual history. She develops this theme by associating each of Christ's fingers with a virtue: by joining one's fingers figuratively to his, one may find a remedy for spiritual ills. For example, the ring finger symbolizes Christ's fidelity. Like a faithful mother he relieves our burdens with inexpressible constancy and keeps us from all evil. 'Join your finger to his by confessing your infidelity toward this gentle and faithful lover.'[33]

In another letter to the same unnamed person she employs military terms with a vigor and assurance which remind us that her name, Mechtild, means strength in battle. She writes: 'Ask of the Saviour armies to strengthen you for victory against the assault of vices. If thieving wicked thoughts try to take you by surprise, run to the arsenal and there clothe yourself with the ever-shining armor of your Savior's passion and death.'[34] Other passages remind her friend that nothing is to be preferred to the love of Christ. If she gives him her heart in joy and confidence, he will give her his. Even when deprived of joy and consolation she must continue to praise and thank him.

Mechtild herself knew what it was to be deprived of consolation. Beloved as she was and extraordinarily gifted, she had nevertheless much to suffer. One can only guess what personal experience and self-conquest inspired her counsel: 'One should be like a trusty little dog who always returns to its master even after frequent rebuffs. If one is wounded by a word, she should not withdraw, or if she does so, she should return at once, relying on God's mercy which for a single sigh pardons everything.'[35]

Mechtild was particularly devoted to the dying. It was a great sorrow to her that illness prevented her from being at the deathbed of her sister the abbess. As substitute chantress Gertrude intoned the antiphon for the dying, *Surge, Virgo*. Mechtild's prayers followed her friends after their death, and she was sometimes privileged to communicate with their departed spirits. Once she saw in the choir a dear friend who had recently died. 'All that you told me is perfectly true,' the friend assured her, 'and now I have found my hundredfold.'[36]

TRIALS

Mechtild's ill health, which often kept her from taking part in community prayers, her disabling headaches, and the three-year illness that culminated in her death at the age of fifty-seven, were probably less painful than her mental sufferings, the conviction of her unworthiness and wasted life. We read that sometimes she could not sleep for sorrow. She feared that the divine communications were only her imagination. When she found that St Gertrude and another nun were recording her intimate conversations with Christ—even though this was by order of the Abbess Sophia, the successor to her sister—she was inconsolable. (Here we might note that conversations between Christ and the soul, as Vernet explains, are not to be taken as literal conversations. The expression, 'Jesus said to me', which one finds in the writings of many mystics, refers to the thoughts which occur during prayer.)[37]

Among her many self-accusations she includes speaking ill of someone and inopportune silence. That she was occasionally scandalized, that she could become indignant at a display of ill temper, that she found it hard to be waited on when she was ill—these are reminders that with all her spiritual gifts she remained one of us, a member of the human family.

Nemo communior—no one more companionable, less singular— St Dominic's brethren said of him. So might the nuns of Helfta have spoken of St

Mechtild. Member of a family that for three generations had been benefactors of the community, sister of a great abbess, Mechtild had no higher title than *Domna Cantrix*. 'The word of command does not become me', she said.[38] Her role was to serve her sisters physically, intellectually, and spiritually, sometimes to the point of exhaustion. By doing so, this nightingale of Christ through a life radiant with the praise and love of God, has cast on the ideal of the common life an enduring light.

NOTES

1. *The Booke of Gostlye Grace of Mechtild of Hakeborn,* ed. Theresa A Halligan (Toronto; Pontifical Institute of Medieval Studies 1979). This is a fifteenth-century translation of an abridged version of the *Liber specialis gratiae.* 'Gostlye' is a mistranslation of the abbreviated *specialis.*

2. *Revelationes Gertrudianae ac Mechtildianae,* ed. Dom Ludwig Paquelin (Paris, 1875–77).

3. Halligan, p. 39.

4. *Révélations de Sainte Mechtilde,* (Tours, 1926) vi.

5. Jean Leclercq, *The Love of Learning and the Desire for God* (New York, 1960) 301.

6. Halligan, p. 298.

7. *Révélations,* IV, ch. 60; p. 306.

8. *Ibid.* I, ch.9; pp. 28–29.

9. *Ibid.* Preamble; p.5.

10. *Ibid.* IV, ch. 35; p. 286.

11. Halligan, p. 93, note 251/17–21.

12. *Révélations,* IV, ch. 11; p. 261.

13. Mechthild von Magdeburg, *Das fliessende Licht der Gottheit,* ed. Margot Schmidt (Einsiedeln, 1956).

14. *Ibid.* VI. 28; p. 307.

15. *Ibid.* 'Mechthilds Kirklicher Auftrag', p. 20.

16. *Révélations,* V, ch. 30; p. 352.

17. *Ibid.* III, ch. 15; p. 208.

18. *Ibid.* IV, ch. 7; p. 257.

19. *Ibid.* III, ch. 27; p. 225.

20. *Ibid.* IV, ch. 6; p. 256.

21. *Ibid.* I, ch. 27; p. 93.

22. *Ibid.* Preamble; p. 4.

23. *Ibid.* III, ch. 45; p. 243.

24. *Ibid.* IV, ch. 50; p. 296.

25. *Ibid.* IV, ch. 32; p. 284.

26. *Ibid.* III, ch. 35; p. 235.

27. *Ibid.* IV, ch. 38; p. 289.

28. *Ibid.* VII, ch. 12; p. 393.

29. *Ibid.* I, ch. 5; p. 20.

30. *Ibid.* IV, ch. 53, p. 297; ch. 15, p. 265.

31. *Ibid.* IV, ch. 40; p. 290.

32. *Ibid.* II, ch. 26; p. 165.

33. *Ibid.* ch. 59; p. 301.

34. *Ibid.* IV, ch. 59; p. 304.

35. *Ibid.* IV, ch. 32; p. 283.

36. *Ibid.* I, ch. 1; p. 10.

37. Félix Vernet, *La spiritualité médiévale* (Paris, 1928) 195.

38. *Révélations,* I, ch. 23; p. 82.

To Be a Full-Grown Bride: Mechthild of Magdeburg

Edith Scholl

'Love grows by loving and loves by growing.'[1] This is true of everyone who tries to love God, but it applies particularly to Mechthild of Magdeburg. Loving God and growing in that love sum up her life and spirituality.

Mechthild's life spanned most of the thirteenth century, that high point of the christian Middle Ages. She was born in Germany about 1209, apparently of noble or well-born parents. All she tells us of her early life is that at the age of twelve the Holy Spirit greeted her so overwhelmingly that she could no longer yield to serious sin.[2] This was apparently an experience crucial to the development of her spiritual life.

In 1230 she went to the city of Magdeburg and lived there as a beguine in an informal sort of religious life which must have suited her temperament better than the more structured atmosphere of a cloister. Although she says that when she arrived she knew only one person in the city, that situation cannot have lasted for long. She attracted attention by her life of fervor and intense prayer, and made friends and disciples. As she felt called upon to denounce in her blunt and forthright manner clerics who were not living up to their obligations, she made enemies, too. Apparently, there were also doubts raised as to her orthodoxy.

Eventually, when she was already old and in poor health, she left Magdeburg and was received into the convent of Helfta, the home of Sts Gertrude the Great and Mechthild of Hackeborn—both so different in character from Mechthild, but like her in their devotion to God. In the congenial atmosphere of that fervent community she remained until her death, which took place in 1282 or 1284.[3]

Though we know little of the outward events of Mechthild's life, her spiritual development can be traced from the writings she left—fragments which she jotted down over her long lifetime and which were collected by her friend, Heinrich von Halle, who assembled them into a book, *The Flowing Light of the Godhead*. In it we can see Mechthild's love for God grow and develop from her young womanhood through maturity to old age.[4] That growth will be the subject of the second and principal part of this paper. The first part will deal with some of Mechthild's characteristics as a writer.

LOVE'S VISION

Mechthild was above all a poet. Her gifts were affective and imaginative rather than intellectual. She saw, rather than reasoned; above all, she loved, and her love gave her vision. This vision she expressed in vivid images. God is a mountain:

> I have seen a mountain
> The base of which was as a shining cloud
> The brightness of which
> No human being could endure
> In his soul for one hour.
> The foot of the mountain was snow-white, cloud covered,
> But its heights were fiery and clear as the sun.
> I could find neither beginning nor end of it. (2.21)

Christ is a hunter who relentlessly pursues her:

> I am hunted, captured, bound,
> Wounded so terribly
> That never can I be healed. (1.3)

Her soul 'found itself in the Holy Trinity as a child finds itself under its mother's breast'. (6.7) After committing a fault, 'I creep back like a beaten dog to the kitchen'. (5.33)

Abstract terms become persons: Understanding (2.29), Contemplation (2.22), above all, Love, and the other virtues (e.g. 1.1, 4.12, 7.48).

Perhaps because of this, Mechthild's characteristic literary genre is the dialogue. She was almost always in conversation with someone; most often with God, sometimes with Love personified, with her own soul, with angels —even with devils. At times the dialogue expands to resemble a scene from a play (1.44). God's plan of creation and redemption she presented as a discussion among the Three Persons of the Trinity (3.9).

Mechthild's main influences, it seems, were those of her times: chivalry; *Minnesänge*, secular love songs which she adapted to her own purposes; the religious ideals promoted by the Dominicans, whom she greatly admired; the mysticism and apocalyptic ideas which were circulating in her day. She rarely quoted the Bible—perhaps a dozen times in all—though a number of passages seem to show the underlying influence of the *Song of Songs.*

We must not expect theology from her; her piety was of a more popular kind. She accepted the doctrines of the Church with no attempt to see their connections or to penetrate them more deeply. She had little or no use for the theoretical; her own experience of God was the starting-point and impetus of all her writings. When something puzzled or troubled her, she did not reason about it, but turned directly to God for an answer (e.g. 2.26, 5.34).

It is interesting to note, however, that images of the Trinity, that most abstract of doctrines, occur frequently under her pen. They are among her most striking and original concepts. They rarely concern the Trinity in itself, but rather its relation to herself, or to others:

> 'I must to God—my Father through nature, my Brother through humanity, my Bridegroom through love.' (1.44)
>
> There [in heaven] the heavenly Father is the cup-bearer, Jesus Christ the chalice and the Holy Spirit the pure wine, and the Holy Trinity together the full plenishing of the chalice and love the mighty cellar. (2.24)
>
> When we receive the Body of the Lord, the Godhead unites itself with our sinless soul and the Humanity of our Lord is mingled with our sinful body and the Holy Spirit makes his dwelling in our faith. (4.8)
>
> Lord and heavenly Father, you are my heart! Lord Jesus Christ, you are my body! Lord Holy Spirit, you are my breath! Lord Holy Trinity, you are my only refuge and my everlasting peace! (5.6)

Obviously this is far from the language of scholastic theology. Yet how vivid and real it makes the Three Persons in their individuality and unity!

It must be admitted that Mechthild's writings are of unequal value: naïve, even grotesque, concepts are mingled with flashes of deep insight and lyrical poetry of a high order. Not everything in her writings will appeal to us, for she was a child of her times, and our mentality is not that of the thirteenth century. Yet a great deal of what she wrote has kept its freshness over seven hundred years. Throughout her work, Mechthild herself remains a very real woman, with a buoyant, resolute, ardent spirit.

LOVE'S BEGINNINGS

Mechthild's early writings are nearly all variations on a theme: her experience of God and their mutual love. Mechthild and her Beloved are completely absorbed in each other; the rest of the world hardly seems to exist. They vie with one another in expressing their love. As soon as she praises God in five things, he returns the compliment (1.17–18). Or else he praises her first, and she replies in kind (2.9–10). Here as elsewhere she used comparisons from all manner of natural objects: flowers, birds, animals, jewels, fire, light. She borrowed the language of court, and, above all, that of bridal love. She loved details of clothing, numerical lists, and descriptions of every sort.

Mechthild gloried in her status as Bride, and expressed herself with the ardor, spontaneity, and freedom of one who knew she was greatly loved. She seems to have been aware already, at least unconsciously, of the dynamism of love, which is never content to remain static, but must be continually reaching out beyond itself:

> Ah Lord! Love me greatly, love me often and long! For the more continuously you love me, the purer I shall be; the more fervently you love me, the more lovely I shall be; the longer you love me the more holy I shall become, even here on earth. (1.23)

We are in the world of the *Song of Songs*—or rather, that of lovers everywhere; a world of mutual desire, searching, longing, and of the bliss of union. It is an enchanted world, a secret place where God plays a game with the soul (1.2). It is a world of paradoxes:

> The richer she becomes, the poorer she is. . . . The more she labors, the more sweetly she rests. The more she understands, the less she speaks. . . . The more he gives her, the more she spends, the more she has. (1.22)

The greatest paradox is that Love is both her joy and her anguish (1.5); 'love can both fiercely scorch and tenderly console'. (1.44)

In fact, though Love has taken from her everything, she feels this has been a small price to pay (1.1); her real suffering comes from her ardent longing for God:

> How long must I endure this thirst?
> One hour is already too long,
> A day is as a thousand years
> When you are absent!
> Should this continue for eight days
> I would rather go down to Hell—
> Where indeed I already am! (2.25)

Summing up her efforts in the beginning she said: 'I saw . . . that were I to escape everlasting death, I must utterly conquer self, and that would be a sore struggle.' (4.2)

Love itself guided her to the asceticism she must practise:

> If I now allow Love to rule over me, that it may bind me in holy patience . . . it will lead me to a noble gentleness that I may be prepared for all good things and held in strict obedience, ever lovingly subject in all things to God and all creatures. (2.19)

For someone of her fiery and impetuous nature, achieving a 'noble gentleness' must have been even more of a struggle than she anticipated. But it was love that motivated and impelled her:

> I rejoice that I must love him who loves me and I pray that till my death I may love him without measure and without ceasing . . . love him so greatly that I would gladly die for love of him. (1.28)

Christ replied by inviting her to follow him to death and described her itinerary in terms of his own passion:

> You shall be martyred with me . . . you shall bear your cross in hatred of sin; be crucified in renunciation of all things by your own will; nailed on the cross by the holy virtues; wounded through love; you shall die on the cross in holy constancy; be pierced to the heart by constant union; taken down from the cross in true victory over all your enemies; buried in meekness; raised up from the dead to a blessed end; drawn up to Heaven by the breath of God. (1.29)

In a later, similar passage (3.10) her sufferings are attributed less to outward agents and more to love. She will be betrayed in true love, clothed with the purple of great love; she will hang high on the cross of love. The dominant note in this first stage of her life remains one of joy and bliss, of high union between her soul and God. 'I am in you and you in me; we could not be closer.' 'You have taken me from myself and hidden yourself in me.' (3.5) Yet God tells her this is only the beginning: 'My deepest searchings, my farthest wanderings, my highest desires, my long expectation I must yet teach you'. For 'whoso would follow God must never stand still. He must ever travel on.' (3.6)

LOVE'S DESCENT

At this point a new stage began in Mechthild's spiritual development. In her earlier ecstasies she may have thought she had reached the heights of divine union, and perhaps she had, but another dimension was to open before her: *the depths*. She saw herself 'like a dusty acre on which little good has grown. . . . All the gifts I have ever received from you stand before me, a heavy reproach, for your highest gift humbles me to the dust.'(4.5)

A little farther on, though she is longing for God, 'yet would I gladly sacrifice the joy of his presence could he be greatly honored thereby'. (4.12) It is she herself who cries out: 'No, dear Lord! Do not raise me too high!" Then begins her descent: 'The soul fell down below the ill-fated souls who had forfeited their reward, and it seemed good to her so.' Yet our Lord followed her, until she begged him:

> 'Leave me, and let me sink further down, to your glory!' Then soul and body came into such gross darkness that I lost light and consciousness and knew no more of God's intimacy; ever-blessed Love also went its way.

The real struggles of her life had begun.

Elsewhere she gives us another description of this experience:

> When the soul walks with love, with eager desire for God in its heart, and when it has come to the Mount of powerful love and blissful knowledge, then it does as pilgrims do who have eagerly climbed a summit: they descend with care lest they fall over a precipice. So it is with the soul. Irradiated by the fire of its long love, overpowered by the embrace of the Holy Trinity, it begins to sink. . . . It sinks swiftly to the lowest place God has in his power. (5.4)

Even here her flair for picturesque phrases remains; the lowest place is 'under the devil's tail'.

> When the soul has thus climbed to the highest to which it may attain while still companioned by the body, and has sunk to the lowest depths it can find, then it is full-grown in virtue and in holiness. But it must yet be adorned with suffering in patient waiting.

This was to be Mechthild's lot for the remainder of her life.

LOVE'S COMPASSION

One fruit of this new stage of spiritual growth was Mechthild's growing concern and compassion for others. We find her praying earnestly for individuals, especially the souls in purgatory. As her heart expanded, she looked upon all humanity as her three children,

> for whom I foresee great trouble. The first child stands for those poor sinners who lie in everlasting death . . . my second child stands for those poor souls who suffer in Purgatory . . . my third child stands for those spiritual people who are not yet perfect. (5.8)

Her loving compassion reached its climax when

> I, poor wretch, was so bold in my prayer as to lift corrupt Christianity in the arms of my soul and hold it up in lamentation. Our Lord said, 'let be! It is too heavy for you!'
>
> No, sweet Lord!
> I will lift it up
> And bear it to your feet
> With your own arms
> Which bore it on the Cross!
> And God let me have my will,
> That so I might find rest. (5.34)

But she had no illusions about the Christendom for whose salvation she longed:

> This poor Christendom when it appeared before the Lord seemed to me as a poor maid. I looked at her and saw our Lord also look at her. And I was bitterly ashamed of her. The Lord said: 'Is it seemly that I take this poor maid to me as my bride? To love her without end?' He answered his own question: 'I will wash her in my own blood and I will protect all the blessed who are truly innocent.'

In fact, Mechthild usually viewed the Church as sinful and in need of redemption.

Of all those for whom she prayed, it was especially with the mediocre that she was concened. 'Of two things I can never lament sufficiently; the first is that God is so forgotten in the world; the second that spiritual people are so imperfect.' (4.16) There is a skillfully constructed dialogue in which Love (a spokesman for Mechthild herself) gently, yet urgently and persistently, strives to rouse a self-satisfied soul from its complacency:

> Where can you find rest if you will not enthrone above your own powers and your own will your God who rejoices in you? (2.23),

Love answers all its excuses until finally the soul capitulates:

> Alas, where have I been? Unblessed, blind . . . I will now go out from all things into God.

Of her three children, the one for whom she showed most anxiety is the third

> because with its outward senses so sadly taken up with passing things, it is so widely separated from heavenly things that it has lost its good habits and sweet trust in God. . . . It is thus sadly turned away from the right course. (5.8)

To this 'third child' she gives advice: her most urgent need is breadth of understanding.

> If . . . you make your need too narrow, then you will never be ready for the height of holy desire, nor the breadth of divine perception nor the depth of the flowing sweetness of God.

Her use of terms of growth and expansion reflects her own continuous striving to enlarge her capacity for God. She gave some instruction on prayer, ending with the counsel: 'Make your heart crystal clear within and keep yourself outwardly small'—love and humility, her constantly recurring themes—'so may you be one with God' (5.11).

Many other parts of her book read like advice to her disciples and spiritual children. To one, evidently a recently appointed superior, she sent a short manual of advice, both spiritual and practical. A prior is to have 'special love for each brother', to share his joys and sorrows ('Suffer? I too suffer! Wound? And I have wounded! Merit God's praise? I sing!'), to give the young disciples all the help in his power. He is to cheer the sick, even 'to be merry and laugh with them in a godly manner'; to watch ever the kitchen that the brethren have sufficient food, 'for no hungry priest may sing sweetly nor study deeply'. (6.1) It is pleasant to find here a more human side to Mechthild than usually appears.

LOVE'S ENLIGHTENMENT

In her maturity Mechthild sang of love as ardently as ever and with new depth:

> Dear love of God! embrace this soul of mine. . . . You make pain and need sweet to me, you give wisdom and comfort to the children of God. . . . Sweet love of God! should I sleep too long, woefully neglecting all good things, do you awaken me and sing; for the song with which you touch my soul delights me as sweet music. Love! fling me down under you; gladly would I be vanquished; should you take my life from me, therein would I find comfort; for you, most gentle love of God, spare me too much. (5.30)

> This is the nature of great love, it does not flow with tears, it rather burns in the great fire of heaven. In the fire it flows swiftly and yet remains in itself in great stillness. It rises almost up to God, yet remains small in itself. . . . Ah, most blessed love! where are those who know you? They are wholly irradiated in the Holy Trinity, they no longer live in themselves. (4.16, Cf. 5.17, 5.35, 6.29)

Though Mechthild used the third person here, she was undoubtedly speaking of her own experience.

With her growth in the knowledge and the love of God, her sense of sin deepened (5.1, 5.29), and she understood the interrelationship between sin and suffering:

> So long as the creature can sin, he requires suffering as much as virtue. . . . No one can escape suffering, for it purifies mankind from hour to hour for their many sins. (5.27) The pain [love] causes me helps me to live without sin. (5.30)

It is sins, even small ones, which 'hinder spiritual people most of all from full perfection'.

Yet even sinfulness can be turned to good account:

> When I, the poorest of the poor, go to my prayer, I adorn myself with my unworthiness and clothe myself with the mud which I myself am. I shoe myself with the precious time I have lost all my days and I gird myself with the suffering I have deserved. Then I throw around me the cloak of wickedness of which I am full. I put on my head a crown of the secret sins I have committed against God. After that I take in my hand a mirror of true knowledge and see myself therein as I am, so that I see nothing but alas! and alas!
>
> But I am happier in these clothes that I could be if I had every earthly gift, even though I am often sad and impatient, for I would rather be clothed with hell and crowned by all devils than be without my sin. [For] I find [Jesus] in no other thing so truly as in my sins. (6.1)

Her greatest discovery, however, was that 'Now is God marvelous to me and his forsaken-ness better even than himself'. (4.2) She realized that 'the noblest of all things' is

> that in poverty, contempt, misery, days of sorrow, spiritual poverty (that most of all), in the demands of obedience, in all kinds of bitterness, inward and outward, one can and will rejoice in praising God from the heart, thanking him with joy, reaching out to him in longing and fulfilling his will in works. (5.25)

Her poverty of spirit extended so far that she could say, 'I have no longer any virtues. They serve me—yet are truly his'. (4.19)

This extreme poverty led to a new experience of God:

> When I awake in the night...
> Sometimes he draws me by another way,
> Without bridge or steps,
> So that I am constrained to follow
> Naked, barefoot and stripped of earthly things. (6.16)

LOVE'S LONGINGS

As she advanced in age, Mechthild dwelt often on the thought of death, both desiring it and fearing it.

> Lord, I still have a great dread as to the way in which my soul shall pass from my body. Then the Lord said: 'It shall be thus: I will draw my breath and your soul shall come to me as a needle to a magnet.' (5.32)

She inquired of him how she was to conduct herself in her last days, and he replied: 'You shall do in your last days as in your first. You shall hold yourself in love and longing, repentance and fear, for these four things were the beginning of your life, therefore they must also be the end.' (6.6)

She composed a leave-taking litany, in which her glance and her compassion ranged over the whole of creation. Even though she here envisaged her death as imminent, she was still concerned to use well any time that remained to her in the service of God and the Church:

> When I am about to die, I take leave of all from which I must part. I take leave of Holy Church; I thank God that I was called to be a Christian and have come to real Christian belief. Were I to remain longer here I would try to help Holy Church which lies in many sins.

I take leave of all poor souls now in Purgatory. Were I to be longer here I would gladly help to expiate their sins and I thank God that they will find mercy. . . .

I take leave of all sinners who lie in mortal sin. . .
of all penitents working out their penance. . .
of all my enemies. . .
of all earthly things. . .
of all my dear friends. . .
of all my wickedness. . .
of my suffering body. . . (6.28).

The thought of death led to that of heaven. Throughout her book she had given many imaginative descriptions of it, but by far the most appealing is this last one, in which she saw it as a place where

. . . the Spirit shafts
Such heavenly floods of light
On all the Blest that they
Filled and enchanted, sing
For joy, and laugh and leap
In ordered dance. They flow
And swim and fly and climb
From tiered choir to choir
Still upward through the height. (7.1)

The themes of play and dance which she used in her early poems have returned, transfigured. There is also a hint that growth in love will continue even in eternity.

But this is in the future, and she had still to remain in this life. As she looked back on her past, she saw only its weaknesses:

My childhood was foolish, my youth troubled; how I conquered it is known only to God. Alas! now in my old age I find much to chide, for it can produce no shining works and is cold and without grace. It is powerless, now that it no longer has youth to help it to bear the fiery love of God. It is also impatient, for little ills afflict it much which in youth it hardly noticed. Yet a good old age is full of patient waiting and trusts in God alone. (7.3)

God answers: 'Your childhood was a companion of my Holy Spirit; your youth was a bride of my humanity; in your old age you are a humble housewife of my Godhead.'

She was conscious of her many failings:

> Unworthiness censures me, indolence convicts me, the inconstancy of my nature reproves my changeableness, the wretchedness of my useless life distresses me and lastly holy fear scourges me so that I creep like a little worm into the earth and hide myself under the grass of the many omissions of my whole life. (7.6)

She uttered the cry of every soul who sincerely seeks to serve God: 'I am not yet what I have so long desired to be!'

> Ever longing in the soul
> Ever suffering in the body
> Ever pain in the senses
> Ever hope in the heart in Jesus alone. (7.63)

This hope was well-founded, for Jesus reassures her:

> All your ways are measured, your footsteps counted, your life sanctified, your end shall be joyful for my Kingdom is very near you. (7.4)

LOVE'S FULFILLMENT

Toward the end of her life Mechthild's anguish and struggle gradually gave way to serenity and confidence. She was filled with 'spiritual poverty, everlasting love and longing. . . . The long waiting is forgotten, in the future it seems possible that God and the soul may be united, never more to be separated. When I think of that, my heart is full of joy!' (7.46)

In the meantime there remained joy of union with Christ in the Eucharist. We catch a glimpse of what that meant to her in this communion song of love and humility:

> Where, then, Lord, shall I rest you,
> All my soul is your house
> Enter, O enter in!
> It is a house of sorrow
> That I had forgotten,
> Remembering only your woe.
> O rest then upon my sorrow,
> My coverlet of longing,
> Pillow your head on my grief! . . .
> Now my sorrow and yours
> Have rested in peace together
> Now is our love made whole.
> O Guest! raised from the dead

Keep me close to yourself
In consolation and bliss.
What more can our love say?
Now that you are houseled
In the house of my sorrow?
Risen from the dead
You come to me,
Comfort me, O my Beloved,
And hold me in your presence
In continual joy....
Now Lord in your ascending
Having given yourself to me
Spare me not too much!
In all ways I must die for love
That is all my desire.
Give me and take from me
What you will, but leave me this,
In loving, to die of love! (7.21)

To die of love had, indeed, been her desire all her life, but as her love grew, this desire had grown too in depth and sincerity.

Her imagination remained as active as ever, and she used it to portray the virtues as officials in a spiritual convent:

> The Abbess is true Love who has much sanctified sense with which she rules the community in body and soul to the honor of God. She gives her Sisters much holy teaching of the Will of God whereby her own soul is set free.
>
> The Chaplain-of-love is divine Humility so utterly subject to Love that Pride has to stand aside.
>
> The Prioress is the holy Peace of God; patience is added to her goodwill that she may teach the community with divine Wisdom....
>
> The Sub-Prioress is Loving-kindness...
>
> Hope is the Chantress filled with holy, humble devotion, so that even temerity of heart in singing before God, sounds so sweetly that he loves the melody sung from the heart....
>
> Gentleness is the Steward always happily doing good...
>
> Watchfulness is the Portress filled with holy desire to do whatever she is bidden. Thus nothing she does is ever lost and she comes quickly to God when she would pray; there he is with her in holy stillness....
>
> Thus the Convent abides in God.... Blessed are they who dwell therein! (7.36)

As always, love was her favorite, ever-recurring theme: 'All who inwardly love fervently, become outwardly still. . . . What the spirit then sings inwardly sounds sweeter far than any earthly song.' (7.34)

> The nature of love is such that it overflows at first in sweetness, then it becomes rich in understanding, thirdly it abounds in desolation. (6.20)

That seems to have been the pattern of Mechthild's life.

> All that is in [this world] can neither comfort nor please me save suffering alone. . . . I live in a country called Exile. That is this world. . . . Therein I have a house called Suffering, that is the body in which my soul is imprisoned. This house is old and small and dark. (7.48)

But into that house came Love, with whom she had been on such familiar terms in her youth, 'in the form of a queenly maid of noble presence, fair skin and with the rosy bloom of youth. She had with her many virtues: they were her handmaidens and were come to serve me if I wished them. . . . As I looked at her closely, my dark house became lighted up.' She speaks to these handmaidens lovingly and confidently, in a mood of great contentment:

> Remorse! Come here to me
> And bring me holy tears
> To wash away my sins. . . .
> Gentleness! Sit under my cloak. . . .
> Come to me Holiness!
> Kiss the mouth of my soul
> And dwell in the depths of my heart. . . .

Her anxiety has been transformed into trust, her impetuosity into peace. She has realized that God is, above all, compassion (7.62), that 'every soul whom God in his mercy serves is dearest to him'. (7.8) God's work has come to perfection in her and she need no longer humble herself to the extent that she did earlier. She is truly a queen, a noble lady, as she calls the human soul and body. (7.62) Truthfully she can cry out: 'I am not my own but belong utterly to you!' (7.63) Even though she must remain a while longer 'in this bitter outcast life', she is 'sure and free, without fear or pain'.

In a last outburst of joy, she ends her life and her book with thanksgiving; thanksgiving for her own utter poverty, and for the goodness of God:

> Lord! I thank you that since in your love you have taken from me all earthly riches, you now clothe and feed me through the goodness of others, so that everything which might clothe my heart in pride of possession, is no more known to me.

> Lord! I thank you that since you have taken from me the sight of my eyes, you serve me through the eyes of others.
>
> Lord! I thank you that since you have taken from me the power of my hands . . . and the power of my heart, you now serve me with the hands and hearts of other. (7.64)

The boast of her youthful ardor had now been truly realized:

> I am a full-grown Bride,
> And must to my Lover's side! (1.44)

NOTES

1. Eugene Boylan, *Difficulties in Mental Prayer* (Westminster, Maryland, 1948) 47.

2. Lucy Menzies, *The Revelations of Mechthild of Magdeburg*, 4.2 (London, 1953). All quotations in this article have been taken from the Menzies translation, and are cited by Book and Chapter. For further information on Mechthild's book and its subsequent history, see Odo Egres, O.Cist., 'Mechthild von Magdeburg, the Flowing Light of God', in E. Rozanne Elder, *Cistercians in the Late Middle Ages*, Studies in Medieval Cistercian History VI (1981) 19–37.

3. *The New Catholic Encyclopaedia*, 9:546, gives the date of her death as between 1282 and 1294. Egres prefers a date between 1281 and 1283.

4. It is not certain that her writings as we have them are in chronological order, but internal evidence would seem to indicate that, in general, they are.

The God of My Life: St Gertrude, A Monastic Woman

Lillian Thomas Shank

'I WAS TWENTY-FIVE years old, and it was the Monday (a Monday most fraught with salvation for me) before the feast of the Purification of Mary . . . at the hour after Compline for which one longs, in the early hours of dusk.' So St Gertrude relates the great event of her conversion. As she turned from her 'preoccupation with the world and the court', the Lord promised her: '. . . you have sucked honey among thorns; return to me at last, and I shall make you drunk with the rushing river of my divine pleasure'. (2.1)[1] This occurred on 27 January 1281.

This remarkable woman, sometimes called 'The Great', was a nun of the benedictine abbey of Helfta, near modern Eisleben, in East Germany. The monastery was not officially under the jurisdiction of Cîteaux, but, as Dom Pierre Doyère states, 'the discipline and spirituality of Helfta were undoubtedly of Cistercian inspiration, while at the same time, thanks to its independence, the monastery observed certain customs of its own'.[2]

Germany, during the years of Gertrude's life (1256–1302 or 1303),[3] was in a state of anarchy; sporadic wars and '. . . the terror of robber-barons demoralized Saxony and Thuringia'.[4] Some have conjectured that Gertrude's own arrival at Helfta at the age of five, without mention of any family, might indicate that she had been orphaned in one of these violent clashes.[5] In all events, the experience of death and violence could not have been foreign to this child, who was eventually to bequeath to us a very rich monastic spirituality—a spirituality full of life, yet giving deep meaning to death.

Although St Gertrude's biographer tells us in Book One of *The Herald* that Gertrude wrote many books and composed many prayers, we now know of only four of these works and only three are extant:

1. Book Two of the *Herald of Divine Loving-Kindness* or *Legatus divinae pietatis* (sometimes known as the 'Revelations of St Gertrude') gives us the clearest picture of her personality. *The Herald* consists of five books. Books One, Three, Four and Five were written by one or more of Gertrude's companions, either at her dictation, or compiled from her notes or in some way immediately inspired by her. They contain many of her characteristic expressions but their style is inferior to that of Book Two[6] written at the Lord's command in 1289, when Gertrude was thirty-three years old. Jean Leclercq argues: 'Book II was surely written by the saint herself and constitutes the authentic and original nucleus around which all the rest was added and according to which the rest has to be interpreted'.[7] In this book, she wrote down her Lord's intimate visitations (as he instructed her), recorded his many gifts of divine love and, while the book abounds in praise and thanksgiving, she simply and sincerely, proclaimed her own weakness and limitations. Book Two begins with the story of her own call to conversion from being a religious 'in name only' (as she describes herself) to a person guided by the power of the Spirit.

2. *The Exercises*, evidently written toward the end of her life, consist of seven retreat experiences. In them she utilized prayers, reflections, and instructions, as a guide to renewal of life. This book gives us a broad picture of Gertrude's mature values and desires.

3. *The Book of Special Grace* was written by Gertrude and another nun sometime after 1292. Because this book is of joint authorship and focuses on the experiences of St Mechthild, I do not refer to it in this present study.

4. *The Remembrance of Death*, a book which has not come down to us, consisted of a sort of retreat of five days intended to be made once a year in preparation for death.[8]

My present study of Gertrude is based on her own two works: Book Two of the *Herald* and the *Exercises*.

As we come to know Gertrude through her writings we notice some outstanding personal traits: a wholehearted, passionate spirit which, in her early years, she dissipated in excessive study and intellectual pride. We find in her a zeal for truth which sometimes caused her anguish and anxiety and sometimes resulted in overly enthusiastic corrections (or so they seemed to others!). Her love of beauty could potentially lead her away from God as well as toward him. A delicate sensitivity to her own moods facilitated her growth in self-knowledge as well as in inner attentiveness to the calls of grace; this sensitivity also reached out in consoling others and giving spiritual direction, to the point that she could become over-committed. We find in Gertrude a spirit of joy and thanksgiving which nevertheless could yield to 'mental darkness' in which she was 'devoured by sadness'. These qualities existed within a basic simplicity that characterized Gertrude's personality. Perhaps it was this simplicity that opened her to the dramatic grace[9] of conversion and led her to begin the journey to poverty of spirit which was to provide the foundations for her growth in love. Of this conversion she said to her Lord: '. . . you were attempting to tear down the tower . . . my pride had erected'. (2.1)

It is this unique person, as woman and monastic woman, upon whom I should like to reflect, and also the monastic values she chose to teach and to live. Finally, in this context, I will consider the meaning she gave to the mysteries of life and death.

GERTRUDE AS WOMAN[10]

The mature Gertrude delineated for us the richly feminine characteristics of wholeness, spiritual receptivity, a sense of being (rather than doing), outgoing love—contemplative attitudes.[11] She also delineated the masculine characteristics of courage, holy boldness and respectful assertiveness, even in her familiar colloquies with Jesus. Here we shall focus on two of Gertrude's personal characteristics: her ability to love and to be loved (traditionally 'feminine'), and her spirit of independence (traditionally 'masculine'). I am not attempting to define 'woman',[12] nor am I saying this is the only way to be woman, but I wish to reflect upon these two ways by which Gertrude lived her womanliness.

TO LOVE AND BE LOVED

The energy of love, when shared, begets life. According to one psychologist: 'Women see love as a process, an energy flow . . . and the love must build, augment and energize in the process; it is a flowing process.[13] Gertrude experienced a divine love which had these qualities; it was, she wrote, the love of Jesus that empowered her.(2.5) In Book Two the Lord says to her:[14] 'I shall now lay you to my divine heart, so that I may flow gently and sweetly into you, rhythmically and in proportion to your capacity, with measured flow'. (2.10) God's love flows inevitably toward the salvation of humankind, (2.8) and Gertrude, as true spouse, participated as God's tool in this work of salvation. After describing a particular experience of God's love she says to Christ: 'You explained to me how it is a great deed if the soul gives up the sweetness of the heart's fulfillment for your sake, keeps vigil in governing her bodily senses and labours over works of charity for the salvation of her neighbors as well'. (2.15) Gertrude prayed and suffered for the salvation of all men and women; she also counseled and encouraged many directly as one of her works of charity. Her love desired selfless purity of mind and heart, and grew through this purification.

The ascesis *of love, when lived, begets mysticism.* Gertrude performed no extreme penances, other than the acceptance of sickness, of various discomforts sent her day by day and the routine of monastic life with its round of vigils, offices, fasting, reading, work, and prayer. Her great *ascesis* lay in striving to love within her ordinary life. She was a mystic seeking to become one with Christ, to go to the Father, through the Son, in the Holy Spirit. Trinitarian imagery is frequent in her spirituality. She prayed:

> God the Father of heaven and King of Kings, deign to wed me within my soul unto Christ the King, your Son . . . Holy Spirit . . . join my heart forever unto Jesus by that connecting tie of love wherein you do unite the Father and the Son (*Ex*, 38).

'Christian mysticism' explains one modern scholar of the phenomenon, 'is nothing else than the process of becoming Christ, of living with Him, of dying with Him, of rising with Him',[15] all done through love. 'Love is the motivation and driving force behind the mystical journey.'[16] In christian teaching, 'God who is love infuses His gift of love into the soul. When a man or a woman responds to this call, s/he receives the Holy Spirit who is love personified.'[17] Being totally open to this call to 'be in love'[18] was one of Gertrude's graces, a grace growing in and transforming her naturally passionate nature. More and more theologians hold that mysticism is a universal call: '. . . if mysticism is knowledge through love and if love is the great commandment, can we not say that mysticism is the core of authentic religious experience and that it is for everyone?'[19]

Christian love, necessarily trinitarian, when lived, begets union. Grafted onto Gertrude's ability to love was Christ's own love. Under the beautiful imagery of the tree of love, she was taught to live [another aspect of] Christ-love, love of enemies. At Mass, overcome with weariness, she was aroused at the sound of the bell at the elevation of the Host, when:

> she beheld Jesus Christ her Lord and King holding a tree in his hand . . . covered with the most beautiful fruit and whose leaves shone like so many stars . . . soon Our Lord planted this tree in the garden of her heart. . . . Having received this deposit she began to pray for a person who had persecuted her a short time before, asking that she might suffer again what she had already suffered to draw down more abundant grace on this person. At this moment she beheld a flower, of a most beautiful color, burst forth on the top of the tree. . . . (3.14)

The flow of love moved from the heart of Jesus to Gertrude; then on to all people, friends and enemies. She pleaded that this love might grow:

> O Love, O God . . . . come let me not be left behind in the school of charity . . . but in you and through you, or rather with you, let me grow into maturity day by day and advance from strength unto strength daily bringing forth fruit unto you, my Beloved, in the new path of your love.' (*Ex*, 98)

As love grew into union, Gertrude became the bride of her Beloved.

Bridal love, when lived, begets transformation. Much of Gertrude's writing speaks of the mystery of union with God under the imagery of nuptial mysticism.[20] In the rich depth of intimate love, raised to the level of holy love and a relationship with the divine, Gertrude reveals a personality ardent and bold, simple and pure. She prays: 'Come, dear Jesus . . . enter now my Beloved, within me and grant me entrance within you. Hide me in the immovable rock of your fatherly protection in the cleft of your most benign heart' (*Ex*, 20–21). 'O Holy and Almighty Spirit,' she continues, ' . . . grant that I may love you with my whole heart, cleave unto you with my whole soul, expend all my strength in loving and serving you . . . ' (*Ex*, 21). She accepts Christ's love for herself with equal simplicity: 'High above the heavens there is a King who is enthralled with desire of you. He loves you with his whole heart and he loves you immoderately, he loves you so dearly, he loves you so faithfully' (*Ex*, 34). Then, in response, she hears these words from Christ: 'In my Holy Spirit I betroth you unto me, I take you unto myself in deathless union. Where I am you too shall dwell; I will seclude you within my living love' (*Ex*, 36).

A mission of love, when lived, begets a 'herald' of love. Her mission in life, the one given her by Christ himself, was to be an emissary, a herald, of God's love. The whole fifth exercise is a series of practices and prayers in which a day is chosen to 'give yourself up to love' (*Ex*, 84ff). As the author of Book One of the *Herald* emphatically states: 'It is beyond dispute that the Lord chose Gertrude as a special instrument to make known through her the mysteries of his loving-kindness' (1.2). Gertrude's experiences of God's love were gifts given her for others, as the Lord often told her when she was experiencing aversion to writing or speaking about these gifts of love.

Gertrude's capacity for love and her mission to be a herald of that love were symbolized in her devotion to the heart of Jesus. The symbol of the wound in Jesus' heart where the lance had pierced and from which flowed out blood and water was for her the great revelation of God's loving-kindness. We should be careful to speak of this love, not in the sense of more modern devotion to the Sacred Heart, but rather with the meaning it had for Gertrude in the thirteenth century. As Barratt explains: '. . . we should note that the title of Gertrude's book contains no mention of the Heart of Jesus. Indeed it is that title, *Legatus divinae pietatis*, which provides the vital clue to an understanding of the saints' teaching. Gertrude should be seen . . . as the apostle . . . of the *divina pietas* of which Christ's heart is the living embodiment. Hence the Heart of Jesus is seen, not as a suffering heart in need of consolation and reparation, but as the loving heart of a risen and triumphant Christ . . . . As used by Gertrude, *pietas* means the attitude of loving concern which God shows towards all his people . . . .'[21]

Jesus' heart manifested to Gertrude both the humanity and divinity of Christ; it was the source of an ardor which both consumes and transforms, a truly devouring fire.[22] As the biographer has Christ say of Gertrude: 'the beatings of her heart are ceaselessly intertwined with the beatings of my love and in this lies my delight' (1.3).

This woman who loved and could receive love became transformed; God's love flowed in and through her. She found that love within herself and she lived that love.

INDEPENDENCE

There is no doubt that Gertrude had a natural sauciness about her, an open upright spirit which could lead her into speaking too hastily or a little too severely. As her biographer admitted: 'She acted and spoke uncompromisingly'. But hers was a free and independent nature which grace used while transforming, and it enabled her to act and speak fearlessly in matters concerning God's honor or the salvation of souls.[23]

Spiritual Independence

In Book One, Gertrude's biographer tells us: 'There also shone in Gertrude such great spiritual independence (*libertas cordis*, literally freedom of heart] that she could never bear for any length of time anything which was against her principles' (1.11). It seems the Lord approved of this spontaneity of heart, for later, when he was asked by someone what he found most pleasing in Gertrude, he replied:

> The independence of her heart . . . she had already achieved greater knowledge and ardent love . . . by means of the grace of independence of heart . . . . For at every single moment she is found fit for my gifts, for she never allows anything to find a place in her heart which could be an obstacle to me (1.11).

Independence of Pride and Independence of Liberty

Gertrude, in the untransformed independence of her early years, was proud and sought to please herself. Redirected through her attentive cooperation with grace she wished 'truly to seek God' (*Rule* of St Benedict, 58). The power for this work, as she tells us, came from God. To him she says: '. . . you exercised your inextinguishable power on my . . . soul, first drying out in her the rising damp of worldly pleasures and afterwards softening the rigidity of her attachment to her own ideas, a position in which she had for some time been completely fixed' (2.7).

HUMILITY

In order to understand this growth from an independence rooted in pride and self-love (for after all original sin was nothing else than Adam and Eve's desire to be "independent" of God) to genuine spiritual independence, the liberty of heart of the spiritually mature, we must look at Gertrude's humility. True humility is growth from the false self of egoism and selfishness to the true self, recreated in Christ, simple and free; it is a basic virtue in the monastic life. Book Two of the *Herald* and the *Exercises* abound in exclamations of her unworthiness:

> I am the least. . .(115) the tiniest of all your creatures (118). . . . I am needy and poor (35). . . I am nothing . . . I know nothing . . . I can do nothing without You (68). . . . I am the most unworthy of all men and women (2.22).

But interestingly, nowhere does St Gertrude attribute her 'unworthiness' to her own womanly nature, to a sense of feminine inferiority, but always to the knowledge that she is creature before God. As the writer of Book One expresses it:

> Set in the midst of the bright light of her virtues which shone like twinkling stars, with which the Lord had made her extraordinarily beautiful for Himself to live in, there shone out with special power the virtue of humility, which is the guest chamber of all graces and the strong-room of all virtues. (1.11)

HUMILIATIONS AND WATCHFULNESS OF THOUGHTS

In an article on humility in the Rule of St Benedict, Thomas Davis explains: 'Union with God is the beginning of an encounter we "know not"; yet it is truly the place where our self belongs. We arrive here by a ruthless campaign against all forms of illusion and the desires that come from self complacency and spiritual ambition.'[24] Formed in the benedictine tradition from childhood, Gertrude was deeply sensitive to any form of vainglory or spiritual pride; using her strong will and independent spirit, she quickly formed a habit of dashing against Christ all these evil thoughts. (2.11, 18; cf. Prologue, Rule of St Benedict) She fully accepted humiliations. She tells of an incident where she was 'in a state of anger . . . that I had failed to repel the enemy's driving me into actions so contrary to you.' Yet she received assurance from the Lord that he loved her '. . . amid all the squalls of her faults', indicating that these weaknesses lead '. . . to the calm of repentance and the harbour of humility' (2.12).

THANKSGIVING

Gertrude's favorite way of cooperating with the graces of humility seems to have been through thanksgiving. Her works abound in expressions of praise and thanks. She describes a charming moment of deep insight:

> I had gone into the courtyard before Prime and was sitting beside the fish-pond absorbed by the charms of the place. The crystalline water flowing through, the fresh green trees standing around, the birds circling in flight and above all the freedom of the dove gave me pleasure . . . . you guided my meditation . . . and you drew its conclusion . . . breathing into me the knowledge that if I poured back like water the flowing streams of your graces with constant and rightful thanksgiving, I would grow in a passion for virtue like the trees and would blossom with a fresh flowering of good works (2.3).

Thanksgiving acknowledges the given, it flows outward and empties us of self-pretensions and self-preoccupations; it is like a gentle but potent fertilizer that helps us grow. Her sixth exercise in the Book of *Exercises* is replete with joyous exclamations of praise and thanksgiving.

Holy Assertiveness

Another aspect of Gertrude's independent character was her assertiveness, her eventually holy boldness. Between Christ and Gertrude, as his bride, we see an equality of relationships between his gifts of grace and her acceptance and use of them with deep humility. With great courage and a sense of responsibility, she received and accepted his gifts of love, of union, and of deepened insight. As her biographer says: '. . . she thought of herself as a channel through which grace flowed to those whom God had chosen . . .' (1.11). She asked for his gifts with a reverent audacity. Soldier-like, she prayed: 'O Jesus . . . confirm me by your almighty power and gird me with the strength of the Spirit . . . that I may ever be victorious over the thousand wiles of Satan, and all my victory may be in you' (*Ex*, 13). Again: 'Fill me with your Spirit and take possession of my whole being in purity of body and soul' (*Ex*, 11). She was not afraid to ask for anything.

Gertrude spoke frankly, both to her sisters and to Christ. In the *Herald* we find several pages of dialogues where, in a very courteous way, she put her holy bridegroom 'on the spot'. She asked, we are told 'How could it possibly come about that he condescended to perform such wonderful miracles through her, totally worthless as she was?'' Also able to make a point, he replied with another question: '. . . why do you not believe with equal faith that I am able or am willing to do anything at the prompting of love?' (1.14) Again, she inquired, 'Lord, if you speak the truth through my mouth as your loving kindness condescends to assert, how is it that my words sometimes have so little effect on people?' (1.14) In Book Three, following a section on the tree of love, there occurs a delightful scene in which the Lord asks Gertrude to gather nuts from this tree and bids her 'place herself in the branches'. 'But, my sweet Lord', she protests, 'why do you ask me to do that which is far beyond the weakness of my virtue and my sex, and which your condescension would rather incline you to do for me?' (3.14) Gertrude, in a simple, direct way, lets her friend and bridegroom know that it is beneath a woman's dignity and physical ability to climb trees.

Daily living this mature spiritual independence, this liberty of heart, by the power of the Spirit, Gertrude exemplied a truly liberated woman. By deliberate decision, she chose humility and living her independence freely and fully. She was a woman totally pliant and supple to all the movements of the Holy Spirit.[25]

ST GERTRUDE AS A MONASTIC WOMAN

The christian monastic life which formed Gertrude originated about the beginning of the fourth century. Two impulses evidently gave rise to it: 1) men and women wanted to express their christian commitment in a radical way; with the cessation of the persecutions and the acceptance of Christianity, a somewhat routine, comfortable discipline had replaced the ardent faith and love needed to sustain the persecuted community; 2) the first monks who fled from persecution to the deserts of Egypt had found this life of solitude, poverty and austerity conducive to deep contemplative prayer.[26] These monks—men and women of prayer—desired to be Christians, to follow Christ, to assimilate his virtues and live by his Word. These successors of the martyrs wished to eliminate all obstacles to growth in Christ, this growth to union with God, and to anticipate on earth the heavenly kingdom, as Cassian was to express it, to seek the kingdom of God [union with God] through purity of heart. (*Conference* One, IV) This purity of heart is described as a loving attention and vigilance over every thought and movement of the heart. This *nepsis*, guarding of the heart, made the monk attentive to the inner movements of God's Spirit.[27]

As a monastic woman, Gertrude lived within this tradition, bringing the individuality of her feminine personhood into the framework of a principally cistercian life-style. Cîteaux had sought to re-express primitive monasticism in terms current in eleventh-century monastic reforms; it emphasised a contemplative life-style through separation from the world, poverty, and austerity. It also uniquely blended the solitary and the common life, prayer and fraternal love. Manual labor was an important aspect of its expression of poverty; by it the monks strove to support themselves and provide for their guests, rich and poor. Simplicity pervaded the whole cistercian renewal, eliminating accretions in liturgical prayers and ceremonies, expressing itself in clothing, architecture, objects used in worship and most of all, as a desire to be free from all superfluity.[28] Spiritually it expressed itself in an undivided search for God. Cîteaux's renewal sought to express exteriorly and interiorly a new breathing of the Spirit. In the *Exordium Parvum*, one of the first cistercian documents, written around 1112–1119[29], we find the remark that the first Cistercians wished to live up to the etymology of their name; they wanted to be 'real' monks, to live the age-old monastic tradition in a new and authentic way.[30] The authentic living of the *Rule of St Benedict* was the key, they believed, to fulfilling this deep desire.

The Cistercians expressed their ideal through the *Rule*, which was interpreted in the light of the Gospel and the monastic tradition of the first ages, Cassian, Basil and the desert Fathers, rather than in the early medieval benedictine tradition of liturgy, study, and active evangelization.[31] Cistercian solitude, silence, simplicity, fraternal love, austerity, and poverty were simply aids to provide the proper purifying environment for 'that return to the heart, that discovery of a deep interior tasting in the depths of the soul where the monk encounters the Lord Jesus'.[32]

Helfta, Gertrude's monastery, while not under the official jurisdiction of Cîteaux, had originated from a cistercian abbey.[33] Its observance was in large part Cistercian, with its own usages mingled in; it could be called partly cistercian and partly benedictine. The *Rule of St Benedict* common to both Cistercians and Benedictines formed the monastic spirituality of Gertrude. Referring to the principal observances of that Rule, I wish to point out how Gertrude lived these values in her daily monastic life and then examine monastic profession and its meaning for her.

Gertrude lived the monastic life from her deepest being; there was no formalism in her.[34] One of the dominant themes of both Book Two of the *Herald* and the *Exercises* is her desire for union with God through the observances of the monastic life. She prays: 'Come then, O Love most true, unite me intimately unto you. . . . O Beloved of my heart . . . that henceforth I may live for you alone. . . . Come, mould my heart after your own heart that I may deserve to be entirely pleasing unto you in my monastic observance' (*Ex*, 22). The observances were a way to show love and to 'become love'. This basic characteristic of Gertrude, to love and to be loved, was directed toward this purity of union with God as she yielded herself to be pruned and shaped by monastic observances.

THE RULE OF ST BENEDICT

Humility and Obedience

We find in the *Rule* two pillars which uphold and strengthen the other observances: the humility and the obedience of Christ. We have already seen Gertrude's zeal for humility, her awareness of her own nothingness, her acceptance of humiliations (and self), watchfulness of thoughts (thereby combating temptations to pride and vainglory), and thanksgiving. In Book Two Gertrude tells of yet another concrete means to grow in humility and hence in union with God: 'You added that if I genuinely considered myself to be less perfect than others, the torrential flood of your honey-sweet divine nature would never cease to flow into my soul' (2.28). Her practice of humility was based on the seventh degree of humility in the *Rule* and the evidence that Gertrude truly lived this interior attitude is found everywhere in her writings. Humility does not exclude a healthy sense of self-worth nor is it to be equated with a sense of psychological inferiority. It indicates rather a happy acceptance of oneself with all one's gifts and weaknesses, and prevents the growth of the attitudes of competition and rivalry. It combats the natural inclination to criticize and judge others and, focusing on the good in the other, turns this ability to criticize into a wondering awe at the beauty of the unique person.

Obedience and humility are interrelated for only the humble can be obedient. Only someone able to risk being stripped of his false self can be receptive to the voice of another, even the Holy Spirit. Gertrude held a simple concept of obedience which pervades her writing: our obedience is Christ's obedience, for he said, 'I came not to do my own will but the will of him who sent me' (Jn 6:38). She quoted Psalm 142: 'Teach me to do your will, for you are my God'. She said simply: 'My heart has fixed itself upon the will of Jesus . . .' (*Ex*, 135). And she exclaimed: 'Oh that in me, contemptible as I am, by the Holy Spirit, that breath of your mouth, you would throw down all barriers to your will and good pleasure' (*Ex*, 157). Then to Christ: 'I vow obedience to you . . . . I pledge myself to do your will because union with you outshines the loveliness of all things else, and love of you is exceedingly sweet and desirable' (*Ex*, 22). The routine obediences of daily life were all encompassed in this deeper motivation and all were a means through faith to find God's will and an expression of love for him.

To divest oneself of the false self, egoism, and selfishness, the virtues of trust and confidence are needed; these come with the sure knowledge that God loves us. Gertrude expressed this confidence in a dynamic way by the constant practice of *suppletio*. The term itself was borrowed by a modern theologian[35] to describe this deep attitude of Gertrude; she *refers to the practice* at least thirty times in her *Exercises* and some ten times in Book Two of the *Herald*.[36] *Suppletio* consists 'in pondering on the merits of Jesus Christ, on his sorrows, desires, prayers, on the love of his most holy humanity; to uniting herself to them and to offering them to the Father so they might "supply" for her unworthiness, her negligences, her faults, her sins . . . . having done this, not withstanding the strong awareness of her own unworthiness, . . . she was perfectly at peace.'[37] When she remembered in a vital way that Jesus truly 'supplies' all fears, all sins were healed and, by this redeeming love, even forgotten. As she expressed it: 'May the power of that love whose fulness lives in him who . . . has become bone of my bone and flesh of my flesh, make up for what ever I have confused and distorted . . .' (2.5). And again: 'Through him . . . I offer my amendment of life, so that through him all that I have failed to do may be made up' (2.16). We see this use of *suppletio* again when she prayed to Jesus: '. . . clothe me in the purity of your most innocent life' (*Ex*, 21). 'By the riches of your bounty cover over my poverty and conceal the neediness of my ignoble life' (*Ex*, 93).

Gertrude lived humility and obedience in Christ and with Christ, with love, confidence, and trust and in the peaceful consciousness that Jesus supplies.

Conversion

The monk or nun following the *Rule* of St Benedict vows conversion of life; s/he promises to keep turning to Christ, to be a real monk, a monk not in name only but from the depths of his/her being. Conversion penetrates much of Gertrude's work. Great mystic that she was, she never represented herself in a self-righteous or spiritually elite way. Her approach to life, though always wholehearted, was simple, down to earth, and honest, especially when she looked at her own faults. Impatience, too sharp a word, anger, negligence, ingratitude, were faults she had constantly to battle. Even St Mechtild, Gertrude's spiritual mother and intimate friend, complained to the Lord about Gertrude: 'My Lord, why is she able to judge the aberrations and failures of others too severely on occasion?' The Lord's reply gives us an insight into the basic monastic practice of vigilance which helped Gertrude to live her *conversio morum*. 'The Lord kindly replied: "I am sure the reason for that is that she herself does not allow any blemish to gain a footing in her heart and she cannot bear the failure of others with equanimity"' (1.11). This careful 'watching' is a way to keep faults and sins from getting a foothold. The Lord had even told Gertrude, through an intermediary: 'If she really wished to find me she should pay attention to keeping watch over her senses' (1.13).

Conversion also involves sorrow for failures. Lamenting her failure to respond more generously to suffering, she wrote:

> But alas! a thousand times alas! that I have given you my consent so little and so rarely. . . . Lord, you know the sorrow, confusion and dejection of my spirit over this, and the desire of my heart that I should make up for my shortcomings toward you in some other way (2.15).

Conversion also expresses itself in prayer: 'Grant . . . that all created things may grow worthless in my eyes, and that you alone may impart sweetness to my heart' (2.4). It also involves asking for God's light: 'I thank you especially for having made me understand . . . how I was corrupting the purity of your gifts' (2.11). She knew that ingratitude and carelessness prevent conversion (2.4) and that: 'if I wished to be bound to you I was obliged above all to work away wholeheartedly at purity of heart and works of loving charity' (2.16).

St Gertrude's second exercise is entitled 'Spiritual Conversion'; it is an exercise designed to help one renew oneself on the anniversary of having received the holy habit. She explains the meaning of conversion when she instructs the reader at the beginning of the exercise:

> Whenever you renew your good purpose, desiring to solemnize the memory of your first conversion whereby you did renounce the world and to convert your heart with its whole strength unto God you shall use this exercise. Let your prayer be that God may build up for himself within you a monastery of love and of all the virtues. (*Ex*, 19)

Silence

Gertrude longed that her heart might be a dwelling place for the Lord. To have a receptive, open, heart was her unique way of expressing the desire to be present to God, to 'dwell' in his presence, and we might say it expresses a traditionally feminine way. Silence implies a contemplative, receiving stance. She speaks of an insight the Lord had given her: '. . . if my outer self with its bodily senses were held aloof from hustle and bustle, my mind would be completely available for you and my heart would offer you a dwelling-place with all that is lovely and joyful' (2.3). The whole monastic *ascesis*—conversion, prayer, humility —is needed if one is to enter into the desire for this presence. As she expressed this in her *Exercises*: 'Come, renew and sanctify me in you that you may take up a dwelling in my soul' (*Ex*, 156), and 'You make your dwelling in the humble. . . (*Ex*, 156)'. Gertrude's silence flowed from her monastic *ascesis*, especially humility and solitude; silence meant not simply not speaking but the recollection needed for carefully guarding the senses and the heart so as to prepare a delightful dwelling place for her Lord and God.

Gertrude explains, in Chapter Three of Book Two, that it was at the end of a day of solitude and silence, of prayer and pondering, that she realized '. . . that you had come and were there present'. Thereafter, she always felt this presence, for whenever 'I returned to my heart, I always found you there'. The one exception she noted was an eight-day absence of his presence when 'you withdrew from me. . . . as a result of a worldly conversation. . .' (2.14)—a breach of the silent watching of the heart and senses. Again, she explains her lived silence when she says that on the Sunday before Ash Wednesday: '. . . you were asking me . . . for a home where you could rest. . . . I did not find any meal I could serve you which was more gladly received than my being constant in prayer, silence and other penitential practices. . . (2.14).

Opus Dei, the Work of God

The renewal of Cîteaux aimed at striking a balance between liturgical prayer, manual work, and spiritual reading. The *Opus Dei*, the liturgical prayer of the Church, helps keep the monk in God's presence and in a state of constant prayer. The medieval monk and nun did not experience the sense of dichotomy between private, personal prayer and liturgical prayer which seems to beset our modern religious minds. As much has been written on St Gertrude as a prime example of a perfect blend of these two types of prayer, our treatment here will be brief.[38] As a cistercian benedictine house, Helfta would have structured its life around the Mass and the Divine Office. As Dom Vaggagini explains: 'The hours of the *Opus Dei* gave a rhythm to the whole day, and the liturgical feasts to the entire year'.[39] All five books of the *Herald* and the *Exercises* express this rhythm as Gertrude seeks God constantly, through love, in this liturgical round. As Dom Leclercq points out:

> Her inner piety vivifies her liturgical office, her liturgical life nourishes her personal piety.... There was a continuous interpenetration in her daily life between liturgy and personal devotion. When Gertrude sings a hymn she lives it, she feels what it says, contains and communicates and these moments of intense prayer influence all other moments.[40]

We see then a woman vitally alive in the prayer of the liturgy and in prayerful touch with the present moment. This blend of personal and liturgical prayer in Gertrude shows a depth of integration of divine and human life which enabled Gertrude to carry this unity and wholeness into the rhythm of every other moment of her day.

Prayer

Women of the twentieth century, as we are, find that St Gertrude has much to offer us as we reflect upon her prayer. 'Contemplation has become an important issue for women', writes Jacquelyn Mattfield, president of Barnard College, and she goes on to quote from Jean Miller's book *Toward a New Psychology of Women*:

> Everyone repeatedly has to break through to a new vision if he/she is to keep living. This very personal kind of creativity, this making of new visions, this continuous struggle, does not usually go on in open and well-articulated ways. But it goes on. Today, we can see this universal process most clearly in women. Women are the people struggling to create for themselves a new concept of personhood. They are attempting to restructure the central tenet of their lives. This effort extends to the deepest inner reaches....[41]

There is no doubt that one of the best means we have of attaining new vision, of finding a new concept of personhood for women even on the level of psychological examination is contemplative prayer, a quieting of our being, whether we are angry or frustrated or simply distracted. 'Be still and know that I am God.' We receive new strength and light in that quietness; we come alive and awake in that inner recess. This is not passsivity but demands the disciplined activity of watching the heart, of turning from what is bright and splashy to the quiet unknowingness of our deep inner self where we are being born again. 'There is a contemplative dimension within the depth of every person that needs to be touched if we are to realize the fullness of our human potential'.[42]

Gertrude had a down-to-earth way of expressing one of her first experiences of contemplative prayer:

> May all . . . thank you for that extraordinary grace with which you led my soul to experience and brood upon the innermost recesses of my heart, which had been of as little concern to me before as, if I may say so, the insides of my feet.'

And then she prayed:

> May I win for myself and all those whom you have chosen, the privilege of enjoying often that sweet union and unifying sweetness which were quite unknown to me before that hour' (2.2).

What can we say about Gertrude's prayer? She was a contemplative and a mystic, certainly; but despite her many visions, and their complicated but beautiful medieval imagery, Gertrude's prayer was utter simplicity. Her writings hold basically one message: she desired to live by God's life, by the Holy Spirit. This she did especially through love, poverty of spirit, and with zeal for the salvation of all persons. Her monastic life-style was simple. Her attention to God was simple. God's will and sensitivity to his calls was an important means of living this simplicity; she trusted in God and not in herself. She received energy and light from the contemplative prayer of faith, hope, and love to discover and live the joy and sorrows of each new moment in decisiveness and faith. 'Come Holy Spirit', she prays,

> Come, O Lord who are God, fill my heart . . . it is empty of anything good. Set me on fire that I may love you. Enlighten me, that I may know you. Attract me that I may delight in you. Arouse me, that I may experience the fruition of you (*Ex*, 20).

MONASTIC PROFESSION

The title of the fourth Exercise in Gertrude's book of *Exercises* is 'Renewal of Monastic Profession'; this is a time 'when the religious soul wishes to reawaken in herself the grace of her donation'. (*Ex*, 57) To do this Gertrude set forth a series of prayers, psalms, and petitions to the Trinity, Our Lady, the angels and saints for guarding chastity, for perseverance, for devotedness, for faith and obedience, a spirit of meekness and docility, to mention only some of the virtues she lists. A prayer to invoke Divine Wisdom is given, and then: 'Now you shall give to the Lord the written bond of your profession'. The prayer that follows states simply what monastic profession meant to Gertrude.

> O Jesus, my dearest beloved, I wish to embrace with you the rule of love, that I may renew my life and may spend it in you. Come, place my life under the care of your Holy Spirit. . . . (*Ex*, 70)

These ideals, growth in Christ, growth in union and submission to the guidance of the Holy Spirit are the rock foundation upon which Gertrude was building her consecrated life. She then instructs: 'Now, take upon you anew the yoke of the Holy Rule' (*Ex*, 71). There follows a threefold prayer to Father, Son, and Holy Spirit. Of the Father she asks:

> . . . that at the end of this course of holy monastic observance (which, for love of You, I have undertaken to run), I may receive You Yourself as my crown and my eternal inheritance.

To the Son she says:

> Receive me, O Jesus most loving, that you may bear with me all the burdens of the heat of the day, and may I have you as my comforter and . . . as my tutor, guide, and companion on my journey.

And to the Holy Spirit:

> May I have you as the master and instructor of my whole life, and the dearest lover of my heart (*Ex*, 71).

Monastic commitment was a covenant commitment to the Trinity; the Father would return that covenant as an eternal inheritance with himself, the Son as comforter and companion, and the Holy Spirit as instructor and lover.

Prostrate before the Lord, the person renewing his covenant was to recite Psalm 50 and then in a spirit of repentance and conversion pray to the Father: 'Come, be merciful to me. . . . and break asunder the wall of my past way of life which withholds me from you; and draw me into you. . .' (*Ex*, 71). Then the monastic cowl was given as a symbol of final commitment and finally communion was received. At this special moment of union Gertrude counselled: 'When you are about to receive communion cast yourself into God that you may live for him alone'; and then pray: '. . . deign to cast me into the impetuous whirlwind of your Spirit. . . . Then shall I truly begin to renounce myself and pour myself, in spirit, O my kind Love, into you' (*Ex*, 73–74).

The act of monastic profession commits the monk or nun radically to God through monastic vows. St Gertrude's ardent nature entered into this mystery with repentance, humble love, and a holy boldness of aspirations.

THE MYSTERY OF LIFE AND DEATH IN THE WRITINGS OF GERTRUDE

Thus far, I have tried to portray St Gertrude as an individual, a woman motivated by a freedom which integrated both the feminine and masculine traits of her personality. I have tried also to situate her within the context of her monastic life, identifying, however summarily, the monastic values by which she chose to live. I have done this through a study of the two works we know she herself wrote, Book Two of the *Herald* and the *Exercises*, with a few references to the other books of the *Herald*.

Within this context I now wish to study the meaning she saw in the great realities of life and death. All men knowingly or unknowingly seek 'a reason to live and a reason to die'.[43] Any study of Gertrude's writings reveals life and death as two of her most dominant themes, encompassing her other more familiar themes. They support and give meaning to one another. They also express her personality, for they pervaded her whole life.

LIFE

Jesus tells us 'I have come that they may have life and have it more abundantly', (Jn 10:10) and 'I am the way and the truth and the life (Jn 14:6) . . . I will not the death of the sinner but that he be converted and live' (Ez 18:23, Prologue *Rule of Benedict*)'. Life, Christ's life, eternal life in all its forms is the most basic gospel promise. So it is not surprising that it is a basic monastic motive. 'Who is the man who will have life and desires to see good days . . . If you will have true and everlasting life . . . decline from evil and do good . . . Behold how in His loving kindness the Lord shows us the way of life.' (Prologue to the *Rule* of St Benedict)

In a conference Thomas Merton once asked: 'What is monastic life?' (putting the emphasis on life). He answered: 'Monastic life is simply life! We have come here to live.'[44] And so it was with St Gertrude. Hardly a page in her *Exercises* does not mention the word 'life' once or several times. And although it is not so explicitly frequent in Book Two of the *Herald* as in the *Exercises* (because of the nature of the content) it pervades her thought and imagery. In her commentary on the translation of the first exercise of St Gertrude, Mother Columba Hart writes:

> In this relatively short book [Gertrude] calls upon God no less than thirteen times, in the words of the psalmist, as 'God of my life!' To her, Christ, who is God, is the source of our true life; by living that life on earth to the best of our ability and in constant dependency on Christ, we shall attain in heaven to that perfect union with the Triune God which is the plenitude of eternal life. . . . This is Gertrude's message. . . .[45]

Gertrude, Fully Human, Fully Alive

It has been said 'the unawakened man is like a puppet. He doesn't live but lets life live in him'.[46] Gertrude was wholly alive. In her style of writing we discern ardor, impetuosity, and passion—a wholehearted aliveness in her attitudes and desires. She was a deeply human person who enjoyed life in the beauty of a rose (2.21) in the brilliance of the sun (2.4), and in sharing a secret with a friend (2.4). Alive intellectually, she was a woman with a keen mind and a love of study. Her preoccupation with studies was one of the main obstacles to be overcome in her first conversion. She also experienced inward distress, mental darkness, sadness, fear, and anguish, but these shadows only cast into focus her natural buoyancy and liveliness and reveal a balanced and normal personality. She was not always on the peaks; her very capacity to live and to enjoy life made her all the more vulnerable. Her inability to be with the community, or to participate in the liturgy, or to live a normal community life during the sicknesses which beset her provided trials in her life.

In her humanness she felt the need of a close friend. She describes this experience: '. . . the secret peace of a secluded place of rest gave me special pleasure. I began to turn over in my mind what I would like which would make my pleasure in that resting place seem complete. This was my request: that I might have a close friend—loving, warm, congenial—who might solace me in my solitude' (2.3). It seemed that this request won for her the gift of the experience of God's loving presence within her, for she says: 'Meanwhile my heart of clay realized you had come and were there present. . . . For although I wavered mentally, and enjoyed certain forbidden pleasures, when after hours, days (alas), even, I fear, weeks (to my great sorrow) I returned to my heart, I always found you there' (2.3). Such graces and her original conversion awakened ever more fully and transformed ever more completely Gertrude's natural ardor of spirit into a deeper experience of God's own life.

God's Life in Gertrude

Many incidents Gertrude relates show her remarkable experience of and growth in God's life. They were his gifts to her to teach others and help their growth in holiness. This was the only reason she finally wrote, with deep repugnance and only under Christ's command, of her experiences of his love. She was quite aware she might somehow 'shock human understanding' (2.10). She begged the Lord not to ask her to write down her experience. But he won the argument: 'It is my wish to have in your writings irrefutable evidence of my loving-kindness for these last days' (2.10).

One of the loveliest of these scenes took place on the Feast of Candlemas (Purification, 2 February) and she described what happened:

> For while they were reading the Gospel: 'She brought forth her first born Son' etc., your spotless mother offered me . . . you, the child of her virginity, a lovely little baby struggling with all his might to be embraced by me. I . . . took you, a fragile baby boy who clung to me with your little arms. I became aware of such life-giving refreshment from the breath of . . . your blessed mouth that my soul should in all justice bless you from that moment forwards . . . (2.16).

Especially in receiving communion, which she liked to call 'your life-giving sacrament', did Gertrude receive the gift of life. Her devotion to the Eucharist was strong and she wished to receive communion frequently, encouraging others to do so as well, in a period of history when communion was generally received only a few days each year on important feasts. She said:

> How often . . . you communicated . . . your saving presence to me! . . . . especially whenever I am permitted to share in your blessed body and blood (2.11). [It was on days] when I came to the life-giving food of your body and blood . . . . [that] you allured my soul . . . that she might be more closely united with you . . . enjoy you more freely (2.2).

One time when Gertrude was sick:

> . . . having received the Bread of Life I was intent on God and myself, when I realized that my soul, like wax carefully softened in the fire, lay on the Lord's chest, as if about to be impressed with a seal. Suddenly she seemed to be seized and partially drawn into that treasury [Sacred Heart] in which the full being of the Godhead lives incarnate, and she was sealed with the indelible mark of the bright and ever-tranquil Trinity. (2.7)

All through her works vivid, descriptive 'life' phrases dot her beautiful prose

—living love . . . living faith . . . He who is the healing of life . . . You are the fount of life . . . living word . . . living letter of his Spirit . . . you who are life . . . you are the life of my soul'[47]. With the gifts of God's life came a growing realization of a deeper sense of the meaning of life.

A Reason to Live

What gave meaning to Gertrude's life? What did she see as life's purpose? We get some inkling when, at the moment of monastic profession, she prayed 'that I may renew my life and spend it in you. . . . place my life under the care of the Holy Spirit' (*Ex*, 70). And elsewhere:

> let the depths of your love engulf me. . . . let me lose myself in the flood of your living love. . . (*Ex*, 74). . . . restore to me a life which lives for you alone. . . . give me a spirit which tastes you, thoughts which think of you, a soul which understands your will, strength which accomplishes your good pleasure and stability which perseveres with you (*Ex*, 169).

Yet, as we have seen, she also experienced the anguish of life, of sickness, of evil, of threats to her monastery and sisters, and of the seeming loss of souls. She responded to these threats with profound confidence in God's power.

> O Love, O God, you yourself are my wall and bulwark. Behold, they who endure anguish in this world know what a shade is spread above them in your peace. . . . But evil shall not approach me, since you yourself are with me. . . (*Ex*, 100–101).

We can recognize in Gertrude what many of us have felt within the depths of our heart. The reason for life is to let God's goodness and love grow within us. This deepened realization is the way to combat evil, hatred, injustice, and absurdities, to renew our lives, to lose our false selves and let our true self, Christ, live in us. This is to transform the world by love. This is our christian witness and mission. Gertrude's own witness took the form of being an emissary—a herald of God's loving-kindness in word, deed, and writing. Her daily living was her means of praising, loving, and thanking him whom she knew experientially to be her life.

Receptivity to Life

Certain attitudes helped Gertrude to be fully open and receptive to God and his gifts of life; certainly the whole of the monastic *ascesis*, already discussed, humility, obedience, conversion, silence, and prayer, contributed. She was especially open to seeking life:

> 'where is the way of life.... You alone know these paths of life and truth.... from you proceeds ... the richest seed of the fruits of life' (*Ex*, 49).

She asked, even begged for life:

> 'Let the life-giving floods that flow from you, I beg you, overwhelm me' (*Ex*, 160); 'O Jesus, fountain of life, come, give me to drink, a cup of the living water which flows from you...' (*Ex*, 10).

Her petitions for life, scattered throughout her works, use poetic, scriptural images to manifest an intensity of desire:

> he has '...regenerated me unto the hope of life ... (*Ex*,6); Give me living faith ... (*Ex*, 7); cleanse ... renew me, O you my true life ... (*Ex*, 64); ...deign to infuse into me the grace, relish and love of the life of the Spirit ... (*Ex*, 68).

She counselled:

> 'Stir up therefore your desire ... to be reborn in God by the holiness of a new life...' (*Ex*, 5).

And finally:

> '[Grant that] I may no longer have any life outside of you' (*Ex*, 74).

'Ask and you shall receive, seek and you shall find'; Gertrude lived this word of God and, as St Benedict prescribed, (RB 4) she desired 'life everlasting' with all the passion of her soul.

Life-giving

As Gertrude grew in the rhythm of God's life, it was natural that she should bear fruit in giving this life to others. Although she was never abbess and held in the monastery no office that we know of, nevertheless, because of her remarkable intellectual gifts, her outstanding eloquence both in speech and in writing, and the many spiritual gifts granted her for winning and converting souls, her influence over others was marked. In her *Exercises* we have the fruit of that life in her prayers and petitions. In Books One and Two of the *Herald* we get a deeper glimpse of how she exercised her remarkable life-giving powers.

In Book Two she lists some of the situations in which the Lord promised her a special grace: consoling and strengthening those who reveal their shortcomings to her; those experiencing doubt and anguish about their worthiness to receive communion; those to whom she promises a blessing or pardons for some fault; those who entrust themselves to her prayers; and all who discuss their spiritual progress with her. Two dispositions were necessary: on the part of the person asking for help, a contrite heart and humbled spirit; and on Gertrude's part, a deep spiritual poverty. This is the single trait that comes through most strongly in all of Gertrude's 'life giving'. She was completely the instrument of the Lord. She longed to be, and fully realized that she was, such an instrument, for she said:

> . . . your loving kindness, aware of my spiritual poverty, made the decision to accomplish this through me. . . . you condescended to adopt me as your tool (most unworthy) . . . that through the words of my mouth you might transmit the grace of victory to other . . . friends of yours.

Then the Lord assured Gertrude:

> As often as you consider your low estate and entrust yourself, unworthy as you are of my gifts, to me—above all, trusting in my loving kindness—you are paying the 'rent' you owe me for my blessings. (2.20)

It is as if the open, humble receptivity of the person in need and the sincere poverty of Gertrude acted as catalyst and conductor for God's grace, and it came, powerful and strong, restoring life, engendering life.

The unidentified biographer of Book One relates: '. . . her advice and example greatly inspired many to an urgent longing for greater devotion. . . . it was God's spirit speaking in her by the miraculous softening which took place in their hearts and changes which took place in their wills' (1.1). Through her words and prayers she was also able to free people from temptation and to touch the rebellious. Yet she was not always successful. She failed with some souls and complained to the Lord, who replied: 'Do not be surprised that your words sometimes toil in vain, when I myself during my earthly life preached many times in the ardor of my divine spirit, and none the less my words brought about no improvement in some people, for in my divine plan all things have their right and proper time' (1.14).

Chapter seven of Book One, entitled 'Her Passion for the Salvation of Souls' explains:

> Both Gertrude's words and deeds provide the clearest evidence as to the way in which a passion for souls and an enthusiasm for the religious life fired her mind. For if she ever noticed some failing in one of her neighbors, she longed to set it right, and if she did not see this longing have any effect, it weighed on her soul so heavily that she was quite inconsolable, until, by her prayers to the Lord and also by her own words of warning, she had won some improvement at least either personally or through intermediaries whom she was able to involve. . . . because one ought to make the attempt now, as an eternal penalty would follow death.

Gertrude's desire to correct was born of sincere love and concern for the person.

It was often through Scripture that Gertrude 'gave' life. Her biographer tells us that she 'read over and over again . . . all the books of the Bible' and that 'she always had an instructive quotation from Scripture at her finger tips' and could easily refute error with Scripture (1.1). She used this gift to help those who found difficulty in understanding the Scriptures, '. . . she would alter the Latin and rewrite it in a more straightforward style, so that it would be more useful for those who read it' (1.7).

Her biographer goes on to explain: 'She spent her whole life in this way, from early morning till night, sometimes summarizing lengthy passages, sometimes smoothing away difficulties. She longed to work for God's praise and her neighbour's salvation' (1.7).

Gertrude's disposition in this role of giving and sharing God's life was first and foremost utter poverty; she let God work through her; she was his tool. She had the beautiful habit of calling God to her side to ask his help in little and big things, her will united to his will. She had a selfless spirit:

> to interrupt the peace and quiet of her sleep, to postpone her meals, to do without anything which concerned the comfort of her own body—she considered this joy rather than work. Not satisfied with this she would also time and again interrupt the sweetness of contemplation when necessity compelled her to go to the assistance of someone in temptation, to encourage the discouraged or to help someone in charity. For as iron placed in fire, so she, burnt up by the love of God became Love longing for the salvation of the whole world (1.4).

Gertrude the monastic woman was becoming Gertrude the saint, Gertrude the bride, sharing fully Christ's own love and zeal for the salvation of all. 'I have come that they might have life and have it more abundantly.' (Jn 10: 10)

Along with her active works, and integrated with them, and surely the power behind Gertrude's influence, we notice her prayers—pure and humble. One is reminded of St Gregory's picture of St Benedict in the *Dialogues*. St Benedict, a poor man, bowed his head in humble intercession before any of his works as he interceded for his monks in temptation, and in his healings and miracles. The power of Gertrude's prayer, too, was her poverty.

She was also warmly human and always showed concern.

> She radiated such a strong feeling of compassionate love that if she . . . came to know of someone . . . who was in trouble, she would immediately do everything in her power to lessen their distress by speaking to them, or put new life into them by writing to them. . . . But it was not only towards people but also towards animals that she experienced a strong feeling of loving-kindness; if she saw any living thing, bird or animal, suffering distress from hunger or thirst or cold, from the depths of her loving heart she immediately felt pity for one of her Lord's creatures. (1.8)

That she might harm a soul by failing to understand God's will and message for this person was Gertrude's greatest fear. The Lord assured her: 'Do not be afraid, daughter. . . . when anyone asks your advice in humility and faith on any matter whatsoever, in the light of my divine truth you will analyse that case and come to the same conclusion as me . . .', and, the Lord added, 'anyone who is oppressed or sad and humbly and honestly looks for strength in your words, will never be frustrated, for I, God, living in you, at the prompting of unbounded loving kindness of my love, long to bring blessings on many people through your words.' (1.14)

Gertrude teaches us to dare to be poor, to be the Lord's instrument; life-givers through love and selflessness, faith and prayer. Gertrude fully alive, receiving God's life, celebrated life with a passionate love for God and all men and women; she then became a life-giver by her union in poverty and love with him who is life.

As men and women of today's world we know that life's meaning is being challenged, misused. One prevalent philosophy holds that: 'Life is a purely biological force that surges up in the organism. Man must remain passive to its promptings, obedient to its rhythm. Spiritual values curb the innocence and purity of this naked life principle.'[48] Gertrude's life, and our lives, should witness that the mystery of life, gradually being transformed, is God's wonderful gift to us to be used responsibly in freedom and love. She shows us the 'whole' person responding to God. If we focus on the biological force only, we stunt our growth to the fullness of human life.

The victory of life over death was won by the Prince of Life for us at Easter. It is Gertrude's view of this victory—the mystery of life in death—that will be the subject of the concluding section of my study of Gertrude.

DEATH[49]

Death in the Modern World

In our own times, a remarkable phenomenon has taken place in the area of death consciousness and confrontation, mainly because of treatises on death and individual eschatology by such scholars as Karl Rahner, Ladislas Boros, and F. X. Durwell in the field of theology. For some years sociologists, psychologists, and historians have been studying contemporary man's attitude toward death. From the medical profession we have the writings of Dr Elizabeth Kübler-Ross on the care of dying patients and of Dr Raymond Moody on after-life experiences. All of this has stirred a wave of speculation on the reality of 'my own death' and how to cope with it. Many of the questions being raised are formulated by Monika Hellwig in her book, *What are They Saying about Death and Christian Hope?*:[50] questions about the meaning of death; 'Why must I die?' And, she asks, 'What will happen to my reflexive self awareness beyond death?' 'Will I continue to be self aware and under what circumstances?' Is 'there an ultimate moral accountability and what [are] the rules...?' If contemporary men and women ask these questions about the apparent meaninglessness of death, and if they are answered with assurances that the meaning of death lies in a divinely appointed task in life, then they naturally raise questions concerning the meaning of life. To die a happy death one must have lived a purposeful life.

ST GERTRUDE'S ATTITUDE TO DEATH

In reflecting on the mystery of life's meaning for Gertrude, we have found her a woman devoted to life and to living. She was a joyous, praising person who prayed: 'Now O love, [my] life, you give life, give me life in that living word of God who is yourself' (*Ex*, 103). These words describe her habitual attitude and we shall find in Gertrude this same attitude when she regarded death.

Thomas Merton once said that our attitude towards death depends on how we look on the earth; if we live for this life our attitude to death will be affected by this fact. Death and life are inextricably interrelated, and so are our attitudes towards them. In St Gertrude we find a life-oriented attitude toward death. How was it formed? How did she cope with and overcome, the fears, the uncertainties, the loneliness of death?

Again, the two works by Gertrude herself will help us answer these questions. Book Two of the *Herald* makes only two or three direct references to death. In her *Exercises*, a work described as 'her masterpiece.... into it, in the full maturity of her powers she poured her deepest reflections and aspirations',[51] we have a treasure house containing both a spirituality and a theology of death. Yet it is best understood within the framework and background of the *Herald*, and especially Book Two. The death references in the *Exercises* (some sixty-seven)[52] far outnumber any of Gertrude's better known themes—her sense of unworthiness, her references to the Sacred Heart, her *suppletio*, even her ardent desires and prayers for union with God (which number about thirty-six).[53]

SPIRITUALITY OF DEATH IN GERTRUDE

When the earliest monks went into the desert to seek God they also chose to enter into combat. As Archbishop Antony Bloom explains:

> this battle which is our vocation is part and parcel of holiness. The desert fathers . . . did not flee the world in the sense in which modern man sometimes tries to escape its grip in order to find a haven of security; they set out to conquer the enemy in battle. By the grace of God, in the power of the Spirit, they were engaging in combat.[54]

This means combat with evil and with the devil; it demands the loss of the false self (the death of egotistical self-love) and entrance into the passion, death, and resurrection of Christ, imitating as the martyrs did, Christ's own conquest of sin, evil, and death by his paschal mystery. This is to enter into the combat of our daily life experiences as followers of Christ.

In Gertrude's *Exercises* we have a series of seven exercises which give us a spirituality of the way to Christ. She turns the spotlight, so to speak, on seven important events in the monastic journey by which we enter the combat—the mystery of the passion, death, and resurrection of Christ. The first exercise focuses on the renewal of our baptism: '. . . be you careful at some appointed season . . . to solemnize the memory of your baptism. Stir up your desire therefore, to be reborn in God by the holiness of a new life . . .' (*Ex*, 5). The second exercise, 'For the Anniversary of Investiture with the Holy Habit', celebrates our conversion totally to God. The third exercise for 'Espousals and Consecration of Virgins', and the fourth, 'Renewal of Monastic Profession', are a renewal of our total commitment to Christ in love. These four events symbolize a complete entrance into the passion and death of Christ within the monastic commitment. The next two exercises, 'To Stir up the Love of God', and 'Praise and Thanksgiving', instruct us in the dispositions of faithful love and ready praise and thanksgiving; they are both the fruit of total commitment already made and supply the strength to live it. They are also the expression of resurrection in our life. Love and joyous praise are the fruits of prayer and humility—the traditional monastic ways of confronting evil and its forces. The final exercise on 'Preparation for Death', prepares us for the fullness of resurrection, our life after death.

In the *Exercises*, penetrated with the spirit of the *Rule*, Gertrude gives us a spirituality of the monastic journey into the mystery of Christ. 'It is tempting to draw a certain comparison between the *Exercises* of Saint Gertrude and the Rule of Saint Benedict, for both books begin with the Divine adoption and guide us onward and upward from this beginning to the summits of perfection.'[55] Both are filled with a sense of God's presence and the goal of perfect love.

Martyrdom and Spiritual or Mystical Death

The spirit of martyrdom is expressed by Gertrude through her benedictine monastic *ascesis*; obedience, humility, and charity grow and yield a full spiritual or mystical death. She prayed:

> Through your passion and death, make me die unto myself and live unto you alone. Through your glorious resurrection and wonderful ascension make me advance daily from strength to strength. (*Ex*, 39)

> The soul which, through imitation of Christ, finds itself dying with him on the cross can again find itself in the depth of his divinity for he himself has made this promise: 'where I am [suffering, death, resurrection] there also shall my servant be' (Jn 12:26).[56]

A sincere desire to die to self completely she coupled with the equally ardent desire to be united to God: 'Let me lose myself in the flood of your living love . . .' (*Ex*, 74). Death to self is not to be thought of as a negation or destruction of self, as we commonly think of death, whether spiritual or physical, but it is a finding of our true identity, our life in Christ.

Why must I die? Whether physically or spiritually, in order truly to live. 'Spiritually speaking there are two kinds of life: one is beatific, consisting of the vision of God, which must be attained by natural death . . . the other is the perfect spiritual life, the possession of God through union of love . . .'.[57]

Face to Face Vision[58]

St Gertrude's whole life was directed toward this union of love, and physical death meant for her a 'face to face' encounter with God, and the very fullness of life forever. In her seventh exercise, 'Preparation for Death', she took the seven Hours of the Divine Office and '. . . avails herself here of the widespread medieval custom of matching the canonical Hours with the stages of Christ's passion . . .',[59] and incorporates the following prayer into each exposition on the seven Hours. She prays: '. . . satisfy me at the hour of death with the immediate vision of your sweet countenance, that I may have eternal rest in you.' (*Ex*, 141, 153, 156, 159, 163, 166) For Gertrude, death was meeting life and light in God's face: 'Come, show me your face and make me contemplate your loveliness' (*Ex*, 86).

With this imagery in mind, let us ask how Gertrude would answer Monika Hellwig's question: 'What will happen to my reflexive self awareness beyond death? Will I continue to be self aware and under what circumstances?' In her sixth exercise, Gertrude prays:

> . . . that I may pass in safety through the narrow gate of death . . . . leave me not . . . that I may behold you face to face, O my God, my Lover, who did create me for yourself. . . . show me in the mirror of unveiled contemplation of yourself, the glory of your Godhead, that my spirit and my soul may be filled with praise of you in all joy and splendor . . . . it will draw its inmost sustenance from the joy of the vision of your glorious face . . . . Then in paradise you will be in me, and I in you . . . I shall praise your name without ceasing, for you are the God of my life, the Redeemer and Lover of my soul. (*Ex*, 140–141)

Perhaps this means that our self-awareness will be totally unselfish, totally free, totally loving in that great face-to-face meeting in total joy and total praise. We cannot really die, for from the moment of our creation we have been made in relationship to God, our creator, the source of being, who is our mother, our father, our spouse, our brother, our sister, our friend. At the moment of death, the narrow gate through which we all must enter leads us to the fullness of relationship with Father, Son, and Spirit and one day to our full redemption in the one body of Christ.[60]

The mystery of death shines as a golden thread all through St Gertrude's *Exercises*. In innumerable images and in beautiful prose-poetry she ponders, describes, anticipates the moment of death, God's protection and strength at death, her need to be purified and truly prepared, Jesus' *suppletio* in this time of trial, death as union with God (often likened to bridal union), death as redemption and death as the true beholding face to face. Interspersed with the expression of joyful longings, these images are intertwined with every aspect of her life.

THEOLOGY OF DEATH

Judgment

Gertrude was deeply conscious of the reality of judgment. Her references are not frequent but they are forceful. She knew fear and dread: 'Come, let me not fear the hearing of condemnation . . .' (*Ex*, 164). She gives us a potent remedy for the fear that can come at the thought of judgment. Here too she is a daughter of St Benedict, who counsels us never to despair of God's mercy. (RB 4) We see again in this all-important moment her use of *suppletio*, the assurance that 'Jesus supplies'. She tells the Lord:

> At the hour of death, do you judge me according to that innocence and stainlessness which you have conferred upon me in you since all my debt has been paid through you. You were judged and condemned for my sake, that I, who of myself am only a poor beggar maid, might have all blessings in abundance through you (*Ex*, 153).

Reward at Death

Gertrude was not enticed by rewards nor dismayed by punishment. In her spiritual maturity she was drawn by the perfect love St Benedict describes in his Rule (RB 7). The one reward she sought was full union with God, which is life. Her deep confidence in God's love banished fear of punishment. But she was realistic and dealt with the conquest of evil in ourselves as simply as did St Benedict, who tells us to dash at once against Christ any evil thoughts that arise in the mind (RB 4). Gertrude says to God: 'If only we cling to you with will's understanding the more prompt our resistance to any evil, the more effective . . . and successful it is' (2.11). We are human, and St Benedict and Gertrude knew this. There are times when we need to be prodded with reminders of judgment or punishment or encouraged with rewards.

But our goal is perfect love which casts out fear and leads us all together to eternal life. This 'life everlasting', this full fruition of love is another constant in Gertrude's writings. Again, she prays: 'O death, you bring forth the fruits of eternal life . . . . I beg you, engulf my whole life in yourself and immerse my death in you' (*Ex*, 160). 'Oh, when will my soul be engulfed in the river of life, she asks elsewhere, 'in the rapturous waters of the eternal fruition of you?' (*Ex*, 139)

In a litany for the renewal of monastic profession, Gertrude asked St Benedict to help her attain eternal life. United to all who follow a monastic rule, she prayed:

> O Benedict, glorious founder of the monastic state, who are my father and one of God's chosen great, obtain for me in monastic observance such constancy that I may receive the crown of eternal life together with you (*Ex*, 67).

Accountability

Having found St Gertrude totally life-orientated, I now wish to ponder this life-characteristic and present it as a part of her theology of death. Life attitudes are formed by our moment-to-moment choices, for all of which we are accountable. Are we hastening to do now what will profit us for all eternity? (RB Prologue) Gertrude's confidant, the author of Book Three of the *Herald* says of Gertrude: 'She remembered what St Bernard has said would happen at the hour of death, when our actions will address us thus: "you have produced us; we are your work; we will never leave you, but will abide continually with you, and appear with you at judgment"' (3.69). Might this not answer Monika Hellwig's question whether there is moral accountability and what are its rules. In Book Five of the *Herald* we are given a series of descriptions of deaths (of the nuns, monks, and lay persons). We see strict moral accountability—reward given for the faithful and pure soul but purification demanded for the stains that remain at death's moment. Gertrude, in deep compassion for these suffering souls, was able to relieve them through fervent prayer and acts of charity. She believed we are all members of that Mystical Body; that each of us needs to pray and do good works for the brother or sister who having passed through death is no longer able to choose or to merit salvation. Gertrude cared for each moment and sensed how this moment tends to, or directs, our final moment. She invites us to prepare now our fundamental option—to do now what will profit us for all eternity.[61]

Christ's Death

I will do one last bit of sewing with that golden thread of the mystery of death in Gertrude's reflections. In her seventh exercise, on 'Atonement for Sin and Preparation for Death', she included a beautful section in which she meditates on Christ's death. She begs, in the prayers of this exercise, that her soul may find a nest in the death of Christ; she prays for his protection, and proclaims his death the source of her heart's confidence: 'O most consoling death of Christ . . . shelter me about when the anguish of death comes . . . . engulf my life; in you, immerse me utterly' (*Ex*, 161). She goes on for several pages, pondering Christ's death and so intertwining it with our own death that one hardly knows sometimes to whose death (Christ or ours) she is referring. At death, she teaches us, we are not alone. He is truly with us, whether in the obscurity of faith or in the tenderness of his love—dying in us, rising again in us. If we have died with him we shall rise with him!

From her consideration of Christ's presence at our death comes Gertrude's devotion to the Sacred Heart. She saw it as an ardent heart of love, a heart of refuge. She prays: 'Come, and at the hour of my death open unto me without delay the door of your most benign heart that through you I may deserve to enter unhindered into the bridechamber of your living love where I shall enjoy and possess you, O you true joy of my heart!' (*Ex*, 169) Here was a woman who had lived the monastic life to the full. Gertrude viewed the moment of death as the most life-filled moment, because it brought to her the gift of eternal life.

EPILOGUE

Concluding this article on the joyous feast of Our Lady's birthday (8 September), I think back three weeks to the Feast of Our Lady's 'death'—her Assumption (15 August) and I think of the Dormition icon which symbolizes this event.[62] On the back of it is written the explanation: 'We behold in this icon the "Mother of Life" being transferred to life by her Son, Our Lord Jesus Christ. . . . This feast celebrates the Mother of God as the Mother of life. . . . Her death and burial show us the completion of God's plan for all mankind.'[63] This same rhythm of life and death runs through the whole doctrine of Gertrude, the monastic woman: life lived to the fullest, with purpose and meaning, leads to life eternal in Christ. In the context of her monastic life, Gertrude was a fulfilled woman; a lover and a life-giver, poor and free; like Christ, whose likeness she bore, she yearned for truth and salvation, life for every person. For her, death was but a totally new and free life. 'Life has not ended but only changed',[64] when we come to meet the life and light of his face. As she expresses it so beautifully in her fifth exercise:

> Come, show me your face and make me contemplate your loveliness. Yes, your face is winning and beautiful, radiant with the fairest dawn of the Godhead. In the color of your cheeks is written in red the wondrous name Alpha and Omega. In your eyes burns the deathless glory of eternity; their light is unto me the lamp of the salvation of God. In you the beauty of charity does enhance the splendor of truth. The fragrance of life breathes forth unto me from you' (*Ex*, 86–87)[65].

NOTES

1. All quotations from the writings of St Gertrude will be briefly indicated within the paper directly following the quotation. Quotations from the *Herald* are noted with Book number and then chapter number—hence (2.1) means book two, chapter one. Quotations from the *Exercises* are cited by *Ex* and then page number, from *The Exercises of Saint Gertrude*, translated by a Benedictine Nun of Regina Laudis [Columba Hart, OSB] (Westminster, Md: The Newman Press, 1956). These quotations have been slightly modified in that 'thy' and 'thee' have been changed to 'your' and 'you'. *Herald* quotations from Books One and Two (the books most referred to in this paper) come from an as yet unpublished translation: *The Emissary of God's Loving-Kindness*, translated by Alexandra Barratt (University of Waikato, Hamilton, New Zealand) for Cistercian Publications. The few references to Books Three, Four, and Five of the *Herald* come from *The Life and Revelations of Saint Gertrude*, translated by M. Francis Clare, PC (second edition, Dublin, 1876; rpt. Westminster, Maryland: Newman, 1952).

2. Benedictine Nun of Regina Laudis, Introduction to the *Exercises*, p. xv, quoting P. Doyère, '*Le Memorial Spirituel de Sainte Gertrude*', (Paris, 1954) 6.

3. See Cyprian Vagaggini, OSB, *Theological Dimensions of the Liturgy*, trans. by Leonard J. Doyle and W. A. Jurgens (Collegeville, Minn., The Liturgical Press, 1976) 740.

4. Mary Jeremy [Finnegan], *Scholars and Mystics* (Chicago: Henry Regnery, 1962) 4.

5. Alexandra Barrett, introduction to *The Emissary of God's Loving Kindness*, manuscript, 4.

6. Mary Jeremy [Finnegan], EP 'Similitudes in the Writing of St. Gertrude of Helfta', *Mediaeval Studies*, 19, (1957) 50.

7. Jean Leclercq, OSB, 'Liturgy and Mental Prayer in the Life of St. Gertrude', *Sponsa Regis*, 31 (1960) 1.

8. M. Jeremy, introduction to *Exercises*, xvi.

9. Gertrude's sense of grace, which she understood as God's spiritual gifts, favours, or blessings, was very acute and is constantly expressed in her writings. See *Exercises* p. 116: 'Let . . . my heart sing jubilantly unto you, and your gifts of so many graces chant your praises'. or in Book Two of the *Herald*: ' . . . you graced me a gift more welcome than, . . . the one I have already described' (2.16).

10. In my references to men and women or masculine and femine traits I do not wish to infer stereotyping! I am following the approach of Mary F. Rousseau in her article: 'The Ordination of Women: A Philosopher's Viewpoint', *The Way*, 21/3 (July, 1981) 217–20. Dr Rousseau says: 'Everyone's person is his or her sexualilty, through and through. Sexuality has meaning for every aspect of each person's life. It pervades one's very existence.' Men and women are different . . . in the very essentials of our humanity'. Men and women can be gentle and loving or bold and assertive but in their living experience of these so called 'traditional' masculine or feminine traits each person will be gentle or bold in a different way. A man's gentleness in expression will be different from a woman's gentleness. Our modern society is in transition to a new vision of masculinity and femininity from role-programming and stereotyping to a fuller understanding of the masculine and feminine in each person. While this is a healthy growth we must be careful to avoid the other extreme of 'unisex'—men and women so artificially the same or equal that they no longer complement each other, grace each other with the uniqueness of their feminine and masculine experience and personhood. See page 217.

11. Dietrich Von Hildebrand, *Man and Woman* (Chicago: Henry Regnery, 1965) 13, 63–64.

12. George H. Tavard, *Woman in Christian Tradition* (Notre Dame University Press, 1973) 210.

13. Ann Wilson Schaef, *Women's Reality* (Winston Press, 1981) 118–20.

14. The actual text here says: you 'refreshed my soul with these words'. Here and in other places when I say 'the Lord says to her', rather than include long quotations I am referring to a sense she had that God was guiding her and speaking to her (the Holy Spirit using her own thoughts and inspirations). Other expressions of this are: 'The Lord guided my understanding. . . . The Lord threw in my way the verse I had read. . .' (2.10)

15. William Johnston, SJ, *Inner Eye of Love* (New York-San Francisco: Harper and Row, 1978) 51.

16. *Ibid.*, 20.

17. *Ibid.*, 21.

18. *Ibid.*, 62.

19. *Ibid.*, 31. See also Garrigou-Lagrange, *The Three Ages of the Interior Life*, 2 (St. Louis: Herder, 1948); John Arintero, OP, *The Mystical Evolution in the Development and Vitality of the Church*, 1 (Herder, 1950) 16–41; Louis Bouyer, *Introduction to Spirituality* (Desclée, *1961)* 287–306, esp. 303; *Catholicisme*, 2: 1085; Ursula King, *Towards A New Mysticism* (New York: Seabury, 1980) 208–18.

20. Cyprian Vagaggini, OSB, *Theological Dimensions of the Liturgy*, 748–49, 743. Father Cyprian explains and clarifies the meaning of nuptial mysticism imagery and deals with the difficulties it might cause modern readers.

21. Alexandra Barrett, introduction to *Emissary*, manuscript, pp. 17–18.

22. *Ibid.*, 20–21.

23. Sr. Jeremy [Finnegan], OP, *Scholars and Mystics*, 170.

24. Thomas X. Davis, ocso, 'Loss of Self in the Degrees of Humility in the Rule of St. Benedict, Chapter VII', in E. Rozanne Elder, ed., *Benedictus, Studies in Honor of St. Benedict of Nursia*, CS67 (Kalamazoo: Cistercian Publications, 1981) 23.

25. See above note 14.

26. John de la Croix Bouton, ocso, *History of the Cistercian Order* Fiche, #2. (privately translated and xeroxed).

27. George A. Maloney, SJ, *Following Jesus in the Real World: Asceticism Today* (Albany, N.Y.: Clarity, 1979) 8.

28. From the conclusions, *The Cistercian Spirit*, CS3 (1970) 270.

29. Chrysogonus Waddell, ocso, 'Notes on the Liturgical and Patristic Resonances of Two Fragments from the *Exordium Parvum*' *Liturgy* ocso 15/2 (1981) 61–107: 'The bulk of the *Exordium Parvum* dates from a period early in the abbacy of St. Stephen Harding, before the era of foundations and expansions; St. Stephen is both author and compiler.'

30. Bouton, *Fiche* #16, 1–2.

31. Bouton, *Fiche* #1, p. 1; *Fiche* #16, p. 1. Here, I in no way wish to infer that the benedictine tradition of seventh to ninth centuries was 'inferior' monasticism but only to clarify two validly different interpretations of the Rule, both leading to lives of constant prayer and fervent love of God and neighbor.

32. Placide Deseilles, ocso, 'Principles of Monastic Spirituality'. Proposed outline for new Spiritual Directory (Privately printed) p. 9.

33. The Cistercian General Chapter of 1228, overwhelmed with requests for affiliation with the Order and unable to cope with the influx, refused all future requests. Helfta was among the many convents seeking a cistercian life but not incorporated officially. See: Sr Jeremy, *Scholars and Mystics*, 9–10; Nun of Regina Laudis, introduction to The *Exercises*, p. xv; Thomas Merton, 'Modern Biographical Sketches of Cistercian Blessed and Saints' (manuscript) p. 287.

34. 'Formalism' meaning a freedom to depart from strict exterior forms i.e. going to Communion without prescribed preparation in this specific case, from Barrett, Introduction to *Emissary*, manuscript, p. 10.

35. Vagaggini, *Theological Dimensions* (n. 20 above) *passim*.

36. *Exercises* 6, 7, 12, 14, 17–18, 21, 33, 40, 86, 92, 93, 97, 100, 103–4, 104, 111, 116, 127–8, 128–9, 138, 149, 150, 152, 154, 155, 157, 161, 162, 165, 168. *Herald* II, 1, 3, 4, 5[2], 11, 16, 18, 20, 23.

37. Vagaggini, p. 758–759.

38. *Ibid.* See Chapter 22 and 23 for his thorough treatment of the union of liturgical and mystical prayer in Gertrude.

39. *Ibid.*, 749.

40. Leclercq, 'Liturgy and Mental Prayer . . .' (see 7 above) pp. 3 and 5.

41. Jacquelyn Mattfield, 'Introduction to "Contemplation and Feminism" Program held at Barnard College, December 1978', from *Anima*, 6/2 (1980) 124.

42. Sr Vilma Seelaus OCD, 'Contemplative Spirituality and Feminine Identity', *Anima* 6/2 (1980) 129.

43. Whittiker Chambers, *Witness* (Gateway, 1952) 11–12.

44. Thomas Merton, *Life and God's Love*, Taped Conference #6.

45. Nun of Regina Laudis, Commentary on *Exercises*, p. 3.

46. Edward Stevens, *Oriental Mysticism* (Paulist, 1973) 8.

47. *Exercises*, 19, 61, 76, 77, 142, 7, 9, 10; 10, 120, 139; 38, 89, 103; 76, 115, 125, 132, 129; 112; 110, 119, 134, 135, 140.

48. J.M. Somerville, 'Life Philosophies', *New Catholic Encyclopedia*, 8, (1966) 746, describing Ludwig Klages' philosophy.

49. The following section is adapted from an unpublished paper: 'The Meaning of Death in the Rule of St Benedict and the Thought of St Gertrude' given by Sr Thomas Shank, OCSO, Sr Regina Keating OCSO Sr Joanna Dailey OCSO, at the St Benedict-St Scholastica symposium held at St Benedict's Center, Madison, Wisconsin, October 1980.

50. New York:Paulist Press, 1978.

51. Nun of Regina Laudis introduction to *Exercises*, p. xii.

52. *Exercises* p. 8, 9, 10, 12, 13, 14, 21, 38, 40^3, 58, 66, 69, 73, 74–75, 77, 87, 90^3, 92, 93^2, 93–94, 97–98, 101, 102, 103, 104, 115, 116, 123, 135, 132–133, 134, 135^2, 136^2, 137^3, 138, 139, 140, 140–141, 141–142, 148, 149, 151^2, 153^2, 155, 156, 158, 159, 161^2, 162, 166^2, 169, 170^2, 172, 173. Elevated numbers indicate number of times death is mentioned in different images or contexts on one page.

53. *Ibid.* p. 19, 20, 22, 41, 59, 64, 66, 67, 71–72, 73, 74, 78, 85, 88, 90^2, 91, 92, 94, 97, 98, 99^2, 103^2, 104, 112, 126, 129, 134, 141, 150, 155, 161, 162, 173.

54. Archbishop Antony Bloom, *God and Man* (New York: Paulist, 1971) 73.

55. A Nun of Regina Laudis, commentary on *Exercises*, 3.

56. J.G. Arintero OP, *Mystical Evolution*, Vol 2 (St Louis; Herder, 1951) 288.

57. Kieran Kavanaugh OCD, 'Introduction' to the *Living Flame of Love*, The Collected Works of St. John of the Cross, (Washington, D.C. ICS Publications, 1973) 570.

58. Gen 32:30. This image enjoyed a long scriptural, patristic and monastic tradition, being used for immediate presence before God, especially after physical death. See below, n. 65.

59. Commentary to the seventh exercise. *Exercises*, p. 145.

60. For a résumé of St Gertrude's Trinitarian spirituality see: P. Doyère OSB, 'St. Gertrude, Mystic and Nun', in *Worship* 34/9 (October 1960) 540–541.

61. Cf. Prologue, *Rule of Benedict.*

62. This icon, 'The Dormition of the Mother of God', is included in the icon series collection of Ger. S. Manetas and Sons (Athens, Greece), #39.

63. This reproduction and prayer are issued by The Byzantine Catholic Archdiocese of Munhall, 3605 Perrysville Avenue, Pittsburgh, Pa. 15214.

64. Preface for Christian Death I, *Roman Missal: The Sacramentary* (Collegeville: The Liturgical Press, 1974) 493.

65. St Gertrude's many references to meeting God 'face to face' were certainly influenced by the experience she relates in the *Herald* Book II, chapter 2 (in some translations chapter 22).

Foundations of Christian Formation in the *Dialogue* of St Catherine of Siena

Susan A. Muto

CATHERINE BENINCASA, the twenty-third child of a prosperous dyer, was born in Siena on 25 March 1347. The patron saint of Italy, she is regarded as the greatest of the fourteenth-century mystics.

At the age of six, Catherine had a religious experience that changed the whole direction of her life. Until 1367, she lived as a contemplative in her own home. During that period, she also became a member of the *Mantellate*, a group of laywomen affiliated with the Dominican Order.

Then slowly, at the Lord's command, Catherine left her solitude, reaching out to help the needy of Siena—the prisoners, the sick, and the poor. By 1370, her world had expanded to include people from all walks of life. She became known as a peacemaker, a healer and, above all, a prophet.

In the short span of ten years, with the help of secretaries, Catherine sent out over four hundred letters, many of them to leaders of both Church and State. These letters and the spiritual treatise known as *The Dialogue* are her legacy to the Church.

During the last five years of her life, Catherine came into close contact with Pope Gregory XI, whom she persuaded to return from Avignon to Rome, and with his successor, Urban VI. More than once, she served as the papal emissary to the city-states in revolt. At the beginning of the Great Schism in 1378, Urban VI called her to Rome, but all Catherine's efforts to prevent the spread of the schism were in vain.

Worn out by her attempts to restore unity and peace, Catherine died in Rome on 29 April, 1380 and her body was laid in the Church of the Minerva where it remains today.

A complete edition of Catherine's works, together with her biography by her confessor, Raymond of Capua, was published in Siena, 1707–1721. Her feast day is April 30.

To seek a clearer comprehension of the foundations of our faith, we do well to use the guidance offered by exemplars in the christian-formation tradition. Among women, we would without hesitation name Catherine of Siena. Her life, her leadership capacity, her influence on the Church, her gift for spiritual communication—all are widely known and revered.[1] Here we wish to concentrate on a perhaps less familiar source, but one which is rich in spiritual insights: *The Dialogue*. What are the foundations of christian formation revealed by and to Catherine in *The Dialogue*? To grasp these is to catch glimpses of truths of timeless value, which deepen our faith and strengthen our commitment to Christ.

At the base of Catherine's teaching is her insight into the central dogma of Christianity, the union of divinity and humanity in Jesus Christ. She met Christ with a rare intimacy during the years she spent at home in seclusion. At the end of this preparatory period, she received a command from him to come out of solitude and practise the second part of the Great Commandment: to love others as God has loved her because, as the Lord tells Catherine:

> . . . it is your duty to love your neighbor as your own self. In love you ought to help them spiritually with prayer and counsel, and assist them spiritually and materially in their need—at least with your good will if you have nothing else. If you do not love me, you do not love your neighbors, nor will you help those you do not love. But it is yourself you harm most, because you deprive yourself of grace. And you harm your neighbors by depriving them of the prayer and loving desires you should be offering to me on their behalf. Every help you give them ought to come from the affection you bear them for love of me.[2]

INTEGRATING LOVE OF GOD AND CARE FOR OTHERS

In Catherine's life and in her writings, we thus witness as a first foundation of spiritual formation the integration of solitude and communion, or, to phrase it differently, of recollection and participation, of contemplation and action—in short, of inner and outer formation.[3]

Once Catherine discovered who she was, she was able to show others the divine compassion that had been shown to her. The Lord assured her that 'to attain charity you must dwell constantly in the cell of self-knowledge. For in knowing yourself you will come to know my mercy in the blood of my only-begotten Son, thus drawing my divine charity to yourself with your love'.[4] The saint could not contain this love within her heart but had to share it with her friends and disciples, with the people of Siena and with the whole Church. At the center of her vision, she proclaimed the mystery of God Incarnate. Her writings for the most part are extended meditations on Christ crucified, a reflection of her christocentric spirituality.

CENTERING ONE'S LIFE IN THE LORD

A second foundation of christian formation, lived intensely by Catherine, is that of centering our lives on Christ, the Way, who shed his blood to redeem a people deadened by sin; on Christ, the Truth, in whose presence we see God as Father; on Christ, the Life, whose Spirit renews the Body, his Church, and wills the well-being of each member.

Because of Jesus, the Bridge, the Mediator between us and God, we can cross over the chasm of sin, or 'selfish sensuality', and return to the Father. The Lord conveyed this mystery to Catherine in these words:

> So first I made a bridge of my Son as he lived in your company. And though this living bridge has been taken from your sight, there remains the bridgeway of his teaching, which, as I told you, is held together by my power and my Son's wisdom and the mercy of the Holy Spirit. My power gives the virtue of courage to those who follow this way. Wisdom gives light to know the truth along the way. And the Holy Spirit gives them a love that uproots all sensual love from the soul and leaves only virtuous love. So now as much as before, through his teaching as much as when he was among you, he is the way and truth and life—the way that is the bridge leading to the very height of heaven.[5]

THE WAY OF RETURN

In the writings of St Catherine, the way of return implies three steps comparable to the traditional path of purgation, illumination, and union. Catherine symbolized these steps in *The Dialogue* by using the imagery of Christ's wounded feet, implying that too often the motivation for our obedience is fear of punishment—a motivation Catherine considered imperfect and mercenary.

The second step, symbolized by Christ's wounded heart or open side, finds us following him not out of fear, but out of love, but a love that is still mingled with selfishness because we lack sufficient understanding of what has been done for us. Still, we are progressing along the way, no longer fearful slaves but faithful servants.

If the first step sparks our desire for God and the second step enlightens our mind, then the third step leads to a profound transformation of heart, imaged by Catherine as the mouth of Christ. He himself claims the soul with a mystical kiss and instills as a permanent disposition of heart the grace of filial love. One is now truly a child of God, enjoying his peace.[6]

Catherine adds to this threefold path a fourth stage, symbolized by the fire of charity toward one's neighbor, thus establishing as a foundation of christian spirituality the obligation not only to hear the word of God in one's heart, but also to proclaim it to the world.[7] The culmination of this journey from love to Love will be presence to the Father in an eternal beatific vision.[8]

An excellent summary of the three ways can be found in one of Catherine's letters to the abbess and nuns of the augustinian monastery of S. Gaggio near Florence. She writes:

> . . . to enable the soul to attain this perfection, Christ has made his body into a staircase, with great steps. See, his feet are nailed fast to the cross; they constitute the first step because, to begin with, the soul's desire has to be stripped of self-will, for as the feet carry the body, so desire carries the soul. Reflect that no soul will ever acquire virtue without climbing this first step. Once you have done that, you come to real, deep humility. Climb the next step without delay and you reach the open side of God's Son. Within, you will find the fathomless furnace of divine Charity. Yes, on this second step of the open side, there is a little shop, full of fragrant spices. Therein you will find the God-Man; therein, too, the soul becomes so satiated and inebriated as to become oblivious of self for, like a man intoxicated with wine, it will have eyes only for the Blood spilt with such burning love. With eager longing it presses on upwards and reaches the last step, the mouth, where it reposes in peace and quiet, savouring the peace of obedience. Like a man who falls asleep after drinking heavily and so is oblivious of both pain and pleasure, the bride of Christ, brimming over with love, sleeps in the peace of her Bridegroom. Her own feelings are so deeply asleep that she remains unruffled when assailed by tribulation and rises above undue delight in worldly prosperity; for she stripped herself of all desire of that kind back on the first step. Here [on the third] she is conformed to Christ crucified and made one with him.[9]

THE SOUL'S GUIDES

Complementing this description of Christ, the Bridge, is Catherine's teaching on the three powers of the soul. She identifies these as our guides across this Bridge and the means by which we avoid falling into the abyss of selfish sensuality or self-willed love. These gifts of memory, intellect, and will are a dowry given us by Christ.[10]

The formative function of memory is not to catalogue faults and failings but to remember God's faithfulness to us, his giving and forgiving love. Deformed memory wallows in its own misery and forgets that creation abounds with his mercy. Christ intends that we use our intellect to perceive and live in the truth. For Catherine, truth is to know oneself as wholly dependent on God and thus to attain deep humility. This disposition is essential for transformation of heart, when God himself draws us into the 'fathomless furnace of divine Charity'.

As self-love or self-willed love is the source of all deformation, so love of God, willing the good, is the source of all formation. Deformed will attaches its affections in an inordinate way to that which is infinitely less than God, thus leading to sins of avarice, gluttony, and lust. Catherine summarized her teachings on the powers of the soul in a letter to the abbot of San Pietro:

> When the understanding has received the light from the fire . . . it is transformed into it so that the two become one: thus, the memory becomes one with Christ crucified, retaining nothing, delighting in nothing, thinking of nothing but the Beloved, for the memory is flooded in an instant with the ineffable love it sees poured out on itself and on all mankind, and the person becomes so great a lover of both God and his neighbor that he would give his life for him a hundred thousand times over . . . The three powers of the soul are at one in this fire: the memory treasuring all God's benefits; the understanding knowing his goodness and his will . . . and the will so expanding with love that it cannot love or even desire anything apart from god. All the soul's movements are centred on God, and it has eyes only for him; its one concern is to do what is most pleasing to its Creator. . . .[11]

THE LIGHT OF TRUTH

Catherine's love of truth led her to passionate affection for Christ crucified as well as to a longing for ever more knowledge of herself and God. In her spirituality there is thus an intermingling of affection and cognition, of love and light.[12] She insisted again and again that nothing is as important for formation as growth in self-knowledge. Such knowledge leads not to isolated egoism but to the light of Christ, who is the deepest form of our being.

Catherine called Christ the Light of truth and explained that his disciples shared in three degrees of this light: ordinary, more perfect, and glorious. The first or ordinary light refers to those who walk in the light of reason, drawn from Jesus, the true Light, through the eye of understanding. Such persons have as well the light of faith, possessed as a gift from baptism unless it is put out by sin. The Lord explained to Catherine:

> In baptism, through the power of my only-begotten Son's blood, you received the form of faith. If you exercise this faith by virtue with the light of reason, reason will in turn be enlightened by faith, and such faith will give you life and lead you in the way of truth. With this light you will reach me, the true light; without it you would come to darkness.[13]

This first light bears fruit in those whose charity is ordinary, but to it Christ would add two other lights, bestowed on those who are seeking a fuller christian life, a life of mystic union. The 'more perfect' light enables one to sense the transitory nature of things in this world. This sense in turn stimulates our desire for God. More perfect light is comparable to spiritual discretion or prudence, gained by persons who live a disciplined life, engaging in mortification not for its own sake but for the sake of mastering their willful selfishness.

Glorious light is that wisdom achieved by those able to recognize the will of God in all the events of their lives. Hence no matter what God sends them they hold it in due reverence. Such a person enjoys the graces of union and lives in intimacy with the Word, accepting suffering in a spirit of Christ-like surrender until this burden is lifted and one enters the 'sea of peace'.

> When the soul. . . has come to taste this light after so delightfully seeing and knowing it, she runs to the table of holy desire, in love as she is and eager with a lover's restlessness. She has no eyes for herself, for seeking her own spiritual or material comfort. Rather, as one who has completely drowned her own will in this light and knowledge, she shuns no burden, from whatever source it may come. She even endures the pain of shame and vexations from the devil and other people's grumbling, feasting at the table of the most holy cross on honor for me, God eternal, and salvation for others.[14]

THE MASTER-DISCIPLE RELATIONSHIP

Catherine went on to apply these lights to the direction between a master of formation and a disciple. From the side of the disciple or directee, the main disposition to cultivate is purity of heart. Three principal things must be done to reach this goal.[15] We must be united with God in loving affection, bearing in our memory the blessings we have received from him. With the eye of our understanding, we must see his affectionate charity, how deeply he loves us and draws us to union. Then, if we consider his will first, we can quell our own evil intentions and approach self and others in charitable service.

From the side of the master or director, perception of the light of Christ's truth calls for a non-judgmental approach. Catherine is adamant on this matter. She says that we must never pass judgment in human terms on anything we see. In our relations with others we must refrain from judging, for no one can see the hidden heart but God. Our stance is to be one of holy compassion. Why is this the case? Because, as the Lord tells Catherine,

> You would think you were judging rightly when in fact you were judging wrongly by following what you saw, for often the devil would make you see too much of the truth in order to lead you into falsehood. He would do this to make you set yourself up as judge of other people's spirits and intentions, something of which, as I told you, I alone am judge.[16]

Astute directress of souls that she was, Catherine explained how judgment should be qualified. We are not to confront others with specific sins but to correct their bad habits in a general way, for instance, by lovingly complementing vices beheld in others by virtues in ourselves. The general rule is gentleness, though she did say that there are times when we must add severity to kindness. Mainly, we are to put the vices of others on our own back and strive gently to understand them. If possible, we must not focus on these vices but hold fast to the sight and knowledge of ourselves and of God's generosity. In short, 'compassion is what you must have, you and the others, and leave the judging to me'.[17]

LIGHT AND DARKNESS

Another important area of Catherine's formative teaching consists of her analysis of experiences of Great Light or Great Darkness, in other words, her teaching on visions and other consolations. We wonder with her, when are they delusionary? The Lord answered Catherine: '. . . when my servants love me imperfectly, they love this consolation more than they love me'.[18] Catherine herself distrusted such phenomena, because the general inclination is to pay more attention to the gift than to the Giver. People become so desirous of spiritual consolations that they do not see, or they refuse to help a neighbor in need. The delusion consists of this:

> Under pretense of virtue they say, 'It would make me lose my spiritual peace and quiet, and I would not be able to say my Hours at the proper time'. Then if they do not enjoy consolation they think they have offend-

> ed me. But they are deceived by their own spiritual pleasure, and they offend me more by not coming to the help of their neighbors' need than if they had abandoned all their consolations. For I have ordained every exercise of vocal and mental prayer to bring souls to perfect love for me and their neighbors, and to keep them in this love.[19]

To test the faith of a person, Catherine explained, God may withdraw his consolations for a time. His intention is to bring the soul to greater perfection, for he withdraws in order to humble us and to help us identify with Christ crucified that we may know the depth of his love. Without this time of testing, in which one lives on faith because the felt sense of God is absent, one might play into the hands of the devil, who spots gluttonous desires for consolation and feeds them with false visions. For, the Lord assured Catherine, the devil can present himself to the mind under the appearance of light:

> He does this in different ways: now as an angel, now under the guise of my Truth, now as one or the other of my saints. And this he does to catch the soul with the hook of that very spiritual pleasure she has sought in visions and spiritual delight. And unless she rouses herself with true humility, scorning all pleasure, she will be caught on this hook in the devil's hands. But let her humbly disdain pleasure and cling to love not for the gift but for me, the giver. For the Devil for all his pride cannot tolerate a humble spirit.[20]

How can we tell if a visitation is of God or of the devil? The sign is this:

> If it is the devil who has come to visit the mind under the guise of light, the soul experiences gladness at his coming. But the longer he stays, the more gladness gives way to weariness and darkness and pricking as the mind becomes clouded over by his presence within. But when the soul is truly visited by me, eternal Truth, she experiences holy fear at the first encounter. And with this fear comes gladness and security, along with a gentle prudence that does not doubt even while it doubts, but through self-knowledge considers itself unworthy.[21]

Thus God's visitation brings fear at the beginning, but this gives way to gladness and a hunger for virtue that remains in the soul after the visitation—especially hunger for the virtues of humility and charity, the main foundations of Catherine's faith. We must not trust consolation itself but test its fruits.

WOMAN OF PRAYER

All of these foundational teachings and their fruits are traceable to Catherine as a woman of prayer. *The Dialogue* itself is a lengthly prayer for self-understanding, for the Church, for the whole world, for God's providential care. Time and again she returned to the absolute necessity of building in one's soul an interior cell into which one can return to be alone with God and attend to his Word and will before venturing out into the world. One seeks in prayer the inspiration that will make one's actions effective and one's witness edifying.

Prayer is not an egocentric contemplation of self leading to complacency, but a clinging to God that strengthens us to serve our neighbor in charity. In prayer we behold the wretchedness of human imperfection, but this only increases our hope of obtaining God's mercy—a gift Catherine never doubted. She believed that continual prayer is nothing else than a ceaseless holy desire for God and a sharing in Christ's hunger and thirst for souls.

Against this background of holy desire, we can understand her dismay at those whose behavior marred the mystic body of the Church.[22] No prayer could be more fervent than hers for its reform and renewal on the eve of the great Western Schism. She pictured the Church as a bride ever cleansed and nourished by sacrificial blood flowing from the heart of Christ's love. God confirmed her intuition that nothing is more necessary for the revitalization of the Church than good ministers of its sacraments who can instruct the faithful in its foundational truths. By the same token, nothing is more detrimental to reform than unfaithful ministers who flow with the pulsations of the times and forget the necessity of ongoing personal and communal formation.

Catherine minced no words in her denunciation of the clergy of her time whose neglect of ministry had led many into disillusionment and deception. She was consoled by God that their sins do not render the sacraments less valid, but she knew that their actions nevertheless hindered the formation of the faithful. Thus Catherine beseeched Christ to reform the guardians of his truth. She recalls their high dignity and the obligation God had placed upon them to guide his people, in imitation of Christ, the good shepherd.

The root of deformation was again identified as selfish self-centeredness, which had bred pride, indiscretion, and the passion for worldly power. Such confused ministers provided for their own needs first and neglected the poor, scandalized the laity by parading with their mistresses and children, shunned just admonitions from superiors, jeered at those who obeyed the Rule, and in place of fraternal love chose gluttony and lust.

In the face of such dissonance with divine directives, Catherine asked the Lord if anything could be done. Here is his answer:

> My daughter, let your respite be in glorifying and praising my name, in offering me the incense of constant prayer for these poor wretches who have sunk so low and made themselves deserving of divine judgment for their sins. And let your place of refuge be my only-begotten Son, Christ crucified. Make your home and hiding place in the cavern of his open side. There, in his humanity, you will enjoy my divinity with loving affection. In that open heart you will find charity for me and for your neighbors . . . Once you see and taste this love you will follow his teaching and find your nourishment at the table of the cross. In other words, charity will make you put up with your neighbors with true patience by enduring pain, torment and weariness no matter what their source. In this way you will flee and escape the leprosy.[23]

The Lord offered Catherine no easy solution to Church reform, saying, in effect, return to the foundation of faith and root your life in constant prayer. Through such faithful souls as Catherine, God will accomplish in due time the renewal of his Church. As protection against the vices of impurity, avarice, and pride, he will grant to his friends purity of heart, generosity, and humility, provided they remember the rule of constant prayer, for this remembrance opens up the channels of God's mercy.

> Now, dearest daughter, I invite you and all my other servants to weep over these dead. Be as little sheep in the garden of holy Church, grazing there in holy longing and constant prayer. Offer these to me on their behalf so that I may be merciful to the world. Do not let either assault or prosperity cause you to abandon this grazing. I mean, I do not want you to raise your heads either in impatience or in inordinate gladness. Rather, be humbly attentive to my honor, the salvation of souls, and the reform of holy Church.[24]

Catherine responded to this invitation with an ecstatic prayer, reminding God as well of his love and mercy for creatures made in his image and likeness. Everywhere she turned she found only his providential concern. Thus she prayed:

> To you, eternal Father everything is possible. Though you created us without our help, it is not your will to save us without your help . . . I ask this of your infinite mercy. You created us out of nothing. So, now, that we exist, be merciful and remake the vessels you created and formed in your image and likeness; re-form them to grace in the mercy and blood of your Son.[25]

THE INNER AND OUTER LIFE IN HARMONY

Formation, reformation, transformation—these are the dynamics underlying the dialogue between Catherine and her God. She saw the whole of life, every person, event, and thing, encompassed by his providential care from the beginning to the end of time.[26] He does all that he can to make possible our joy of being with him eternally, sending us his Son and our Saviour; giving us the Eucharist as the sacrament of tender care; presenting us with Mary as the sign of his redeeming love. Trust in providence is the final, all-encompassing foundation of Catherine's faith and ours.

God cares lovingly for the whole world and for each person, whom he knows by name. In light of his forming love, a mystery never to be fathomed by us, Catherine saw the meaning behind many formative and deformative experiences. For instance, trials and consolations are given for love and to provide for our salvation. Thus we need to hold everything in reverence and be patient. Selfish sensuality blinds one to the hidden judgments of God, preventing us from opening our mind's eye to his mysteries. So much is made clear in this final section of *The Dialogue*, for the Lord assured Catherine that no matter where his faithful ones turn, they will find nothing but his deep burning charity, nothing but the greatest, gentlest, truest, most perfect providence. Such is the width and breadth of his forming mystery.

In his providence God treats each person uniquely, responding to different needs and desires. He wakes up worldly souls with a 'pricking of conscience' or by the weariness they feel in their hearts. He rewards the virtuous by making them fall more deeply in love with his mystery. He encourages those on the way to bring their disordered memory, understanding, and will into consonance with his revelation, orchestrating their spiritual unfolding as a conductor draws forth all the beauty of a symphony. The farther one progresses, the more one learns to walk perfectly along the way of Christ's gentle but firm teaching. All of this leads to harmony between the inner and outer life, between praising God's name and serving one's neighbor. Each of us needs one another and all of us need God.

> Thus you see the artisan turn to the worker and the worker to the artisan: Each has need of the other because neither knows how to do what the other does. So also the cleric and religious have need of the layperson, and the layperson of the religious; neither can get along without the other. And so with everything else.
>
> Could I not have given everyone everything? Of course. But in my providence I wanted to make each of you dependent on the others, so that you would be forced to exercise charity in action and will at once.[27]

CONCLUSION

On the basis of these revelations, Catherine concluded that we must turn from selfish concern to care for others. All of us are sent by God into the vineyard of life to work at ongoing formation. This work continues from birth until death and thereafter in the life of purgatory. If we trust in God, he will not fail to hear our prayers, as he heard those of Catherine. She asked for four things, four essentials of christian formation, and each petition was answered in full by God. For he explained to her how to attain knowledge of the truth through knowledge of herself and him in the light of faith. He heard her plea for mercy for the world and explained how this mercy was granted to her and the whole Church through the entrance into history of Christ, the Mediator. He showed how this Bridge is mounted by the soul's three powers and how he does everything to facilitate our journey from pride to humility, from death to new life. Lastly, he revealed to her the glory of his providence, the inclusivity of his love and care for all of creation. He asked Catherine to pray always and to show mercy to others.

No more fitting conclusion could be found for these reflections on foundational christian formation than Catherine's prayer to the Holy Trinity for the grace of final consummation:

> O eternal Trinity, fire and abyss of charity, dissolve this very day the cloud of my body! I am driven to desire, in the knowledge of yourself that you have given me in your truth, to leave behind the weight of this body of mine and give my life for the glory and praise of your name. For by the light of understanding within your light I have tasted and seen your depth, eternal Trinity, and the beauty of your creation. Then, when I considered myself in you, I saw that I am your image. You have gifted me with power from yourself, eternal Father, and my understanding with your wisdom—such wisdom as is proper to your only-begotten Son; and the Holy Spirit, who proceeds from you and from your Son, has given me a will and so I am able to love.
>
> You, eternal Trinity, are the craftsman; and I your handiwork have come to know that you are in love with the beauty of what you have made, since you made of me a new creation in the blood of your Son.
>
> O abyss! O eternal Godhead! O deep sea! What more could you have given me than the gift of your very self?[28]

NOTES

1. Among more recently published materials, see Alice Curtayne, *Saint Catherine of Siena* (Rockford, Illinois: Tan Books, 1980); Raymond of Capuda, *The Life of Catherine of Siena*, trans. Conleth Kearns (Wilmington, Delaware; Michael Glazier,

1980); Igino Giordani, *Saint Catherine of Siena —Doctor of the Church*, trans. Thomas J. Tobin (Boston: Daughters of St Paul, 1975); Benedict Ashley, 'Guide to Saint Catherine's Dialogue', *Cross and Crown* 29/3 September 1977) 237–49; and *Spirituality Today* 32/1 March 1980).

2. Catherine of Siena, *The Dialogue*, trans. Suzanne Noffke (New York: Paulist Press, 1980) 33–34. All further references to the text of *The Dialogue* (hereafter abbreviated *D*) are taken from this edition.

3. Adrian van Kaam points to the same inextricable unity between what he calls 'intra' (unique) and 'extra' (communal) formation. He describes the ultimate aim of christian formation, therefore, as the 'realization of the fully consonant Christ form in one's life which opens the life of the Christian uniquely and communally to the fullness of divine peace and joy through participation in the eternal Trinitarian formation mystery'. *Studies in Formative Spirituality* 1/3 (November 1980) 462. I am indebted to him for certain insights into the problems of spiritual formation pertinent to this paper. Readers interested in a contemporary treatment of formation as an art and science may consult his glossary of terminology in the to-date issues of *Studies in Formative Spirituality*, published tri-yearly by the Institute of Formative Spirituality, Duquesne University, Pittsburgh, Pennsylvania, 15282.

4. *D*, p. 118.

5. *D*, p. 70.

6. See *D*, pp. 64–65; 111–16; 118–20; and 145.

7. See *D*, pp. 136–37.

8. See *D*, p. 152.

9. *I, Catherine: Selected Writings of St. Catherine of Siena* Letter 18 of March 1376, Trans. Kenelm Foster & Mary John Ronayne (London: Collins, 1980) 105–106.

10. See *D*, pp. 103–5; 108; and 148.

11. Letter 13 of May 1375, *I, Catherine*, pp. 85–86.

12. See *D*, pp. 161–83 for a treatment in her doctrine of tears of the affective side of transcendence; her doctrine of truth, pertaining to the cognitive side, begins on p. 184ff.

13. *D*, p. 185.

14. *D*, pp. 188–89.

15. See *D*, pp. 191–92

16. *D*, p. 193.

17. *D*, p. 197.

18. *D*, pp. 127–28.

19. *D*, pp. 130–31.

20. *D*, p. 133.

21. *D*, p. 133.

22. See *D*, pp. 205–276.

23. *D*, pp. 238–39.

24. *D*, p. 272.

25. *D*, p. 276.

26. See *D*, pp. 277–326.

27. *D*, pp. 311–12.

28. *D*, p. 365.

Julian of Norwich

Julian of Norwich, one of England's greatest woman mystics, was just thirty and a half years old when she received her first *Showing*—a 'bodily sight' of the passion of Christ. Studies on her have increased in recent years, as her simple heartfelt sharings and the brilliance of her theological intuitions attract the interest of the scholarly and the devout. Speaking as she does from the confusion and disunion of late fourteenth-century England, she gives all ages a message of confident tender love and trusting faith. Sr Ritamary Bradley traces Julian's growth in prayer, the gentle rhythm of moving 'ever more deeply into the goodness of God and all creation'. In this tracing she touches on Julian's 'Christ-Mother' theme.

Fr Charles Cummings then elaborates upon this image of 'the Motherhood of God', describing Julian as a sound and reliable spiritual guide who drew deeply from the authentic traditions of biblical and patristic spirituality. Her womanly descriptions of 'our true mother' refresh and stimulate us to new intuitions, new depths. Fr Charles, a cistercian monk, shows sensitivity to and an appreciation of the feminine dimension in his reflective and prayerful treatment of Julian.

These two articles offer us an opportunity to appreciate this remarkable medieval woman.

Julian on Prayer

Ritamary Bradley

JULIAN OF NORWICH (1345–1415?) took care that we should know very little about her, in order that we should not be distracted from the message she had to transmit. Consequently, we indeed know little about her personally. We have only the short version of her *Showings*, an account of an intense visionary experience which took place on 8 May 1373; the long version of the same work, the fruit of some twenty or more years of prayerful reflection; and a brief passage of spiritual counsel preserved in the *Book of Margery Kempe*. To these sources may be added what has been deduced from the facts of her environment.[1]

Even what facts are known about her from a few scanty records, and from her *Showings*, are dimmed by mystery. She lived as a recluse in a cell attached to the church of St Julian of Norwich. But since the structure now standing on the site of the original anchorhold was built to replace the original church, nearly destroyed in World War II, we can only try to imagine the exact circumstances under which she lived. We know that she had some contact with the nearby abbey of benedictine nuns at Carrow, but there is no evidence that she ever lived there.

She was unswervingly faithful to the medieval Church. She was at pains never to deviate from official ecclesiastical teachings, and her theology, though at times misunderstood, has never been definitively faulted.[2] Though her illness and visions opened her up to depths of consciousness which might have disoriented her, her writings reveal a mind completely sane and balanced and a heart probing but at peace. This balance and peace are even more extraordinary when we recall that she did not hesitate to consider the most unsettling questions: the mysteries of God's ways with humanity, the impact of evil, the contradictions that seem to confuse belief in how all things will be restored in Christ. It seems to be primarily through her visions and her reflections that she arrived at a vivid grasp of a theological principle basic to christian mysticism: our humanity is incorporated in Christ and thereby joined to divinity (the Trinity). Yet humanity—and all creation—though joined to Christ is clearly other than divinity.

Because Julian expresses this principle and its assumptions and corollaries so simply, it is easy to miss much of her teaching. Many, for example, focus solely on her well-known theme that 'all will be well'.[3] It is a mistake to go to Julian for an optimism based on simplistic faith. Yet the consoling theme of the final restoration of all that is now imperfect is nonetheless a key to her mind.[4] As Thomas Merton says:

> One of her most telling and central convictions is her orientation to what one might call ***an eschatological secret***, the hidden dynamism which is at work already and by which 'all manner of thing shall be well'. This secret, this act which the Lord keeps hidden away, is really the full fruit of the *Parousia*. It is not just that 'He comes,' but He comes with this final answer to the world's anguish, this answer which is already decided, but which we cannot discover. . . . Actually, her life was lived in the belief in this 'secret,' this 'great deed' that the Lord will do on the Last Day . . . all partial expectations will be exploded and everything will be made right. . . . It is the great deed of 'the end' which is still secret, but already at work in the world, in spite of all its sorrow, the great deed 'ordained by our Lord without beginning.'[5]

Merton perceived the teachings of Lady Julian as a mystery which must be approached through prayer and reflected on through theology. He rejoiced in his own discovery of Julian, whom he praised highly: 'She is a true theologian with greater clarity, depth and order than St Teresa: she really elaborates, theologically, the content of her revelations'.[6] Through her help he hoped to obtain a 'wise heart', a grasp of the great secret and its impact on life.

Not only Merton but generations of readers have gone to Julian's book to pray for a wise heart. This has been true from the beginning of what we know of the reception of her writings. In fact, we possess copies of the manuscripts, as well as the earliest printed edition (1670), only because english Benedictines, in exile after the expulsion of religious from England in the sixteenth century, thirsted for contemplation. At the request of Dom Augustine Baker, to accommodate Dame Gertrude More, descendant of St Thomas More, manuscripts of Julian's book found their way to Cambrai. There the work of transcription began, in a setting of prayer.

I review these basic facts about Julian primarily for those who are learning of her for the first time, as well as for those who have heard of her only as an important figure in the history of english prose. I have oriented the review towards the place of prayer in Julian's teaching, a focus which is drawing an ever widening audience who seek to learn from her.[7] Recent research has shown that her way of prayer is in continuity with the ancient tradition of prayer practised by the desert Fathers and with the scriptural and patristic teachings of the Church.[8] What I propose to add to this research is evidence that her way of prayer unfolds sequentially in the text of the *Showings* as Julian herself learned more about prayer and grew in interiority. I will explore Julian's growth through what happened to her in the first showing, through what changes took place in her under the impact of the eighth and ninth showings, and through what she says explicitly about prayer in the fourteenth revelation. In the course of this re-examination I will add some new evidence which shows that her prayer is rooted in the early contemplative tradition of the Church.

THE BEGINNINGS OF JULIAN'S PRAYER

Julian introduced the story of her revelations with an overview of the sixteen showings, together with a brief account of what had gone on in her interior life prior to 8 May 1373, the day of the revelations. Further, she makes clear that the visionary events centered on the passion of Christ illuminated by the mysteries of the Trinity and the Incarnation.

Before her showings, Julian already possessed considerable spiritual maturity. Her petitionary prayers were rooted in a desire to know the passion of Christ in such a way as to enter more fully into his life through grace. She asked to have the mind—or memory—of Christ's passion, thus using a prayer which is in some way analogous to the practice of the desert Fathers who hoped, through repeating a short prayer, to have a continuous remembrance of Jesus' sufferings. But Julian was seeking more: she wished to know, vividly and interiorly, what Christ's closest friends, especially Mary, his mother, knew when they stood near the cross. She desired no other vision. With the same disposition she wished to come near death so that she might afterwards live better. Here again, she was in harmony with the ancient tradition of spiritual guides who taught that affliction and sickness can serve to heal those who desire to be united with God. But knowing these are unusual prayers, she wanted them fulfilled only if God so wills (Chapter 2).

These desires passed from her mind. But there persisted in her will the desire for another gift which she asked for unconditionally, for she knew it originated in God's grace and harmonized with the teachings of the Church. The occasion for this third petition was hearing the story of St Cecilia, who, according to legend, received three wounds to her neck at the hands of her tormentors.[9] Julian interpreted these wounds symbolically, already giving us a hint as to the quality of her mind and the nature of her devotion. She wanted, like Cecilia, also to have three wounds—not physical ones, but wounds of contrition and of human compassion, crowned with a 'sincere longing for God' (Chapter 2). This longing, as the ongoing text of the *Show-*

ings makes clear, was not an emotive feeling, but a stirring of the heart, a motion of the whole being towards God, an impulse of the will. Julian wished to see God in all things through compassion, and, in a paradoxical sense, to see only God: 'I wanted his pain to be my pain: a true compassion producing a longing for God. I was not wanting a physical revelation of God, but such compassion as a soul would naturally have for the Lord Jesus, who for love became a mortal man. Therefore, I desired to suffer with him' (Chapter 3).

Yet something may be missing from these first prayers, or at least one ingredient of prayer is not yet fully articulated: that is, a consciousness of the corporate christian community in her relation to God. It is in this direction she was to grow.

In a significant way the experience of being close to death precipitated that growth. Her prayer for a near-fatal illness was answered, and in the midst of that illness her visions took place. In her dark room only light from the crucifix was visible, but with the showings an interior light flooded her soul. As Roland Maisonneuve says:

> . . . the proximity of death can burst the limits of perception. . . . In Julian's case it pulverizes her first universe, which was more limited spiritually; she is confronted, as a starting point, with the emptiness of the divine darkness which is light: it is this paradox which the darkness of the room and the light of the crucifix symbolize.[10]

The first revelation is a starting point in more senses than one. Julian tells us that the first vision contained all the rest in some way. This showing, which was a bodily vision of Christ crowned with a garland of thorns, was permeated by a spiritual vision which centered on the Trinity, who entered her life in the Incarnation:

> And at once I saw the red blood trickling down from under the garland, hot, fresh, and plentiful, just as it did at the time of the passion when the crown of thorns was pressed on to the blessed head of God-and-Man, who suffered for me. And I had a strong and deep conviction that it was himself and none other that showed me this vision.
>
> At the same moment the Trinity filled me full of heartfelt joy, and I knew that all eternity was like this for those who attain heaven. For the Trinity is God, and God the Trinity; the Trinity is our maker and keeper, our eternal lover, joy and bliss—all through our Lord Jesus Christ (Chapter 4).

Likewise, in the context of the first revelation Julian establishes a relationship to Christ that threads through all the showings. This is a relationship to Christ as the one divine teacher. In placing herself in this manner in God's presence, she entered into an established tradition of mystical spirituality which extended from the New Testament through the works of St Bonaventure († 1274) and of St Gertrude the Great(† 1301).[11] Of the first revelation as applied to prayer she says: 'The purpose of this revelation was to teach our soul the wisdom of cleaving to the goodness of God'. (Chapter 6). And she calls the showing a 'lesson of love' (Chapter 6). At a later point she elaborates on the complex meaning of teacher as applied to Christ: 'He is the ground, he is the substance, he is the teaching, he is the teacher, he is the taught, and he is the reward' (Chapter 34).

Moved by the impetus of the first showing Julian persevered under the tutelage of Christ, the teacher, as she grew in the understanding of prayer. She did not explain her progress, however, by expressions which mystics sometimes relied on, such as Walter Hilton's comparison of spiritual change to scaling a ladder. Rather, she kept on learning in three modes: through bodily or imaginative figures, centered on the face of Christ in his passion and transfigured in his glorified state; through reason, by which she reflected, raised doubts, revised tentative positions, and drew firm conclusions based on what she knew and believed, and on what she had seen; and finally through spiritual sight. Her growth was never a steady ascent. It was more like the seasonal cycles of fruit-bearing plants, which are sometimes dry and death-like, and are at other times transformed into beauty and productive life.

The first showing clearly marks a stage of her growth in prayer. The purpose of that showing was 'to teach our soul the wisdom of cleaving to the goodness of God' (Chapter 6). Such an insight taught her the limitations of those customary practices of prayer whereby 'we go on making as many petitions as our souls are capable of'. 'For in his goodness is included all one can want, without exception' (Chapter 6). Yet she makes clear that such a stance before God does not mean that our human needs are not placed in his care. For she says: 'He does not despise the work of his hands, nor does he disdain to serve us, however lowly our natural need may be'. Therefore '. . . let us in spirit stand and gaze, eternally marvelling at the supreme, surpassing singleminded, incalculable love that God, who is goodness, has for us. Then we can ask reverently of our lover whatever we will' (Chapter 6).

That grasp of goodness moved her to go beyond the personal focus of her earlier prayers (the three petitions) to reach out spontaneously to others. She realized that she was not going to die of the mysterious sickness, since the showing was for the living, and she must communicate it to them. This forward step was embodied in the lesson of the first showing, for she says: 'All that I say of myself, this I mean to say of the person of my fellow Christians. For I was taught in the showing of our Lord that such is his meaning' (Chapter 8).

What is it that she now had to share? It is a prayer directed to the goodness of God, but springing from a sense that God is in all things. She cried out simply: 'God, of thy goodness, give me yourself; for you are enough for me' (Chapter 5). This goodness, she taught, is closer to us than clothing is to the body (Chapter 6). It pervades all things, as her vision of a nut-sized globe in the palm of her hand signified. In the nut (a word which comes from the same root as our modern terms nucleus and nuclear)[12] she sees all visible creation sustained by the maker, the keeper, the lover (Chapter 5). In this vision sense does not disappear to make room for the divine, for God is present to all forms of our need, even to the humblest bodily functions; '. . . he is everything that we know to be good and helpful'. Yet the large, beautiful world looks very small in the presence of the Maker: '. . . we have got to realize the littleness of creation and to see it for the nothing that it is before we can love and possess God who is uncreated' (Chapter 5).

Julian also shared the theological underpinnings of this prayer to God's all-pervasive goodness. For in the first showing, she says, 'was included and demonstrated the Trinity, the Incarnation, and the unity between God and the soul of man' (Chapter 1). Looking on the face of Christ she saw the Trinity which is love; she did not see God as being (a mystery), but she saw what the divine one does in the world and in ourselves.

Julian's prayer, then, as inspired by the first showing, is not a piercing of the cloud of unknowing.[13] Rather, she beheld the Trinity in Jesus on the cross. She unveiled her vision of the suffering Jesus in vivid terms, continuing to focus on the garland on Christ's head:

> Great drops of blood rolled down from the garland like pellets, seemingly from the veins; and they came down a brownish red color, and as they spread out they became bright red, and when they reached the eyebrows they vanished . . . their abundance was like the drops of water that fall from the eaves after a heavy shower, falling so thickly that no one can possibly count them; their roundness as they spread out on his forehead was like the scales of herring (Chapter 7).

While the *Cloud* author in his youth was at his theological studies, learning the metaphor of the cloud of unknowing from the writings of Denys, Julian may have been cleaning fish somewhere in England, watching the heavy rains flooding down the eaves in a sudden rainstorm. Perhaps she had seen stray pellets (the small stones shot from cross bows) lying in the grass. It is from such experiences that she drew her language for the bodily visions. Yet, she says, she could find no image for the beauty and vitality which emanated from the divine face. So great is this beauty that she broke out in a prayer of joy and thanksgiving: 'I could never stop saying, "bless the Lord"' (Chapter 8).

EIGHTH AND NINTH SHOWINGS

Though, as Julian says, all the showings were in some sense contained in the first revelation, nonetheless each of the other visions brought its own special insights. For Julian's growth in prayer, the eighth and ninth showings were crucial. These were the most explicit answers to her early petitions, embodying a vivid sight of the passion, followed by her own deepening experience of contrition and compassion. The eighth showing spoke of Christ's final sufferings and his cruel death; the ninth related the comfort that flows to us from the passion, and the joy that awaits us in heaven (Chapter 1).

During these showings Julian felt the pain of the passion and regretted her prayer for this terrible experience: '. . . wretch that I am, I at once repented, thinking that had I known what it would have been like, I should have hesitated before making such a prayer' (Chapter 17). But the new insight which was burned into her consciousness at this point of the revelations is that Jesus still suffers with us in his glorified state: 'All the time that he could suffer, he did suffer for us. . . . Now that he is risen and is impassible, he still suffers with us' (Chapter 20). How this is true is obviously a mystery and can only be spoken of in the language of symbols.

She spoke of this insight in terms of two crowns. She saw two garlands on the head of Christ: the first is a garland of thorns; the second is a garland of blood, which takes on the colorlessness of Christ's head. This second garland is dried out, because Christ was hanging in the air 'like some cloth hung out to dry' (Chapter 17). This garland of blood which dyes the crown of thorns stands for those who are to be saved: it is the Church. This meaning of the second garland is underlined in another place, when she describes the suffering Church in the same terms used to speak of the crown of blood: 'Holy Church shall be shaken as one shakes a cloth in the wind'.

In fact, Julian referred a number of times to the crown, explaining it as both the suffering which Christ bears for us and the sign of his victory: 'This was a singular source of wonder, and a beholding of delight—that we should be his crown' (Chapter 22).

The symbolism of the crowns can best be understood in the light of a long spiritual tradition. Clement of Alexandria contemplated this symbol and said of it:

> For the Lord's crown prophetically pointed to us, who once were barren, but are placed around Him through the Church of which He is the Head.[14]

Clement saw the crown as a mystical symbol and explicates its meaning in Trinitarian terms:

> This crown is the flower of those who have believed in the glorified One.... It is a symbol, too, of the Lord's successful work ... when the Almighty Lord of the universe ... wished His power to be manifested to Moses, a godlike vision of light ... was shown him in the burning bush (the bush is a thorny plant....) On His departure from this world to the place when He came, He repeated the beginning of His old descent, in order that the Word beheld at first in the bush, and afterwards crowned by the thorn, might show the whole to be the work of one power. He Himself being one, the Son of the Father, who is truly one, the beginning and the end of time.[15]

With this deepened grasp of the extent and effect of Christ's work in the passion Julian resolves the conflict she felt between her outward part which shrank from pain and her inward part which chose Jesus for her heaven: '... it was shown that the inward should by grace draw the outward, that by the power of Christ both might be eternally and blessedly one' (Chapter 19). In other words, heaven is for the whole person—not just for separated spirits. 'We shall be blessed indeed' (Chapter 21). The experience then lifted her mind to heaven (Chapter 22), where she beheld all things in the humanity of Christ, and where the whole Trinity rejoices in the perfect work of Jesus: Father, Son, and Holy Spirit, for whom she used the words, 'joy, happiness, and eternal delight' (Chapter 12).

Thus, through the lesson of the eighth and ninth showings, Julian's prayer expanded to a further grasp of God's goodness, that goodness which causes the planets and all of nature to work for our benefit (Chapter 18). She also learned of the deepest part of the inner self, which is felt secretly and which is always in peace and love, even though there be tumult in the senses, reason, imagination, and ordinary consciousness: 'All the intent of the will is set endlessly to be united with Jesus' (Chapter 19). Why this is so is shown in Julian's reflections on the fourteenth revelation, especially in the parable of the Lord and the Servant.

THE FOURTEENTH REVELATION

While in the first showing the basis and nature of prayer is unfolded and in the eighth and ninth the contemplative experience is deepened, it is in the fourteenth revelation that Julian speaks of prayer at length, explicitly and fully. 'And after this Our Lord showed me about prayer', she says, introducing this section of her book (Chapter 41). Given their connection with prayer, Chapters 41 through 63, including the treatise on the motherhood of Christ and the parable of the Lord and the Servant, are rightly considered part of the fourteenth revelation.[16] For only in these parts does the true doctrine of prayer emerge, together with its theological base.

What does she now say of prayer? She says that God is the source of our prayers for he wills that we pray in accord with what he is working out in our lives. In this sense our whole lives, and not just certain moments, are a continuous prayer and grow out of his love for us. We cannot in this life know our true self—what we are intended to be—apart from seeing ourselves in Christ. We are united substantially to him and have been from the beginning. Hence sin, though it is not illusory, need not stand in the way of God working out his plan. This is because there is a godly will in us—an unbroken, sinless desire for God—which is indivisibly united with God's will. This point of union touches both our sensuality and our substance—that is, the human mental structure, and all that depends on the body, and the spiritual structure, that which shares in the life of God. Though sensuality and substance were broken off from one another by sin, leaving a state of disharmony, they can achieve unity again through Jesus Christ. How can we grasp this mystery? The parable of the Lord and the Servant throws light on these concepts.

This parable shows how, in God's sight, Adam, Christ, and we ourselves are seen in one timeless unchanging love. Julian visualized a Lord clothed in the sky and seated in a desert. Before the throne stands a servant in ragged clothing. The servant turns to do the bidding of the Lord but instead falls into a chasm. (This signifies both that Adam fell and that Christ fell into the womb of Mary). The Lord lifts the servant out of the chasm, and he is at once transfigured, clothed in a shining garment, and summoned to the right side of the Lord's throne. 'In all this', Julian explains, 'the good Lord showed his own son and Adam as one man. Our virtue and goodness are due to Jesus Christ; our weakness and blindness to Adam; and both were shown in the one servant' (Chapter 51).

Julian could then say that we are absolutely loved by God, despite our sin: 'God judges us according to our essential nature, which is for ever kept whole, safe, and sound in him' (Chapter 45). 'Christ in his mercy works within us, and we graciously cooperate with him through the gift and power of the Holy Spirit. This makes us Christ's children . . .' (Chapter 54).

Elaborating on this basis for her prayer, Julian developed her metaphor of the Christ-mother.[17] The Christ-mother surpasses the best of other mothers in that he gives birth to his children not into a life which closes with death, but into a life that never ends. The Christ-mother is the mother of all the living. Consequently, though as individuals we often experience brokenness and pain, the Church will never be utterly broken. Its purpose, like that of the mother, is to surround us with the love of Jesus, who sends his spirit into our heart so that we also love one another.

Julian's direct references to Jesus' motherhood cover the range of christian mysteries and the heart of mysticism: the deep Wisdom of the Trinity is our Mother; in him we are enfolded (Chapter 54). Jesus is the true mother of our nature because he made us, and he is mother by grace because he took created nature on himself (Chapter 59). We grow and develop in our Mother Christ: his mercy reforms and restores us, and through his passion, death, and resurrection he has united us to our being (Chapter 57). We are ever being born of him and will never be delivered (Chapter 57). Jesus feeds us with himself in the Blessed Sacrament, like the human mother who feeds her child with milk (Chapter 60). Our separate parts are integrated into a perfect human being in our merciful mother, Jesus (Chapter 58). Holy Church is our mother's breast (Chapter 62). And throughout, God rejoices to be our mother (Chapter 52).

Julian connected these insights of the fourteenth revelation with what she had learned in the first: 'the deep wisdom of the Trinity is our Mother, in whom we are enfolded' (Chapter 54).

> Indeed, our Saviour himself is our Mother for we are forever being born of him, and shall never be delivered. All this . . . is referred to in the first revelation where it is said, 'We are enfolded in him and he is us' (Chapter 57).

She also connects her expanded understanding of how we are united to Christ—both in substance and sensuality—with what she had seen in the eighth showing: 'These two parts were shown in the eighth revelation when my whole being was absorbed by the recollection and experience of Christ's passion and death' (Chapter 55). Hence, all the insights are drawn together in prayer.

Julian then gives explicit advice about prayer.[18] She counsels confidence and trust:

> Our Lord . . . said: 'I am the foundation of your praying' ('Ground of thy beseeching'). In the first place my will is that you should pray, and since it is I who make you pray, and you do so pray, how can you not have what you ask for?' (Chapter 41).

God's acts of creation and redemption are the ground of that confidence (Chapter 42). By prayer one can share in the work going on now:

> He means that we ought to know that the greatest deeds are already

> done. . . . Gratefully realizing that we ought to be praying for the deed now in process, which is that he should rule and guide us in this life for his glory, and bring us to bliss (Chapter 42).

One should persevere through dryness and distaste, not hesitating to ask for what is humanly needed, confident that our prayer does not perish: '. . . he sends it up above, and puts it in the treasury where it will never perish. There it remains continually . . . ever helping our needs' (Chapter 41).

It is love which gives shape to prayer—the love, created and uncreated, which is the primary meaning of the *Showings* as a whole. Consequently, 'Instead of telling God, "Things ought to have been this way"—which is how we often feel like praying—we are free to say, "Lord, bless you."'[19] To this disposition of gratitude is finally added a true contemplative sight:

> . . . when our Lord in his courtesy and grace shows himself to our soul we have what we desire. Then we care no longer about praying for any thing, for our whole strength and aim is set on beholding. This is prayer, high and ineffable, in my eyes (Chapter 43).

Hence, as a recent writer has noted, Julian learned to integrate the prayer of petition with contemplative adoration of God's goodness, thus bringing full-circle the basic insight of the first revelation: '. . . she contrasts the prayer that is based on the consciousness of human need—and so is man-centered—with the prayer of adoration which is not indeed forgetful of human need but is first and foremost centered in God, so that human needs are taken into the offering of Christ in worship'.[20]

When she concluded her short treatise on prayer, Julian had not forgotten the lesson of the hazelnut which brought to her mind God's sustaining and loving presence in all things. Nor had she left behind the teaching that even in the painful suffering of the passion and the permitting of sin, God is at work doing all things well. All these spiritual sights were taken up into her prayer:

> . . . I saw and knew that his marvelous and utter goodness brings our powers to their full strength. At the same time I saw that he is at work unceasingly in every conceivable thing, and that it is far greater than anything we can imagine, guess, or think. Then we can do no more than gaze in delight with tremendous desire . . . and to delight in his goodness. . . . This is achieved by the grace of the Holy Spirit, both now and until the time that, still longing and loving, we die (Chapter 43).

Through the showings, then, Julian had grown in her understanding of the basis of prayer. Nonetheless, she distinguished what she learned through revelation, what Holy Church commonly teaches, and what will only be revealed in heaven:

> Our Lord showed secrets [hidden truths] of two kinds. One is the great secret on which all other secrets depend. His will is that we recognize these to be hidden until such time as he declares them. The other consists of those secrets he is willing to reveal and make known. . . . They are secrets not merely because that is his will, but because we are blind and ignorant. This he greatly pities, and accordingly himself opens them up to us, so that we may know him thereby and love and cling to him. All we need to know and understand our Lord will most graciously show us, both by this means and by the preaching and teaching of Holy Church (Chapter 34).[21]

In heaven there will be revealed that inner self which she had learned about in part in the fourteenth showing, and, of course, the face of God:

> On that day we shall come to our Lord knowing our Self clearly, possessing God completely. Eternally 'hid in God' we shall see him truly and feel him fully, hear him spiritually, smell him delightfully, and taste him sweetly. We shall see God face to face, simply and fully (Chapter 43).

Julian at prayer, then, was Julian moving ever more deeply into the goodness of God and all creation, drawing closer by irregular growth cycles to union with Christ. This growth was expressed in part in her transformation through a feeling of compassion and pain for the physical thirst of Christ on the cross to knowing interiorly that God's thirst is to have all humankind, generally, within himself. Thus she could say—and invite all to say—'Lord, bless you'.

NOTES

1. See Brant Pelphrey, *Julian of Norwich: A Theological Reappraisal*, Elizabethan and Renaissance Studies 92 (Salzburg: Institut für Englische Sprache und Literatur, 1982) introductory chapters. See also Katherine Brégy, 'The Lady Anchoress', *Catholic World* 135 (1932) 9–15, and H. R. Flood, *St. Julian's Church, Norwich, and Dame Julian* (Norwich: Wherry Press, 1936).

2. See especially Paul Molinari, *Julian of Norwich: The Teaching of a Fourteenth-Century Mystic* (London: Longmans Green & Co., 1958); and Deryck Hanshell, 'A Crux in the Interpretation of Dame Julian', *Downside Review* 92 (1974) 77–91.

3. 'The writings of Julian of Norwich may be said to have entered into the mainstream of Engish literature at that moment in 1943 when T. S. Eliot quoted from the *Revelations of Divine Love* in the last of his *Four Quartets, Little Gidding*. '—A. M. Allchin, *The Living Presence of the Past* (New York, Seabury Press, 1981) 3.

4. *Ibid.*, 'The words which Eliot chose from her book: 'Sin is behovely, but all shall be well and all manner of thing shall be well' . . . stand very close to the heart of our book, and evidently they have spoken in a particular way to men and women of our own time.'

5. *Confessions of a Guilty Bystander*, as quoted in *Julian of Norwich, Four Studies to Commemorate the Sixth Centenary of the Revelations of Divine Love*, (Oxford: Fairacres Press, 1975) 37.

6. *Ibid.*

7. Evidence for this growing popularity is the reception of *Enfolded in Love, Daily Readings with Julian of Norwich* (London: Darton, Longman and Todd, 1980). Over seven thousand copies were sold within three years.

8. See Roland Maisonneuve, *L'Univers Visionnaire de Julian of Norwich* (Dissertation, University of Paris-Sorbonne, 1978) 1:3–4.

9. Recounted in the Short Version, Chapter 1.

10. Maisonneuve, 1:51–2 (My translation).

11. See Ritamary Bradley, 'Christ the Teacher in Julian's *Showings*: The Biblical and Patristic Traditions', in Marion Glasscoe, ed., *The Medieval Mystical Tradition in England*, Papers Read at Dartington Hall, July, 1982 (Exeter: University of Exeter, 1982) 127–42.

12. An observation made by A. T. Robinson, *The Roots of a Radical* (London: SCM 1980) (from a typescript copy).

13. For an overview of the approach to mysticism in the *Cloud of Unknowing* (in the latter part of the fourteenth century), see Harvey D. Egan, 'Mystical Crosscurrents', *Communio* 7 (Spring, 1980).

14. *The Instructor*, 2.8, translated in *Ante-Nicene Fathers* (New York: Scribners, 1925) 2:256.

15. *Ibid.*, 257. Julian's intricate symbolism, and Clement's, point to two aspects of doctrine and the mystical life. First, God shines through creation—for Moses in the burning bush, for Julian in the little ball. Then, under the transforming work of the passion, God's union with humankind shines out in the crown of thorns (reminiscent of the bush) and in the crown of blood, which is Jesus at one with collective humanity. Jesus' claim to kingship was mocked by the thorns; now his triumph is signified by a crown of thorns covered with blood—the humanity of which he is king by grace and glory. With the victory of the passion all creation and restored humanity are his glorious crown.

16. This position is convincingly maintained by Edmund Colledge and James Walsh, in *A Book of Showings to the Anchoress Julian of Norwich*, 2 vols. (Toronto: Pontifical Institute of Medieval Studies, 1978) 1:114.

17. See Ritamary Bradley, 'Patristic Background of the Motherhood Similitude in Julian of Norwich', *Christian Scholar's Review* 8 (1978) 101–13; and Jennifer P. Heimel, '"God is Our Mother": Julian of Norwich and the Medieval Image of Christian Feminine Divinity', (Ph.D. Dissertation, St John's University, 1980). For a study of the image of the Christ-mother before Julian (together with some observations on Julian's use of it) see Carolyn Walker Bynum, *Jesus as Mother: Studies in the Spirituality of the High Middle Ages*. Berkeley, Los Angeles, and London: University of California Press, 1982.

18. For further commentary on this section see Pelphrey, and John H. P. Clark, 'Julian of Norwich and the Monastic Tradition', (London: The Church Literature Association and the Catholic League, 1981) 9.

19. Pelphrey, p. 150 (typescript copy).

20. Clark, p. 10.

21. Pelphrey, pp. 179, 180 (typescript): '. . . it is necessary to speak of uncreated love paradoxically, as both hidden and known. Julian therefore describes two kinds of truths or "secrets," so to speak, in God. One of these is the being of God in himself, the indwelling Love of the Trinity which is really beyond our idea of 'being' or

of 'love' (the apophatic Trinity). The other "secret" is the being of God towards man—the Love which is the Son of God made man, making known the Trinity to us. One is the Father, Son and Holy Spirit so living in one another that they are perfectly one; the other is the Son of God born into creation, yet so living in the Father, in the Holy Spirit, that they are perfectly one . . . . It is possible . . . to know the Trinity in this life, intimately and personally (in the person of Jesus), according to God's will to make himself known. The second "secret" of the Trinity is meant to be revealed, and is revealed in Love."

Translations from the *Showings* (*Revelations of Divine Love*) are from the edition by Clifton Wolters (Baltimore, Maryland: Penguin Books, 1966), with a few changes made by the writer where greater closeness to the Middle English text is desirable for the purposes of this paper.

The Motherhood of God According to Julian of Norwich

Charles Cummings

ACCUSTOMED AS MANY of us are to imagine God exclusively as a male figure, the language of Julian of Norwich has an unfamiliar ring. 'As truly as God is our Father, so truly is God our Mother', wrote Julian in the commentary on her fourteenth revelation.[1] A few lines later, Julian asserted: 'Jesus is our true Mother' (Chapter 59, p. 296). Far from being isolated instances, these remarks are found in the context of an elaborate and carefully constructed reflection on the motherhood of God.

How is the modern reader to understand Julian's teaching? Should we label it a quaint product of fifteenth-century english spirituality that has nothing in common with our more enlightened, twentieth-century mentality? Should we dismiss it kindly and quickly as a flight of fancy in the vivid imagination of a female recluse who chose to live walled up in a cell attached to her village church? Or should we acknowledge Julian of Norwich as a sound and reliable spiritual guide with a theological intuition about the mystery of God that she drew from her own contemplative experience and from the common tradition of biblical and patristic spirituality? This article will explore the third alternative as the most fruitful and instructive approach.

CONTEXT OF HER TEACHING

Julian's teaching on the motherhood of God is developed only in her reflections on the allegory of the lord and the servant, in Chapters 51 to 63 of the Long Text. We may be dealing with an intuition that came to Julian late in her process of writing, was treated exhaustively, and did not surface again in the remaining twenty chapters of her work except for one passing reference in Chapter 83 (page 340). If this view is correct, the teaching represents an insight of Julian's spiritual maturity when she had reached a highly integrated and transcendent image of the Holy Trinity as Father, Mother and Lord.

Julian did not think of God solely as mother, but as mother in a way that complements other designations. 'And so I saw that God rejoices that he is our Father, and God rejoices that he is our Mother, and God rejoices that he is our true spouse, and that our soul is his beloved wife' (Chapter 52, p. 279). Nor did Julian think of Jesus solely as mother, although in these chapters that seems to have been her favorite title. She could also write: 'Christ rejoices that he is our brother, and Jesus rejoices that he is our Saviour' [*ibid.*].

Julian showed that she was aware of the traditional description of the Church as a mother to whom her children owe devotion and loyalty: 'Now I submit myself to my mother, Holy Church, as a simple child should' (Chapter 46, p. 259; also pp. 301, 302, 303). She also referred to Mary as mother: 'So our Lady is our mother, in whom we are all enclosed and born of her in Christ, for she who is mother of our saviour is mother of all who are saved in our saviour' (Chapter 57, p. 292). Typically, Julian was quick to add: 'Our Saviour is our true Mother, in whom we are endlessly born and out of whom we shall never come' (*ibid.*).

The motherhood of God, as Julian understood it, is inclusive rather than exclusive of all other titles. It can be disconcerting when the reader first discovers that divine motherhood is compatible even with masculine designations of God in the same sentence. For example: 'Our courteous Mother does not wish us to flee away, for nothing would be less pleasing to *him*' (Chapter 61, p. 301). Consistency of gender might seem to have required 'her' rather than 'him', but our courteous, heavenly Mother transcends gender entirely. Julian habitually used a masculine pronoun with the name mother because her image of God easily integrated masculinity and femininity while pointing to a reality that lies beyond sexual differences. Julian's thought ranged within an expansive concept of motherhood.

THE CONTENT OF HER TEACHING

Julian's teaching about the divine motherhood arises as an explanation of a parable about the creation and redemption of humanity out of the merciful love of the Trinity. Merciful love spoke to Julian of motherhood. 'Mercy is a compassionate property, which belongs to motherhood in tender love. . . . Mercy works, protecting, enduring, vivifying and healing, and it is all of the tenderness of love' (Chapter 48, p. 262). God's tender love is a mother's love for all her children, a love which never leaves them even when they offend: 'There is no created being who can know how much and how sweetly and how tenderly the Creator loves us' (Chapter 6, p. 186; see also pp. 130, 183, 241).

Among the three divine persons of the Trinity, it is always the second person to whom Julian attributed the quality of motherhood. 'All the lovely works and all the sweet loving offices of beloved motherhood are appropriated to the second person' (Chapter 59, p. 296). Never did Julian attribute motherhood to the first or third person of the Trinity. When motherhood is attributed simply to 'God', the broader context usually shows that Julian was thinking of the second person of the Trinity (Chapter 59, pp. 296–97). God as a Trinity of persons she sometimes called true Mother as well as true Father and Lord because these are qualities of the substantial divine goodness shared by all three persons (Chapter 60, p. 299; Chapter 62, p. 302).

Julian attempted to explain the unity of shared nature and the appropriation of particular properties when she wrote:

> I contemplated the work of all the blessed Trinity, in which contemplation I saw and understood these three properties: the property of the fatherhood, and the property of the motherhood, and the property of the Lordship in one God (Chapter 58, p. 293).

A related text describes the indwelling of the Trinity with all its properties in us and our indwelling or enclosure in the Trinity:

> For the almighty truth of the Trinity is our Father, for he made us and keeps us in him. And the deep wisdom of the Trinity is our Mother, in whom we are enclosed. And the high goodness of the Trinity is our Lord, and in him we are enclosed and he in us (Chapter 54, p. 285).

The second divine person, who is our mother in nature, grace, and mercy, is called 'the deep wisdom of the Trinity'. Elsewhere Julian wrote: 'God all-wisdom is our loving Mother' (Chapter 58, p. 293; Chapter 58, p. 295). The wisdom literature of the Old Testament personified *Sophia* as a female figure and close collaborator with Yahweh. The New Testament saw in Christ the Wisdom of God incarnate. Julian clarified the notion of Christ's divine motherhood by referring to the wisdom theme: 'I am he, the wisdom and the lovingness of motherhood' (Chapter 59, p. 296).

As a wise mother, Jesus watches carefully over our growth and formation in virtue. 'He kindles our understanding, he prepares our ways, he eases our conscience, he comforts our soul, he illumines our heart' (Chapter 61, p. 299). As a wise mother he even permits us to fall, to be distressed and chastised, 'for if we did not fall, we should not know how feeble and how wretched we are in ourselves' (Chapter 61, p. 300). Julian was confident, however, of this mother's protection: 'Our heavenly Mother Jesus may never suffer us who are his children to perish, for he is almighty, all wisdom, and all love' (Chapter 61, p. 301). We will be frightened of dangers but we must act like children who do not trust their own strength but run quickly to their mother for help, and call to her with all their might: 'My kind Mother, my gracious Mother, my beloved Mother, have mercy on me. I have made myself filthy and unlike you, and I may not and cannot make it right except with your help and grace' [*ibid.*].

Julian's childlike prayer also illustrates her fondness for adding a descriptive adjective to the name 'mother' as applied to Jesus. For example: 'our precious Mother Jesus', 'our precious Mother Christ', 'our courteous Mother', 'our tender Mother Jesus', 'our loving Mother'. Her most frequent description is 'our true Mother'. Each of us has a mother who brought us to birth physically, but only because our divine Mother was at work with and in our human mother. Therefore, Julian reasoned, Jesus is our *true* mother:

> This fair lovely word 'mother' is so sweet and so kind in itself that it cannot truly be said of anyone or to anyone except of him and to him who is the true Mother of life and of all things. To the property of motherhood belong nature, love, wisdom and knowledge, and this is God (Chapter 60, pp. 298–99).

It was 'because he wanted altogether to become our Mother in all things' that God became a human being in Jesus Christ, 'all ready in our poor flesh himself to do the service and the office of motherhood in everything' (Chapter 60, p. 297). For Julian, motherhood represented the closest, most loving, most faithful approach to human beings; she saw that 'no one ever might or could perform this office fully, except only him', Jesus our true Mother [*ibid.*].

ROLE OF THE DIVINE MOTHER

The meaning Julian perceived in the divine motherhood becomes clearer when we study the role or functions she assigned to Christ, 'our Mother of mercy' (Chapter 58, p. 294). Her language is resonant with love but free of sentimentality as she reflects on the works of this Mother:

> Our Mother is working on us in various ways . . . for in our Mother Christ we profit and increase, and in mercy he reforms and restores us, and by the power of his Passion, his death and his Resurrection he unites

> us to our substance. So our Mother works in mercy on all his beloved children who are docile and obedient to him . . . (Chapter 58, p. 294).

A mother is the source of life, as Eve was known as 'the mother of all the living' (Gen 3:20). The mother's biological functions of bringing to birth and nursing a child have their counterpart 'in our spiritual bringing to birth' (Chapter 61, p. 299; see Chapter 59, p. 295). Julian summarized these functions:

> In our true Mother Jesus our life is founded in his own prescient wisdom from without beginning. . . . And in accepting our nature he gave us life, and in his blessed dying on the Cross he bore us to endless life. And since that time, now and until the day of judgment, he feeds us and fosters us, just as the great supreme lovingness of motherhood wishes, and as the natural need of childhood asks (Chapter 63, p. 304).

In another text Julian described the 'cruel pains' of childbirth that Jesus endured on the cross, but these were not the end of his 'motherhood of love, a mother's love which never leaves us' (Chapter 60, pp. 297–98). 'He could not die any more', Julian explained, 'but he did not want to cease working: therefore he must needs nourish us' (Chapter 60, p. 298). Julian could perceive the protecting, nourishing divine Mother in the preaching, teaching, and sacramental structures of the Church: 'The mother can give her child to suck of her milk, but our precious Mother Jesus can feed us with himself, and does, most courteously and most tenderly, with the blessed sacrament, which is the precious food of true life . . .' [*ibid.*].

To 'our beloved Mother' also belongs the function of gently healing and cleaning the wounds of sin (Chapter 63, p. 304). His too is the motherly role of comforting and consoling in time of trouble (Chapter 74, p. 325). Julian recommended 'mightily praying to our Mother for mercy and pity', 'committing ourselves fervently to the faith of Holy Church', and 'attaching' all our love to 'our mother Holy Church, who is Christ Jesus', for 'he wants us to love him sweetly and trust in him meekly and greatly' (Chapter 59, p. 296; Chapter 61, pp. 301–302). Christ exercises his role of motherhood through the Church with which he is identified. Through the Church, 'the sweet gracious hands of our Mother are ready and diligent about us' (Chapter 61, p. 302).

THE SOURCES OF HER TEACHING

Julian of Norwich was not the first to present Christ or the triune God as mother, but no christian writer before Julian elaborated the image so powerfully and comprehensively. This insight was God's gift to Julian in her contemplative experience, and her gift to the world in theological synthesis. What on the natural level predisposed Julian to think of God as mother we cannot say because we do not know enough about her life and personality. She did mention the presence of her own mother at her bedside as she lay at the point of death, and we might speculate that her mother was a particularly strong, positive influence in Julian's life.

Julian had a long familiarity with the latin Bible, but she did not quote chapter and verse literally in her reflections on the motherhood of God. Similarly, she seems to have known a number of patristic and medieval monastic texts, but she did not choose to refer to any particular author by name in these chapters. Consequently the 'sources' indicated below may or may not have had a direct influence on Julian. They do indicate the presence of a tradition that recognized God as mother long before Julian wrote.

Witnesses to this tradition listed by the editors of the *Showings* include the anonymous author of the *Ancrene Riwle*, St Bridget of Sweden, St Mechtild of Hackeborn, St Catherine of Siena, some early Franciscans. In his ninth sermon on the Song of Songs, St Bernard spoke of 'the breasts of the Bridegroom, sweeter than wine' (cf. Is 66:9–13). St Anselm addressed to St Paul a prayer in which he referred to Paul's description of himself as a mother [Gal 4:19, 1 Thess 2:7] and then went on to address Jesus as mother: 'But you, too, good Jesus, are not you also a mother? Is not he a mother who like a hen gathers his chicks beneath his wings? Truly, Lord, you are a mother too.'

One of the early patristic sources of this terminology was Clement of Alexandria. A master of rhetorical language, Clement identified masculine and feminine qualities both in God and in Jesus Christ. Christians are the children of Christ our parent: 'The Word is everything to his little ones, both father and mother, educator and nurse'.[2] In a homily on a text from Mark, Clement related the loving tenderness of God to femininity:

> God himself is love, and out of love to us he became feminine. In his ineffable essence he is Father; in his compassion to us he became Mother. The Father by loving became feminine; and the great proof of this is he whom he begot of himself.[3]

Clement saw motherhood and fatherhood as complementary aspects of the divinity, like concavity and convexity. Fatherhood characterizes the ineffable transcendence of God; motherhood denotes God's intimate nearness and tenderness.

In the Old Testament, as we have noted, wisdom is a feminine figure related both to heaven and to earth (see Prov 4:5–9, 8:12–9:11, Sir

24:1–31, Wis 7:21–8:21). Ben Sirach portrayed *Sophia* as mother and bride: 'She will meet him as a mother, and as a youthful wife will she receive him; and she will feed him with the bread of understanding, and will give him the waters of knowledge to drink' (Sir 15:2–3).

Does the Old Testament give Yahweh the name mother? Some texts could be the speech of either a mother or father figure: 'When Israel was a child I loved him, out of Egypt I called my son' (Hos 11:1), or 'Is Ephraim not my favored son, the child in whom I delight. . . . My heart stirs for him, I must show him mercy, says the Lord' (Jer 31:20). But the Psalmist compared his humble trust in Yahweh to 'a weaned child on its mother's lap' (Ps 131:2). Jerusalem was clearly depicted as mother: 'To Zion each says "Mother", for in her each one is born' [Ps 87:5, see Gal 4:26]. And Isaiah associated Yahweh closely with Jerusalem: 'As a mother comforts her son, so will I comfort you; in Jerusalem you shall find your comfort' (Is 66:13). Isaiah came closest to calling God 'mother' in an inspiring comparison: 'Can a mother forget her infant, be without tenderness for the child of her womb? Even should she forget, I will never forget you' (Is 49:15, cf. 63:16). The 'tenderness' characteristic of a mother's love is denoted by the Hebrew word *rahamim*, from *rehem*, the womb. The Old Testament did not hesitate to ascribe this tender, maternal love to Yahweh (Ex 34:6, Ps 25:6, 116:5, Hos 11:8, 14:5, Dn 9:9).

Early New Testament writers identified Jesus with wisdom without stressing *Sophia's* femininity. St Paul proclaimed Christ as 'the power of God and the wisdom of God' (1 Cor 1:24, see 1:30, 2:7–11, Lk 7:35). In his lament over Jerusalem, Jesus compared himself to a sorrowing mother bird: 'How often have I wanted to gather your children together as a mother bird collects her young under her wings, and you refused me!' (Lk 13:34, Mt 23:37). The synoptic gospels portray Jesus as the incarnation of divine mercy and tenderness in his compassion for the crowds, for the lepers and other afflicted persons, for the bereaved and the repentant. Far from being vindictive, judgmental, and hard hearted, Jesus could suffer and weep with the poor and could pardon those who crucified him (Lk 23:34).

John's gospel seems particularly sensitive to the maternal role of Jesus without prejudice to his masculinity. The *logos* of the prologue is perhaps to be understood as the masculine form of *Sophia* in the Old Testament. The 'I am' statements of Jesus are reminiscent of the claims of *Sophia*, as is his identification with bread, water, and light, his origin from the Father, and his gift of himself as a living banquet to satisfy all human hunger (Jn 6:35). In his dealings with John and Lazarus, with Martha and Mary, Mary Magdalen, and the Samaritan woman, Jesus behaved in a caring, nourishing way, sometimes to the consternation of others (Jn 4:27). On the final day of the feast of Tabernacles, Jesus made a bold allusion to a nursing mother when he cried out: 'If anyone thirsts, let him come to me; let him come who believes in me. Scripture has it: "From within him rivers of living water shall flow"' (Jn 7:37–38). John adds that 'he was referring to the Spirit' (see Jn 19:34). During the farewell discourse, after washing his disciples' feet, Jesus addressed them as 'my little children' (Jn 13:33) and compared their distress, as well as his own, to that of a woman in labor (Jn 16:21). On the cross, after giving his own mother to the disciple whom he loved, Jesus said to the disciple 'Behold your mother', a word which may have more than one referent in the context of Christ's life-giving death (Jn 19:27). In a post-resurrection appearance, Jesus entrusted to Peter the role of tending and feeding the sheep as he himself had done in his pastoral, nurturing ministry (Jn 21:15–17, 10:14–16).

EVALUATION

We do not know to what degree Julian of Norwich was influenced by any of these biblical or non-biblical sources because her synthesis of God's motherhood is stamped with her own personal intuition, and developed in a highly original way. In evaluating her contribution we can say that she was faithful to the existing tradition but even more faithful to her own contemplative insights.

Even deeper than her insight into the motherhood of God was Julian's conviction that God is love. Motherhood was the most effective image she had at her command for teaching God's love. After explaining the 'three ways of contemplating motherhood in God' as she understood it, Julian shared her deepest conviction: 'And in that by the same grace everything is penetrated, in length and in breadth, in height and in depth without end; and it is all one love' (Chapter 59, p. 297). The primacy of love also shines through the following text:

> Our great Father, almighty God, who is being, knows us and loved us before time began. Out of this knowledge, in his most wonderful deep love, by the prescient eternal counsel of all the blessed Trinity, he wanted the second person to become our Mother, our brother and our saviour. From this it follows that as truly as God is our Father, so truly is God our Mother. Our Father wills, our Mother works, our good Lord the Holy Spirit confirms (Chapter 59, p. 296).

It is evident from this text that Julian did not wish to play off motherhood against fatherhood in God. Divine motherhood completes the image of divine fatherhood, while God transcends both in unfathomable oneness and allness. Contemplating God as both mother and father leads to an appreciation of the fullness of divine reality in the inexhaustible fecundity and energy of his mystery. Seeing God as both mother and father is a way of hinting at possibilities and realizations beyond all ordinary limits, a way of describing the indescribable perfection of God. God is always more than everything we can say about the divine totality, yet God never ceases to be utter simplicity.

It is characteristic of Julian that she did not make ethical applications of her teaching on the divine motherhood, for example, by exhortations to act in a motherly and compassionate way towards other people and to foster life in the concrete situations of our daily existence. Her reflections seem to be aimed simply at unfolding the meaning of her personal intuition and eliciting a response of loving gratitude towards God for his self-revelation. Julian was, after all, a recluse and her primary orientation was towards contemplation rather than apostolic ministry. Nor did she draw any conclusions applicable to a fifteenth-century feminist movement. In any such movement Julian deserved by her theological brilliance to be in the forefront, but she was content to remain quietly turned towards the mystery of God, our true Father and true Mother, in whom she found fulfilling bliss.

CONCLUSION

Julian's image of God as transcendent father and mother may have contributed to the integration, balance and human wholeness of her spirituality. Hers was a felt, experiential piety springing from heart as well as head, under the inspiration of grace. She desired a place among 'the children of grace' with all the virtues of gentleness, meekness and trustfulness that belong naturally to children. One who knows God as father and mother knows himself or herself as child on some central level that does not exclude functioning as a mature, responsible adult on other levels. In this sense we can understand Julian in the following, difficult text with which she concludes this section of her *Revelations*:

> I understood no greater stature in this life than childhood, with its feebleness and lack of power and intelligence, until the time that our gracious Mother has brought us up into our Father's bliss. And then it will truly be made known to us what he means in the sweet words when he says: All will be well, and you will see it yourself, that every kind of thing will be well. And then will the bliss of our motherhood [i.e. 'our having been mothered'] in Christ be to begin anew in the joys of our Father, God, which new beginning will last, newly beginning without end (Chapter 63, p. 305).

NOTES

1. Julian of Norwich, *Showings*, Chapter 59, trans. Edmund Colledge and James Walsh (New York: Paulist Press, 1978) p. 295. All subsequent references to Julian's text will quote this edition, giving chapter and page number.

2. Clement of Alexandria, *Christ the Educator* 1.6, trans. Simon P. Wood, *The Fathers of the Church*, 23 (New York, 1954) 40.

3. Clement of Alexandria, *Who is the Rich Man That Shall Be Saved?* 37, trans. William Wilson, *The Ante-Nicene Fathers* (New York, 1905) Vol. 2:601.

Teresa of Avila

Teresa of Avila's extraordinary gifts of mystical prayer have so inflamed the imaginations of some artists that they have portrayed a Teresa of their own misunderstanding—a woman so out of the ordinary as to seem out of touch with reality.

The authors of the three following articles have not fallen into this trap. Theirs is the authentic Teresa of history, seen through her writings. They present carefully documented studies based on primary sources and showing patient care for accuracy in interpretation.

Each article stresses a specific aspect of St Teresa's spirituality and personality, but all three possess certain emphases which serve to unify them within the triad. Brother Laurin Hartzog's discussion of the christocentric nature of Teresa's spirituality is a motif repeated in both Keith Egan's and in Sr Margaret Dorgan's treatments of the specific contents of diverse teresian texts. All three writers are at one in their efforts to keep St Teresa's message within its proper context; they understand the importance of remembering that she wrote her works under obedience; that the language of her day was still in process of development; that she addressed a clearly defined audience; that the era in which she lived was undergoing theological and ideological foment. To ignore these facts, they warn us, is to run the risk of distorting Teresa's teachings.

These three articles offer valuable stimuli for further study of St Teresa of Avila's inspired and inspirational guidance in one's spiritual life.

Teresa of Jesus: The Saint and Her Spirituality

Laurin Hartzog

He then left to make his way as usual to the Mount of Olives, with the disciples following. When they reached the place he said to them, 'Pray not to be put to the test.'

Then he withdrew from them, about a stone's throw away, and knelt down and prayed. 'Father', he said 'if you are willing, take this cup away from me. Nevertheless, let your will be done, not mine.' Then an angel appeared to him, coming from heaven to give him strength. In his anguish he prayed even more earnestly, and his sweat fell to the ground like great drops of blood.

Luke 22:39–44

UNABLE TO REASON logically with her mind when she was praying, St Teresa tells us that her method of prayer consisted in trying to make pictures of Christ inwardly. She especially liked those parts of his life when he was most alone, for it seemed easier to approach him when he was afflicted and in need. She was particularly attached to his agony in the garden. She would go and keep him company, wishing to wipe the sweat from his face, but never daring to do so because of the gravity of her sins. She would remain with him there for as long as her thoughts permitted. For many years, before going to sleep, she would recall this scene (and this even before she was a nun) and so she found herself practising prayer without even knowing what it was.[1] Thus began the prayer life of a young girl who would attain the heights of mystical prayer and who would become the first woman doctor of the universal Church.

St Teresa's drawing close to Christ to keep him company and her devotion to his sacred humanity was to become the hallmark of her spirituality.

Her intimate conversations with him were to lead her to define mental prayer as nothing more than friendly intercourse and frequent solitary converse with him who we know loves us.[2]

St Teresa confessed that, unlike many others, she had great difficulty in using her imagination in prayer and she never fully succeeded in forming a picture of Christ as man.[3] Yet it was by recalling certain scenes from his life and Passion and pondering them in her heart that she had her most intense experiences of her intimate companion.

> When picturing Christ in the way I have mentioned, and sometimes even when reading, I used unexpectedly to experience a consciousness of the presence of God, of such a kind that I could not possibly doubt that He was within me or that I was wholly engulfed in him.[4]

St Teresa always began her prayer by meditating on some incident from the passion. She felt that meditation was compatible with the sublimest types of prayer and that usually the higher forms of prayer followed the lower. She saw clearly that if we are to please God and if he is to grant great favors to us, this will happen through the humanity of Christ, in whom, as God himself said, he was well pleased. Not only had she learned this by experience, but the Lord himself had told her that if great secrets were to be revealed to the soul, they would be revealed through the sacred humanity of Christ.[5]

The idea that at certain stages of the life of prayer all corporeal things should be excluded, including the sacred humanity of Christ, was very prevalent during St Teresa's time and she attacks this idea very forcefully both in her *Life* (Chapters XXII–XXIV) and in the Interior Castle (Chapter VI).

> This withdrawal from the corporeal must doubtless be good, since it is advised by such spiritual people, but . . . What I should like to make clear is that Christ's most sacred humanity must not be reckoned among these corporeal objects. Let that point be clearly understood. . . .[6]

St Teresa was adamant on this point: the sacred humanity should never be excluded no matter how sublime one's prayer might be. And she was speaking from a sad experience here:

> As I had no director, I used to read these books, and gradually began to think I was learning something. I found out later that, if the Lord had not taught me, I could have learned little from books . . . I tried to put aside everything corporeal . . . O Lord of my soul and my Good, Jesus Christ crucified! Never once do I recall this opinion which I held without a feeling of pain: I believe I was committing an act of high treason, though I committed it in ignorance.[7]

Teresa felt that she had been deceived by the devil to give up her meditations on the sacred humanity, for '. . . though angelic spirits, freed from everything corporeal, may remain permanently enkindled in love, this is not possible for those of us who live in this mortal body'.[8] Some souls complain that they cannot dwell upon the passion; she agreed that there are times in one's life of prayer when meditation (and by meditation here she meant prolonged rational reflection)[9] would be a hindrance. But to reason with the understanding is one thing; it is quite another, she says, for the memory to represent truths to the understanding.[10] In this latter activity she encouraged all of us to participate. The understanding, she says,

> . . . will picture them to itself, and they will be impressed upon the memory, so that the mere sight of the Lord on his knees, in the garden, covered with that terrible sweat, will suffice us, not merely for an hour, but for many days. We consider, with simple regard, who he is and how ungrateful we have been to One who has borne such pain for us. Then the will is aroused, not perhaps with deep emotion but with a desire to make some kind of return for this great favor, and to suffer something for One who has suffered so much himself.[11]

She counsels that all should attempt to meditate in this way, for even the most sublime kind of prayer will be no obstacle to meditation, and if while the soul is meditating the Lord should suspend meditation, well and good.[12]

She assures all that they will not enter the last two Mansions—those in which the highest mystical union is experienced[13]—if they lose their guide, the good Jesus. And not only will they be unable to enter the last two Mansions, but they will do well if they are able to remain securely in the other Mansions. 'For the Lord himself says that he is the Way; the Lord also says that he is light (John 14:6) and that no one can come to the Father save by him; (John 14:6) and that "he that seeth me seeth my Father".'[14]

HUMILITY IS TRUTH

Teresa was of the opinion that there were two main reasons why those who had succeeded in experiencing the prayer of union did not make further progress and achieve great spiritual freedom. One is that they ceased to meditate on the sacred humanity; the other is that they were somewhat lacking in humility.[15]

She was convinced that prayer must be entirely grounded and established in humility, and that the more a soul abases itself in prayer, the higher God raises it. She could not remember a time when our Lord had granted her any of the outstanding favors she had received, except when she had been consumed with shame at realizing her own wickedness. Christ had actually helped her in this by revealing to her things about herself that she could never have imagined on her own.[16]

> One night, when I was at prayer, the Lord began to talk to me. He reminded me how wicked my life had been and made me feel very confused and distressed; for, although he did not speak severely, his words caused me to be consumed with distress and sorrow. A single word of this kind makes a person more keenly aware of his advance in self-knowledge than do many days spent in meditating upon his own wretchedness, for it bears a stamp of truth the reality of which none can deny. He pictured to me the earlier movements of my will, showed me how vain they had been. . . .
>
> As the Lord began to remind me of the wickedness of my past life, . . . I wondered if he was about to show me some favour. For it is quite usual for the Lord to grant me some special favour after I have been beside myself with shame . . . Soon after this, my spirit became so completely transported that it seemed to have departed almost wholly from the body; . . . I saw the most sacred Humanity in far greater glory than I had ever seen before. I saw a most clear and wonderful representation of it in the bosom of the Father.[17]

St Teresa was careful to point out what humility is not, however, and she exhorted her daughters to acquire true humility.

> We may think it humility not to realize that the Lord is bestowing gifts upon us. Let us understand very, very clearly, how this matter stands. God gives us these gifts for no merit of ours. Let us be grateful to his Majesty for them, for, unless we recognize that we are receiving them, we shall not be aroused to love him. And it is a most certain thing that, if we remember all the time that we are poor, the richer we find ourselves, the greater will be the profit that comes to us and the more genuine our humility.[18]

So long as we remain in this world, nothing is more important than humility. However high a state the soul may have attained, humility and self-knowledge are incumbent upon it. Yet we will never succeed in knowing ourselves unless we seek to know God: 'think of God's greatness and then come back to our own baseness; by looking at his purity we shall see our foulness; by meditating upon his humility, we shall see how far we are from being humble'.[19] Nor shall we achieve true humility until our own will is simply and wholly united with that of our Creator:

> The highest perfection [says the saint] consists not in interior favours or in

> great raptures or in visions or in the spirit of prophecy, but in the bringing of our wills so closely into conformity with the will of God that, as soon as we realize he wills anything, we desire it ourselves with all our might, and take the bitter with the sweet, knowing that to be his majesty's will.[20]

Many ills come to us from a lack of humility and self-knowledge. We get a distorted idea of our own nature, and, if we never stop thinking about ourselves, we will experience all kinds of fears. We must set our eyes on Christ, from whom we shall learn true humility, and also upon his saints.[21] If we turn from self towards God, our understanding will be ennobled, and self-knowledge will not make us timorous and fearful.[22]

> His majesty desires and loves courageous souls if they have no confidence in themselves but walk in humility; and I have never seen any such person hanging back on this road, nor any soul that, under the guise of humility, acted like a coward, go as far in many years as the courageous soul can in few.[23]

Humility, the heart of St Teresa's spirituality, is not a matter of being pusillanimous and cowardly and stifling our good desires. On the contrary! Far from cramping our good desires, humility should inspire us with great confidence that we too can attain to what many saints attained through God's favor. St Teresa was convinced that if the saints had not resolved to attain perfection and continually to put their desires into effect, they would never have risen to as high a state as they did. 'With regard to this matter of desires', she admitted, 'my own were always ambitious . . .'[24] At one time in her life she found encouraging St Paul's conviction that everything is possible in God.[25] She used often to reflect that St Peter had lost nothing by throwing himself into the sea, though after he had done so he was afraid. (Mt 14:29)[26]

Once, while St Teresa was wondering why our Lord so dearly loved this virtue of humility, all of a sudden, without her having previously considered it, the following thought struck her:

> . . . it is because God is Sovereign Truth and to be humble is to walk in truth, for it is absolutely true to say that we have no good thing in ourselves, but only misery and nothingness; and anyone who fails to understand this is walking in falsehood. He who best understands it is most pleasing to Sovereign Truth because he is walking in truth.[27]

To be humble then is to see things and oneself in truth, to see things as God sees them.

Once, when she was in prayer and felt a great joy within, she started meditating on how unworthy she was of such joy and how much more she deserved to be occupying the place she had once seen prepared for her in hell. And in the Divine Majesty into which she was plunged, and which she knew to be Truth itself, she was given to understand a truth which is the fulfilment of all truths. Truth itself said to her:

> 'This that I am doing for thee is no small thing, but one of the things for which thou are greatly indebted to me; for all the harm which comes to the world is due to a failure to know the truths of Scripture in the clarity of their truth, of which not a tittle shall fail'[28]

She thought that she and all the faithful had always believed this. Then he said to her:

> 'Ah, daughter, how few are they who love me in truth! If people loved me, I should not hide my secrets from them. Knowest thou what it is to love me in truth? It is to realize that everything which is not pleasing to me is a lie.'[29]

From this experience Teresa derived great benefit. She began to look upon all that was not directed to the service of God as vanity and lies. She firmly resolved to carry out with all her might the very smallest thing contained in holy Scripture, and it gave her a very great desire to speak only of things that were very true and which went far beyond any that were treated of in the world. She came to understand what a blessing it is for a soul to place no value on anything that will not bring it nearer to God. She also understood what a blessing it is to be walking in truth in the presence of Truth itself. In short, God showed her that he is Truth itself, that this Truth is without beginning or end, and that upon it all other truths depend.[30]

VISIONS: ST TERESA'S PATH

These great truths were revealed and experienced by St Teresa through visions, visions that were to last some twenty-seven years and accompany her to her death in 1582.

Our Lord began to awaken her soul and grant her favors again about 1555. She began to think she was being addressed by interior voices and that she was experiencing visions and revelations. She saw nothing with her bodily eyes, but a picture would come to her as if in a lightning-flash, and so deeply would the impression of it remain with her, and such effects would it produce, that it was clearer than if she had seen it with her physical eyes.[31]

As the number of these locutions and visions increased, her confessors became more and more incredulous. The sheer number alone was enough to raise doubts. Teresa, in her great humility, made much of her faults and could not understand how God would grant such favors to anyone as wicked as she. The discernment of spirits by her confessors went on for six years, but the self-questioning by St Teresa went on for the rest of her life. When she was actually experiencing the visions, she could not doubt that they came from God. But once they were past, she would return to her self-questioning, and this heavy burden caused her to seek learned men to whom to open her soul and from whom to seek advice lest she be deluded by the devil.

Some time between 1555 and 1557, Teresa experienced her first locution. While reciting the Hours, she began pondering the verse '*Justus es, Domine*. . . '

> While I was wondering how in thy justice thou couldst ordain that so many of thy faithful handmaidens . . . should not be given the graces and favours which thou didst bestow on me, being such as I was, thou didst answer me, Lord, saying 'Serve thou me, and meddle not with this'. This was the first word which I ever heard thee speak to me and so it made me very much afraid . . . .[32]

St Teresa says that these words were perfectly formed, yet they were not heard with the bodily ear; and yet they were understood much more clearly than if they had been. It is impossible, she says, for one to fail to hear them, even if one were to resist, and the understanding has to devote itself completely to what God wishes it to understand.[33] When these words are addressed to the soul they are accompanied by effects, and whether they are words of devotion or reproof, they prepare the soul and move it to affection, they give it light and make it happy and tranquil. If the soul has been afflicted with aridity and unrest, the Lord frees it so that the soul realizes his power and the efficacy of his words.[34] Nor do these words vanish from the memory for a very long time; indeed, some of them never vanish at all.[35] They impress us with their complete certainty, and although they might seem quite impossible of fulfilment, yet within the soul itself there is a certainty which cannot be overcome. The soul cannot doubt that the words will come true because it knows that they come from God who is Truth itself. The soul is anxious for the event to come to pass and experiences great joy when the words are fulfilled.[36]

After two years of continually praying that the Lord would either lead her by another path or make plain the truth, she had the following experience:

> I was at prayer on a festival of the glorious Saint Peter when I saw Christ at my side—or, to put it better, I was conscious of him, for neither with the eyes of the body nor with those of the soul did I see anything. I thought he was quite close to me and I saw that it was he who, as I thought, was speaking to me. Being completely ignorant that visions of this kind could occur, I was at first very much afraid, and did nothing but weep, though, as soon as he addressed a single word to me to reassure me, I became quiet again, as I had been before, and was quite happy and free from fear. All the time Jesus Christ seemed to be beside me, but, as this was not an imaginary vision, I could not discern in what form: what I felt very clearly was that all the time he was at my right hand, and a witness of everything that I was doing, and that, whenever I became slightly recollected or was not greatly distracted, I could not but be aware of his nearness to me.[37]

When Teresa reported this to her confessor he wanted to know in what form she had seen Christ and how she knew it was Christ. She could only say that she could not help realizing that Christ was beside her and that she saw and felt this clearly; that now, in the prayer of quiet, her soul was much more deeply and continuously recollected; that the effects of her prayer were very different from those which she had previously been accustomed to experience. She could only draw comparisons, despite the fact that for such visions, no comparison is much to the point. This is what she was told later by Peter of Alcantara and other learned men. Of all the kinds of visions it is this kind in which the devil has the least power of interference.

Though this type of vision is not seen with the eyes either of the body or of the soul, since it is not an imaginary vision, yet the seer knows with utmost certainty that the Lord is present. Neither is it like the consciousness of the presence of God which is experienced in the prayer of union or the prayer of quiet. Though these are lofty forms of prayer and come from God, they are not visions. In a vision the soul distinctly sees that Jesus Christ, the Son of the Virgin, is present. In this experience, besides receiving the influences that come with the prayer of union, the soul finds that the sacred humanity becomes its companion and is pleased to grant it favors.[38] This knowledge implanted deep within the soul is impressed in such a way that the truth of it cannot be doubted.

There is another way in which the Lord instructs the soul with such a celestial language that it is difficult to explain it; one needs to experience it to understand it. The Lord introduces into the inmost part of the soul what he wishes that soul to understand, and presents it as an intellectual vision—a vision, that is, which is not communicated by means of images, symbols, or words of any kind. The soul here does nothing and accomplishes nothing—the whole thing is the work of the Lord.[39]

> It is like one who, without having learned anything, or having taken the slightest trouble in order to learn to read, or even having ever studied, finds himself in possession of all existing knowledge; he has no idea how or whence it has come, since he has never done any work, even so much as was necessary for the learning of the alphabet.
>
> This last comparison, I think, furnishes some sort of explanation of this heavenly gift, for the soul suddenly finds itself learned, and the mystery of the Most Holy Trinity, together with other lofty things, is so clearly explained to it that there is no theologian with whom it would not have the boldness to contend in defence of the truth of these marvels. So astounded is the soul at what has happened to it that a single one of these favours suffices to change it altogether and make it love nothing save him who, without any labour on its part, renders it capable of receiving such great blessings, and communicates secrets to it and treats it with such friendship and love as is impossible to describe.[40]

St Teresa says some of the favors bestowed upon the soul are so wonderful in themselves that only someone with a lively faith could believe them. She, therefore, limited herself to revealing only a few of these favors, and these because she thought they would be of benefit to others, and would show the method and the road by which the Lord had led her, for that is the subject on which she had been commanded to write.[41]

It seemed to Teresa that it was the Lord's will for the soul to have some idea of what was happening in heaven, and, just as the souls in heaven understand one another without speaking, even so do God and the soul understand each other now, simply because God's will is that this be so. No other means is necessary to express the mutual love of these two friends.[42]

One night, when Teresa was so unwell that she had meant to excuse herself from mental prayer, she took a rosary, so as to occupy herself in vocal prayer, trying not to be recollected in mind.

> But, when the Lord wills it otherwise, such efforts are of little avail. I had been in that condition only a very short time when there came to me a spiritual impulse of such vehemence that resistance to it was impossible. I thought I was being carried up to heaven: the first persons I saw there were my father and mother, and such great things happened in so short a time—no longer than it would take to repeat an *Ave Maria*—that I was completely lost to myself. . . .[43]

As time progressed, the Lord continued to show her further great secrets. Though the soul may wish to see more than is pictured to it, she wrote, there is no way in which it may do so.[44] When speaking of imaginary visions, she says that one has to look at such a vision when the Lord is pleased to reveal it to us. Nor is there any possibility of subtracting from it or adding to it; nor any way in which one can obtain it, or look at it when one likes, or refrain from looking at it. If she tried to look at any particular part of it, she at once lost the vision:

> Though I saw that he was speaking to me, and though I was looking upon that great beauty of his, and experiencing the sweetness with which he uttered those words—sometimes stern words—with that most lovely and divine mouth, and though, too, I was extremely desirous of observing the colour of his eyes, or his height, so that I should be able to describe it, I have never been sufficiently worthy to see this, nor has it been of any use for me to attempt to do so; if I tried, I lost the vision altogether. Though I sometimes see him looking at me compassionately, his gaze has such power that my soul cannot endure it and remains in so sublime a rapture that it loses this beauteous vision in order to have the greater fruition of it all. So there is no question here of wanting to see the vision. It is clear that the Lord wants of us only humility and shame, our acceptance of what is given us and our praise of its Giver.[45]

She claimed that this refers to all visions, none excepted. There is nothing one can do about them; one cannot see more or less of them at will; neither can one call them up nor banish them by one's own efforts. It is the Lord's will that the person see quite clearly that they are produced, not by the soul, but by the Lord. Still less can one be proud of them; on the contrary, they make one humble and fearful, because they make one realize that these favors and this grace can be withdrawn by God, with the result that the soul is completely lost.[46]

Almost invariably the Lord showed himself to her in his resurrection body, and it was this way also that she saw him in the host. Only occasionally, to strengthen her in her tribulation, did he show her his wounds, and he would appear sometimes as he was on the cross and sometimes as in the garden. She always considered these visions a great favor from the Lord, a great treasure; and often the Lord himself would reassure her about them. She found her love for Christ growing exceedingly, and she would go to him and tell him of her trials—not least the trials that came from telling the visions to others—and he would comfort and strengthen her.[47]

A long time after the Lord had granted her many of the favors she describes in her *Life*, together with other very great ones, she was

> at prayer one day when suddenly, without knowing how, I found myself, as I thought, plunged right into hell. I realized that it was the Lord's will that I should see the place which the devils had prepared for me there and which I had merited for my sins . . . The entrance, I thought, resembled a

> very long, narrow passage, like a furnace, very low, dark and closely confined; the ground seemed to be full of water which looked like filthy, evil-smelling mud, and in it were many wicked-looking reptiles. At the end there was a hollow place scooped out of a wall, like a cupboard, and it was here that I found myself in close confinement. But the sight of all this was pleasant by comparison with what I felt there...
>
> My feelings . . . could not possibly be exaggerated, nor can anyone understand them. I felt a fire within my soul the nature of which I am utterly incapable of describing. . . . To say that it is as if the soul were continually being torn from the body is very little, for that would mean that one's life was being taken by another; whereas in this case it is the soul itself that is tearing itself to pieces. The fact is that I cannot find words to describe that interior fire and that despair, which is greater than the most grievous tortures and pains . . . I felt . . . as if I were being both burned and dismembered; and I repeat that that interior fire and despair are the worst things of all.[48]

Teresa considered this vision one of the most signal favors the Lord had bestowed upon her. She said that to read a description of it is nothing compared to the reality. It is like a picture set against reality, and any burning on earth is a small matter compared with that fire. This vision was of the greatest benefit to her, for not only did it take from her all fear of the tribulations and disappointments of this life, but it also gave her the strength to suffer them and to give thanks to the Lord who had delivered her from such terrible and never-ending torments. It seemed to her that anything we can suffer here on earth is wholly trivial compared with what we deserve to suffer, and that if we complain we do so without reason.[49]

One day when she was at prayer, the Lord revealed to her nothing but his hands, the beauty of which was indescribably great. A few days later she also saw his divine face, which seemed to leave her completely absorbed. She could not understand at first why the Lord revealed himself gradually like that, since he was later to grant her the favor of seeing him wholly, but then she realized that his majesty was leading her according to her natural weakness. So much glory all at once would have been more than she could have endured, and knowing this, the Lord prepared her for it by degrees. The saint explained the matter to her confessor in this way:

> Your Reverence may suppose that it would have needed no great effort to behold those hands and that beauteous face. But there is such beauty about glorified bodies that the glory which illumines them throws all who look upon such supernatural loveliness into confusion...

> . . . I will only say that, if there were nothing else in Heaven to delight the eyes but the extreme beauty of the glorified bodies there, that alone would be the greatest bliss. A most especial bliss, then, will it be to us when we see the humanity of Jesus Christ . . . .[50]

In the imaginary visions, our Lord revealed to St Teresa that he is both man and God. Sometimes he would come with such majesty that no one could doubt he was the Lord. Christ was pleased to reveal the power of his sacred humanity in union with his divinity—a clear picture of what the Day of Judgment will be like. Though the intellectual vision is a higher form of vision and reveals God without presenting any image of him, yet, if the memory of the vision is to last and if the thoughts are to be well-occupied, it is a great thing that the divine Presence should be presented to the imagination and should remain within it. St Teresa claimed that these two kinds of visions almost invariably occur simultaneously, and, as they come in this way, the eyes of the soul see the excellence and the beauty and the glory of the most holy humanity.[51]

In explaining why the Lord granted her so many favors in this life Teresa said,

> For His Majesty can do nothing greater for us than grant us a life which is an imitation of that lived by his beloved Son. I feel certain, therefore, that these favours are given us to strengthen our weakness . . . so that we may be able to imitate him in his great sufferings.
>
> We always find that those who walked closest to Christ Our Lord were those who had to bear the greatest trials. Consider the trials suffered by his glorious Mother and by the glorious apostles. How do you suppose Saint Paul could endure such terrible trials? . . . I am very fond of the story of how, when Saint Peter was fleeing from prison, Our Lord appeared to him and told him to go back to Rome and be crucified . . . How did Saint Peter feel after receiving this favor from the Lord? And what did he do? He went straight to his death; and the Lord showed him no small mercy in providing someone to kill him.[52]

When she herself was dying, her sisters begged her earnestly to speak to them some word for their profit:

> . . . and she said that she entreated them, for the love of God, to keep strictly to their Rule and Constitutions. There was nothing that she wished to add to this.[53]

Shortly afterwards, at nine o'clock in the evening on the fourth of October 1582,

> . . . she breathed forth her soul so gently that it was difficult to tell the precise moment, it was just as they had often seen her in the highest prayer. Her face was gloriously young and beautiful. The little sigh that escaped her lips was like the sound they had heard so many nights during the summer. . . . When she sighed her last, one of the sisters saw something like a white dove pass from her mouth. And while Sister Catalina de la Concepción, who was very holy and had less than a year to live, was sitting by the low window opening on the cloister by La Madre's cell, she heard a noise as of a throng of joyful and hilarious people making merry, and then saw innumerable resplendent persons, all dressed in white, pass the cloister and into the room of the dying saint, where the nuns gathered about her seemed but a handful in comparison; and then all advanced toward the bed. And this was the moment when Teresa died.[54]

CONCLUSION

Though there are many ways to perfection, there is only one Way, Jesus Christ our Lord. St Teresa's way included visions and revelations. It was through visions and revelations that this bride of Christ was instructed, humbled, and made perfect. But these were only means to an end and should not be confused with the end. Perfection does not consist in extraordinary phenomena but in the closeness of conformity between our will and the will of God. Everyone is led by a different path but the three essentials common to all paths are prayer, humility and self-knowledge, and the love of God and neighbor.

NOTES

In the following notes, the works of St. Teresa are quoted in the translation of E. Allison Peers and are cited according to the following abbreviations:

Life—The Life of the Holy Mother Teresa of Jesus in E. Allison Peers, *The Complete Works of Saint Teresa of Jesus* (London/New York, 1944) I. 1–300.

Relations—Spiritual Relations Addressed by Saint Teresa of Jesus to Her Confessors in *ibid.* I. 304–17.

Perfection—Book Called Way of Perfection in *ibid.* II. 1–186.

Castle—Interior Castle (*The Mansions*) in *ibid.* II. 187–351.

Foundations—Book of the Foundations in *ibid.* III. 1–206.

1. *Life*, I. 54–55.
2. *Life*, I. 50.
3. *Life*, I. 55.
4. *Life*, I. 58.
5. *Life*, I. 139.
6. *Life*, I. 139–40.
7. *Life*, I. 137.
8. *Castle*, II. 304.
9. Cf. *Castle*, II. 307: 'By meditation I mean prolonged reasoning with the under-

standing'. In using the term 'meditation' in this way, St Teresa stands within the whole medieval monastic tradition.

10. *Castle*, II. 306.
11. *Castle*, II. 307.
12. *Castle*, II. 307.
13. For those who may be unfamiliar with the seven mansions, the seven stages of prayer of St Teresa, the sixth mansion is the spiritual betrothal and the seventh mansion is the spiritual marriage. These last two, of course, are the higest stages of mystical prayer. For further materials on this matter, the reader may be referred to the excellent summary in the relevant chapter of E. Allison Peers', ***Studies in the Spanish*** *Mystics: Volume I* (London, 1927; second edition 1951).
14. *Castle*, II. 304.
15. *Life*, I. 138.
16. *Life*, I. 141.
17. *Life*, I. 273.
18. *Life*, I. 59. Cf. also *ibid*., 197–98 and *Perfection* II. 169–70.
19. *Castle*, II. 209.
20. *Foundations*, III. 23.
21. *Castle*, II. 208–9.
22. *Castle*, II. 209.
23. *Life*, I. 74.
24. *Life*, I. 76.
25. *Life*, I. 74. This is presumably a reference to Philippians 4:13, unless she is attributing our Lord's words in Matthew 19:26 to St Paul.
26. *Life*, I. 75.
27. *Castle*, II. 323.
28. *Life*, I. 290.
29. *Life*, I. 290.
30. *Life*, I. 291.
31. *Relations*, I. 319.
32. *Life*, I. 115.
33. *Life*, I. 156–7.
34. *Life*, I. 157–8.
35. *Castle*, II. 281.
36. *Castle*, II. 282.
37. *Life*, I. 170.
38. *Life*, I. 171.
39. *Life*, I. 172.
40. *Life*, I. 173.
41. *Ibid*.
42. *Life*, I. 173–4
43. *Life*, I. 267.
44. *Ibid*.
45. *Life*, I. 187–8
46. *Ibid*.
47. *Life*, I. 187–8.
48. *Life*, I. 215–16
49. *Life*, I. 217.
50. *Life*, I. 179.
51. *Life*, I. 181–83.
52. *Castle*, II. 345.
53. The Venerable Ana de San Bartolomé, *The Last Acts of the Life of Saint Teresa*, translated in Peers, III: 361.
54. Walsh, William Thomas, *Saint Teresa of Avila* (Milwaukee, 1944) 580.

The Foundations of Mystical Prayer: Teresa of Jesus

Keith J. Egan

TERESA OF AVILA, a woman whose inspiration for the reform of her order came from the carmelite hermits of the thirteenth century,[1] lived in an age that straddled the medieval and the modern. Since her time she has been a central figure in the roman catholic understanding of the mystical life. Now, in the wake of the four-hundredth anniversary of her death, October 1982, it is apparent that Teresa of Jesus is becoming a classical figure and writer not only throughout Roman Catholicism but well beyond even christian circles. Like the classics, the works of this woman of the Spanish Golden Era have become ageless and crossed many boundaries. To commemorate the fourth centenary of the death of Teresa, who died on the feast of St Francis, 4 October 1582[2] Pope John Paul II travelled to Avila, her hometown. There, in a homily on 1 November 1982, he paid special attention to St Teresa as a christian woman:

> Dear brothers and sisters, we have recalled the luminous and ever present figure of Teresa of Jesus the daughter singularly loved by the divine wisdom, God's vagabond, the reformer of Carmel, Spain's glory and a light to holy Church, an honor to Christian women, a distinguished presence in universal culture.[3]

Earlier in the same address the pope made an extraordinary claim for Teresa of Jesus: 'Among the holy women of the church's history, Teresa of Avila is undoubtedly she who responded to Christ with greatest fervor of heart. . .'.[4]

Doña Teresa de Ahumada, known from the time of her first foundation in 1562 as Teresa de Jesús[5] was the granddaughter of a jewish Christian of Toledo who was reconciled with the church and moved to Avila after an alleged relapse into judaizing.[6] Nonetheless, his granddaughter became very conscious of her place as a woman of this church. Those at her deathbed heard her remark in various ways the sentiment that sums up the meaning of her life: 'Finally, Lord, I die a daughter of the church'.[7] Though her writings betray a denigration of women, resulting from what John Paul II has described as a 'time of accentuated anti-feminism',[8] Teresa rose on occasion to eloquent eulogies of womanhood.[9]

Born in 1515, Teresa entered the carmelite monastery of the Incarnation at Avila in 1535. For almost twenty years she lived a prayerful, although not a fully satisfying religious life in a very large community. At the age of thirty-nine she experienced a conversion that initiated a lifetime's journey in the mystical life. In 1562 Teresa made her first foundation, San José in Avila. Before she died, she had made sixteen more foundations for carmelite nuns besides fostering some fifteen foundations of carmelite friars during the same period. After her death the church quickly honored Teresa with beatification in 1614 and with canonization in 1622, on the same day that it so honored Saints Isidore the Farmer, Ignatius of Loyola, Francis Xavier, and Philip Neri. Moreover, in 1617 the Spanish Cortes chose Teresa as patroness of Spain.[10] Finally, on 27 September 1970 Pope Paul VI declared Teresa of Jesus to be the first woman doctor of the Roman Catholic Church.[11]

The modern world has come to know Teresa of Jesus through her writings, chiefly through those in which she presented descriptions of her own experience and also provided guidance for the sisters of her reformed monasteries; namely, *The Book of Her Life, The Way of Perfection,* and *The Interior Castle.* The last named is the concern of this paper; in fact, we shall specifically focus on the first three Mansions of *The Interior Castle.*[12] Teresa of Jesus composed *The Interior Castle* in 1577, a year of illness and a very troublesome time for her reform,[13] just five years before she died. It is estimated that, from the time she began this book, on 2 June, the feast of the Holy Trinity, until she completed it on 29 November, Teresa effectively had only two months to work on what has come to be acknowledged as her masterpiece.[14] Because the *Book of Her Life* had been in the hands of the Inquisition since 1576,[15] she was ordered by her friend and advisor, Father Jerome Gracián, to whom she had made a vow of obedience in 1575,[16] to write another book. He instructed her to '. . . put down the doctrine in a general way without naming the one to whom the things you mention there happened'.[17] Gracián's directive accounts for the narrative of *The Interior Castle* being in the third person, a fact that ought not becloud the autobiographical character of this book.

Teresa's audience in *The Interior Castle* is her carmelite sisters. On the reverse side of the first page of her manuscript she writes: 'This treatise, called "Interior Castle", was written by Teresa of Jesus, nun of Our Lady of Mount

Carmel, to her sisters and daughters, the Discalced Carmelite nuns.'[18] Moreover, in her prologue, Teresa writes:

> The one who ordered me to write told me that the nuns in these monasteries of our Lady of Mt. Carmel need someone to answer their questions about prayer and that he thought they would better understand the language used between women, and that because of the love they bore me they would pay more attention to what I would tell them.[19]

Teresa's intention of writing for her nuns needs to be kept in mind. Their life as enclosed women living in solitude with a commitment to asceticism and regular periods of prayer is the special context to which Teresa directed herself. Though she did not by any means reserve solitude, asceticism, or even mystical prayer to nuns, monks, or friars,[20] *The Interior Castle* must be read in the light of Teresa's intended audience.

Teresa's theme in *The Interior Castle* is clear from the quotation from the prologue above. In another statement in the prologue, Teresa wrote: 'Not many things that I have been ordered to do under obedience have been as difficult for me as is this present task of writing about prayer'.[21] Yet Teresa's doctrine of prayer here and elsewhere goes far beyond instruction in the techniques of prayer. She speaks rather of God becoming active in prayer in accord with St Paul's doctrine: '. . . the Spirit himself intercedes for us with sighs too deep for words'.[22] Only a week after she finished *The Interior Castle*, Teresa wrote to the Jesuit Gaspar de Salazar to say that this book '. . . does not treat of anything other than that which He is'.[23] *The Interior Castle* is about God and God's activity, first through ordinary grace (described in Mansions One–Three) and more spectacularly through what Teresa calls supernatural grace (described in Mansions Four–Seven). More on this point later, but, for the present, let me say that I speak of mansions in this essay as a translation for Teresa's *moradas* rather than accept the suggestion of Kavanaugh and Rodriguez that this word be translated as dwelling places.[24] With an appreciation for their arguments in favor of dwelling places, I demur. For me the King James' and Douay's translation of the greek text's *μοναί* and the latin Vulgate's *mansiones* as mansions has a richness that conveys Teresa's notion of the soul (castle) as spacious, with not just a few rooms but more like a 'million' of them.[25] Teresa said: '. . . the soul must always be considered as plentiful, spacious, and large',[26] with a 'marvellous capacity'.[27] True enough, mansions refer to rooms within the spacious castle. However, the metaphorical character of the room itself should not be curtailed. In addition, the translation of *moradas* by E. Allison Peers has extended the classical rendering of mansions from John 14:2 of the King James and Douay versions into the modern spiritual vocabulary. There is something to be said for the symbolic power that has thus been achieved for the modern reader of *The Interior Castle*.

It must be admitted that *The Interior Castle* is best known for Teresa's uncommon descriptions of the stages of the mystical life, that is, what is contained in Mansions Four–Seven. Moreover, Teresa herself dashed through the first three Mansions and hurried along to the later. In the translation of *The Interior Castle* published by the Institute of Carmelite Studies, a uniformly printed text without any notes at the bottom of its pages, Mansions Four–Seven take up 137 pages while only 30 pages are devoted to Mansions One–Three.[28] The first three Mansions thus constitute only eighteen percent of the text, excluding the prologue and the epilogue. On the other hand, Teresa devoted eighty-two percent of the text to her descriptions of the mystical or, in her word, supernatural life contained in Mansions Four–Seven. Why explore the earlier Mansions when Teresa herself did not give them evenhanded attention? Why look at Mansions One–Three when modern readers seem less concerned about them than they are about the later Mansions? Teresa of Jesus saw the virtuous and prayerful christian life as both a prelude to the mystical journey and at the same time a description of the good christian life as far as one can advance with the help of ordinary grace. It seems to me that we ought to pay more attention to the first three Mansions precisely because they are a prelude to the mystical graces and also because they describe a life of ordinary and therefore usual spiritual achievement.[29] In regard to the latter, it helps to know more about what we can do and what God can do. We need to be able to recognize the difference. Teresa of Jesus is a gifted narrator of both ways. Closer attention to Mansions One–Three increases our understanding of the way of ordinary grace and human response. It also puts into sharper relief Teresa's description of the mystical or supernatural way of Mansions Four–Seven.

CONTEXT FOR MANSIONS ONE–THREE

The Book of Her Life

The reader of Mansions One–Three has to keep in mind that Teresa covers there in abbreviated form ground given much more extensive treatment in her previous writings. The earlier texts, especially certain sections of them, constitute a necessary background and context for the briefer treatment in Mansions One–Three of the non-mystical stages of Teresa's journey to God. The first broader treatment of these stages appears in *The Book of Her Life*.

Chapters One–Nine of *The Book of Her Life* describe Teresa's own good, virtuous, and prayerful life until the time of her conversion at the age of thirty-nine. Chapter nine is the story of this conversion at the time God broke into her life to give her what she sought, life. Teresa closed chapter eight with the lament: 'I wanted to live—for I well understood that I was not living but was struggling with a shadow of death—but I had no one to give me life. . . '.[30] Signs of this new life are the 'supernatural' favors that she experienced. In chapter ten Teresa speaks of these favors and says: 'I believe they call the experience "mystical theology".'[31]

Chapters eleven–twenty-two constitute a Treatise on Prayer which Teresa inserted into *The Book of Her Life*. She used in this treatise the now classical imagery of the four waters to demonstrate the growing activity of God in the life of prayer. The first waters, chapters eleven–thirteen, are equivalent to the content of Mansions one–three of *The Interior Castle*. The stage of the first waters is characterized by human but graced effort. Like drawing water from a well, praying is hard work. Teresa says: 'Beginners in prayer, we can say, are those who draw water from the well. This involves a lot of work on their own part. . . '.[32] It is at this stage that one practises 'discursive reflection'[33] or, if one is like Teresa, a prayer that does not require much reasoning. For her this prayer is a simple attention to the presence of Christ within, a picturing of Christ present.[34] She calls this prayer elsewhere the prayer of recollection.[35] More precisely, it is the prayer of active recollection.

Chapters one–nine and eleven–thirteen of *The Book of Her Life* describe what Teresa did on her own with the help of ordinary grace in her journey to God.[36] This good and prayerful life she lived in her monastery until she was thirty-nine, when the new life she was seeking was given her by God with absolute gratuity. When she returns to the story of her life after the Treatise on Prayer, Teresa emphasizes that all was changed with this gift from God:

> This is another, new book from here on—I mean another, new life. The life dealt with up to this point was mine; the one I lived from the point where I began to explain these things about prayer is the one God lived in me. . . .[37]

These chapters of *The Book of Her Life* tell the story of how Teresa lived before God began to visit her regularly with mystical experiences in prayer. There she recounts her struggles and conflicts and her inability to give herself to God completely.[38] She could do only so much, and all she could do was not sufficient to obtain for her the gift of life which she so earnestly desired. Life on her own consisted for Teresa in the acquisition of virtue and perseverance in prayer.[39] It was a kind of life but nothing like what she experienced once God entered her life more fully. These years of effort provided for Teresa the background out of which she was able, when she took up this task in the first three Mansions, to pass on more concisely advice to those who set out on the inner journey. That is why it is necessary to make one's way through chapters one–nine, and eleven–thirteen of *The Book of Her Life* in order to understand Mansions one–three.

THE WAY OF PERFECTION

Another task awaits one who wishes to understand more fully Teresa's brief threatment of the non-mystical spirituality of Mansions one–three: to become acquainted with Teresa's *The Way of Perfection*, where for the most part, except for chapters thirty–thirty-one in which Teresa treats the Prayer of Quiet, she covers stages of the spiritual life equivalent to those in Mansions one–three. Teresa herself was aware of the issue raised by her writing *The Interior Castle* after she has already covered much of this ground elsewhere. Typically, she faced the problem head-on. In the prologue to *The Interior Castle* she says:

> Indeed, I don't think I have much more to say than what I've said in other things they ordered me to write; rather I fear that the things I write about will be nearly all alike. I'm, literally, just like the parrots that are taught to speak; they know no more than what they hear or are shown, and they often repeat it. If the Lord wants me to say something new, His Majesty will provide. Or, he will be pleased to make me remember what I have said at other times, for I would be happy even with this. My memory is so poor that I would be glad if I could repeat, in case they've been lost, some of the things which I was told were well said.[40]

In fact, Teresa did have 'something new' to say in *The Interior Castle* and she said in a new way much of what she had said before. What is new, for sure, in *The Interior Castle* is her description of spiritual marriage, a grace that she had received only in November 1572.[41] Moreover, Teresa speaks with new vigorous imagery in *The Interior Castle* of the Prayer of Quiet.[42]

In *The Way of Perfection*, Teresa stayed rather close to the fundamentals of the spiritual growth of the carmelite nuns of her reform. Her confessor at the time, Domingo Báñez, did not consider *The Book of Her Life* suitable reading for the nuns of Teresa's first foundation, San José at Avila, not because of faulty doctrine but seemingly because the book might be open to misrepresentation.[43] In answer to Báñez's objection, Teresa composed for these sisters a very down-to-earth book about 'ordinary things',[44] a book which she referred to as her little book (*librillo*).[45] *The Way of Perfection* is very much a handbook on the rudiments of cloistered carmelite life. It was written explicitly for the sisters at San José in Avila[46] but it served as a primer on this way of life for subsequent foundations of Teresa's reform.

Teresa of Jesus began *The Way of Perfection* with a statement to the effect that her new foundation at Avila was a response to the needs of a troubled church.[47] She then moved into a discussion of the foundations of the spiritual life of the reform: 'three things', she says, 'which are from our own constitutions.'[48] She went on to enumerate these three foundations of prayer in the carmelite cloister:

> The first of these is love for one another; the second is detachment from all created things; the third is true humility, which, even though I speak of it last, is the main practice and embraces all the others.[49]

These three foundations for a life of prayer in the solitude of a monastery of carmelite nuns are elaborated extensively by Teresa in chapters four–fifteen of *The Way*. In Mansions one–three Teresa endorsed the virtues of detachment and humility as essential to these stages of the spiritual life. In Mansions one–three, however, she did not elaborate on the necessity and nature of the love for one another that she so strongly emphasized in *The Way*. Why? Teresa insisted in Mansions one–three that '. . . true perfection consists in love of God and neighbor . . .'.[50] She omitted in the Mansions this particularized treatment of love for one another probably because she presumed the nuns had access to *The Way*, the first redaction of which was completed probably no later than 1566.[51] By 1577, when she wrote *The Interior Castle*, Teresa could also have been aware of a wider interest in her writings. She may well have decided not to be so specific in the Mansions about the kind of love needed among the enclosed sisters so that she could also include in her purview others who were interested in her doctrine. Thus the second redaction of *The Way* is less intimate with her sisters than the original.[52] Mansions one–three, moreover, do take into account laypersons who take up the inner journey of prayer.[53].

There are numerous other themes in *The Way of Perfection*, with much on prayer, e.g., she teaches her way of (active) recollection in chapters twenty-eight–twenty-nine. *The Way* also contains in chapters twenty-seven–forty-two, her commentary on The Lord's Prayer, an enterprise that puts her into a long tradition of christian commentators on this central prayer of the christian life.[54] In *The Way* Teresa also gives advice on the diverse paths of prayer taken even within the enclosed monastery. God gives contemplation or mystical prayer to those whom he chooses and may not grant it to enclosed nuns. Yet, Teresa, who always cared deeply about her readers, reassured them, when she said:

> Be sure that if you do what lies in your power, preparing yourselves for contemplation with the perfection mentioned, and that if he doesn't give it to you (and I believe he will give it if detachment and humility are truly present), he will save this gift for you so as to grant it to you all at once in heaven.[55]

The Way of Perfection was written for the nuns of her first monastery who had no sophisticated training. The direct and simple book covers the basics of the spiritual life of these nuns. It is a life that may well be a prelude to mystical graces. Certainly this life is a struggle to live in conformity with the will of God. In *The Way*, as in her other writings, Teresa does not see holiness as constituted by mystical graces and certainly not in the phenomena of mysticism.[56] For Teresa holiness is living the will of God.[57]

The Book of Her Life and *The Way of Perfection* constitute the context for reading Mansions one–three: *The Life* out of a largely autobiographical approach and *The Way* in a didactic fashion. These two books provide extensive treatment for what is rather more briefly presented in Mansions one–three. The cursory doctrine of Mansions one–three takes on flesh and blood and comes fully alive only if one comes to these Mansions after a careful scrutiny of the previous texts. The fuller and less hurried treatments in these books are, I think, necessary formation for the reader of Mansions one–three. Although these first Mansions seem lackluster in comparison with Mansions four–seven and, in fact, pale in the light of the later Mansions as the human pales before the divine, they have, nonetheless, a sparkle all their own.

MANSIONS ONE–THREE

Even though my emphasis has been on the need to come to Mansions one–three by way of Teresa's earlier writings, I am not suggesting that these Mansions have no independent meaning. While Teresa was anxious to move on to the story of God's supernatural activity in human life, she had a profound respect for those who entered the castle through the door of 'prayer and reflection',[58] but have not experienced mystical favors. Those in the early Mansions live in an '. . . upright and well-ordered way both in body and soul . . .'.[59] The Third Mansions constitute the good, mature christian life, deepened by the practice of the prayer of active recollection. Life in the Third Mansions has all the fullness that ordinary grace and human effort can achieve. It is, indeed, the good life.[60]

In Mansions one–three Teresa characterizes this good life as rooted in humility and self-knowledge and detachment. Humility, as it has been throughout the history of christian spirituality, was the foundation of spiritual growth for Teresa of Jesus. 'With humility present', she says, 'this stage [Third Mansions] is a most excellent one. If humility is lacking, we will remain here our whole life. . . .'[61] Humility is, then, the *sine qua non* for Mansions one–three, the prelude to union with God in the mystical life. In Mansions one–three Teresa gives special attention to self-knowledge, and in Mansions one–three she connects self-knowledge with humility. Thus Teresa stresses that 'knowing ourselves is something so important that I wouldn't want any relaxation ever in this regard, however high you may have climbed into the heavens. While we are on this earth nothing is more important to us than humility.'[62] She adds: 'Because elsewhere I have said a great deal about the harm done to us by our failure to understand well this humility and self-knowledge, I'll tell you no more about it here, even though this self-knowledge is the most important thing for us.'[63] Yet knowledge of self is incomplete unless we '. . . strive to know God'.[64]

Along with self-knowledge and humility Teresa calls for detachment. In the Third Mansions we hear her say: 'There is no doubt that if a person perseveres in this nakedness and detachment from all worldly things he will reach his goal'.[65] In Mansions one–three Teresa puts emphasis on other virtues, such as obedience; however, for her, humility and detachment constitute the true prelude to mystical prayer. This is a point that she makes in the Fourth Mansions:

> I really believe that whoever humbles himself and is detached—I mean in fact because the detachment and humility must not be just in our thoughts —for they often deceive us—but complete—will receive the favor of this water from the Lord and many other favors that we don't know how to desire.[66]

Summaries of the content of Mansions one–three can be read elsewhere,[67] and limitations of space make one here impossible. Yet no one should leave the subject of Mansions one–three without remarking on the beautiful and positive anthropology which Teresa of Jesus articulates in the first two Mansions and which is the foundation for the journey to God, mystical or otherwise. Listen to Teresa's anthropology:

> I don't find anything comparable to the magnificent beauty of a soul and its marvelous capacity. Indeed, our intellects, however keen, can hardly comprehend it, just as they cannot comprehend God; but He Himself says that He created us in His own image and likeness.[68]

For Teresa the soul is a 'beautiful and delightful castle. . .,'[69] and the human person has '. . . so rich a nature and the power to converse with none other than God. . . .'[70] She was lyrical about the beauty of this castle, the soul:

> Before going on I want to say that you should consider what it would mean to this so brilliantly shining and beautiful castle, this pearl from the Orient, this tree of life planted in the very waters of life—that is, in God—to fall into mortal sin.[71]

Teresa of Jesus spoke of sin in a way alien to our current sensibilities. Yet, she did so in the context of a positive and rich anthropology that is entirely faithful to the jewish-christian tradition of accepting the human person as created in the image and likeness of God.

We have argued that, in order to understand Mansions one–three, we need to know their context and background. However, the deceptive brevity of the first three Mansions and the exciting character of the later Mansions should not sidetrack us from a meticulous study on their own of these foundational Mansions. A re-reading of these early Mansions produces things new and old that reveal what a gifted and perceptive spiritual writer Teresa of Jesus was.

MANSIONS ONE–THREE
RECAPITULATION, ANAGOGY, AND ESCHATOLOGY

Mansions one–three do not and cannot stand entirely on their own, just as no segment of reality does. This is much more than a question of general relatedness. Teresa of Jesus in *The Interior Castle* describes a recapitulative journey, one in which each stage is a step forward into a new reality, but at the same time each gathers up all that has been. The meaning of the lower stages of the journey emerges from the horizons and perspectives of the new and higher stages. A few examples from other sources may throw some light on what happens in the evolving Mansions of *The Interior Castle*. Dante's *Commedia* is one example of the recapitulative character of such a journey. The *Inferno* is not fully understood until one has journeyed through the *Purgatorio* and the *Paradiso*.[72] In the anagogical interpretation of reality and of Scripture as it developed under the influence of Pseudo-Dionysius in the twelfth century,[73] the end gives meaning to all that precedes it. Contemporary theology speaks of the eschatological perspective in somewhat the same way.

In like manner, Mansions one–three, which describe the life of the good, spiritually mature Christian who enters within to pray, who is humble and detached, can be understood fully only from the perspective of the rest of the journey to God, as described in Mansions four–seven. The beginning stages of the journey to God are illuminated by the gifts and the charisms of the later Mansions.

Teresa's delightful and colorful comparison of *contentos* with *gustos* is an example of the later stages giving understanding to the earlier and the higher illuminating the lower. In her discussion of the Fourth Mansions where 'supernatural experiences begin',[74] Teresa tells us that *contentos* describes the happiness that comes from what is well done through graced human effort. She says:

> . . . the term 'consolations' [*contentos*], I think, can be given to those experiences we ourselves acquire through our own meditation and petitions to the Lord, those that proceed from our own nature—although God in the end does have a hand in them; for it must be understood, in whatever I say, that without Him we can do nothing.[75]

'In sum', Teresa goes on, 'joyful consolations [*contentos*] in prayer have their beginning in our own human nature and end in God.' *Contentos* describes the joy that comes 'during meditation'[76] in the life of those who have not been gifted with the favors of the higher Mansions. From the perspective of the Fourth Mansions Teresa speaks of the earlier Mansions:

> For the most part, the souls in the previous dwelling places are the ones who have these devout feelings, for these souls work almost continually with the intellect, engaging in discursive thought and meditation. And they do well because nothing further has been given them. . . .[77]

The origin of *gustos*, however, are divine not human:

> The spiritual delights [*gustos*] begin in God, but human nature feels and enjoys them as much as it does those I mentioned—and much more. O Jesus, how I long to know how to explain this! For I discern, I think, a very recognizable difference, but I don't have the knowledge to be able to explain myself. May the Lord do so.[78]

Mansions four–seven are filled with *gustos* and with the lively images through which Teresa attempts to hint at what God begins and does in the mystical life. These *gustos*, by comparison, help us to understand the *contentos* of Mansions one–three where the good life of the prayerful, humble, and detached Christian is a happy, but not a supernatural or mystical, life. *Gustos*, in Teresa's vocabulary, is what is supernatural, what God alone can do, what is impossible for the human person on her own.[79] What is divine thus gives meaning to what is human.

Ultimately, spiritual marriage in the Seventh Mansions provides meaning to the rest of the journey, not only for the recipient but for the rest of the community of believers and for all who look to such a journey for further understanding of human existence. Spiritual marriage, union with God in love as described in the Seventh Mansions, is a gift for all, giving meaning to the lives of others and, as Teresa says, calling forth praise from all of us.[80] This union with God in love celebrated in the symbolism of mystical marriage opens up meaning for all who seek God, and in a special way helps one to understand Mansions one–three.

CONCLUSION

Mansions one–three describe the foundations of mystical prayer and at the same time describe the mature christian life that is informed by interior prayer, humility, and detachment. To understand these stages of the journey to God, one needs to have travelled through much of *The Book of Her Life* and *The Way of Perfection*, to have dialogued with the text of Mansions one–three, and to be willing to let the meaning of these Mansions unfold more fully as one travels through Mansions four–seven. Although Teresa cast no aspersions on the mature, non-mystical, christian life of Mansions one–three, the perspective from which she composed these Mansions was clearly the mystical or supernatural. In Mansions one–three Teresa of Jesus primarily presented the foundations of mystical prayer. For Teresa these Mansions are the usual introduction to the mystically favored life; indeed, for her Mansions one–three were the prelude to mystically gifted prayer.

NOTES

1. *Way of Perfection*, 11.4, 13.6; *Book of Foundations* (Peers, volume 3) p. 66. Unless otherwise noted, the following english translation of the writings of Teresa of Jesus is used: K. Kavanaugh and O. Rodriguez, trans., *The Collected Works of St. Teresa of Avila*, 2 vols. (Washington D. C.: Institute of Carmelite Studies, 1976, 1980). When necessary, the following english translation is used: E. Allison Peers, trans., *The Complete Works of St Teresa of Jesus*, 3 vols. (London: Sheed and Ward, 1946). Spanish edition: Efrén de la Madre de Dios and Otger Steggink, edd., Santa Teresa de Jesús, *Obras Completas*, Biblioteca de Autores Cristianos (6th ed., Madrid: La Editorial Católica, 1979).

2. With the introduction in 1582 into Spain of the Gregorian Calendar, the day following October 4 became October 15, the feast day of St Teresa.

3. *Origins* [National Catholic News Service weekly] 12 (11 November 1982), 360; see also *L'Osservatore Romano* (Weekly edition in English), (29 November 1982), p. 4.

4. *Origins*, p. 359; *L'Osservatore Romano*, p. 4.

5. Efrén de la Madre de Dios and Otger Steggink, *Tiempo y Vida de Santa Teresa*, Biblioteca de Autores Cristianos 2d. ed., (Madrid: La Editorial Católica, 1977) 237.

6. *Ibid.*, pp. 4–5. On Teresa's jewish heritage see *Horizons* 11 (1984) 163–4.
7. *Ibid.*, pp. 983–4.
8. *Origins*, p. 359; *L'Osservatore Romano*, p. 4.
9. *Way of Perfection*, 3, 7; *Foundations* (Peers p. 98).
10. 'Chronologia de Santa Teresa', *Obras Completas*, pp. 16–24.
11. On Teresa's doctorate, see Karl Rahner, 'Teresa of Ávila: Doctor of the Church', *Opportunities for Faith*, tr. E. Quinn (New York: Seabury, 1974) 123–6, and Keith J. Egan, 'The Significance for Theology of the Doctor of the Church: Teresa of Avila', in R. Masson, ed., *The Pedagogy of God's Image*; Essays on Symbol and the Religious Imagination (Chico, CA: Scholars Press, 1982) 153–71.
12. For an introduction to *The Interior Castle*, see Keith J. Egan, 'A Castle for these Times; *The Interior Castle'*, J. May, ed., *The Bent World; Essays on Religion and Culture* (Chico, CA: Scholars Press, 1981) 95–107.
13. *Obras Completas*, p. 363.
14. *Ibid.*
15. *Ibid.*
16. *Ibid.*, p. 21.
17. *Interior Castle*, Introduction, p. 263.
18. *Interior Castle* (Peers II: 199, n. 1).
19. *Interior Castle*, Prologue 4.
20. *Interior Castle*, 3.1.5.
21. *Interior Castle*, Prologue, 4 and 1.
22. Romans 8: 26–7. See George MacRae, 'Romans 8:26–27', *Interpretation* 34 (1980) 288–92.
23. Letter 209 (7 December 1577): *Obras Completas*, p. 886 n. 10.
24. *Collected Works*, 2: 484.
25. *Interior Castle*, 1.2.12.
26. *Ibid.*, 1.2.8.
27. *Ibid.*, 1.1.1.
28. *Collected Works*, 2.
29. *Interior Castle*, 3.1.5, where Teresa says that she believes that 'many in the world' dwell in Mansions Three.
30. *Book of Her Life*, 8.12.
31. *Ibid.*, 10.1.
32. *Ibid.*, 11.9.
33. *Ibid.*, 13.11.
34. *Ibid.* and 12.2–4.
35. *Way of Perfection*, 28–9.
36. *Book of Her Life*, 11.9.
37. *Ibid.*, 23.1.
38. *Ibid.*, 9.8.
39. *Ibid.*, 7.2, 8.10.
40. *Interior Castle*, Prologue, 2.
41. *Spiritual Testimonies*, 31.
42. *Interior Castle*, Mansions 4.
43. *Way of Perfection*, Introduction, p. 15.
44. *Way of Perfection*, Prologue, 3.
45. Letter 288 (22 July 1579); *Obras Completas*, p. 972; and Spiritual Testimony, 53a, p. 476, n. 8.
46. *Way of Perfection*, Prologue 1.
47. *Way of Perfection*, 1–4.1.
48. *Ibid.*, 4, 4. The primitive Constitutions of St Teresa have not survived. See *Obras Completas*, p. 633.
49. *Way of Perfection*, 4.4.
50. *Interior Castle*, 1.2.17. See also 1, 2, 18: 'This mutual love is so important that I would never want it to be forgotten'.

51. *Way of Perfection*, Introduction, p. 17.
52. *Ibid.*
53. *Interior Castle*, 3.1.5.
54. Jean Carmignac, *Recherches sur le 'Notre Père'* (Paris: Letouzey et Ané, 1969) p. 387, n. 5.
55. *Way of Perfection*, 17.7.
56. *Interior Castle*, 6.9.16.
57. *Ibid.*, 2.1.8; 3.2.4; 5.2.10; 5.3.5 and 7.
58. *Ibid.*, 1.1.7.
59. *Ibid.*, 3.2.1.
60. Ernest Larkin compares Mansions Three to Kohlberg's conventional morality. 'Saint Teresa and Women's Liberation', *Sisters Today* 45 (1974) 566, 568.
61. *Interior Castle*, 3.2.9.
62. *Ibid.*, 1.2.9.
63. *Ibid.*, 1.2.13.
64. *Ibid.*, 1.2.9.
65. *Ibid.*, 3.1.8.
66. *Ibid.*, 4.2.10.
67. See Kieran Kavanaugh's Introduction to *The Interior Castle, Collected Works*, 2: 270–8.
68. *Interior Castle*, 1.1.1.
69. *Ibid.*, 1.1.5.
70. *Ibid.*, 1.1.6.
71. *Ibid.*, 1.2.1. See also 7.1.1, and Epilogue 3.
72. Keith J. Egan, 'Dante's Divine Comedy: an Introduction to Medieval Theology,' *Horizons* 4 (1977) 90.
73. M.-D. Chenu, *Nature, Man, and Society in the Twelfth Century*, tr. J. Taylor and L. K. Little (Chicago: University of Chicago Press, 1968) 123–4.
74. *Interior Castle*, 4.1.1.
75. *Ibid.*, 4.1.4.
76. *Ibid.*, 4.1.6.
77. *Ibid.*
78. *Ibid.*, 4.1.4.
79. For what Teresa means by supernatural see *Interior Castle*, 1.2.7 and Spiritual Testimony 59. 2 and 3.
80. *Interior Castle*, 7.1.1.

St Teresa of Avila: A Guide for Travel Inward

Margaret Dorgan

ON 27 SEPTEMBER 1970, St Teresa of Avila, foundress of the Discalced Carmelite reform, was the first woman to be declared a Doctor of the Church. One of the most fascinating of christian mystics, her marvelous sense of language and right-on-target humor bring her down from the rarefied realms of ecstasy and rapture where artists like Bernini have loved to place her. Far from flying high above us, Teresa is the kind of saint and guide that wants to pluck our sleeves and hold us by any hook that is effective.

In her writings, she enters at once into a conversation with her reader. Her works, then, have the advantages and disadvantages of a style close to ordinary speech. Actually, the written Spanish of her sixteenth century had not developed to the level of sophistication of French or English. The masterworks of Spanish literature at that time are lonely examples in an unpopulated field, not crowding on each other as in some nearby european cultures. A language still in its primitive stage has a raw, elemental quality that gives more scope to an untrained mind like Teresa's. She was not urged to imitate a prevailing style as the nineteenth-century french Carmelite Thérèse of Lisieux was unhappily forced to do in the sentimental, artificial phrases of her bourgeois middle class.

Teresa's spontaneity, her disregard of capitalization and punctuation, the obvious urgency to compress what she had to say into time stolen from work—all contributed to the freshness of her message. Her digressions are not leisurely meanderings, mere wordiness, but are based on her quick, alert realization that other important points should be made. She rarely apologizes for her parenthetical observations, for she saw them as necessary threads woven into the whole cloth of her message. Not to have said them would have left the fabric incomplete. When she adds 'May God deliver us from foolish devotions',[1] we can see her press harder on her pen.

Her letters contain the full sparkle of humor and the flow of her affection, as well as thrusts of anger and impatience. The more formal works, addressed for the most part to her nuns, seem patterned on the letters. For all her disclaimers about being a woman, she shows how much she cherished the company of the women who joined her in the carmelite reform. It was obviously a source of joy for her that her daughters, while detached in regard to almost all created beings, were not detached in their love for *la Madre*.

She never lost sight of her potential readers. In Teresa's writing, we sense a kind of personal imperative that says in each line: I'm writing this because it's so important for you. Without psychological training or even familiarity with the appropriate terms of her own day, this unlearned spanish nun devised images and amazingly apt descriptive phrases for inner experience. Her unique empathetic capacities helped her put into words the whole flow of human longings, apprehensions, and subtle subterfuges. She could describe psychological states at firsthand, not clinically, but with the sympathy of a friend who tells us that whatever we are going through can be used for the Lord.

She invites us to an interior journey: 'Turn your eyes inward and look within yourself. . .'.[2] Once we have taken the first step, she urges us to keep moving. When we stop, it is only for the sake of taking stock of where we have arrived. We check our supplies and pause to make sure we are traveling in the correct direction.

> It is very important for you to know that you are on the right road. When a traveler is told that he has made a mistake and lost his way, he is made to go from one end to another, and all his searching for the way tires him, and he wastes time and arrives late.[3]

The beginning she tells us is 'the most important part for everything'.[4] Later she insists:

> They [those who want to pray] must have a great and very resolute determination to persevere until reaching the end, come what may, happen what may, whatever work is involved, whatever criticism arises. . .[5]

Travelers on this road of prayer are to stay en route even "if the whole world collapses."[6]

She lists the objections to praying. These warning spanish voices have their echo today.

> 'There are dangers'; so-and-so went astray by such means'; 'this other one was deceived'; '. . . it's not for women, for they will be susceptible to illusions.'[7]

At this point in *The Way of Perfection*, Teresa dismisses the protesters, but as the work progressed, she was to take up their arguments and deal with them in detail. Here, however, she wanted to instill confidence in the value of praying. It is food for the journey; further on she would explain where to find the best nourishment and what should be avoided. But for now, 'Should anyone tell you that prayer is dangerous, consider him the real danger and run from him'.[8]

At the same time, she urged discrimination. In Teresa's day, as in our own, purveyors of spirituality offered a variety of wares. In spite of the Inquisition or perhaps to some extent because of it, quack mysticism flourished —sometimes in an ecclesiastical underground and sometimes in the open. The pathetic Alumbrados and Illuminati were hounded by church officials once their presence was uncovered. Yet bizarre experiences, especially when accompanied by extraordinary phenomena like levitation, attracted throngs of admirers who flocked to convents or other centers where such happenings occurred. In a country with one-quarter of the population vowed to the church as priests or religious,[9] the very atmosphere was electric with spiritual enthusiasm. That Teresa could walk a path of common sense and intense religious fervor is all the more remarkable. We can be grateful for her careful sifting out of the counterfeit in order to preserve the genuine.

Popularity and widespread acceptance, she says shrewdly, are no indication of authentic spirituality.

> Never pay attention to the opinion of the crowd. Behold these are not the times to believe everyone; believe only those who you see are walking in conformity with Christ's life.[10]

The last simple statement embodies the two strict empirical criteria that Teresa consistently applied to any spiritual experience:

(1) The focus should be on Christ or on some aspect of reality related to him.

> O Lord, how true that all harm comes to us from not keeping our eyes fixed on You; . . . we meet with a thousand falls and obstacles and lose the way because we don't keep our eyes . . . on the true way.[11]

(2) The worth of prayer is guaranteed not by the form it takes but by the increase of virtue that flows from it.

> In humility, mortification, detachment and the other virtues there is always greater security.[12]

Careful as she was to test the validity of experience, still she urged us to dare to seek living experiential contact with God. It is not enough simply to know about him; through love we enter into vital union with the Lord. Some of us will be offered the inebriating wine of this union; none of us will be refused drink for our thirst.

Especially for persons who are beginning to pray, Teresa urged contact with those who have had experience. While the great reformer of Carmel is usually quoted as preferring a learned director to one with experience, she made no such choice at the start of the spiritual life. 'I say that if these learned men do not practise prayer their learning is of little help to beginners.'[13] She recognized that 'the beginner needs counsel so as to see what helps him most'. Without experience, a person giving advice 'can be greatly mistaken and lead a soul without understanding it or allowing it to understand itself'.[14].

Years later, when she was writing her final work on prayer, ***The Interior Castle***, she affirmed the same need: '. . . in my opinion, it is very important to consult persons with experience'. But at the end of her life, she realized the difficulty of finding such pesons and added, 'Provided that we don't give up, the Lord will guide everything for our benefit, even though we may not find someone to teach us'.[15] For many people, direction cannot be an on-going person-to-person relationship because the experienced director, though sought, will not be found. Direction will have to come through other avenues. Teresa has provided one such avenue in her writings.

The busy foundress often complained about the toil of writing when she had other things to do. But later reflecting on what she had written, she noted with honesty that it was bound to be helpful to others. She even ruefully mentioned she wished she herself had been given such assistance when she needed it.[16]

> Although when I began writing this book I am sending you I did so with the aversion I mentioned in the beginning, now that I am finished I admit the work has brought me much happiness, and I consider the labor, though I confess it was small, well spent.
>
> If you find something good in the way I have explained this to you, believe that indeed His Majesty said it so as to make you happy . . .[17]

Reluctant as she was to take up her pen, Teresa left behind a corpus of writing that covers all the stages of prayer. The pages of her works are like the gathering of many candles. Wherever we are in the spiritual life, we can select the particular tapers that cast light on our personal difficulties. She is famous for her penetrating chapters on contemplation, which for Teresa always signified the infused, mystic favor. But she deserves as much gratitude for her practical advice about non-contemplative forms of prayer.

> It is important to understand that God doesn't lead all by one path, and perhaps the one who thinks she is walking along a very lowly path is in fact higher in the eyes of the Lord.
>
> So, not because all in this house practise prayer must all be contemplatives; that's impossible. And it would be very distressing for the one who isn't a contemplative if she didn't understand the truth that to be a contemplative is a gift from God; and since being one isn't necessary for salvation, nor does God demand this, she shouldn't think anyone will demand it of her.[18]

In looking at the non-contemplative way, Teresa suggested that because the traveling is harder, more merit might be gained. '. . . the Lord leads her as one who is strong. . . .'[19]

She then considered those who cannot even meditate and are at a loss to pray other than vocally.

> I know an elderly person who lives a good life, is penitential and an excellent servant of God, who has spent many hours for many years in vocal prayer, but in mental prayer she's helpless; the most she can do is go slowly in reciting the vocal prayers. There are a number of other persons of this kind. If humility is present, I don't believe they will be any the worse off in the end but will be very much the equals of those who receive many delights; and in a way they will be more secure. . . .[20]

Contemplative prayer, then, is not guaranteed to all. Spiritual authors who offer a universal invitation to passive experience would find no support in her careful instruction.

> Those who do not receive these delights walk with humility, suspecting that this lack is their own fault, always concerned about making progress . . . . And perhaps they are much more advanced. . . . There is nothing to fear; don't be afraid that you will fail to reach the perfection of those who are very contemplative.[21]

Teresa's caution, however, is directed both ways. We cannot force open the door to contemplation. To attempt to do so would be to lose whatever prayer we have and to gain nothing for the loss. At the same time, we must be ready to walk through that door when we see the Lord has set it ajar in the small beginning of infused prayer which is passive recollection.

> I don't say that we shouldn't try; on the contrary, we should try everything. What I am saying is that this is not a matter of your choosing but of the Lord's.[22]

Leaving the matter to God, we are willing to meet him in whatever contact he arranges.

> The judgments are His, there's no reason for us to become involved in them. It is good that the choice is not up to us, for then—since contemplation seems a more restful path—we would all be great contemplatives.[23]

Yet everyone will not become a contemplative, and for those who do not taste passive prayer Teresa offered many positive, reassuring statements about the prayer that can move with ease from one thought of God to another. Of this way of praying which is within our power to do, she writes:

> There is nothing for me to say to anyone who can form the habit of following this method of prayer [meditation], or who has already formed it, for by means of so good a path the Lord will draw him to the haven of light. . . . All who are able to walk along this path will have rest and security, for when the intellect is bound one proceeds peacefully.[24]

The great spanish mystic esteemed this kind of prayer-through-thinking because she saw it as a way of truth. 'Let truth dwell in your hearts as it should through meditation . . .'.[25] The pondering of divine realities keeps the mind occupied and less susceptible to illusion. Distractions are warded off through the protective shield of reflections.

Though she valued meditation prayer, she admitted she had little facility for this process. 'God didn't give me talent for discursive thought or for a profitable use of the imagination.'[26] Not being able to think holy thoughts about God during prayer, Teresa substituted for her own sluggish thinking the words of a book. This gave her roaming mind some kind of focus.

She stated that 'this way of inability to work discursively with the intellect [is] most laborious and painful', and yet she pointed out 'if one perseveres, one reaches contemplation more quickly'.[27] Perseverance will be at cost, however; dryness and distractions often weigh down the pray-er. Teresa wisely advised special care to keep the conscience pure: the inability to use the mind actively during prayer makes the inner attention vulnerable to anything that enslaves the heart. Attachments for such pray-ers, then, become the source of a wearisome bombardment that exhausts and harries.

Authentic spirituality walks a sober path from prayer in the thinking, discursive mode to simplified awareness of God, not of the self. Here love and understanding are purged together. As the mind deals less and less with distinct ideas, the heart is urged to let go of selfish delights.

Distractions are experienced but not in the way they are encountered by someone who holds on to self-centered satisfactions. Wandering thoughts buzz obtrusively like flying insects that bite, then wing off. They tend not to gather around a particular target which the pray-er can honestly identify as something he or she strongly covets.

Of the mercurial flow of fancies not based on a disordered will, Teresa wrote:

> Whoever experiences the affliction these distractions cause will see that they are not his fault; he should not grow anxious, which makes things worse, or tire himself trying to put order into something that at the time doesn't have any, that is, his mind. He should just pray as best he can; . . . This advice now is for persons who are careful. . . .[28]

The afflictive restlessness often gives way to deepening calm; and even if the whirl of wandering impressions returns, the pray-er senses that peace is being estabished within him or her at a depth far below the surface. The presence of God during ordinary times of the day taps at the attention, arousing a longing for him. Recollection becomes more continuous. New resources of virtue and discernment are evident in behavior. Here we are in the region of Simple Regard, which is either the prelude to contemplation or the onset of that infused gift in its first purifying phase.

While every subsequent historical period has had its particular preference for Teresa as guide and teacher, today's special interest seems to be this spiritual territory covered by simplified prayer. The mystic of Avila has carefully delineated the peaks and valleys of the passageway between the discursive and the infused—as well as the ditches where a traveler can get stuck. Her pages describing this transition should be well thumbed by contemporary spiritual directors and by those who find themselves described.

Words from the past, when spoken with Teresa's impassioned insight into the mysteries of the spirit, have perennial power to inflame and enlighten. Much contemporary writing seems lukewarm and cloudy in comparison with the old castilian fires that burn so intensely in her lines.

She is a guide for the heights, those moments on the mount of unitive embrace; for the lowlands, when we wonder if we can ever climb up again; for the plateaux, when we would just as soon set up a tent and stop moving. In every situation, positive or negative, Teresa is with us, urging us to see where we are as simply another starting point for further journeying inward to God.

And if [a] person should do no more than take one step, the step will contain in itself so much power that he will not have to fear losing it, nor will he fail to be very well paid.[29]

NOTES

All references to the writings of St. Teresa of Avila are taken from *The Collected Works of St. Teresa of Avila*, trans. by Kieran Kavanaugh and Otilio Rodriguez, Washington, ICS Publications.

Volume One (1976): *The Book of Her Life*; *Spiritual Testimonies*; *Soliloquies*

Volume Two (1980): *The Way of Perfection*; *Meditation on the Song of Songs*; *The Interior Castle*

1. *Life*, 13.16; p. 94.
2. *Way*, 29.2; p. 146.
3. *Ibid*., 22.3; pp. 122, 123.
4. *Ibid*., 20.3; p. 115.
5. *Ibid*., 21.2; pp. 117, 118.
6. *Ibid*.
7. *Ibid*.
8. *Ibid*., 21.7; p. 119.
9. See Reginald Trevor Davies, *The Golden Century of Spain* (London, 1937) 289.
10. *Way*, 22.10; p. 121.
11. *Ibid*., 16.11; p. 97.
12. *Ibid*. 17.4; p. 100.
13. *Life*, 13.16; p. 94.
14. *Ibid*., 13.14; p. 94.
15. *Interior Castle* 2.1.10; p. 303.
16. *Life*, 14.7; p. 99: 'To see itself described brings it intense joy, and then it sees clearly the path it is walking on. It is a great good to know what one must do in order to advance in any of these stages. For I have suffered much and have lost a great deal of time for not knowing what to do. . . .'
17. *Interior Castle*, Epilogue, 1, 3; pp. 451, 452.
18. *Way*, 17.2; p. 99.
19. *Ibid*.
20. *Ibid*., 3; pp. 99, 100.
21. *Ibid*., 4; p. 100.
22. *Ibid*., 7; p. 101.
23. *Ibid*.
24. *Ibid*., 19.1; p. 106.
25. *Ibid*., 20.4; p. 115.
26. *Life*, 5.7; p. 44.
27. *Ibid*.
28. *Way*, 24.5; pp. 129, 130.
29. *Ibid*., 20.3; p. 115.

Two Faces of Christ: Jeanne de Chantal

Wendy M. Wright

'MT CALVARY IS the Academy of Love,'[1] her spiritual director and intimate friend, François de Sales, had written. And this indeed is what Jeanne de Chantal discovered. In the confluence of two vivid images of Christ—the crucified and the beloved—this early seventeenth-century contemplative found a voice for her longings, a direction for her energy and a vehicle for her spirit's soaring.

It will be the purpose of this essay to explore the ways in which this one woman's life experience was made fruitful by being articulated through these two dimensions of Christ passed on by the christian contemplative tradition. It is not intended to be primarily a study of her spiritual teachings, nor is it first and foremost a biographical sketch set in the context of the historical era in which she lived. It will, rather, attempt to probe the hidden recesses that lay between the outer and inner experience of this one individual and touch upon the role that Christ as crucified and Christ as beloved played there.

HER LIFE

Jeanne François Frémyot de Chantal[2] was born into a prominent family of Dijon in the year 1572. These were years in France when the lines between Catholics and Protestants were sharply drawn. The serious religious orthodoxy of the family household was a formative influence on her young character. She was to remain all her life a devout Catholic. Jeanne was an attractive, proud, capable and firm-willed young woman with a wide capacity for loyalty and affection. Left motherless as a child she was raised by a father who saw to it that her practical abilities, resourcefulness, and intelligence were cultivated. A lively zest for life combined in her with an innate reflectiveness which could at times become a brooding inwardness. Most of all, Jeanne felt life vividly. Of all that could be said of her, the intensity and immediacy of her feeling is very important, for it was around this that her spiritual journey revolved. Her feeling was not sentimentality but a vast reservoir of response and reflection which seems always to have been available to her and which made it impossible for her to take her experiences lightly and made it possible for her to plumb the depths of those experiences.

She is somewhat unusual in the annals of female contemplatives because in the course of her life she successfully negotiated a wide variety of feminine roles—roles that we would consider both traditional and nontraditional for a pre-twentieth-century woman. In her early years she accepted without hesitation the idea that her place in life was to be wife and mother. In her social position this entailed being an educated, cultivated individual who was capable of managing the affairs of large estates and multiple households, attending to the education of children and the needs of the local population, and fulfilling the social obligations that accompany such a position. She was married to a young baron—Christophe de Rabutin Baron de Chantal—for whom she had immense affection and respect. They enjoyed a full and compatible relationship. She bore him six children, the first two of whom died at birth. The remaining children she treasured and attended with great energy and concern.

But she was not destined to occupy these traditional roles for long. After eight years of marriage her husband was killed in a hunting accident, leaving the shattered fragments of her life to be arranged in a new way. It was at this time that she began to conceive the possibility of a new self, a self still shadowy and undefined but whose central tenet would be dedication to a life lived solely for God. Long solitary walks produced in her the desire to receive some sort of guidance in the interior life and, after an unsuccessful attempt to find help from a local priest, she came under the tutelage of François de Sales, a charismatic young savoyard bishop whose direct and heartfelt preaching was gaining attention all over France. She became his spiritual daughter. Recognizing the religious depth of this young widow, François de Sales for several years acted as her guide in the inner life, not superimposing his own personality on hers but helping her discover her own gift, gently directing her away from all that seemed to hinder her flowering, giving her confidence in her own emerging self. During this time she lived in difficult circumstances—with her children in the home of her father-in-law, a household tyrannized by the will of a housekeeper who dominated the elderly man and resented the intruding Baroness and her offspring. She spent the time giving abundantly of herself to her children and to the poor and convalescent in the vicinity. In these same years she managed to settle the troubled estate of her late husband and, without much help from family members or others, provide for the futures of her children.

After these years in which she was cast as the obedient daughter to the principle men in her life, Jeanne de Chantal emerged in a new guise. Her mentor revealed to her that he had long had hopes of founding for women a new type of religious community, suitable for those who showed a gift for the radical spiritual demands of the contemplative life but who were not constitutionally suited for the harsh ascetic climate of a reformed convent or interested in the life in a more relaxed house. It would be a community that combined a life of prayer with a life of charitable activity. She was to be its co-founder. She recognized this plan as the fulfillment of her own dreams. So Jeanne became a parent to the new Order of the Visitation of Mary and the spiritual mother of the women who joined her in this new enterprise. A maturity and practical wisdom were required of her now for the founding years of the Order were fraught with difficulties administrative, financial, interpersonal, and spiritual. By the time of her death in 1641 there were over eighty houses of the Order, an indication of her energy, capacity and vision.

It was as superior of the new Order that Jeanne de Chantal came to realize the depth of her own inner resources. She and the small group of women who made up the first generation of Visitandines often met in the garden of their convent in Annecy to discuss with François de Sales the nature of the contemplative life. It was out of these conversations that his great work on spirituality, *The Treatise on the Love of God*, was fashioned. To a large extent, it is Jeanne's book, for it was his contact with her that had first hinted to him of the rich possibilities of the life of prayer and his continuing friendship with her that confirmed those first intimations.[3] She stood in relation to him now less as daughter than as friend, *femme inspiratrice*, and fellow pilgrim. Theirs was a relationship marked by its mutuality, its intimacy, and its warmth.

With her nuns she was both sister and mother. She undertook not only the administration of the Order but its spiritual governance as well.[4] It was she who was most responsible for determining the direction of the community and maintaining it on its course. It was her task to exercise the subtle discrimination required in the spiritual direction of her little band, her task to teach each new superior of a new foundation the pain and joy of spiritual motherhood. She was to achieve wide recognition for her accomplishments. By the end of her life she was admired and her advice sought at all levels of french society.

On the one hand, Jeanne de Chantal's life appears as one of unfolding potential, a life of a woman whose circumstance allowed her to gain the fullness of her own personal vision. While this is true, it is also true that the backdrop behind this vocational scenario was the experience of great personal loss. It should be remembered that this was a woman with deep affection for those closest to her. Life did not spare her grief on that account.

The death of her adored husband was only one in a long series of losses that were to cut cruelly through the fabric of her life. Of her children she lost two infants at birth, a nine-year-old daughter Charlotte to illness, another daughter, and a premature grandchild, in childbirth, her only son to the dark horseman of war. Only one daughter, Françoise, survived her. Other early passings affected her: the death of François de Sales' young sister who had been entrusted to her care; the death of her young son-in-law; the unexpected death of François de Sales himself when he was in his early fifties. She outlived him by almost twenty years. And she bemoaned the fact that she outlived many of her dearest companions; most of the founding members of the Visitation went before her, each mourned with the deep feeling of which she was capable.

To this sad history of loss must be added the experience of loss in the interior life. For the sensible impression of great consolation, warmth, and surety belonged only to the early years of Jeanne's religious pilgrimage. For most of her adult life she suffered from what she called 'temptations', doubts of faith that merged into an intense experience of inner pain and turbulence. But this constant interior suffering was not reflected in her daily life. Her letters, the advice she gave others, the reports of those nearest her suggest that this was a hidden experience. And there is nothing to indicate that her difficulties were a hindrance to her increasing maturity, sensitivity, capability, or capacity to love. Rather, these mysterious and troubling temptations were part of what the christian contemplative tradition calls the 'dark night of the soul', the perceived experience of the loss of God, which, in the understanding of that tradition, is a purifying process that results in a deepening conformity of the individual human nature to the nature of God. It was with this understanding that Jeanne lived in an inner atmosphere of loss.

THE RELIGIOUS MILIEU

From this skeletal portrait of our subject's history we turn to the religious atmosphere that gave shape to her inner life. Jeanne de Chantal lived in France during the early, dynamic years of the Counter-Reformation, years when interest in authentic christian devotion and the integrity of the spiritual life was keen. She derived her concepts of spirituality most particularly from François de Sales. He in his turn drew upon the wide range of christian spiritual writings then circulating in France. He managed to distill the essence of benedictine, augustinian, franciscan, spanish and rhino-flemish sources into an elixir both classic and contemporary in its flavor. He stood firmly within the historical progression of the christian contemplative heritage while at the same time rendering traditional values vital and appropriate to the contemporary situation in which he found himself.[5] The model of the interior life that emerged from this blend is the one through which Jeanne de Chantal achieved personal integrity.

From whatever religious tradition or whatever historical era it emerges, each model of spirituality presents a particular map of the interior landscape. It outlines a particular set of assumptions as to the goal and method of the journeying that must take place there, a particular image of the selfhood that is to be achieved. For the christian contemplative the chief model for the self is Jesus Christ.[6] Most often he is the crucified and risen Christ. It is around this image of dying to an old self and being refashioned to the image of God that the majority of the tradition revolves. A life given to the process that is contemplative prayer is to be a life that conforms more and more to the Christ-image, less and less to the self-willed personality. The experiences of death, of loss, and of abandonment are central to this achievement. In this context, the cross is not some distant, if noteworthy, event but a central dynamic of the life of prayer, an ever-present reality reenacted in the inmost part of the human person: transforming the person into the image of God.

It is this crucified Christ that first and foremost compelled the attention of François de Sales. In a letter to Jeanne in 1607 (when she was living in the world as a widow) he offered the cross as the means by which she was to advance toward the model of selfhood to which she aspired. He wrote in response to her anxiety about her spiritual ills:

> How I desire your consolation, my dear daughter. Provided that it is his divine majesty's pleasure; because if he wishes you to be on the cross, I acquiese to it. And you do too, don't you, my beloved daughter? Yes, I have no doubt. But aren't God's crosses sweet and full of consolation? Yes, provided that one dies there, like the Saviour. So, let us die there, my dear daughter, if it is necessary.[7]

Ten years later he was still impressing upon her, now the Mother Superior of their Order and a woman of emotional and intellectual maturity, the importance of the cross as a means of growth:

> Our Lord loves you, my Mother, he wants you to be completely his. From now on let his arms alone carry you, let his breast and his providence be your resting-place . . . Do not think any more about the friendship in which God has joined us, nor about your children, nor your body, nor your soul, nor indeed anything whatever; for you have given everything to God. Clothe yourself in our crucified Saviour, love him in his suffering, offer up aspirations on this subject.[8]

But there is another face of Christ that was well known to the contemplative tradition and appropriated by François de Sales: Christ as the beloved. From earliest christian times the biblical love poem, the *Song of Songs* had been given various spiritual interpretations.[9] Commentators read in the erotic drama of a betrothed couple the stories of the relationship between God and the church, the Virgin Mary, and/or the individual soul. This last reading, that of the love between God and the soul, was given full expression by Bernard of Clairvaux and his cistercian followers in the twelfth century and from then on it became a standard reading of the text in christian contemplative literature.

The *Song's* sensuous and emotional language became the language of the soul. Desirous of union, seeking the beloved, the soul seeks its God. This lover/beloved relationship became the basis for François de Sales' entire formulation of the christian life. In his *Treatise on the Love of God* he outlined this reciprocal life in eloquent prose. He spoke of the affinity that exists between humans and God.

> The sacred Spouse wished for the kiss of union; oh, she said, 'let him kiss me with the kiss of his mouth'. But is there enough affinity, o well-loved Spouse of the beloved, between you and your loved one to bring to the union you seek? Yes, she says: give it to me, this kiss of union, dear friend of my soul: for your breasts are sweeter than wine, smelling of the sweetest ointments. . . .
>
> So our soul, seeing that nothing can perfectly content her and that her capacity cannot be filled by anything in this world, since her understanding has an infinite inclination to know more and her will an insatiable appetite to love and find the good; does she not have reason to exclaim: Ah, so I am not made for this world! There is some sovereign good on which I depend, some infinite craftsman who has placed in me this endless desire to know and this appetite which cannot be sated. That is why I must yearn and extend toward him, to unite and join myself to the Goodness of him to whom I belong and whose I am! Such is the affinity that we have with God.[10]

Beyond this direct borrowing of imagery from the *Song of Songs* the Bishop of Geneva conceived of love as the means and the end of a life lived fully in Christ. One participates both in the crucifixion and in the love that was the essence of Christ's life on earth. From another letter to Jeanne in 1607:

> Let us be forever attached to the cross and may a hundred thousand arrows pierce our flesh, provided that the burning shaft of the love of God has first pierced our heart. May this arrow make us die that holy death that is worth a thousand lives. I will go, begging the Archer who carries the quiver, through the intercession of St Sebastian whose feast-day we

> celebrate today. Open your heart wide, my dear daughter, and with the love of God as your desire and his glory your aim, live joyously and courageously always. Oh God, how I long for the Saviour's heart to be king of our hearts![11]

EXPERIENCE AND THE IMAGES OF TRADITION

Jeanne de Chantal was the spiritual daughter of the great genevan bishop and breathed with him the same religious atmosphere. For her, as well as for him, the crucified and the beloved were the two faces of Christ that most fully articulated her inner life. But she was quite a different personality from her mentor. Where he was moderate, she was intense, where he was deliberate, she was impulsive. But she was also a woman of great courage and strength of character, whose keen intelligence and practicality qualified her more flamboyant tendencies. She loved unreservedly but not lightly or thoughtlessly. Passion, loyalty, perseverance, devotion all flowed freely and visibly from her towards those she trusted and loved.

She chose as her heroes the early martyrs of the church, feeling a special relationship with those men and women who literally gave up everything for their God. For her, martyrdom was the essence of the christian experience. She spoke to her nuns of the type of martyrdom to which she felt the Order of the Visitation was called. At recreation on a feast-day of St Basil, she informally communicated her thoughts. In her description one can clearly see the interaction of the two Christ motifs that guided her inner imagery.

> 'St Basil, my dear daughters, was not a martyr nor were most of our holy Fathers, the pillars of the church. Why do you suppose this is the case?' After each of us had answered, our blessed Mother said, 'I believe that it is because there is a martyrdom called the martyrdom of love in which God sustains the lives of his servants to make them work for his glory, this makes them martyrs and confessors at the same time. I know that this is the martyrdom to which the Daughters of the Visitation are destined and which God allows to those who are fortunate enough to wish it.' One sister asked her how this martyrdom was achieved. 'Give your absolute consent to God and you will experience it.' She added, 'Divine love thrusts its sword into the most secret and intimate parts of the soul and separates us from our very selves. I know a soul,' she continued, 'whom love had treated in this way so that she felt it more than if a tyrant's sword had separated her body from her soul.' We knew that she was speaking of herself.
>
> Someone asked her if this martyrdom of love could ever equal physical martyrdom. 'Let's not bother about their equality, although I think that

> there is not much difference because love is strong as death and martyrs of love suffer a thousand times more by staying alive to do the will of God than if they had given a thousand lives in witness of their faith, love and loyalty.'[12]

This martyrdom of love made itself known to her in the temptations she suffered for many years. Inner desolation, lack of spiritual consolation, and the experience of hopeful perseverance were subjects upon which she was well suited to elaborate. She spoke of them to her charges when they asked her advice on prayer.

> Do not concern yourselves with your pains or confusion, nor with the dismay or terror that this may cause you although they feel violent or frightening. Instead, look to God patiently and let it be, as our Blessed Father advises: this is an important lesson. Remain steadfast in suffering without reflecting upon what is going on inside you, leave it to God's care without giving it attention; God requires that you sacrifice your Isaac, not once but continually by losing yourself in him. You have only from time to time to say a few words, especially these which are and ought to be your only words: my God, into your hands I commend my spirit, or better: my God, my spirit is in your hands, I no longer see what goes on there, but I leave it all to your care, I no longer desire to give my attention to anything except you alone. . . .
>
> My solace is to have none at all; my death is not to die; my wealth is the poverty and nakedness of the cross where my Saviour died stripped of the consolation of both heaven and earth: this is my path, I do not wish any other.[13]

Loving and dying were the dynamics on which her interior growth was founded. These were her two primary impressions of Christ as well as her two means of self-definition and self-actualization. The beloved and the crucified gave form and content to the event of her interior world. They also supplied meaning to the events of her outward-facing world. In this way they created a unified symbolic field by means of which her life was integrated and transformed.

For Jeanne de Chantal, the central experience of life, both inner and outer, was the experience of relationship. Because of the immediacy of her feeling, her intense commitment to and need for the varied relationships presented to her during her life, this could not be otherwise. She adored her husband, was devoted to her children, and relied upon the friendship, support, and encouragement of François de Sales to an extreme degree. The people closest to her compelled her attention, commanded her love, and bound her to them surely and completely. It was the particular nature of her being to find her self and to grow through relationships. This is not to suggest in any way that her unique unfolding was dominated by or subservient to the others in her life. She did not suffer from a lack of self-determination. Yet she did discover herself through relationships, not outside of them. In the rich texture of interpersonal exchange she was cut and fashioned.

Any evaluation of religious imagery must finally rest upon its ability to give expression creatively to an individual's inner and outer experiences and provide the mechanism to grow through those experiences into a more fully realized sense of one's own potential. One's nascent self must be mirrored and then given the opportunity for expansion. For Jeanne, life was a complex network of love, the revelation of being inexorably joined to others. It was also a painful process of severance, the revelation of that network being broken. When she embraced the contemplative life she embraced a God who proclaimed both the depth of love's potential and the reality of loss of love. She embraced a tradition which had as its central dynamic the very experiences that were primary in her own life.

It was the confluence of her own intimately felt experience of love and death with the highly articulated imagery of love and death found in the contemplative understanding of the crucified and beloved Christ that enabled Jeanne de Chantal to discover her potential for growth, maturity, and wisdom. First, the tradition she embraced placed value upon her capacity to love fully. This is in part because the christian God is perceived as a person with whom one must fashion a relationship, in part because the contemplative tradition has a long history of interpreting that human/divine relationship through the imagery of erotic love, in part because François de Sales himself admired and encouraged her strength of feeling, although he sought to redirect its focus. Thus her emotional predisposition found a home in the tradition.

Similarly, her openness to and need for relationship was called upon. For the contemplative, Christ is not only model of death and resurrection but the object of desire and partner in love. This makes of the Christ-image not only an exemplar to be imitated but a spouse with whom to be intimately related. While it might be questioned if the image of a male is an appropriate model of selfhood for a woman, it is unquestionable that the figure of a spouse is a particularly fertile image through which a woman might articulate her inner life. It should be noted that underpinning the entire marriage drama played out in the commentaries on the *Song of Songs* is the notion, common in western thought, that the soul is feminine. That this notion is implicit in the christian contemplative tradition is seen in the vast monastic literature that describes the soul (men's souls as well as women's) as a desirous bride awaiting the coming of the bridegroom, as well as in the numerous references to the Virgin Mary as the prototype of the soul in relation to God. It is particularly the receptive Mary of the annunciation who provides a prevalent metaphor for the soul.

Jeanne, in the metaphorical language provided by her tradition, was called upon not only to emulate Christ but to love him, to form with him a type of relationship that contained within itself the seeds of new life, of creativity, and of growth. The feminine surrender implied in such marriage symbolism produces an image of the soul not as subservient or oppressed but as potential partner in creation. It is a symbol of mutuality and equality. It is a symbol that can bestow dignity and integrity. Jeanne understood that the dying and rising Christ who was to become the rhythm and source of her own interior music was also the Christ to whom she was betrothed, with whom she brought herself to birth, and whom she bore within herself as a reality yet unborn. This imagery gave full reign to her rich capacity for relationship. Thus her innate mode of being in the world was fully drawn out through the tradition.

However, the Christ-image that she accepted as her model in its crucified form showed her the way in which her feeling and her relationships were to be modulated and recast, ways that her own predispositions would not in all probability have chosen. The image of this forsaken God suggests to its imitators a life that is at once both radically dependent upon the will and destiny of God and radically independent of the usual human supports. This extreme positing of a single-focused dependence requires that the followers of the Crucified slash all ties of relationship that bind them to others or at least reform those relationships so that the single dependence is always uppermost. The deep affections she felt were to be redirected toward one object.

To further this process her mentor taught her a spiritual discipline which entailed a radical death to self—to use his term, annihilation. For all the warmth and familiarity of its language, the fact remains that François de Sales' spiritual teaching is one of the most subtly austere and rigorous teachings of the tradition. His goal was utter denudation (the nakedness of the cross is implied here), his method to strip oneself of all props, inner and outer, and cast oneself unreservedly onto the mercy of God. He counseled indifference, not only to the events of one's life but to the very state and workings of one's own soul. This annihilation was not a passive or fatalistic acceptance of what is, but a daring leap of freedom. It required great love, great capacity for feeling, and immense strength for Jeanne to attempt an authentic enactment of his teaching.

Her deep feeling had to die an anguished death to itself in order for it to discover its own resilience and transcendence. She never ceased to be closely bound to those for whom she was responsible. She was incapable of the type of indifference that springs from either lassitude or self-preoccupation. But she embarked upon the project of re-envisioning her attachments, of slowly, painfully detaching herself from them for their own sakes. She surrendered herself bit by bit, layer by layer, to another relationship which alone could draw from her the immensity of love of which she was becoming capable. She died to herself to discover herself. And in the process the facts of her life, especially the deaths of those whom she loved so dearly, as well as the interior loss she perceived in her 'temptations', were made luminous. This is partly because she was creating a love of wider proportion and greater resilience—a love which could both feel death fully yet transcend death with new vision and power. She was assimilating a religious image—Christ—which became the medium through which she could expand to the farthest perimeters of her own nascent life. Through the love and death proclaimed in the image of self to which she clung, she was able to articulate, widen, and transform the love and death that were the central facts of her experience.

NOTES

1. *Oeuvres de Saint François de Sales. Éditions complète d'après les autographes et les éditions originales.* Par les soins des Religieuses de la Visitation du Premier Monastère d'Annecy, 26 vols. (Annecy, 1892–1932) 5:345.

2. The primary source for the works of Jeanne de Chantal is the eight volume edition, *Sainte Jeanne Franoise Frémyot de Chantal, Sa Vie et Ses Oeuvres*, Édition authentique, Publiée par les soins de Religieuse du Premier Monastère de la Visitation Sainte-Marie d'Annecy (Paris: E. Plon, (1874–1879). See also Wendy Wright, *Bond of Perfection: Jeanne de Chantal and François de Sales.* (New York: Paulist, 1984).

3. There is some debate on the nature of Jeanne's influence on Francois de Sales. On the one extreme, Henri Bremond, the great french scholar of the religious revival of the seventeenth century, who seems to have felt that the spirit of women is dominant in most religious consciousness, gave Jeanne an indispensable place in his vision. Other scholars feel his thought is more his own. It seems more true to their relationship to credit them both in the inspiration of the book. Jeanne, on her part, claimed that the section on prayer was a self-portrait of her mentor. He, on his, recognized the intimacy of their shared vision, for him their hearts were one heart, their souls, one soul.

4. See Émile Bougaud, *Histoire de Sainte Chantal et des Origines de la Visitation*, 2 vols. (Paris, 1863).

5. Francis, Vincent, *Saint François de Sales, Directeur d'Âmes: L'Éducation de la Volonté* (Paris: Beauchesne, 1923).

6. Christ is not the only model for the contemplative process in the west. At times, the Virgin Mary runs a close second and various saints stand as exemplars for contemplatives. Nevertheless, Christ looms always in the background. It is perhaps worth noting that it is not always the crucified Christ that one sees as the center of christian experience. The Eastern Orthodox tradition tends to enshrine the risen Christ and its spirituality reflects this emphasis. In the west, however, it is the crucified that is most visible. The writings of Francis of Assisi, John of the Cross, and Thomas à Kempis exhibit this tendency. For some understanding of differing christian views of the interior landscape see the article 'Âme (Structure d'après les mys-

tiques) in ***Dictionnaire de Spiritualité ascetique et Mystique, doctrine et histoire*** (Paris: G. Beauchesne, 1932–) 1:435–66.

7. François de Sales, *Oeuvres*, 13:294.

8. *Ibid.*, 17:218.

9. See Marvin H. Pope's commentary on the *Song of Songs* in the Anchor Bible series (New York: Doubleday, 1977).

10. François de Sales, *Oeuvres*, 4:76.

11. *Ibid.*, 13:252–53.

12. Jeanne de Chantal, *Sa Vie et Ses Oeuvres*, 1:356–57.

13. *Ibid.*, 3:293–94.

EPILOGUE

Cistercian Monastic Life/Vows: A Vision

Jean-Marie Howe

MONASTIC LIFE-IMMERSION

CISTERCIAN MONASTIC LIFE is an immersion in the Mystery of Christ. It is an immersion of the substance of the person into the substance of the Mystery. One can be penetrated by the Mystery of Christ; one can be transformed and divinized by it. Of course, all life is an immersion in this Mystery; it is not reserved to those in monastic life. Yet, monastic life is rooted in and filled with the Mystery. That is its *raison d'être*.

In cistercian life immersion takes place on several levels. There is what one could call a physical immersion. This is the concrete and basic insertion of the person into the monastic structure, the observance of the Rule and of tradition, interaction in a community founded on monastic norms, the practice of the vows, the exercise of a certain asceticism, participation in the liturgy, the Office, work, prayer, and *lectio divina*. On this level, all the facets of the life are experienced by a person on a more or less exterior or surface level.

Intellectual immersion involves the study of Scripture and monastic doctrine, ranging from the Desert Fathers to the Cittercian Fathers to contemporary theologians and spiritual authors who echo the essence of monastic thought. It complements the previous level and deepens knowledge and understanding.

It is, however, essential to monastic formation that there be a real spiritual immersion, and this spiritual immersion begins with the awakening of the heart. It is in the heart that the whole person can be attained. It is from the heart that the whole person can be transformed. In this context, the heart is to be understood as the center of all the powers of the body and soul, the totality of the human person. It is the primal root of our being. This life of the heart is nurtured and deepened by prayer, *lectio divina*, the liturgical and sacramental life. It is here in the heart that all the various aspects of the monastic experience can be integrated, deepened and assimilated, and then lived out at this much deeper level.

Nevertheless, there is a still deeper level of spiritual life. It is none other than participation in the Mystery of Christ, an immersion in Christ himself. Here there is a profound transformation, a divinization of the whole being. It is toward this level that all the previous levels tend, but it is pure gift, pure mystery.

The fundamental point to be made here is that depth is the key. Everything has levels: prayer, *lectio*, the vows, the Rule, the liturgy; and the human person also has levels. Monastic life can therefore be described as a journey into the depths—going deeper and deeper into our own being and into the realities of the Mystery in which we are immersed.

CONSCIOUSNESS OF IMMERSION

It is one thing to be immersed in a life-style that is rooted in and filled with the Mystery of Christ and quite another thing to be conscious of it. One must really know, really be conscious, that there is a powerful spiritual dynamic inherent in monastic life itself. One must know that simply by being immersed in that life—given certain conditions—one can be transformed. Without consciousness of this truth, one might feel a void and be tempted to fill it with things that, even though they may be positive in themselves, could be quite exterior to the real life that is going on. In that case, it could be possible that the life would have little or no effect on the person. That is why it is so crucial that we be conscious that the Mystery is present and acting in our life. Then it is possible for us to yield to the life and, by so doing, to be immersed ever more deeply in the Mystery and be transformed by it.

Yielding to the Mystery can be compared to taking a journey. The road may often seem to lead nowhere, but we must always keep going. Yielding to the Mystery through the monastic life is a journey that requires fidelity, continuity, trust, and patience. Imperceptibly, immersion deepens and consciousness grows. Even more imperceptibly, transformation can take place.

AWAKENING CONSCIOUSNESS

This consciousness which we have spoken of in the preceding paragraphs is not an intellectual penetration of either the monastic life or the Mystery of Christ. It is a knowledge springing from the heart. It is a consciousness that derives its acuity from a sort of deep connaturality with spiritual realities. It is a consciousness that exists in the human heart, a consciousness that can be awakened and progressively deepened throughout one's life.

Essential to the opening of this consciousness is the awakening and development of a *sens intime*, a deep affinity for spiritual realities. It is here that one finds the aim and goal of both initial and ongoing formation. This *deep affinity* is like a tiny seed lying dormant in our deepest heart. It can be awakened and grow into consciousness that progressively takes over and transforms our being. One could say therefore that consciousness transforms and is itself transformed.

The awakening of this *affinity* is, in effect, the awakening of the heart. It is this that makes a real spiritual journey possible—a journey toward the heart, into it, and through it into a new world; a world where consciousness of reality is other, where one has new eyes, new ears, new thoughts. One exists and moves then in a world that is really different. Thomas Merton speaks of an 'inner transformation, a deepening of consciousness toward an eventual breakthrough and discovery of a transcendent dimension of life beyond that of the ordinary empirical self and of ethical and pious observance'.[1]

POROUSNESS

Transformation through immersion and consciousness depends on our capacity to be penetrated by the Mystery of Christ. Our being, our substance, must be porous in order for the Mystery to enter, to penetrate. That is the crux of the matter. It is not enough simply to be immersed in monastic life. We must let ourselves be plowed so that the furrows of our person become deeper and deeper, so that our earth becomes softer and softer. This is something our being craves, but this plowing is *kenosis* and *kenosis* is not easy.

In the measure that our being becomes porous, open, grace can penetrate us. Depth is possible. Transformation is possible. Thus an ever deepening penetration by the Mystery can fill us with spiritual being.

KENOSIS

Kenosis is the emptying, the death which must precede new life, rebirth. Without *kenosis* there can be no transformation, just as without death there can be no new life. Since transformation is what monastic life is all about, *kenosis* is essential to it, inherent in it. In choosing to live in a monastery, a person chooses to participate in the Mystery of Christ which leads through the cross into the light and life of the resurrection. This passage is the supreme *kenosis* which engages the whole being.

One could say that there is an initial *kenosis* by which one renounces the 'world' in order to enter the monastery. Then there is the continuing *kenosis* implicit in living out the various aspects of monastic life. Finally there is an ultimate *kenosis*—a grace offered to some. This is a point of absolute consciousness, of ultimate liberty, which precedes holocaust and divinization. It is then that *kenosis* becomes *pleroma*.

This preliminary discussion is very important for understanding monastic vows because immersion, depth, and transformation are all key elements inherent in the essence of the vows.

VOWS

This is not a formal study of the vows. It is only an attempt to present a vision of the vows as seen in the context of the benedictine tradition and also as seen in themselves. What is important—and what is perhaps the *leitmotif* of this short article—is that the dynamic of monastic life is transformation and the vows are included in that dynamic.

The vows taken at profession in the benedictine tradition, to which Cistercians belong, are obedience, poverty, chastity, stability and conversion of manners.[2] Although only obedience, stability, and conversion of manners are mentioned explicitly, in the Rule of St Benedict, poverty and chastity have come to be included in the benedictine/cistercian tradition as well as among mendicants. Actually, obedience, poverty and chastity are inseparable, and at a deep level, they are one. In the context of monastic life they are absolutely essential for the experience of God and nothing can be substituted for them. They make our heart, our substance, capable of being penetrated by the Mystery of Christ and they themselves become part of that Mystery. Stability gives continuity and conversion of manners gives depth to our relationship with God. That is why one could say that all these vows are one: union with God.

UNION WITH GOD

The contents of the vows are indispensable to union with God. Poverty, chastity, and obedience are our way of being with God, of being united to him. Stability concerns the continuity of that union and conversion of manners, its depth. The taking of vows and the exercise of those vows are means, but the contents of the vows themselves—poverty, chastity, obedience—have finality. They can become substantial states through the penetration of our heart by the Mystery and as such they are our union with God. If we do not live our vow of poverty, union with God is impossible. If we do not live our vow of chastity, union with God is impossible. If we do not live our vow of obedience, union with God is impossible. Through transformation, poverty can become total loss of self; chastity—energy, fire; obedience—union of wills; stability —duration of union; conversion of manners—depth of union.

TRANSFORMATION/KENOSIS

The vows, as means, are a radical *kenosis*. Each one, in its own way, empties us of self. Thus they can render us porous and penetrable by the Mystery. In this way, they can be transforming. However, they themselves can also be deepened and transformed. The vows, too, have levels.

The vows can reach down into the heart. It is there that poverty can go to terrible depths, as can chastity and obedience. Stability would be continuity in those depths, and conversion of manners their continual deepening. They can take us into the heart of *kenosis* where our immersion in the Mystery of Christ progressively changes into a participation in this Mystery. When transformed, the vows become substantial states.

PERFECTION OR TRANSFORMATION

There seem to be two possible ways of understanding the vows: 1) perfection and 2) transformation. The distinction between the two is a very important one.

1) The vows have often been presented as virtues to be practised more and more perfectly. The perfection of the practice of the vows can become the goal of the spiritual life and thus the principal object of our efforts at conversion. The problem, however, is that this tension toward perfection may well be understood or limited to the perfecting of only one level of the vows: an exterior level with an accent on doing rather than on becoming or being.

2) The vows understood in the light of transformation are something quite different. Here it is a matter of being. The vows, as they are interiorized, deepen our being by taking us into our heart. The Mystery transforms the vows in transforming our being. Vital to the understanding and practice of the vows is radicality, going to the root of the Mystery of Christ. Rigidity is often its substitute. Rigidity is surface strictness; radicality is a life totally immersed in the Mystery, the radicality of *kenosis*, death, and rebirth.

CONVERSION OF MANNERS

The vow of conversion of manners in particular can be understood 1) as a continual effort toward perfection in the practice of the vows and the attainment of virtues, or 2) as a vow of the assimilation of values, a vow of interiority, a vow that aspires toward transformation.

In *The Asian Journal* Thomas Merton wrote:

> When you stop and think a little bit about St. Benedict's concept of *conversio morum*, that most mysterious of our vows, which is actually the most essential, I believe, it can be interpreted as a commitment to total inner transformation of one sort or another—a commitment to become a completely new man. It seems to me that that could be regarded as the end of monastic life. . . .[3]

This vow can be described as a journey into depth, an interiorization, an assimilation which can facilitate transformation. Since it is a vow to go ever deeper into the whole monastic life, it gives depth to poverty, depth to chastity, depth to obedience.

The vow of conversion of manners urges us to go beyond the level of doing in order to penetrate more and more deeply into the realm of being. Only at this level can a substantial transformation of the person take place. Thomas Merton said that this vow is a 'commitment to become a completely new man'; that means rebirth, passage to another order, transformation of being. The dynamism and importance of this vow become most evident when seen in this light.

DEPTH

Each person's being reaches to unfathomable depths. Living in contact with that depth can be a life-time endeavor or a sudden, grace-given entry into it. Depth is essential to transformation and transformation is essential to monastic life. The whole of monastic life is organized to attain this depth, without which there can be no transformation. The monastic life is a journey toward the heart, that which is deepest in us.

We must recognize the value of the different dynamics of monastic life which take us into depth—*kenosis*, assimilation, interiorization—and yield ourselves to them. It is a spiritual endeavor that is eminently dynamic. The static does not lead into depth. Only if we live our life existentially from the level of depth which is ours at a given moment can there be a progressive descent. Our poverty is as deep as our heart. Our chastity is as deep as our heart. Our obedience is as deep as our heart.

CONCLUSION

Monastic life aims at union with God. If we really live that life, if we let ourselves be fully immersed in it, if we allow our substance to become porous and penetrated by the Mystery of Christ present in it, then the life itself can transform us. It can bring us to a certain level of spiritual being, a being that is deeply poor, chaste, and obedient—and it is that being which experiences God.

It becomes obvious, therefore, that our life cannot be reduced to a level of practising vows or acquiring virtues. We must go further. We must, as it were, become the vows that we take, become poor, chaste, obedient.

NOTES

1. Thomas Merton, *The Asian Journal* (New York, New Directions, 1973) 309–10.

2. The vow of obedience implies the renunciation of one's own will. The vow of poverty entails the renunciation of all personal temporal possessions. The vow of chastity implies voluntary celibacy. The vow of stability commits one to remain faithful until death to the community in which one is incorporated by the vow. The vow of conversion of manners is a commitment to the monastic way of life which aspires to spiritual transformation.

3. Thomas Merton, *The Asian Journal* (New York, New Directions, 1973) 337.

AFTERWORD

Concord Homespun

Agnes Day

ETYMOLOGICALLY, *concord* means *with heart*, and surely that aptly describes the dedicated christian women of the past whom we in these essays have called peace weavers. All of them were very strong characters, by nature and by grace. Some of them Balthild, Radegund, Clotilde and others—worked actively to prevent war and unite belligerents, as we see in the first two articles, and in fact the origin of the term 'peace weaver' is to be found in this context. But others did not hesitate to upset what they saw to be false peace: speaking or acting as prophets, antagonizing the self-indulgent and slothful, and rousing the negligent out of their spiritual torpor. To this category belong St Hildegarde, St Elizabeth of Schönau, St Mechthild of Magdeburg, St Catherine of Siena, and, to some extent, St Teresa of Avila, who are the subjects of other studies in this collection. Their common primary interest, though, was the peace of Christ, the reconciliation of man with God through the acceptance of God's ever ready grace, and loving cooperation with his design. Such peace does not come whole or all at once. It is woven by a long series of consents, in the colors of joys or sorrows, as God presents them.

Weaving on a hand loom was a commonplace activity of medieval life, a familiar part of the experience of the women who are the subjects of these essays. It is not so familiar to us, citizens of the computer age, and perhaps not many of us have seen a weaver at work. Weaving is not a quiet, gentle occupation like sewing. It takes strength to set up the loom and pull the warp threads to the proper tension, and the weaving itself is very active. Hand weaving has been compared to organ playing, for although the artist is seated, her hands and feet fly, and her body sways back and forth rhythmically in a great output of energy. Her mind is not idle either, for she has an intricate pattern to follow. It is really an occupation that requires total involvement if it is to produce the desired wholeness and beauty in the union of the disparate. It seems an apt image for the women presented in these articles, who wove with love and prayer on the loom of their lives, reading and following God's master-plan of peace, Jesus, as he revealed himself to them in their hearts. It took everything they had, and they rejoiced to give it.

These were great women, but they were also people very conscious of their personal weaknesses and need for God. They came to see the very lacks in their characters as space for the shuttle of God's power to pass through, carrying the weft thread of his love. This is another side of St Hildegarde, and in fact one preceding and underlying her prophetic activity. She is not unique in this—it is an effect of the life of prayer, and just as characteristic of St Gertrude or Julian of Norwich, leading as a logical consequence to that steadfast faith in divine providence which shone in St Clare and St Jeanne de Chantal.

But how did these women, many of whom were cloistered nuns or recluses, serve the cause of bringing Christ's peace to their fellow men and women? Isn't solitude a strange habitat for an apostle? The answer lies in a paradox. In solitude, solidarity with all humankind is experienced most intensely, and so the burning desire to help everyone can lead to the 'desert', physical or metaphorical. In the solitude of prayer, compassion springs from the inescapable experience of inner poverty in which the contemplative identifies with all her brothers and sisters in their sinfulness and need before God. By the same token, her radical choice of God, and the purification of her heart which he effects, are also in solidarity with all humanity. She heals the wounds of others, as she is herself made whole, by her oneness with them in Christ.

Another way of reaching out to help people, illustrated by these lives, lies in giving spiritual direction or advice. The anchoresses were in an excellent position to do this because they were clearly outside the power structure of society, and their lack of self-interest was obvious. They were able to admonish and console, and their insights, which often came in visions, were accorded a recognized place in a society to which faith was no stranger. Of course the giving of advice was part of the service of non-recluses too. The spoken word, the written word, played their part, given weight by the example of a holy life. Sometimes prophetic dramatization was the medium of a message. Christina Mirabilis, who strikes us as simply bizarre, apparently had such a strong message for her contemporaries which she conveyed primarily by her actions. It is interesting that the study of her life included in this volume ends with an experience of peace and unity among the people crowded at her tomb.

Most of our peacemakers had special tools to help them in their weaving:

vows. Some made only one vow, chastity or virginity. Others made the traditional three vows of religion, and those of the benedictine family added two more; stability and conversion of manners. The emphasis differed—for instance, for St Clare, Lady Poverty was queen; for SS Gertrude and Mechtild von Hackeborn, as followers of St Benedict, obedience held the key position—but for all of them the vows led to the same reality: union with Jesus. In particular, the vows led them to an immersion in the mystery of Jesus on the cross: his absolute fullness of love, his perfect response to the Father's will, and his trust through death. This is where the definitive act of peace weaving was accomplished and is accomplished still, through the members of his Body. Jesus' cross reaches out to the whole world and draws all into unity.

Let us look again at the women weaving, crossing thread over thread thousands upon thousands of times. It takes a lot of patience. The cloth grows slowly, and what is finished is rolled up on the take-up bar. The whole will not be seen until it is cut from the loom and spread out. Growth is the specific focus of articles on Mechthild of Magdeburg and Julian of Norwich, and it is a fascinating subject, because it touches each of us personally. It is the dynamic of life. Growth is hard to see in ourselves, both because we are too close to the process and because we cannot see and can hardly imagine the fullness and integrity the finished whole will have. Though every human tapestry is unique, the consideration of completed patterns can shed light for us on our own, and enlarge our awareness of the interdependence of all of our lives, which are working toward the plenitude of one great whole—'the fullness of him who fills the universe in all its parts' (Eph 1:23).

CONTRIBUTORS

Rita Bradley, sfcc, is Professor of English at St Ambrose College, Davenport, Iowa. She holds M.A. and Ph.D. degrees in English from St Louis University. From 1954 to 1964, she was active in the Sister Formation Movement as founder and editor of the *Sister Formation Bulletin*. She has edited five books and published articles in both scholarly and popular journals. In 1975, she was the co-founder of the *Fourteenth Century English Mystics Newsletter*, now the *Mystics Quarterly*, and continues to be interested in the subjects of women's studies and mysticism.

Charles Cummings, ocso, is a monk of Holy Trinity Abbey, Huntsville, Utah. After completing studies for the priesthood at his monastery, he received a graduate degree in formative spirituality from Duquesne University. In the monastery he serves on the formation team. His article, 'God's "Homely" Love in Julian of Norwich', was published in *Cistercian Studies* in 1978.

Agnes Day, ocso, entered the cistercian Order at Mount Saint Mary's Abbey in Wrentham, Massachusetts in 1956. A graduate of Middlebury College in Vermont, Sr Agnes has been a member of the vocational team for the abbey, and served as the prioress and monastery cobbler before being elected abbess by her community.

Margaret Dorgan, dcm, is a member of St John of the Cross Monastery Hermitage, a small carmelite community near Orland, Maine. The emphasis at this house is on simple contemplative living in rural solitude. A graduate of Radcliffe/Harvard University, Sr Margaret writes for a number of spiritual periodicals. NCR Credence Cassettes has published two sets of her work: *Guidance in Prayer from Three Women Mystics*, and *The Way to Divine Union: Self Direction for Stages of Prayer*.

Keith Egan is director of The Center for Spirituality, Saint Mary's College, Notre Dame, Indiana. He earned an M.A. degree in medieval studies at the Catholic University of America and his Ph.D. in religious history from Cambridge. He is the author of a number of articles on medieval english Carmelites and Teresa of Avila, as well as other subjects.

JEREMY FINNEGAN, OP, is a member of the English Department of Rosary College, River Forest, Illinois. A graduate of the University of Chicago and Yale University, where she received her doctorate, she is the author of *Scholars and Mystics* (Chicago, 1962) as well as numerous articles on medieval literature and contemporary poetry.

FIDELIS HART, OSC, is a Poor Clare nun of the Monastery of St Clare, New Orleans, Louisiana. A Clare since 1952, she holds a bachelor's degree in philosophy from Loyola University (New Orleans), one master's degree in theology and another in religious education from St John's University, New York. Active in formation work within her Order, she is also engaged in spiritual direction and retreat work within her diocese, and is chairperson of the Research Committee of her Poor Clare federation.

BROTHER LAURIN HARTZOG, OCSO, is a cistercian monk of Our Lady of New Clairvaux Abbey in Vina, California. Formerly a member of The Brothers of the Christian Schools, he received undergraduate degrees from Southeastern Louisiana University and the College of Santa Fe, and an M.A. in economics from St. Mary's University, San Antonio, Texas. He serves his community at Vina as bookkeeper, buyer, and spray-rig operator in the orchards.

JEAN-MARIE HOWE, OCSO, is the abbess of Notre-Dame de L'Assomption d'Acadie in Rogersville, New Brunswick. She studied at Queens College and Columbia University where she earned her B.A. and M.S. degrees. She entered monastic life in 1954, and before being elected abbess in 1978 served as novice mistress for many years.

MADGE KARECKI, SSJ-TOSF, lives in a small, intentional community in the inner city of Chicago where she does volunteer work with the mentally disturbed and provides hospitality for 'street people'. She entered the religious life in 1966, and earned her M.A. degree in Franciscan Studies from St Bonaventure University. In addition to teaching novices and directing retreats, she works at writing articles, and is a consulting editor for *The Cord*.

MARGOT KING obtained her Ph.D. at the University of California at Berkeley in Comparative (medieval) Literature in 1967, and her early training at the University of Saskatchewan (B.A.) and the University of Toronto (B.L.S., M.A.). A librarian by profession and mother of three by vocation, she never forgot her early love of medieval monastic spirituality. Arising out of her interest in the largely unknown female eremetical tradition, she has recently been involved in studies and translations of the lives of medieval women saints. As a direct result of this interest, she has begun a new journal called *Vox Benedictina* in which the lives of early benedictine women will be translated and studied.

JEAN LECLERCQ, OSB, is a benedictine monk of the Abbaye Saint-Maur-e-Saint-Maurice, Clervaux, Luxembourg. A professor of the history of medieval spirituality at the Gregorian University, Rome, he is a prodigious author of books and articles, his best-known being *The Love of Learning and the Desire for God* (1961). A listing of his publications to 1973 can be seen in *Bernard of Clairvaux: Studies Presented to Dom Jean Leclercq*.

JANEMARIE LUECKE, OSB, belongs to the benedictine community of Red Plains Priory, Oklahoma City. She has been a professor of English at Oklahoma State University since 1966. Her Ph.D. was earned at Notre Dame University, and her M.A. at Marquette. A versatile writer, she began in journalism, and presently publishes both scholarly and popular articles as well as poetry. She is the author of two books: *Measuring Old English Rhythm: An Application of the Principles of Gregorian Chant Rhythm to the Meter of Beowulf,* and *The Rape of the Sabine Women*, a collection of poems. She has been a leader and lecturer in the women's movement, and in peace and justice activities since the sixties.

JO ANN MCNAMARA is professor of History at Hunter College in New York City, a founding member of the Institute for Research in History, and an active organizer of the Berkshire Conferences on the History of Women. Her research has led her in recent years from the Middle Ages to the early centuries of Christianity. *A New Song: Celibate Women in the First Three Christian Centuries* is now in press. She is working on a sequel covering the fourth and fifth centuries and on a series of translations of the lives of female merovingian saints.

SUSAN MUTO is the Director of the Institute of Formative Spirituality at Duquesne University. She earned her M.A. and Ph.D. degrees in English Literature at the University of Pittsburgh. She is the author or co-author of ten books on christian formation, and the managing editor of two journals, *Studies in Formative Spirituality* and *Envoy*.

BARBARA NEWMAN received her Ph.D. and M. Phil. degrees from the Department of Medieval Studies at Yale. Now an assistant Professor of English at Northwestern University, she is preparing her dissertation, '*O Feminea Forma*: God and Woman in the Works of St. Hildegard (1098–1179)', for press, as well as planning an edition of *Speculum Virginum* (twelfth-century manual for nuns) and book titled *Sophia: A History of Personified Wisdom from Solomon to Suso* for publication.

JOHN A. NICHOLS, professor of History at Slippery Rock University of Pennsylvania, received his Ph.D. in medieval history at Kent State University in 1974. He has published a number of articles on cistercian nuns in medieval England: 'The Internal Organization of English Cistercian Nunneries', *Citeaux* (1979), and 'Medieval English Cistercian Nunneries: Their Art and Physical Remains', *Mélanges Anselme Dimier* (1982). He is currently completing a book on the *Cistercian Nuns of Medieval England*.

COLMAN O'DELL, OCSO, is a nun at the community of Mount Saint Mary's Abbey, Wrentham, Massachusetts where she is an advisor to the junior professed sisters, and a member of the liturgy commission. She was a participant in a symposia for the Benedictine Centenary in 1980, and is the author of several poems and plays. Sr Colman earned her M.S. degree from Pennsylvania State University.

PATRICIA J. F. ROSOF is a member of the Institute for Research in History, and was co-editor of the journal *Trends in History* from 1978–1984. She received her Ph.D. in 1978 from New York University, and is currently teaching at the Hunter College High School in New York. Rosof's most recent article is 'The Anchoretic Bases of the Gilbertine Rule' in the *American Benedictine Review*.

EDITH SCHOLL, OCSO, was educated at the University of Michigan before she entered Mount Saint Mary's Abbey at Wrentham in 1956. Her main interest lies in music in which she is both a talented composer and performer. Her other interests are the history of spirituality and gardening.

LILLIAN THOMAS SHANK, OCSO, is a cistercian nun of Our Lady of the Mississippi Abbey, Dubuque, Iowa. She entred the cistercian Order at Mount Saint Mary's Abbey in Wrentham, Massachusetts, in 1956, and she was sent eight years later to Wrentham's first foundation at Dubuque. She is a graduate of Mount Saint Joseph College near Cincinnati, Ohio, and received her R.N. degree in the Mount Saint Joseph-Good Samaritan Hospital nursing program. She has taught monastic history for the past fourteen years and served her community as infirmarian, prioress, bookkeeper, manager of their candy business, candy cook, and tractor driver on the abbey farm.

FRANCES ANN THOM, OSC, was solemnly professed as a Poor Clare in 1982. She earned M.A. degrees in English from The Catholic University of America, and in Franciscan Studies from St Bonaventure University. She is the author of a number of published poems, and has two books of poetry on St Francis, *Two Prayers for Two Stones* (Herald Press, 1976). She lives in the monastery of St Clare in West Andover, Massachusetts, where she performs office work and is the infirmarian, seamstress, and part-time portress.

SUZANNE F. WEMPLE is professor of History at Barnard College, New York. She is the author of numerous articles on medieval and women's history, and has published two books to date: *Atto of Vercelli* (Rome: Edizioni di Storia e Letteratura, 1979) and *Women in Frankish Society* (Philadelphia: University of Pennsylvania Press, 1981). The latter work received the Berkshire Historial Prize of 1981. Wemple is currently working on a massive project on the accumulation of information on women religious.

WENDY M. WRIGHT earned her doctorate in an Interdisciplinary Program in Contemporary Studies at the University of California, Santa Barbara, where she teaches in the Department of Religious Studies. She is co-author of *Silent Fire: An Invitation to Western Mysticism* and has published in *The Feminist Mystic, The Journal of Studia Mystica,* and The Spirituality of Western Christendom II.

INDEX OF PERSONS AND PLACES

Abra, 22
Adolph of Nassau, emporor, 216
Aelfflaed, abbess, 60
Aelred of Rievaulx, 70, 78–9, 132–3
Aethelbert, king, 55, 57
Aethelburh of Barking, 55, 58–59, 61
Aethelthryth, 56, 59
Agatha, 3–4
Agnes, 3–4, 59, 139
Agnes, abbess, 40
Agnes of Prague, 170–1, 179, 184–7, 189, 192, 198, 200
Aidan, bishop, 63
Alardus, 116
Alboflede, 24
Alboin, king, 24
Aldegund, recluse, 6, 31, 39, 41–2 45–9
Aldhelm, 55–6, 61–3
Aldrith of Northumbria, 61
Alexander III, pope, 89, 94, 97
Alexander IV, pope, 177, 207
Alhflaed, 58
Alhfrith, 58
Alpais, 129, 135–7
Alumbrados, 347
Alyscamps, 26
Amalric, king, 24
Ancelet-Hustache, Jeanne, 93
Angeluccia, nun, 200–1
Anna, king, 56
Anna the prophetess, 3, 7, 77, 80
Annecy, convent of, 355
Anstrude, 27
Arles, convent at, 26, 28, 32
Arian, 24, 26, 31
Assisi, 167–8, 204, 207
Auria, 127, 136
Avila, convent of, 332, 336–7
Avitus, saint, 24

Baker, Augustine, 292
Baldwin, 27
Balthild (Baltilda), queen, 28, 39–42, 45, 47–9, 373
Banez, Dominigo, 336
Barking, convent of, 60–1, 63
Bastia, 197
Baudinivia, nun, 27, 40–5, 47–8
Beatrice, 156
Begu, nun, 61
Beguines, 145
Belgium, 46, 138, 145
Bellarmine, cardinal, 147
Benedicta, 135
Benedictines, 124, 157, 249, 292
Benincasa, Catherine, 275–86
Beowulf, 56–7
Bercharius, bishop, 28
Bermersheim bei Alzey, 103
Bernard, prior, 133
Bernard of Clairvaux, 88, 106, 193, 358
Bertha, queen, 25, 55, 57
Bertilla, abbess, 29, 33, 40, 42–3
Blake, William, 148
Blandina, slave, 3, 20
Bloom, Anthony, archbishop, 265
Bohemia, 170, 184
Bollandists, 42, 147, 184
Boniface, pope, 58, 63
Bonn, 89

Brie, convent of, 56
Brunhilda, queen, 24, 31, 40
Bruizo, Philip, 74
Bugga, 63
Burgandofara, abbess, 29, 31
Burgundy, 23
Byzantium, 40

Caesaria, abbess, 26
Caesaria II, abbess, 32
Caesarius of Arles, 26–8, 31–2, 40
Caesarius of Heisterbach, 133, 138
Cambrai, 292
Carmelite, order of, 332–4, 336–7, 345–6
Carolingian, 26, 41, 46
Carthusians, order of, 124
Catalina de la Conception, nun, 329
Cathari, 89
Catherine of Siena, 7, 9, 11, 373
Catholics, 353
Cecilia, martyr, 3, 4, 59, 202, 293
Celano, 181
Chartres, 31
Chelidonia, 126
Chelles, convent at, 28, 33, 40, 42–3 45, 48
Childeric, king, 23
Chlotar (Clothar) I, king, 27, 30, 32, 40
Christ, 45–7, 317–8, 324, 347, 353 357–63, 365–71, 373–4
Christina of Markyate, 71–2, 75, 79–80, 126, 128
Christina Mirabilis, 13, 145–58, 374
Christophe de Rabutin, baron, 354
Chrona, 24
Cistercian, order of, 123–4, 127, 130 139, 141, 147, 149, 151, 214, 239, 248, 249, 358, 365, 368
Citeaux, 87, 92–3, 239, 248, 252
Clairvaux, 107
Clement of Alexandria, 297, 310
Clotilda, queen, 24–7, 32, 373
Clotsinde, 24
Clovis, king, 24, 26, 30, 32, 40
Clovis II, king, 28, 40
Cluniac, order of, 70, 131
Coldingham, convent of, 60
Cologne, 4, 89, 116–7
Columbanus, 30–1
Comestor, Peter, 90
Constantine, emperor, 63
Corbie, 40, 43
Corinth, 103
Corpus Christi, 78, 137
Cortes, 332
Craon, 123
Cudot, 129
Cuthburg, nun, 61
Cynewulf, 63

Dante, 340
Deborah, 86, 106
Denis le Chartreux, 147
D'Escornaix, Marguerite, abbess of Nivelle, v
Diana, goddess, 21
Dijon, 353
Disibode, saint, 97
Disibodenberg, 77, 93–4
Dominicans, order of, 145, 148, 225, 275
Donatus of Besancon, 31
Douay version, 333
Durscher, Agnes, 72

Ealdwulf, king, 60
Eanflaed, 56, 58
Eangyth, abbess, 63
Earcongota, 56, 59
Eberbach, 103
Ecclesia, 117
Ecgfith, king, 56, 59
Edwin of Northumbria, 56–8
Egbert, 74
Egbert of Schonau, 12, 88–9
Egypt, 219, 248, 311
Eisleben, 239
Elene, 57, 63
Elias, 186, 201
Elijah, 133
Elizabeth of Hungary, 92
Elizabeth of Schonau, 4, 7, 12, 85, 87–94, 96, 98–9, 105, 109, 117, 373
Ely, convent of, 60
England, 28, 33, 64, 92, 124, 289, 292, 296, 345
Eorcenberht, king, 59
Ermentrude of Bruges, 184

Ethelburh, 56, 59
Eugene III, pope, 96
Europe, 19, 21, 24, 39
Eustatius, 31
Eva, 72, 77–8
Eve of St Eutrope, 127, 130, 132, 135
Eve of St Martin, 135, 137

Fara, 31
Faro, bishop, 31
Favarone, 167–8
Flanders, 124, 184
Florence, 128, 145, 200, 278
Fontevrault, convent of, 123
Fontis Ionannis, 135
Fortunatus, Venantius, 40, 42–4
France, 20, 26, 31, 34, 124, 129, 345 353–4, 356
Franciscans, order of, 184, 202, 310
Francis Xavier, saint, 332
Francois de Sales, 12, 353–8, 360–2
Francoise, 356
Franks, 19, 22–4, 27, 30, 39
Frederick II, emperor, 184
Frederick Barbarossa, emperor, 88–9, 97
Frye, Northrop, 148

Gaspar de Salazar, 333
Gaul, 19–23, 26–7, 30, 49, 60
Geneva, bishop of, 358–9
Genovefa, saint, 21–3, 26
Germain of Paris, bishop, 40
Germany, 42, 87, 89, 93, 211, 223 239
Germanus of Auxerre, 22, 26
Gertrude of Hackeborn, 211–2, 214–20
Gertrude of Helfa, 93
Gertrude of Nievelles, 32, 374
Giles, 202
Gottweig, Ava, 77
Gougaud, 136
Gracian, Jerome, 332
Gregory IX, pope, 172, 180, 184, 188, 191, 206–7, 212
Gregory XI, pope, 275
Gregory the Great, 25–6, 47, 263
Gregory of Tours, 23
Grendel, 57
Grimlaic, 67
Guibert of Gembloux, 97, 108, 118
Guido, bishop, 170

Hackeborn, 211
Hagneric, 31
Halberstadt, 216
Hartlepool, monastery of, 60
Helfta, 12, 14, 211–2, 214, 216, 219–20, 223, 239, 248, 253
Henry IV, 105
Hereswith, 60
Hereteu, 63
Herveus, 72
Heschel, Abraham, 109
Hilarion, 72
Hilary of Poitiers, bishop, 22
Hild, abbess, 56, 60–1, 63
Hildeburgis, 126, 138
Hildegard of Bingen, 4, 6–7, 12, 77, 80, 85, 87–90, 93–4, 96–9, 103–18, 135, 373–4
Hildelith, abbess, 59, 61
Hilary of Poitiers, bishop, 22
Holy Roman Empire, 87
Holy Spirit, 46–7
Honorius III, pope, 180
Hrabanus, 46
Hrostwitha, nun, 74
Hrothgar, 57
Hugelac, 57
Hugh of St Victor, 186, 212
Hugolino (Gregory IX), 145, 198, 206
Hugolino di Segni, 180–1
Humilitas, 126
Huns, 4, 23
Huy, 138–40
Hygd, 57

Ida, saint, 73–4
Illuminati, 347
Innocent III, pope, 172, 180, 199, 204
Innocent IV, pope, 181, 207
Isaac of Stella, 70
Isaiah, 71
Isidore the Farmer, saint, 332
Islam, 87
Israel, 91
Italy, 21, 24, 87, 123, 128
Iustina, 126

Iutta, 154
Ivetta of Huy, 12, 138–41

Jacques de Vitry, 145–7, 199
Jeanne de Chantal, 6, 12–3, 353–63 374
Jerusalem, 3
Jesus of Nazareth, 2–14, 296, 308, 319, 326, 374–5
Joachim of Flora, 97
John Cassian, 22, 26, 248
John of the Cross, 193
John the Evangelist, 12
John Paul II, pope, 7, 332
Judith, 57, 63
Juliana, 57, 63
Juliana of Mont Cornillon, 78, 135, 137
Julian of Norwich, 4, 8, 11, 13, 149 289, 291–302, 305–10, 312–3, 374–5
Jutta of Sponheim, 104

Kavanaugh, K, 333
Kent, 25
King James Bible, 333
Krusch, Bruno, 41–3
Kuno of Disibodenburg, 12

Lainati, Chiara, 199
Laon, 27. 33–4
Langres, 34
Lazarus, 311
Leclercq, Jean, 86, 99, 214, 240, 253
Leo, 202
Lerins, 26
Les Andelys, 26
Levison, Wilhelm, 41, 46
Liege, 72, 77–8, 139
Liliola, abbess, 28
Lioba, nun, 63
Liudhard, bishop, 57
Logos, 81
Lombards, 24
Louis of Looz, count, 155
Louis the Pious, king, 46
Lucia, 127
Lutgard of Aywieres, 145, 147, 154
Luxeuil, 31
Lyminge, 55
Lyons, 20, 27, 124

Macon, synod of, 28
Magdeburg, 223
Marcigny, 131
Marcus Aurelius, emperor, 20
Margaret of Ypres, 145
Marie d'Oignies, 145–6
Marseilles, 22, 26
Martha of Bethany, 71, 132–3, 311
Martin of Tours, 20–2, 25–6, 30
Mary, mother of Jesus, 2, 9, 11, 13 46–7, 59, 72, 74, 111–2, 115–6, 136–7, 141, 179, 190, 219, 239, 285, 293, 362 (*see also* Our Lady)
Mary of Bethany, 3, 71, 131–3, 141 311
Mary Magdalen, 2, 3, 77, 311
Matthew Paris, 137
Maubeuge, convent at, 31, 41, 46
Meaux, 31
Mechtild of Magdeburg, 7–8, 13, 93, 211–2, 214–7, 223–6, 228–31, 234, 236, 373, 375
Mechtildis, recluse, 135
Mechtild von Hackeborn, 10–3, 212–21, 223, 240, 251, 310, 375
Medard of Noyon, bishop, 40
Melania the Great, 5
Merovingian, 27, 29, 39, 41–3, 46, 48–9
Merton, Thomas, 367, 370
Micheline de Fontette, 127
Minerva, 275
Minstery, convent of, 60
Monegund, recluse, 31
More, Gertrude, 292
More, Thomas, 292
Mount Carmel, 332–3, 348
Mt Subasio, 199

Nantes, 31
Nazareth, 219
Nelson, Janet, 43
Neri, Philip, saint, 332
Neustria, 40
Nicetius, bishop, 24
Nivelles, 41, 46
Nonnemielen, 157
Northumbria, 56
Nyoiseau, 123

Olivi, Peter John, 97

Olympias, 5
Origen, 7
Ortolana, 168
Orval, 139
Osburg, nun, 61
Ostia, 180
Oswiu, 56, 58
Ottokar, king, 170, 184
Our Lady, 2, 93, 190, 255, 270

Pacifica, 206
Panzo, 197
Paphnutius, 68–9, 74–5
Paris, 23, 42, 72, 193
Paris, Matthew, 137
Paul, 62
Paul VI, pope, 332
Paulinus, chaplain, 58
Paulinus of Nola, 25
Peada, 58
Peers, E. Allison, 333
Pentecost, 88–9
Perugia, 207
Peter Abelard, 72, 88
Peter of Alcantara, 324
Peter Damian, 78, 80, 123, 180
Peter the Venerable, 133–4
Pietro di Bernardone, 168
Pinius, 147, 153
Protestants, 353
Poitiers, convent at, 27, 32, 40, 43, 127
Prague, 170–1, 179, 184
Premonstratensians, order of, 123–4
Psuedo-Dionysius, 340
Puellemoutier, convent of, 28

Rachel, 185, 187–8
Radegund, saint, 9, 12, 21, 27, 30, 32, 39–45, 47–9
Rainaldus, cardinal, 133, 207
Raymond of Capua, 276
Ranieri di Bernardo d'Assisi, 168
Rennes, 123
Repten, convent of, 60
Rhineland, 92
Richard of St Victor, 89, 188
Robert of Arbrissel, 123
Rodriguez, O., 333
Roger of Ford, 92
Roger of St Albans, 72
Romans, 20–1, 49
Rome, 3, 22, 24, 124, 172, 275
Rudolf of Cologne, 134
Rudolph of Hapsburg, 212
Rufino, 168
Rufinus, 5
Rupert, saint, 97
Rupertsburg, 12, 94
Rusticula, abbess, 26–7, 32

Sadalberga, 28, 31, 33–4
Saethryth, 56, 59
St Agnes, 3–4, 40, 59, 139
St Ambrose, 61
St Angelo, 197
St Anselm, 310
St Anthony, 47, 68–9, 133
St Augustine of Canterbury, 57, 61–2
St Augustine of Hippo, 212
St Bartholomew, 138
St Basil, 248, 359
St Benedict, 10, 13–4, 31, 85, 95, 97, 133, 136, 153, 180, 198, 212, 245–6, 251, 256, 260, 263, 266, 268, 368, 370, 375
St Bernard of Clairvaux, 70, 93, 97, 186, 211–2, 269, 310
St Bonaventure, 176–8, 190, 193, 295
St Catherine, 156–7, 277, 310
St Clare of Assisi, 2, 7, 9–12, 165, 167–73, 175–93, 197–207, 374–5
St Dominic, 220
St Francis of Assisi, 10, 12, 145, 165, 167–70, 175–93, 197–207,
St Gaggio, 278
St Gertrude, 5, 10–3, 213, 220, 223 239–40, 242–3, 245–63, 265–70, 295, 374–5
St Ignatius of Loyola, 332
St James, 193
St Jerome, 61, 133
St John the Baptist, 90, 193
St John the Evangelist, 140–1
St Mark, 127
St Martin, convent of, 78
St Martin of Cologne, 116
St Opportune, 72
St Paul, 97, 103–4, 106, 116, 133, 310–1, 321, 328, 333
St Peter, 46–7, 193, 312, 321, 324, 328

St Romuald, 75, 123
St Sebastian, 358
St Ursula, martyr, 4, 91, 117
Samuel the Prophet, 90
San Aemiliano of Suso, 127
San Damiano, 167, 170, 172, 180–1, 185, 190, 198–9, 202–4
San Francesco, 201
San Paulo, 180, 197
San Pietro, 279
San Rufino, 167–8
San Silvestro, 180
Saix, 40
Saxony, 212, 239
Schonau, 85–9, 94, 135
Seaxburh, 56, 59
Seine, 23
Sicily, 3, 204
Siena, 275–7
Sigebert, 12, 40
Sigismund, 24
Solesmes Benedictines, 213
Spain, 332, 345–6
Spoleto, 207
Subnius of Nivelles, abbot, 41, 46
Sulpicius Severus, 21–2
Syria, 69

Talida, 5
Terence, 74
Thaïs, saint, 68, 75
Theodefrid, abbot, 43
Theodelinde, 24
Theodoric, 24
Theudemanda, 31
Thomas of Cantimpre, 145–58
Thomas of Celano, 168, 176–7
Thuringia, 27, 39, 212, 239
Teresa of Avila (Jesus), 7–9, 11–2, 292, 315, 317–29, 332–42, 345–51, 373
Thérèse of Lisieux, 345
Todi, 74
Toulouse, 70
Tours, 22, 26
Trier, 88, 92, 97

United States, 39
Urban IV, pope, 137
Urban VI, pope, 275
Urs von Balthasar, Hans, 217

Vaggagini, 253
Vandals, 23
Van der Essen, 46
Venantius Fortunatus, 40, 42–4
Venerable Bede, 55–6, 59–63
Venus, 21
Verdiana, 71, 128–30
Victor IV, antipope, 89, 97
Victricius of Rouen, 21
Villiers, 139
Virgin, Mother of Christ, 46–7, 74 89, 114, 129, 131–2, 140–1, 358, 362
Visigoths, 24
Visitandines, order of, 355, 359
von Dassel, Rainald, archbishop, 89
von Halle, Heinrich, 224

Waldebert, 31
Waldetrude, 31, 41, 46
Wales, 124
Waltrud, 41, 46
Wealtheow, 57
Wenceslas, 184
Wenlock, convent of, 60
Westermann, Claus, 90
Wiborade, saint, 75
Whitby, convent of, 56, 60
Wilfrid, bishop, 60
William of St Thierry, 13, 149–50, 153–4, 186

Yahweh, 310–1

SUBJECT INDEX

abandonment, 10
and perfect joy, 202ff
ascesis,
monastic, 252, 259ff, 266
of love, 242
abbess, 29, 31, 183, 198, 203, 235
academics, collaboration with religious, ix, xi, 1
acceptance, 326, 359
acedia, 134
adoration, 301
advocate, 215
agony in the garden, 317f, 326
anawim, 6ff, 15n24
see also **poverty of spirit**
anchoresses, 9, 14, 123ff
and ecclesiastical authority, 130ff
see also **recluses**
Ancrene Riwle, 132, 133, 136, 310
angels, 255
anger, 246, 251
anglo-saxon nuns, 55ff
anthropology, 339ff
see also **supernatural anthropology**
ascetic communities, and women, 21
ascetical life, 5, 227, 333, 365
austerity, 248

baptism, 265
of Clovis, 24
beguines, 145
Blessed Sacrament, 11, 300
see also Eucharist
bride of Christ, 4, 5, 6, 125, 185, 187, 192, 226, 229, 237, 243, 246f, 278, 329, 361

call of Spirit, 188
celibate married, 61
charity, x, 10, 11, 20, 45, 48, 60, 183, 187, 217ff, 276f, 282, 284, 285
fire of, 278
works of, 67, 218, 241, 243, 251, 355;
see also **love**
chastity, 368, 369, 370, 371
child of God, 278
childhood, 313
Christbearers, 13ff, 191
Christ's children, 299, 310
Christ-Mother, 13, 289, 299ff, 306ff
christian formation, in St. Catherine of Siena, 275ff
christian witness, 259
church, as Christ Jesus, 309
prayer for, 283f
claustration, 26ff, 33
at Caesaria's monastery, 26
see also **enclosure**
commitment, 1, 4
common life, 10
at Helfta, 214ff, 248
communion, reception of, 218, 258, 261, *see also* **Blessed Sacrament; eucharist**
community, 10, 183, 192
Mechtild and, 213ff
compassion, 276, 281f, 293, 294, 374
concord, 373
confidence, 250f, 259, 300, 308, 321

conformity with Christ, 189, 347, 357
consecrated life, 255
consolations, 281ff, 285, 341, 357
constant prayer, 178, 252, 253, 283, 284f, 299
contemplation, 349ff
  and action, 276f
contemplation, 91–92, 165, 186f, 193, 292
continents, 21–22
conversion, 10, 11, 14, 20, 67, 259, 265, 325, 332
    of Gaul and consecrated women, 19ff
    of Frankish monarchy, 20ff
    of Frankish people, 29ff
    of Frankish women, 28ff
    in St. Gertrude, 239, 241
    vow of, 251ff, 368, 369
conversion of manners, 370f
  see also **conversion,** vow of
convictions, 1
courage, 247, 277, 321, 359f
cross, 11, 137, 189, 227, 280, 284, 302, 309, 357f, 358, 360, 368, 375
crown of blood, 397f, 303n15
crown of thorns, 397f, 303n15

daughter of church, 332
death, 132
  in St Clare, 200
  in St Gertrude, 256, 264ff
  in Jeanne de Chantal, 355–356
  in Julian of Norwich, 293, 294
  in Mechtild of Magdeburg, 232ff
  in Mechtild of Hackeborn, 215, 220
  in Teresa of Avila, 328ff
  to self, 362, 363, 370
delight, in God's goodness, 301, 302, 349
dependence on God, 202f, 279, 362
desert mothers, 4ff
desires, 278f; for God, 280, 301
detachment, 337f, 338, 339f, 341, 342, 348
devil, 265, 280, 281, 282f, 318, 326
  and Aldegund, 47
  and virgins, 118
director of souls, 280f, 348
  as non-judgmental, 281f
  see also **spiritual guide**
discernment of spirits, 323
disciple, 280f
Divine majesty as truth, 322
Divine Office, 14, 253, 365
  and Mechtild, 214ff
  see also **liturgy**
divine power and weakness, 103ff
divine will, 150, 152, 250f, 375
  see also **God's will**
double monasteries, 59, 60, 64

echo within, 2
enclosure, 131, 199, 333
  see also **claustration**
eternal life, 256, 257, 268, 269, 270
eucharist, 234, 285
  anchoress' devotion to, 137f, 140
  Clare's devotion to, 178ff
  Gertrude's devotion to, 258f
  see also **Blessed Sacrament**
eucharistic devotion, 14
evangelical counsels, 15n17
evil, 265, 266, 268, 281, 291
experience, 1, 322
  of God, 226, 232, 348, 368

face of God, 302
face to face vision, 266ff, 270, 302
faith, v, 1, 13, 133, 134, 172, 187, 189, 250, 254, 263, 280, 282, 286, 325, 374
false self, 250f, 259, 265
fasting, 192
fatherhood in the Trinity, 307f, 312
  in Clement of Alexandria, 310
faults, 246, 251
fear, 232, 321, 349
  in St Gertrude, 257, 263
female authors, 42
female religious, lives of, ix, 42
  modes of sanctity, 39
feminine, beauty of, 12
  in Clement of Alexandria, 310
  in Gertrude, 241
  inferiority, 245;
  see also **woman**
fiery love, 233
following Christ, 171, 172, 175ff, 181, 189, 248, 265, 362
fools for Christ's sake, 151, 153

formation, 276, 287n3, 365, 367
ongoing, 286f, 367
fraternal love, 248, 276ff, 300, 329, 337
freedom of heart, in St Gerturde, 244ff, 247
friends, 12, 216
fundamental option, 269

glorified bodies, 327f
God's goodness, 298, 301f, 302, 307, 358
God's life, in St Gertrude, 258ff, 260
in *The Interior Castle*, 333
God's love for us, 219, 226, 243, 250, 281, 299f, 307, 312, 318
God's presence, 1, 252f, 257, 266, 270, 295, 301, 318, 328, 350, 351
God's secrets, 302, 303–304n21, 318, 322, 325
God's will, 250f, 254, 259, 280, 281, 293, 299, 300, 321, 325, 329, 338, 360
see also **divine will**
God's word, 2
Gospel, living the, 169, 177f, 183, 189, 197, 207, 248
promise of, 256
values of, 10
grace, 261, 276, 284, 293, 298, 312, 313, 326, 373
and breasts, 150f, 153
of filial love, 278
in St Gertrude, 271n9
and holy joy, 154
and oil, 153
ordinary, 333, 334, 338
and sweetness, 157, 162n44
supernatural, 333, 334
gratitude, 301, 320
growth, 13, 151, 176, 223, 230, 233, 241, 243, 246, 248, 255, 259, 279, 289, 375
gustos, 341f

hagiography, 2, 19, 29, 41f, 46, 50n5, 50n6, 70, 97, 146, 147
female values in, 43, 49
handmaid, 6, 7, 182, 191
prophets as, 86
healer, 275
heart of Gertrude, dwelling place for the Lord, 252
heart of Jesus, 234, 243f
heart, 366f, 368, 371
knowledge coming from, 367
heaven, 9, 233, 257, 298, 325
hell, 9, 322, 326f
history, 2
Holy Spirit, x, 233, 242, 243, 247, 250, 254, 255, 301, 312
greeted by, 223
impregnated by, 187
kiss of, 193
human effort, 338, 341
human-divine, (humanity and divinity) 1, 2, 6, 14, 17n66, 244, 253, 276, 284, 291, 328, 361
humanity of Christ, 6, 9, 15n23, 151, 298, 317, 318f, 320, 328
humble service, 205
humility, x, 5, 6ff, 10, 11, 20, 48, 111, 133, 135, 187, 230, 245ff, 249ff, 252, 263, 266, 278, 279, 282f, 284, 286, 319ff, 321f, 326, 329, 337, 339ff, 341, 342, 348, 349; *see also* **poverty of spirit**
humor, 346

identification with Christ, 3, 266
crucified, 278
in obedience, 250
image and likeness, 284, 339, 340
imaginary vision, 324, 325, 328
imitation of Christ, 165, 186, 189, 266, 328
incarnation, 293, 294, 296
ingratitude, 251
intellect, in Catherine of Siena, 275f 279, 285
intellectual vision, 324, 328
Interior Castle, 332ff, 336, 340
interior cell, 283
interior voices, 322

joy, 190, 192, 233, 234, 296, 322, 346, 359, 373
judgment, 268, 269

kenosis, 165, 187, 367, 368f, 370
kingdom of heaven, 234; possessed, 171

lay vocation, 14,n1
leader, St Clare, 200ff
Catherine of Siena, 276
liberty of spirit, 5
see also **freedom of heart**
life, in writings of St Gertrude, 256ff
in Jeanne de Chantal, 354
in Teresa of Avila, 335
meaning of, 259
light, 254, 277, 278, 350
of truth, 279ff, 322f
liturgical feasts, 253
liturgical prayer, 252, 253
see also **prayer**
liturgy, 2–4, 33, 365
in Hildegard of Bingen, 97
in Mechtild of Hackeborn, 214
see also **divine office**
locution, 323
longing for God, (desiring God), 226, 228, 230, 232, 234, 293, 299, 301
lord and servant allegory, 299f, 305f
love of enemies, 242
love, 4, 5, 49, 223, 230, 232, 234ff 242, 254, 277, 279, 280f, 325, 326, 329, 374
in Algegund's vision, 47
in Clare, 171
in Francois de Sales, 358f
in St Gertrude, 241ff, 259
in Jeanne de Chantal, 359–63,
in Julian of Norwich, 295, 301, 306ff, 312f
in Mechtild of Magdeburg, 231f, 236
in truth, 322f
loving kindness, 243ff, 258–9, 261, 263
St Gertrude's, 263

Mansions **one–three,** 334ff, 336, 338ff, 340ff, 342
manual labor and work, 199, 215, 248, 252, 365
martyrdom, 3, 117f, 266
of love, 359ff
as witness of christian virgins, 75
martyrs, 3ff, 359
and spiritual verve, 4
of Lyons, 20
and hermits, 75
masculinity and femininity, 306, 310
mass, 253
medieval saints' lives, 34, n2, 47
see also **hagiography**
meditation, 318, 319f, 341, 349, 350
on sacred humanity, 319
memory, in Catherine of Siena, 275f, 279, 280, 285
men and women, 271n10
Hildegard on the nature of, 115, 118
spiritual friendship between, 12, 72, 176–77, 355
needed one another, 32f
mental prayer, 318
mercy, 276, 279, 283, 284, 286, 306, 308
merovingian kingdom, monastic women in, 39, 48, 49
merovingian, culture, 41; Baudinivia, 41; saints' lives, 42ff
miracles, in life of Christina Mirabilis, 150, 152
missionaries, nuns as, 67
missionary efforts, 19
models for religious men, 133
monachae, 10ff, 5
monasteries of women, 25ff
monastery of love, 252
monastic commitment, 255f, 265
monastic communities, 52
foundation of, 28
monastic cowl, 255
monastic life, 256, 270, 365, 370f
monastic observances, 249ff, 255, 269, 365
monastic profession, 254ff
monastic rules, 10, 268, 365
monastic women, ix, 248
St Gertrude as, 239ff
see also **religious woman**
monasticism, 5
meaning of, 81
monks, 248, 251
moral accountability, 269f
mother of God, 270
motherhood of God, 13, 289, 305ff, 310, 312
sources in tradition, 310ff
in old testament, 311
in new testament, 311, 312

motherhood of Jesus, 308f, 313
meaning of, 308ff
see also **Christ-Mother**
mystery of Christ, 3, 6, 11, 12, 14, 15n22, 17n65, 265, 365ff, 368, 370, 375
mystical union, 280, 319f
mystic, 275, 345, 347
mystical kiss, 278, 358
mystical life, 331, 334, 341, 342
mystical theology, 335
mysticism, 242f, 291, 300
thirteenth century, 147, 148
nuptial, 243
quack, 347

obedience, 10, 20, 182, 232, 249ff, 277, 309, 332, 333, 368, 369, 370, 371; to the church, 207, 291, 306
old age, 233
oneness with all, 11
opus dei, 252, 253
see also **divine office**

pagan practices, 21
passion, death and resurrection of Christ, 265, 266, 300, 308
passion, remembrance of, 293; suffering of, 301; *see also* **Christ; Cross**
pastoral guidance for women, 20
peace, x, 1, 60, 157, 278, 280, 351f, 373f
peacemaker, 9ff, 275
peaceweavers, x, 1, 56ff, 373
penance, 170
perfect love, 267
perseverance, 187, 259, 335, 346, 350, 359
pilgrims, 13f
porousness, 367f
poverty of spirit, 6ff, 11, 111, 165ff, 189, 199, 232, 234, 241, 254, 261, 263, 374
poverty of womanhood, 12, 13
poverty, 167ff, 171, 172ff, 178, 187, 199, 202, 248, 368, 369, 370, 371
powerlessness, womanly, 12, 138
praise, 200, 232, 259, 265, 326
prayer of quiet, 324, 336f
prayer, x, 3, 4, 11f, 48, 67, 68, 248, 251, 252, 266, 269, 276, 289, 355, 374
contemplative, 253, 254, 298, 310
of human need, 301
mystical, 317, 331ff, 333, 337, 338, 339, 342
private, 253
of union, 324
in St Catherine of Siena, 283ff
in Clare of Assisi, 167, 170, 171ff, 178
in Julian of Norwich, 291ff, 298ff
in Teresa of Avila, 317ff, 330n13, 331ff, 335f, 341, 342, 347–352
preaching, task of men, 32; anchoress visons as a medium, 135ff, 291
present moment, 253
pride, 283, 284, 286
priesthood, in Hildegard of Bingen, 115ff
prophets, religious women as, 7ff; St Catherine of Siena as, 275; Elizabeth of Schonau and Hildegard of Bingen, 85ff, 105; message of, 99; as overshadowed ones, 111; what are, 86
prophecy, 3
prophetess, 3, 7, 80
prophetic mission, 7; of Hildegard of Bingen, 105
prophetic spirit, of anchoresses, 135
providence, 285f, 286, 357, 374
providential care, 284, 285
purgatory, 286; and Christina Mirabilis, 147, 151; souls in, 233
purity of heart, 248, 251, 280, 284

queens, and conversion, 24f

reader of hearts, Mechtild, 219
recluses, 31; and devotions, 78, 136–137
and freedom, 71
and interior life, 73
lifestyle of, 70ff
and liturgy, 78
as prayers, 77, 78, 79

doing penance, 76
reconcilers, 78
repentant sinner, 77
as sinners, 76
as widows, 74
women, 67ff
reclusion in primitive times, 68f
during middle ages, 69ff
and prophecy, 79ff
reform, 284
Regula reclusorum, 134
relationships, lifegiving, 1, 261f
human, 4, 12, 263, 360
to God, 267, 362
to Christ as teacher, 295
relic of true cross, 44–45
religious woman, ix, 1, 2;
as anawim, 6ff
as Christbearers, 13ff, 111
desires of, 6, 260
forming Christ, 2
friends, 12f, 216, 251, 346
foundresses and rulers of monastic communities, 19, 41
liturgy as formative, 3–4, 14, 90, 214
models for, 1, 2ff, 132
monache, 10ff
origins of, 1, 2ff
as peacemakers, 9ff, 204, 374
as pilgrims, 13, 228f
as prophets, 85, 7ff, 85ff
as sponsa Christi, 5ff
as teachers, 7, 215
as theologians, 8ff
theme patterns of, 5
values, x, 1
women, 12ff
work nurtured within, 2
religious life, 5
repentance, 232, 246, 255
repentant prostitutes, 68, 74
return to the heart, 252, 257
revelations, Julian, 293, 294, 296, 297
rosary, 11
Rule of St Benedict, 10, 14, 248, 249, 251, 266, 268, 368
Rule of St Clare, 181, 203

sacramental witness, 148ff, 156, 157
sacred heart, 258, 270
sacred humanity, in Teresa of Avila, 324
salvation, 241, 254, 280, 284, 285;
of souls in Gertrude, 261ff
scripture, 2, 4, 10, 19, 60, 105, 365;
in Francis and Clare, 177ff
in Gertrude, 262
in Mechtild of Hackeborn, 215
in Teresa of Avila, 322f
scripture models, 2ff
self knowledge, 276, 279f, 286, 320, 321, 329, 338ff
self will, 278, 279, 280, 357
selfless, 262
servant of christ, 4, 116
Seven Mansions, 333f
Showings, Julian of Norwich, 289, 291f, 301
silence, 132ff, 189, 252f
simplicity, 5, 248
in St Gertrude's prayer, 254
sin, 231f, 277, 279, 280, 284, 299, 301, 309, 317, 326
mortal, 340
solidarity with others, x, 76ff, 374
solitude, 252, 333, 374
its meaning, 80–81
spiritual reality at core, 76ff
sophia, 307, 311f
sorrow, 251, 293, 320, 356, 357, 373
spiritual guide, 332, 345, 351f, 374; *see also* **director of souls**
spiritual immersion, 365
consciousness of, 366
spiritual marriage, 192, 336, 342
spiritual motherhood, 44, 165, 230, 251
spiritual mothers, 12, 13, 202, 229, 230, 355f
spirituality, women's, 1, 45
desert, 5
female, in Frankish monasteries, 39ff
trinitarian, 8, 242
sponsa christi, x, 5ff
spousal imagery, 171, 362
spouse, Christ as, 186, 188, 358, 361; *see also* **bride of Christ**
stability, 368, 369

strength, 254, 259, 265f, 267
study, 215
in St Gertrude, 257
suffering, 231, 234, 236, 251, 280, 327, 328, 360
vicarious, 154f, 155
with Jesus, 294
Christ's, 297
see also **Christ; Cross**
supernatural anthropology, Teresa of Avila's, 12
suppletio, (Christ's virtues supply for our deficiencies), 219, 250f, 267, 268
surrender to God, 176, 280

temptations, 219, 356, 360, 363; to be freed from, 261, 263
thanksgiving, 236, 246ff, 259, 265, 296
The Book of Her Life, 332, 334f, 335f, 336, 338, 342
theologians, 8ff
theology, as experienced, 9, 16n35, 225; as prayer, 9, 292
thoughts, evil, 246, 268; carnal, 133; distracting, 351f
transformation into Christ, 170, 242, 243, 278, 293, 357, 366, 368, 370f
transformation of heart, 279, 367
Treatise on the Love of God, 355
tirals, 285, 326, 327, 328, 335
in life of St Gertrude, 257, 259
trinity, 9, 224ff, 228, 242, 255, 258, 286, 293, 294, 296f, 298, 300, 306, 307f, 312, 325
truth, 279, 322
as humility, 7, 279, 321ff

union with Christ, 3, 6, 14, 171, 175–76, 217f, 227, 234, 258, 278, 298, 299, 300, 302, 375
union with God, 48, 157, 230, 243, 248, 249f, 256, 266, 267, 268, 293, 339, 342, 348, 368, 369f, 371
union with the divine, x, 4, 6, 8, 11
unworthiness, 234

vigilance, 248, 251f, 254
virgin martyr, v, 3
virgin, 4, 21, 56, 61, 186; *see also* **virginity**
virginity, 3, 59, 62f, 117f; and pride, 61
virtues, 236, 245, 246, 248, 252, 255, 278, 299, 307, 335, 347f, 369, 371
visionary, 148; mode of perception, 148
visions, 281ff
Aldegund's, 46f
anchoresses', 135ff
Christina Mirabilis', 148
Clare's, 201
Elizabeth of Schonau's, 89ff
Hildegard of Bingen's, 94ff, 113f
Julian's *Showings*, 294f
Teresa of Avila, 322ff, 329
Visitation of Mary Order, 355
vows, 365, 368ff, 371
profession of, 1, 14f, 17n64, 188
practice of, 369f, 370

Way of Perfection, 332, 336ff, 338, 342, 347
Lord's Prayer in, 337
weakness, v; human, 1, 268, 307–308, 328
womanly, 4, 103ff, 16n32, 374
weaving, 373
widows, 21, 61, 74
will, in Catherine of Siena, 275f, 279, 285
wisdom, of the Trinity, 307f
in old testament, 310
womanhood, 1, 106, 332; meaning of, in Hildegard, 118
women, 12ff
airy temperament in Hildegard's view, 109ff
consecrated, 22
as counselors, 63, 136, 141, 217, 242
and the feminine divine in Hildegard, 113ff
holy, 1
and the humanity of Christ, 112ff
identity, 2, 12
integraged, 1
living sermon, 32, 158
monks, 4

personhood of, 253
as passive in prophecy, 109
as peacemakers, 43, 44, 45
as promoters of dynastic cult centers, 43
as recluses, 67ff, 123ff
redistribution of wealth by, 32ff
saints, as mother figures, 43, 45
whole, 1
wounded feet, 277f, 278
wounded side, 277, 278, 284

CISTERCIAN PUBLICATIONS INC.

Kalamazoo, Michigan

TITLES LISTING

THE CISTERCIAN FATHERS SERIES

THE WORKS OF BERNARD OF CLAIRVAUX

- Treatises I: Apologia to Abbot William, On Precept and Dispensation . . . . CF 1
- On the Song of Songs I–IV . . . . CF 4,7,31,40
- The Life and Death of Saint Malachy the Irishman . . . . CF 10
- Treatises II: The Steps of Humility, On Loving God . . . . CF 13
- Magnificat: Homilies in Praise of the Blessed Virgin Mary [with Amadeus of Lausanne] . . . . CF 18
- Treatises III: On Grace and Free Choice, In Praise of the New Knighthood . . . . CF 19
- Sermons on Conversion: A Sermon to Clerics, Lenten Sermons on Psalm 91 . . . . CF 25
- Five Books on Consideration: Advice to a Pope . . . . CF 37

THE WORKS OF WILLIAM OF SAINT THIERRY

- On Contemplating God, Prayer, and Meditations . . . . CF 3
- Exposition on the Song of Songs . . . . CF 6
- The Enigma of Faith . . . . CF 9
- The Golden Epistle . . . . CF 12
- The Mirror of Faith . . . . CF 15
- Exposition on the Epistle to the Romans . . . . CF 27
- The Nature and Dignity of Love . . . . CF 30

THE WORKS OF AELRED OF RIEVAULX

- Treatises I: On Jesus at the Age of Twelve, Rule for a Recluse, The Pastoral Prayer . . . . CF 2
- Spiritual Friendship . . . . CF 5
- The Mirror of Charity . . . . CF 17†
- Dialogue on the Soul . . . . CF 22

THE WORKS OF GILBERT OF HOYLAND

- Sermons on the Song of Songs I–III . . CF 14,20,26
- Treatises, Sermons, and Epistles . . . . CF 34

THE WORKS OF JOHN OF FORD

- Sermons on the Final Verses of the Song of Songs I–VII . . . . . . CF 29,39,43,44,45,46,47

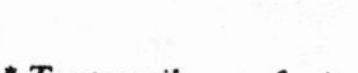

** Temporarily out of print*

Texts and Studies in the Monastic Tradition

OTHER EARLY CISTERCIAN WRITERS

- The Letters of Adam of Perseigne, I . . . . CF 21
- Alan of Lille: The Art of Preaching . . . . CF 23
- Idung of Prüfening. Cistercians and Cluniacs: The Case for Citeaux . . . . CF 33
- Guerric of Igny. Liturgical Sermons I–II . . . . CF 8,32
- Three Treatises on Man: A Cistercian Anthropology . . . . CF 24
- Isaac of Stella. Sermons on the Christian Year, I . . . . CF 11
- Stephen of Lexington. Letters from Ireland, 1228–9 . . . . CF 28
- Stephen of Sawley, Treatises . . . . CF 36
- Baldwin of Ford. Spiritual Tractates . . . . CF 38,41

† Forthcoming

THE CISTERCIAN STUDIES SERIES

MONASTIC TEXTS

Evagrius Ponticus. Praktikos and Chapters on Prayer . . . CS 4
The Rule of the Master . . . CS 6
The Lives of the Desert Fathers . . . CS 34
The Sayings of the Desert Fathers . . . CS 59
Dorotheos of Gaza. Discourses and Sayings . . . CS 33
Pachomian Koinonia I–III:
  The Lives . . . CS 45
  The Chronicles and Rules . . . CS 46
  The Instructions, Letters, and Other Writings of St Pachomius and His Disciples . . . CS 47
Besa, The Life of Shenoute . . . CS 73
Symeon the New Theologian. Theological and Practical Treatises and Three Theological Discourses . . . CS 41
The Venerable Bede: Commentary on the Seven Catholic Epistles . . . CS 82
The Letters of Armand-Jean de Rancé (A.J. Krailsheimer) . . . CS 80, 81
Guigo II the Carthusian. The Ladder of Monks and Twelve Meditations . . . CS 48
The Monastic Rule of Iosif Volotsky . . . CS 36
Theodoret of Cyrrhus. A History of the Monks of Syria . . . CS 88
Anselm of Canterbury. Letters . . . CS 94,95†

CHRISTIAN SPIRITUALITY

The Spirituality of Western Christendom . . . CS 30
Russian Mystics (Sergius Bolshakoff) . . . CS 26
In Quest of the Absolute: The Life and Works of Jules Monchanin (J.G. Weber) . . . CS 51
The Name of Jesus (Irénée Hausherr) . . . CS 44
The Roots of the Modern Christian Tradition . . . CS 55
Abba: Guides to Wholeness and Holiness East and West . . . CS 38
Sermons in a Monastery (Matthew Kelty–William Paulsell) . . . CS 58
Penthos: The Doctrine of Compunction in the Christian East (Irénée Hausherr) . . . CS 53
The Spirituality of the Christian East. A Systematic Handbook (Tomas Spidlik SJ) . . . CS 79
From Cloister to Classroom . . . CS 90
Fathers Talking. An Anthology (Aelred Squire) . . . CS 92

MONASTIC STUDIES

The Abbot in Monastic Tradition (Pierre Salmon) . . . CS 14
Why Monks? (François Vandenbroucke) . . . CS 17
Community and Abbot in the Rule of St Benedict I (Adalbert de Vogüé) . . . CS 5/1
Consider Your Call: A Theology of the Monastic Life (Daniel Rees et al.) . . . CS 20
The Way to God According to the Rule of St Benedict (E. Heufelder) . . . CS 49
The Rule of St Benedict. A Doctrinal and Spiritual Commentary (Adalbert de Vogüé) . . . CS 54
Serving God First (Sighard Kleiner) . . . CS 83
Monastic Practices (Charles Cummings) . . . CS 75
St Hugh of Lincoln (David Hugh Farmer) . . . CS 87

CISTERCIAN STUDIES

The Cistercian Way (André Louf) . . . CS 76
The Cistercian Spirit (M. Basil Pennington, ed.) . . . CS 3
The Eleventh-Century Background of Citeaux (Bede K. Lackner) . . . CS 8
Contemplative Community . . . CS 21
Cistercian Sign Language (Robert Barakat) . . . CS 11
The Cistercians in Denmark (Brian P. McGuire) . . . CS 35
Soul Athirst for God. Spiritual Desire in Bernard of Clairvaux's Sermons on the Song of Songs (Michael Casey) . . . CS 77†
Saint Bernard of Clairvaux: Essays Commemorating the Eighth Centenary of His Canonization . . . CS 28
Bernard of Clairvaux: Studies Presented to Dom Jean Leclercq . . . CS 23
Bernard of Clairvaux and the Cistercian Spirit (Jean Leclercq) . . . CS 16
Image and Likeness. The Augustinian Spirituality of William of St Thierry (David N. Bell) . . . CS 78
Aelred of Rievaulx: A Study (Aelred Squire) . . . CS 50
Christ the Way: The Christology of Guerric of Igny (John Morson) . . . CS 25
The Golden Chain: The Theological Anthropology of Isaac of Stella (Bernard McGinn) . . . CS 15
Nicolas Cotheret's Annals of Citeaux (Louis J. Lekai) . . . CS 57
The Occupation of Celtic Sites in Ireland by the Canons Regular of St Augustine and the Cistercians (G. Carville) . . . CS 56
The Finances of the Cistercian Order in the Fourteenth Century (Peter King) . . . CS 85
Rancé and the Trappest Legacy (A. J. Krailsheimer) . . . CS 89
Fountains Abbey and Its Benefactors, 1132–1300 (Joan Wardrop) . . . CS 91†

Medieval Religious Women

Distant Echoes: MRW, I (L.T. Shank and J.A. Nichols, edd.) . . . CS 71

** Temporarily out of print*

† Forthcoming

Peace Weavers. MEW II
(L. T. Shank-J. A. Nichols, edd.) . . . . CS 72†

Studies in Medieval Cistercian History sub-series

Studies I . . . . CS 13

Studies II . . . . CS 24

Cistercian Ideals and Reality (Studies III) . . . . CS 60

Simplicity and Ordinariness (Studies IV) . . . . CS 61

The Chimera of His Age: Studies on St Bernard (Studies V) . . . . CS 63

Cistercians in the Late Middle Ages (Studies VI) . . . . CS 64

Noble Piety and Reformed Monasticism (Studies VII) . . . . CS 65

Benedictus: Studies in Honor of St Benedict of Nursia (Studies VIII) . . . . CS 67

Heaven on Earth (Studies IX) . . . . CS 68

Goad and Nail (Studies X) . . . . CS 84

Studies in Cistercian Art and Architecture

Studies in Cistercian Art and Architecture, I (Meredith Lillich, ed.) . . . . CS 66

Studies in Cistercian Art and Architecture, II (Meredith Lillich, ed.) . . . . CS 69

Studies in Cistercian Art and Architecture, III (Meredith Lillich, ed.) . . . . CS 89†

THOMAS MERTON

The Climate of Monastic Prayer . . . . CS 1

Thomas Merton on St Bernard . . . . CS 9

Thomas Merton's Shared Contemplation: A Protestant Perspective (Daniel J. Adams) . . . . CS 62

Solitude in the Writings of Thomas Merton (Richard Anthony Cashen) . . . . CS 40

The Message of Thomas Merton (Brother Patrick Hart, ed.) . . . . CS 42

Thomas Merton Monk (revised edition/ Brother Patrick Hart, ed.) . . . . CS 52

The Legacy of Thomas Merton (Brother Patrick Hart, ed.) . . . . CS 92

Thomas Merton and Asia: His Quest for Utopia (Alexander Lipski) . . . . CS 74

THE CISTERCIAN LITURGICAL DOCUMENTS SERIES

The Cistercian Hymnal: Introduction and Commentary . . . . CLS 1

The Cistercian Hymnal: Text and Melodies . . . . CLS 2

The Old French Ordinary and Breviary of the Abbey of the Paraclete: Introduction and Commentary . . . . CLS 3

The Old French Ordinary of the Abbey of the Paraclete: Text . . . . CLS 4

The Paraclete Breviary: Text . . . . CLS 5-7

The Hymn Collection of the Abbey of the Paraclete: Introduction and Commentary . . . . CLS 8†

The Hymn Collection of the Abbey of the Paraclete: Text . . . . CLS 9†

STUDIA PATRISTICA

Papers of the Oxford Patristics Conference 1983 (Elizabeth A. Livingstone, ed.)

1. Historica-Gnostica-Biblica
2. Critica-Classica-Ascetica-Liturgica
3. The Second Century-Clement and Origen-The Cappodocian Fathers †
4. Augustine-Post Nicene Latin Fathers-Oriental Texts-*Nachleben* of the Fathers †

FAIRACRES PRESS, OXFORD

The Wisdom of the Desert Fathers

The Letters of St Antony the Great

The Letters of Ammonas, Successor of St Antony

A Study of Wisdom. Three Tracts by the author of *The Cloud of Unknowing*

The Power of the Name. The Jesus Prayer in Orthodox Spirituality (Kallistos Ware)

Contemporary Monasticism

A Pilgrim's Book of Prayers (Gilbert Shaw)

Theology and Spirituality (Andrew Louth)

Prayer and Holiness (Dumitru Staniloae)

Eight Chapters on Perfection and Angel's Song (Walter Hilton)

Creative Suffering (Iulia de Beausobre)

Bringing Forth Christ. Five Feasts of the Child Jesus (St Bonaventure)

Distributed in North America only for Fairacres Press.

DISTRIBUTED BOOKS

La Trappe in England

O Holy Mountain: Journal of a Retreat on Mount Athos

St Benedict: Man with An Idea (Melbourne Studies)

The Spirit of Simplicity

Vision of Peace (St. Joseph's Abbey)

The Animals of St Gregory (Paulinus Press)

Benedict's Disciples (David Hugh Farmer)

The Christmas Sermons of Guerric of Igny

The Emperor's Monk. A Contemporary Life of Benedict of Aniane

Journey to God:. Anglican Essays on the Benedictine Way

* *Temporarily out of print*

† *Forthcoming*